The Dynamics of Victorian Business

The Dynamics of Victorian Business

Problems and Perspectives to the 1870s

edited by

Roy Church

Professor of Economic and Social History,
University of East Anglia

London
GEORGE ALLEN & UNWIN
Boston   Sydney

First published in 1980

GEORGE ALLEN & UNWIN LTD
40 Museum Street, London WC1A 1LU

© George Allen & Unwin (Publishers) Ltd., 1980

British Library Cataloguing in Publication Data

The dynamics of Victorian business.
  1. Business enterprises – Great Britain – History
  – 19th century
  I. Church, Roy Anthony
  338'.0941   HF5349.G7   79–41410

ISBN 0–04–330300–5

Typeset in 10 on 11 point Times by Trade Linotype Ltd., Birmingham
and printed and bound in Great Britain
by Biddles Ltd, Guildford and King's Lynn

Contents

Contributors

R. A. Church, Professor of Economic and Social History, University of East Anglia

E. W. Cooney, Reader in Economic and Social History, University of York

P. L. Cottrell, Lecturer in Economic History, University of Leicester

T. R. Gourvish, Senior Lecturer in Economic and Social History, University of East Anglia

C. H. Lee, Senior Lecturer in Economic History, University of Aberdeen

A. E. Musson, Professor of Economic History, University of Manchester

P. J. Riden, Lecturer in History, University College, Cardiff

E. M. Sigsworth, formerly Professor of Economic and Social History, University of York

A. Slaven, Professor of Business History, University of Glasgow

A. J. Taylor, Professor of Modern History, University of Leeds

R. B. Weir, Lecturer in Economic and Social History, University of York

Introduction

When reviewers differ sharply over whether a thesis repeats a self-evident orthodoxy or heralds a controversy which the thesis is likely to withstand, an author may surely be forgiven for accepting the challenge and resuming the initiative.[1] For if scholars cannot agree on what constitutes a conventional interpretation of the characteristics and dynamics of change in the British economy of the nineteenth century, it seems unlikely that students, for whom *The Great Victorian Boom* (Church, 1975) was written, will reach a consensus. The purpose of this collection of essays is to explore further that part of the thesis, tentatively advanced in interrogative mode in 1975, concerning the course of industrial development during the second and third quarters of the nineteenth century. Contributors were invited to consider the dynamics of change in particular sectors and industries selected mainly for their importance within the economy, the range being limited necessarily by constraints on space and the finances of publishing. The degree to which the chapters cohere has been dependent largely upon the availability of sources helpful in elaborating upon the unifying themes. Slight variation in chronological emphases reflects the differences in development from one industry or sector to another, though one of the principal aims was to establish whether the second quarter of the century possessed distinctive characteristics in contrast to those of the third quarter. For these various reasons the chapters vary in scope and emphasis, but the fact that each lends itself to reference in Chapter 1, 'Problems and Perspectives', is an indication that those contributors who delivered the goods also endeavoured to observe the editor's guidelines. I am grateful to those who did, and those to whom my thanks are due especially are my colleague Dr T. R. Gourvish, who read and commented upon the introductory section (though who should not be held responsible for the conclusions), and to Mary Gurteen for providing incomparable secretarial service in a frustrating exercise which editing such a collection tends to be.

The University of East Anglia   ROY CHURCH
Norwich

NOTE TO INTRODUCTION

1 Dr Wray Vamplew (*Economic History Review*, 2nd series, vol. XXIX, no. 4,
  1976) was somewhat less impressed than Professor William Ashworth (*History*,
  vol. 61, 1976) with the novelty of the thesis that the period 1850–73 did not
  possess a unity exhibiting economic characteristics markedly dissimilar from
  those identifiable in the early and later nineteenth century.

1 Problems and Perspectives

by R. A. Church

DIMENSIONS

By the second quarter of the nineteenth century the shift of human resources associated with industrialisation had already advanced to the extent that the mining, manufacturing and building groups of industries employed a major proportion of the labour force. Admittedly defective estimates based on Census data suggest that whereas 24·6 per cent of the total occupied population were in agriculture, forestry and fishing in 1831, 40·8 per cent were in mining, manufacturing and building, with 12·4 per cent in trade and transport. After the Napoleonic Wars the hugely expanded agricultural sector could hardly be expected to have absorbed a rapidly growing population to work on the land, thus the industrial workforce expanded both in absolute numbers and in relative terms. In 1841 the picture becomes clearer, though the Census data still affords only an approximation of the industrial distribution of the labour force (Table 1.1). Whereas between 1841 and 1881

Table 1.1 *Estimated industrial distribution of the British labour force 1821–81, as percentage of occupied population*

	Agriculture and Fishing	Mining and Quarrying	Building	Manufacturing	Transport	Trade	Total Occupied Population (millions of persons)
1821	28·4		38·4			12·9	
1831	24·6		40·8			12·4	
1841	22·6	2·4	4·8	32·1	3·6	10·7	8·4
1851	21·6	4·1	5·2	32·9	5·2	10·3	9·7
1861	18·5	4·6	5·6	33·3	5·6	11·1	10·8
1871	15·0	5·0	6·7	32·5	5·8	13·3	12·0
1881	12·9	4·6	6·9	32·1	6·9	14·5	13·1

Source: Derived from Deane and Cole 1969, table 31.

agriculture lost labour at an increasing rate, the principal gainers were trade and transport. Mining and quarrying, which meant principally coal mining, expanded rapidly in the 1840s and retained a higher, albeit relatively small, percentage of the total occupied population. The transport sector also grew fast in the 1840s and again in the 1870s. The building trades experienced their most rapid expansion in the 1860s, continuing to exceed mining as an employer of labour and maintaining a size of labour force similar to that in transport. Finally, the manufacturing sector remained virtually static in relative terms throughout the period, employing roughly one-third of the total occupied population.

Measured in terms of the industrial distribution of national income manufacturing, mining and building together recorded an increase by about 14 per cent in their contribution between 1851 and 1871 and 1881. This compared with an estimated expansion in the trade and transport sector by 21 per cent between 1851 and 1871 and by 28 per cent between 1851 and 1881.

Table 1.2   *Industrial distribution of the national income of Great Britain as percentage of Total Domestic Income*[1] *1821–81*

	Agriculture	Manu- facturing, Mining and Building	Trade and Transport	Housing	Total Domestic Income £m.
1821	26·4	32·3	16·1	6·2	288·0
1831	23·7	34·8	17·6	6·5	336·1
1841	22·4	34·9	18·7	8·3	446·1
1851	20·7	34·9	19·0	8·3	514·9
1861	18·3	37·6	20·2	7·8	648·1
1871	14·9	39·9	23·0	7·9	877·1
1881	11·0	39·9	24·4	8·9	991·7

[1]Total national product less income from abroad.
Source: Derived from Deane and Cole 1969, table 37.

Relative stability in the size of the industrial workforce during the period was possible only because of the considerable absolute increase in the numbers employed by non-manufacturing sectors. The numbers in mining and quarrying and in transport more than doubled between 1841 and 1861, rising by more than one-half as much again between 1861 and 1881. Due to the prevailing mode of industrial organisation in the mid-nineteenth century it was often difficult to distinguish with any confidence between manufacturing and the distributive trades, which explains why in Booth's tabulation the manufacturing sector included dealers in a given material as well as those who worked upon it (Armstrong, 1972, p. 231.) Depending upon the extent to which such classification occurred, it seems likely that the size of the manufacturing sector was understated. Furthermore, economic activities became more specialised as industrial organisation altered and outwork declined, bringing about an increase in the proportion of industrial employees devoting the whole of their working time to making, rather than to fetching and carrying raw materials and finished goods. This trend suggests that the downward bias of those classified as employed in manufacturing assumed greater significance during the later decades in the period as economic differentiation progressed, and that the relative growth in the proportion of the labour force engaged in manufacturing is concealed by the census returns.

Despite the deficiencies of our information relating to the composition of the labour force in the nineteenth century, we can be certain that after 1841 the picture presented by the census figures is reasonably accurate. No such confidence may be attached to our view of the size, rate of growth, and composition of capital. The three scholars who have taken pains to assemble national estimates of capital formation – Deane (1962, 1969), Pollard (1968), and Feinstein (1972) – disagree in detail, but more importantly Deane's estimates conflict fundamentally with those of Pollard and, more recently, with the highly detailed figures published by Feinstein (1978) both of which *suggest* a considerably higher level of capital formation throughout the series. The published estimates of both Deane and Pollard have attracted adverse criticism, and subsequently those of Feinstein (1978), intended to remedy the deficiencies of previous figures, received a sceptical reception when they were first exposed to the scrutiny of scholars in 1976, principally because of the alleged unrepresentativeness of micro data which provided the basis for assumptions relating to industries and sectors. Despite weaknesses, however, due as much to the paucity of data as to the assumptions the author found it necessary to adopt in the course of estimation, they cannot be ignored; neither can the implications which the estimates might have for our interpretation of historical change. While acknowledging, therefore, the provisional character of Feinstein's figures (which he readily admits), and emphasising the tentative nature of statements which they may seem to justify, we propose to incorporate these recent estimates in our introductory review, drawing attention to the ways in which they might alter conventional interpretations of the period.

Feinstein's reconstruction of the structure of national wealth and of investment is congruent with that presented by Deane and Pollard. His estimates show that in 1830 agriculture accounted for 37 per cent of domestic reproducible capital (compared with 46 per cent in 1800); industry and commerce 25 per cent (compared with 18 per cent in 1800); and transport 9 per cent (compared with 8 per cent in 1800). By 1860 the share attributed to agriculture had fallen to 25 per cent, while industry and commerce accounted for 33 per cent and transport

18 per cent (Feinstein, 1978, table 24). These figures suggest a high rate of transformation for industry and commerce during the first thirty years of the century, though it was during the three decades after 1830 that the balance tipped in favour of industry and commerce. The alteration in the ratio of fixed to circulating capital in industry and commerce from approximately 1·5:1 in 1800 to 2·5:1 in 1830 and slightly more than 3:1 in 1860 reflects changes in industrial organisation and in the structure of production, the doubling in the size of the reproducible capital of the transport sector again underlining the significance of the period between 1830 and 1860 as one of marked structural change.

Given the decisive shift in the distribution of human and capital resources in this period, the question of the changing level of capital formation requires consideration, for this has been central to the debate on industrialisation initiated by W. Arthur Lewis and W. W. Rostow. They hypothesised that a rise in the rate of capital formation to between 10 and 12 per cent was typically associated with the 'take-off' stage of industrialisation. Empirical evidence on this hypothesis has been difficult to assemble. Deane's earlier estimates (1965) pointed to a gradual rise in the long-term average rate of net capital formation reaching a sustained average of 5 per cent by 1800, a rate maintained until after the 1800s and the coming of the railway which within twenty years boosted the figure to about 10 per cent. When Feinstein's capital formation figures (1972) were applied to Deane's new estimates of Gross National Product (1968) it appears that it was not until the 1860s that the critical ratio was achieved (Church, 1975a, p. 37). More recently, Feinstein has related revised estimates of investment levels to a newly constructed gross domestic product series (which in a context of less than robust estimates Feinstein notes is *very* uncertain (1978, p. 28). The conclusion he draws is that a rise in the overall investment ratio in excess of 10 per cent occurred even before the Napoleonic Wars, and that the rise in investment which occurred during the second and third decades of the nineteenth century represented merely a return to prewar levels of relatively high rates of capital formation (tables 21 and 24). His explanation for such a surprising conclusion is that the growth of income kept pace with rising investment in the first half of the nineteenth century, leaving the ratio of investment to income virtually unaltered (pp. 66*ff*). If Feinstein's estimates and conclusions are valid, then in terms of the ratio of investment to domestic product the period between the end of the first and the seventh decades of the nineteenth century appears to have witnessed no substantial change. The composition of investment, however, was transformed. Historians will now have to consider whether the 'critical' ratio of 10 or 12 per cent was reached in the 1840s or in the 1860s – or even before the century began.

Like the estimates for capital, the course of industrial production, as indeed of total output, has formed the subject for debate, though almost all attempts to measure industrial growth in the nineteenth century are derived to some extent from the production index constructed by W. Hoffman (1955). In a critical review of this index W. A. Cole (1958, p. 314) observed that the likelihood of error before 1830 and after 1870 seemed greater than in the intervening decades, therefore the conclusions drawn from it regarding long-term trends in the nineteenth century down to 1870 must continue to command some respect. The index shows rapid rates of growth in industrial output occurring in the years between the end of the Napoleonic Wars and the 1850s, the annual rate of growth of industrial production falling from between 3 and 4 per cent for the decades before 1855 to below 3 per cent between 1856 and 1876. More critical of Hoffman's index than Cole, J. F. Wright (1956, pp. 362–3) has suggested that the higher growth rates for the earlier period might be exaggerated due to the predominance of the major export industries contained in the index, while the smaller domestic industries were excluded.[1] Partly offsetting this bias is the changing ratio of outputs to inputs and the resulting downward bias which is likely to have increased as the century progressed and as output per unit of physical inputs (adopted by Hoffman as output indicators), rose.[2]

Beginning with values, rather than physical outputs and deflating by a price index, Deane and Cole's attempt (1969) to estimate growth in real product has likewise received criticism. For the deflator adopted was the Rousseaux price index, which while described as an index of principal industrial goods comprised in fact mainly raw-material prices, coal and pig iron, representing net values added. The difficulty posed by such an approach was compounded by differences in the movement of raw-material prices compared with the prices of manufactured goods between 1831–41 and 1861–71. For these reasons Deane and Cole's attempt to revise the conventional picture of the output curve in the nineteenth century has proved unsuccessful, and their claim to have located an actual dip in the rate of industrial production in the mid-century followed by a considerable recovery has been rejected. In the absence of further information to illuminate the course of industrial growth, historians are disposed to accept, albeit with serious particular reservations, the general picture presented by the Hoffman index which showed a deceleration, probably beginning in the 1860s (Table 1.3).

STRUCTURE AND DIFFERENTIATION

If the rate of industrial growth began to slacken towards the end of our period, the degree of industrialisation, measured by the direct

Table 1.3 *Percentage increase in industrial production between successive decades*

Deane and Cole		Hoffman	
	Manufacturing, mining, building, percentage		Industrial products, percentage annual
Decades compared	annual growth	Decades compared	growth
1801–11 and 1831–41	4·7	1800–09 and 1830–9	3·1
1811–21 and 1841–51	3·7	1810–19 and 1840–9	3·5
1821–31 and 1851–61	2·3	1820–9 and 1850–9	3·5
1831–41 and 1861–71	3·0	1830–9 and 1860–9	3·0
1851–61 and 1871–81	2·7	1840–9 and 1870–9	2·9
1851–61 and 1881–91	3·5	1850–9 and 1880–9	2·4
1861–71 and 1891–1901	3·5	1860–9 and 1890–9	2·1

Source: J. F. Wright (1965, p. 407). Neither the coverage of the two indices nor the periods compared are identical. They are considered sufficiently similar, however, for a general comparison of the kind made here.

contribution of industry to the total domestic national income, increased, especially between 1851 and 1871, when the proportion reached 40 per cent. The distribution of the labour force gradually shifted still further in favour of industry (manufacturing, mining and building) from round about 36 per cent in 1841 to nearly 43 per cent by 1881. From the mid-century, therefore, industrial activity came to dominate economic life, stimulating the growth in transport and distribution which the expansion of industrial goods required and reflected in the rise in the share of these sectors, both in their contribution to the national income and as employers of labour.

Within the industrial sector some changes occurred in the relative importance of particular industries, though not to a very large extent. While textiles, including dyeing and dress, still employed over half the total number of people in manufacturing in 1881, the proportion had declined by about 11 per cent since 1841, mainly due to the relative fall in numbers employed in textiles and dyeing, excluding dress. The detailed figures for England and Wales reveal that within textiles, employment in the silk and cotton industries declined more in relative terms than did employment in woollens and worsted, which dropped barely a percentage point. The growing importance of the metallurgical and engineering industries provides part of the explanation for the relative, if modest, decline in textiles, for whereas in 1841 they employed 14 per cent of the manufacturing population, by 1881 that figure exceeded 21 per cent.

The change in the structure of output implied by shifts in the occupational structure is not easy to corroborate in terms of the value of industrial output, for the estimates of Deane and Cole, the best available, are expressed in terms of gross output for some industries, and net output, or value added, for others. None the less, the estimates suggest that textiles, in which cotton output continued to predominate by a wide margin, retained its leading importance, with iron expanding steadily from *c.* 1840 and very rapidly in the 1860s. The rate of coal output increased enormously from the 1850s, but remained well behind textiles, cotton and iron, achieving a comparable importance in terms of net output, to the woollen and worsted industries in 1870 (Deane and Cole, 1967, ch. 6). While the group of manufacturing industries which dominated economic activity in the 1870s were broadly the same as those which in 1840 bulked largest in the industrial structure, their range and quality of production had altered considerably, especially in woollen and worsteds, iron and steel, and engineering within which the railway, shipbuilding and machinery sections had assumed much greater importance, while the production of finished metal goods had been transformed. British linen production appears to have grown during the second quarter of the century and its decline during the third quarter was offset by the expansion of the jute industry, though this was almost entirely a Scottish development. Silk production likewise grew in the second and third quarters, reaching a peak in the 1860s (Deane and Cole, 1967, pp. 207–11).

Some of the new industries, numerically small but which were symptoms of the general process of differentiation, developed from the handling of waste products, and some from the appearance of raw materials hitherto intractable or unknown. The most spectacular example of this is seen in the growth of the chemical industry, which in the second quarter of the century began to expand both in scope and dimensions. One of the more readily identifiable 'new industries' of the nineteenth century, the chemical industry altered radically in character as the traditional markets for alkali, soda, alum, sulphuric acid, phosphorous and borate underwent massive expansion. The production of heavy chemicals also expanded hugely from the vast Leblanc plants. Growth brought substantial internal economies of scale through integrated production, the cost reductions and resource economies stimulating diversification of output by utilising waste and bringing about cumulative expansion in the production of heavy inorganic chemicals. 'Newer', though less impressive in scale and organisation, was the light and organic branch of the industry, the development of which dates from the 1840s, which brought to consumers various coal-tar derivatives, synthetic dyes and fertilisers, paint, high explosives and pharmaceuticals (Miall, 1931, chs 1–9). Refinements in chemical processes and the application of improved engineering techniques also provided the basis for a growth and diversification of rubber manufacture, stimulated in part by the railways (Payne, 1961).

Table 1.4 *Occupational Distribution in Great Britain 1841–81*

Totals in thousands   Percentages of self-supporting — a) Manufacturing b) Total population

Total occupied in	1841	1851	1861	1871	1881	1841 a	1841 b	1851 a	1851 b	1861 a	1861 b	1871 a	1871 b	1881 a	1881 b
AGRICULTURE AND FISHING	1,580	2,096	2,016	1,790	1,636		20·4		21·5		18·6		14·8		12·2
MINING	236	387	487	551	646		3·0		3·9		4·5		4·5		4·8
BUILDING	413	530	631	758	907		5·3		5·4		5·8		6·3		6·8
TRANSPORT	174	392	492	597	739		2·2		4·0		4·5		4·9		7·8
DEALING	400	621	763	944	1,047		5·2		6·4		7·0		7·8		7·8
MANUFACTURE															
Machinery and Tools	62	112	177	220	259	2·9		3·5		4·9		5·7		6·2	
Shipbuilding	26	32	53	61	72	1·2		0·9		1·47		1·6		1·7	
Metal Workers	213	332	422	496	549	9·9		10·3		11·7		12·8		13·2	
Earthernware, glass etc.	33	49	60	72	77	1·5		1·5		1·7		1·7		1·9	
Fuel, gas and chemicals	7	21	30	44	54	0·3		0·6		0·8		1·1		1·3	
Furs, leather, glue etc.	38	56	61	65	69	1·8		1·7		1·7		1·7		1·7	
Wood, furniture and carriages	171	211	241	260	270	8·0		6·5		6·7		6·7		6·5	
Paper, floorcloth and waterproof	14	27	31	42	60	0·6		0·8		0·9		1·1		1·4	
Textiles and dyeing	785	1,182	1,181	1,182	1,153	36·5		36·5		32·8		30·5		27·7	
Dress[1]	597	979	1,033	1,019	1,062	27·8		30·3		28·7		26·3		25·6	
Food, drink and smoking	105	153	172	190	212	4·9		4·7		4·8		4·9		5·1	
Watches, instruments and toys	22	27	39	42	49	1·0		0·8		1·1		1·1		1·2	

					percentage of population				
Printing and bookbinding	27	39	55	76	102	1·3	1·2	1·5	1·9	2·5
Unspecified (chiefly connected with machinery)	48	15	43	107	168	2·2	0·5	1·2	2·8	4·0
Others in industrial occupations, including 'general labour'	408	427	432	703	887	19·0	13·2	12·0	18·1	21·3
Total Manufacturing	2,148	3,235	3,598	3,876	4,156	27·8	33·2	33·2	32·0	31·0
Total 'self-supporting'	7,739	9,745	10,827	12,116	13,361	41·2	46·8	46·8	46·5	44·9
Total Population	18,532	20,816	23,128	26,072	29,710					

[1] Dress includes boot, shoe pattern and clog makers, which are not separately classified in Booth's tables relating to Scotland, but were as follows for England and Wales:

1841	1851	1861	1871	1881
190·8	244	256·1	224·6	224·1

It also included hosiery, the figures for which for England and Wales were:

1841	1851	1861	1871	1881
36·0	58·9	45·9	42·1	40·4

Source: Booth (1886, pp. 414-19).

Other minor, though long established, industrial activities to expand during the second and third quarters of the century include the small metal trades of the west midlands. As demand for certain of their products increased the older industries had split up to form a number of new trades. To the production of hardware made of iron or brass, and of hollow-ware, guns, jewellery, buttons, edge tools, locks, wrought nails, leather, saddlery, ironmongery and glass manufacture, were added the new industries producing cut nails, railway rolling stock, pens, enamelled hollow-ware and electro-plate, wrought-iron tubes, nuts and bolts, malleable iron castings, anchor chains, galvanised iron-work, springs and safes (G. C. Allen, 1929, pp. 41–2). Increasing differentiation is also indicated by the growth in employment in a number of minor industries which more than kept pace with population. In addition to chemicals and glass, these included earthenware, gas, glass, paper, floor-cloth and waterproofing, printing and book-binding, though none of this group employed more than 2·5 per cent of the occupied population in 1881 (Table 1.4). It is possible that the employment figures understate the relative growth of these activities, for in some industries, hosiery and footwear for example, a fall in the numbers employed after the mid-century was accompanied by con-siderable expansion of output achieved by technical change and reorganisation of production methods.

Indeed, the relatively gradual introduction of steam-powered machinery and the adoption of factory production in these industries after 1850 is a reminder of the uneven progress of the revolution in technical processes and organisation which we associate with 'industrial revolution'. For while the proportion of capital formation had risen to levels associated with the transformation to an industrial economy sometime before 1870, the distribution of steam power was heavily concentrated within a narrow range of industries, and before 1870 very unevenly. Steam power had been applied to cotton spinning before 1830 and weaving was completely mechanised in steam-powered factories during the following two decades. Worsted powered spinning was completed by about 1840, weaving slightly later, and in woollens both occurred a decade later. The need for pumping and winding machinery explains why coal mining was a major sector attracting investment in steam power in the nineteenth century, as the depth of mining increased, while the only other industries where mechanical power was introduced on anything approaching a similar scale were iron smelting, founding and forging, and engineering. In 1870 this group together accounted for a combined horsepower estimated at between one-quarter and one-third of the total manufacturing horse-power (Musson, 1976, p. 435).

Musson compared his estimate of less than 100,000 total industrial horsepower in the mid-1820s, with something less than 300,000 nominal horsepower in 1850, and with 513,335 revealed by the Factory and Workshop Returns for 1870 (Musson, 1976, pp. 23–4, 435–7), a figure which Kanefsky's research suggests should be revised upwards by about 15 per cent (Kanefsky). The First Census of Production recorded a comparable figure of 9·65 million horsepower in 1907, which led to Musson to conclude that, 'even allowing for inadequate statistics and under-measurements of horsepower in the late eighteenth and early nineteenth centuries, it seems clear that the really massive growth of steam power occurred in the later nineteenth century' rather than in 'the heroic age of the early Industrial Revolution'.[3] It is true that probably more people in industry worked outside steam-powered factories than within them in the 1870s, an arrangement which was due in part to the demand for labour-intensive subsidiary processes and services generated by sectors affected by power, but also because the character of the trade restricted the scope for motive power – or made the substitution of steam for handpower uneconomic. Important though such industries as building and woodworking, small metals manufacture, chemicals, glassmaking, pottery, printing, leather and footwear, clothing, food and drink were, except in large breweries steam power was virtually unknown; only the building, clothing and footwear industries employed substantial numbers of people, and building was the only activity to contribute a sizeable proportion of the national income. In one sense, therefore, it is true to claim as Musson does, that 'British industry had not been revolutionised by the mid-nineteenth century' (p. 436), for even in the aforementioned industries where steam power had been introduced, its extent was limited before 1870, and widespread domestic outwork in manufacturing continued to persist, notably in the clothing, hosiery and footwear industries. None the less, it seems likely that sometime before 1870 by far the greatest proportion of the national product derived from manufacturing and mining was produced in factories, plants and collieries employing steam power. Whether this constitutes a 'revolution' is a question of definition, as is the notion of 'maturity', a term which some historians have used to describe the stage of development by which time the technology of basic industries had been transformed (Landes, 1969, p. 229). Musson's analysis, however, does emphasise once again the immense dependence of British industrialisation, and particularly of the progress of steam power, upon the textile industries, especially cotton, well into the third quarter of the nineteenth century.

While the character of innovation in the second and third quarters of the century was dominated by the application of steam-powered machinery across a gradually wider range of manufacturing industries, a few key inventions were especially important to industrial development – Robert's self-acting mule in the cotton industry (1830), in which the moveable carriage as well as the spindles were operated by power,

Lister and Donnisthorpe's wool-combing machine (1851), of critical importance in both the worsted and woollen industries, and Neilson's 'hot blast' (1828), which made possible direct and economical smelting with new coal, and cheap Bessemer steel introduced in 1856, but whose impact upon the output of the iron industry before 1870 was relatively small. Steam-powered hosiery frames were devised during the third quarter of the century and applied widely only from after 1870. Similarly, and even more tardily, the introduction of the sewing machine from the USA in the 1850s ushered in changes in the methods of producing footwear and ready-made clothing. Most far-reaching in its implications for the economy was the application of steam to rail and sea transport.

Coal, of course, had been critical in the early development of steam power in the eighteenth century, but the history of technical innovation in the nineteenth century took the form of extending the mechanisation of winding and underground haulage in order to deepen and raise the capacity of pit shafts, and to introduce mechanically operated fans to help in this process (see Taylor, Chapter 2). As for the building trades, the other major industrial activity outside manufacturing, these were even less affected by novel technical developments in the nineteenth century. Beginning in the 1830s and 1840s the gradual introduction of machines to cut and shape wood, fashion stone and make bricks, and steam-driven machinery for sawing, planing, and shaping timber, together represented the limited extent to which mechanisation had affected construction before the 1870s (see Cooney, Chapter 7). In shipbuilding, that other important construction industry, the application of steam power from the late 1840s was to revolutionise the performance of ships but did little to alter the technical efficiency of shipbuilding (see Slaven, Chapter 5).

Indeed the growing use of steam power contributed to the process of increasing differentiation within industries, for whereas before 1830 the steam engineering industry was small and largely concentrated in Birmingham and London, the requirements for steam power stimulated a separate section of engineering whose location in the 1840s was gradually developing in those regions generating specialist demands, for steam-driven machinery for textiles production in the north, for coal and iron production in South Wales and the north midlands, for coal and steamship construction in Scotland and the north-east, and agricultural machinery in the east. The location of railway engineering, another important speciality, was less influenced by the need for the railway companies to service rolling stock within their respective regions. Much of the technical advance in engineering took the form of piecemeal improvements rather than revolutionary change, though Nasmyth's direct-acting steam hammer made possible the production of massive forgings and die stampings. The development of boring engines, improved upon by Smeaton, Wilkinson and others, also played a vital role in ensuring accuracy and greater efficiency of cylinders for steam engines, while the application of steam power to drilling, grooving, filing, grinding, slotting, and metal planing machines enormously enlarged the range and contribution of mechanical engineering from the 1820s. Perhaps exaggerating their positions, Musson has argued that Habakkuk, Rosenberg, and others have underestimated the extent of standardised engineering and machine-tool progress before 1850, that contemporaries exaggerated the lag by paying too much attention to woodworking machinery and light engineering, and that subsequent historians have tended to ignore the British lead in steam and heavy mechanical engineering throughout the period (see Musson, Chapter 4).

TECHNOLOGY AND ORGANISATION

Certainly the contemporary sources, upon which so much of the subsequent analysis has been based, are important if we wish to place the Anglo-American comparisons in perspective, for the reports of the two groups of Englishmen visiting the USA in the 1850s drew most of their evidence relating to labour-saving machinery from three specific areas – woodworking, hardware and ordnance manufacture (Temin, 1966*a*, pp. 281–4). The observations on woodworking were not intended to be applied generally to American manufacturing industry, and while the implications of the mechanised manufacture of standardised products and interchangeable parts extended far beyond the particular branches of hardware and ordnance, the remarks were specific to the advances in those particular industries which were not representative. Temin has suggested that the lack of evidence about whole areas of American industry, and the known American backwardness in the production and fabrication of iron, renders plausible the hypothesis that the American and British economies at the middle of the nineteenth century were using essentially the same technology, i.e. that due to differences in factor prices between the two countries it would not have been advantageous for British manufacturers to have used the methods employed by Americans (Temin, 1966*a*, pp. 279, 283). Machinery used differed in some instances, but the widely observed sturdiness and enduring qualities of British machinery, so often contrasted with the relatively flimsy capital equipment of the Americans typically adopting rapid depreciation rates, he explains in terms of the lower internal rate of interest in Britain (p. 295).

Were British manufacturers slow to devise and introduce cost-reducing techniques until the later nineteenth century? Habakkuk has remarked that 'compared to the last forty years of the nineteenth century the first half of the nineteenth century was not a period of major technological breakthroughs in English industry . . . It was not until the 1870s and 1880s that additions to fundamental knowledge assumed technological significance' (Habakkuk, 1962*a*, p. 182). He acknowledged that considerable 'technical progress' accrued down to the mid-nineteenth century, in improving basic processes, and in the application of known principles outside the industries in which the inventions occurred, and that these developments were economically important. But the qualifications he makes are considerable and the overall impression of his view is that in comparison with the developments in the USA 'technical potentialities were not always fully exploited', that the nature of much of the technical progress of the period took forms which were not capable of wide application outside the industries in which they originated and that because of this they limited the pace of investment (Habakkuk, 1962*a*, pp. 184–5). Added to this, 'innovation in one sector was less likely to have had wide repercussions because there was a good deal of slack in the economy'.

If, like Habakkuk, we regard steam technology as having possessed the greatest potentiality for widest application in industry then this view receives support from Musson's estimates of steam power in British industry at the mid-century. By 1850 steam had affected only a narrow range of productive activity and was limited in extent, still, in 1870 (Musson, 1976, pp. 434–6). But, with the exceptions of woodworking and sugar production, a not dissimilar pattern has been drawn of the employment of steam power in America at the mid-century: 'Although steam power was used widely in manufacturing by 1840, most of its use was concentrated in a few industries and it provided the main power supply for almost none' (Temin, 1966*b*, p. 204). Temin has explained the limited concentration of steam power in the USA in terms of higher direct costs of steam compared with water power, and underlines the relative slowness with which steam was applied to urban industries, cotton excepted. This similarity between the two countries may seem surprising, given the generally unfavourable comparisons drawn between British and American technology at the mid-century.[4] Indeed, it seems likely that future empirical research will further undermine the picture of an economy in which, at least until the second half of the nineteenth century, the inducements to British manufacturers to mechanise were dampened significantly more than were their American counterparts by relatively lower wage rates. Habakkuk's assertion that 'inventions which save labour are likely to be more widely applicable, or to suggest possibilities of new methods over a wider range of processes than are those which save specific raw materials' (Habakkuk, 1962*a*, p. 159) has yet to be demonstrated, but should that contention be valid then it follows that a disincentive to develop and invest in labour-saving technology is likely to have been a major factor in impeding the rate of technical progress, at least in the first half of the century.

An empirical study produced evidence that by 1830 wage rates for comparable kinds of labour were perhaps 20 per cent lower in Britain than in the USA, the differential having fallen from a somewhat larger figure at the end of the French Wars (Adams, 1970, p. 510); an examination of the differential wages of skilled and unskilled workers does not show skilled workers in Britain to have been better paid relative to unskilled workers than their American counterparts, and no change in these relationships. Adams thus dissents from Habakkuk's view that the cheapness of skilled labour relative to unskilled in America, combined with the greater need for skilled labour in capital-intensive techniques, provided less of an incentive for British entrepreneurs to adopt such techniques than their American counterparts. Adams also argues that if Habakkuk's assertion is true, and that in many cases the capital-intensive technique required for its construction and operation more skilled labour per unit of output than the labour-intensive technique than his own evidence indicates, then 'the advantages pursuant to the adoption of capital intensive techniques was greater in England' (Adams, 1970, p. 510). Such an incentive, if it did exist, was strengthened by the higher interest rates prevailing in Britain than in the USA (Temin, 1966*a*, p. 291).

Zabler questions Adams's evidence and his conclusions, presenting data which supports Habakkuk's view that American skilled labour was less expensive than British, in comparison with their unskilled counterparts (Zabler, 1972, p. 117). This is also the position adopted by Brito and Williamson who cite evidence to suggest that unskilled wages were probably 20 per cent higher in the USA in the 1820s and 30 per cent higher in the 1850s. They argue that one effect of a relative decline in skilled wages which they identify in the USA during the first half of the nineteenth century was the substitution of skilled labour for capital. This meant that American entrepreneurs tended to share higher fixed stock utilisation rates, implying higher observed rates of depreciation, which would explain the contrast between the higher rate of technical progress characteristic of American industry with an apparent lag on the part of British industrialists (Brito and Williamson, 1973, pp. 249–50). As for the key innovation of the nineteenth century, von Tunzelmann doubts that a more rapid adoption of steam power by British manufacturers would have been rational before the 1840s and 1850s, for not until then did improved technology in high-pressure steam engine design and production offer them significantly cheaper and more efficient steam power than was available hitherto (von Tunzelmann, 1978, pp. 289–91).

Ames and Rosenberg have stressed the relatively low price of wood in the USA in explaining why American labour-saving woodworking machinery was not taken up in Britain, where the prodigal use of raw materials characteristic of those woodworking machines would have been economically unacceptable (Ames and Rosenberg, 1968, p. 831). A similar concern to economise on relatively high-cost raw materials can also help to explain why the American ring spinning machinery was not substituted for the mule by British manufacturers except for the spinning of lower-cost short staple yarns of low count (Sandberg, 1968*a*, pp. 34–9). Even where British ironmasters were using relatively cheap fuel (and the price of coal fell considerably to the late 1860s) technological change was designed to economise on coal inputs. Hence the invention in 1828 and the diffusion in the 1830s of Neilson's hot blast, and the introduction in the 1860s of the very tall blast furnace, which was pioneered in Cleveland in the 1860s. It has been argued that there is evidence to indicate that innovations which exploited the differences in resource characteristics – Scottish 'flint' coal in the 1830s, and the Cleveland ores thirty years later – explain why the productivity of British blast furnaces may have risen between the 1830s and 1870 (Allen, 1977, pp. 626–32). Increasingly it seems that the antithesis of Habakkuk is supported by as much, or as little, empirical evidence as the original thesis.

Economists have stressed the irrelevance of differences in factor prices as an explanation for the particular factor-saving bias of technological change. 'The entrepreneur is interested in reducing costs in total, not particular costs such as labour costs or capital costs. When labour costs rise any advance that reduces total costs is welcome, and whether this is achieved by saving labour or capital is irrelevant' (Salter, 1960, pp. 43–4). Furthermore, Rosenberg has argued that economic incentives to reduce cost *always* exist in business operations, but because they are so pervasive and so diffuse prove to be unhelpful in explaining the particular sequence and timing of innovative activity (Rosenberg, 1976, p. 110). Incentives, however, are guiding mechanisms, and whether a response to incentives occurs depends much upon the ease with which it is possible for an entrepreneur to reduce costs. Thus, while raw-material costs accounted for a relatively high proportion of total costs in a wide range of industries, and a given percentage reduction in raw materials could often yield a greater absolute saving than an equivalent percentage cut in labour or over-head costs, none the less labour economies were simply easier to achieve – and in mining and iron production of major importance in percentage terms.

Until a great deal more detailed research is carried out to remedy the lack of adequately corroborated generalisations concerning British and American technology, our perception of the dynamics of British industrial development in the nineteenth century will remain very confused. Nearly ten years after Saul's review of the debate on British and American technology his agnostic conclusions remain valid and merit repetition. Emphasising the diversity and variety of experiences, both between and within British and American industries, the need which he identified was for a clearer delineation of each separate problem; in effect an exhortation for research to be directed at the level of the industry and of the firm, with attention to the comparative developments in more than two countries (Saul, 1970, pp. 17–21). None the less, while we are condemned to remain uncertain on these issues for the foreseeable future, it is possible to identify inducement mechanisms which were manifestly at work in stimulating invention and innovation, and which do assist in the explanation of the sequence and timing of innovative activity (Rosenberg, 1976, pp. 108–25).

The impulse to resolve a technical imbalance between interdependent processes, a change in one component of an interdependent system creating a stimulus for changes elsewhere in this system, has long been acknowledged as a fruitful source of technical change, the disequilibria involving compulsive sequences inducing innovation; but technical imbalances, strictly defined, are inherent in technology itself and do not differ, in general, from one society to another – though it may take a Bessemer to achieve a breakthrough. This is not the case with the hostility, or otherwise, of labour towards innovation, yet labour militancy was a powerful inducement to devise and to introduce labour-saving machinery in the nineteenth century. Habakkuk has drawn attention to this (Habakkuk, 1962, pp. 50–1, 142–4), while Rosenberg has remarked upon the unexpected agreement of Karl Marx and Samuel Smiles in the opinion that strikes and innovation were closely related as cause and effect, and there are numerous testimonies to this effect by inventors themselves. Richard Roberts's self-acting mule was invented in 1825 as a result of a strike by mule spinners, as was his Jacquard machine. W. Fairbairn's riveting machine patented in 1837 was designed for a similar reason in the 1830s; and Nasmyth's response to the lengthy engineering strike of 1851 was to devise self-acting tools to reduce his labour force, hence the invention of the planing machine, the slotting machine, Nasmyth's steam arm, and many others. Lister and Donnisthorpe's wool-combing machine is another example whereby labour recalcitrance acted as a powerful stimulus to the search for new techniques in a particular direction, the substitution of capital for skilled labour. In such instances, where innovative response was triggered by labour hostility and inseparable from the motive to lower production costs, was the desire to reduce the disruptive effects on production which a strike would bring about (Rosenberg, 1976, pp. 117–20).

But if labour hostility stimulated invention and innovation (and sometimes delayed it), especially after the mid-century when the unionisation of skilled workers grew appreciably, there were also other influences which, it has been argued, tended generally to inhibit the diffusion of new technology, notably the market which faced British entrepreneurs. The critical difference between the British and American markets in the mid-nineteenth century was not size, for in the 1850s the American market was still smaller than the British, while the greater dispersion of the American population meant that the market in which any single manufacturer could sell for a given transport cost was actually smaller in the USA than in Britain (Temin, 1966a, p. 294). Habakkuk stressed the importance of the *rate* of market expansion which in the case of Britain, at least until the third quarter of the century, he interprets as having been inadequate to impose sufficient pressure on resources and to provide a spur to 'innovation'. His emphasis on this retardative feature of the economy is explained by his insistence that factor shortages are more powerful influences on investment and innovation than pressure on profit margins, explained by the inability of the market to absorb additional production except at much reduced prices (Habakkuk, 1962a, pp. 181–7). The evidence relating invention to labour shortage and labour hostility suggests that there was an important causal relationship and that to some degree the rate of invention in our period is explicable in these terms. We shall argue below, however, that investment and the diffusion of new technology was very strongly influenced by profit margins, not only in the 1830s, as shown by Matthews (1954), but in succeeding decades, too.

Rosenberg has stressed the inhibiting influence on the composition of demand and the malleability of public taste in Britain (Rosenberg, 1976, pp. 157–61). He argues that earlier industrialisation introduced a widening range of consumer goods manufactured on the basis of a highly intensive handicraft technology, which in the mid-nineteenth century may well have constrained British producers with respect to the exploitation of machine technology. This was noticeably the case in the hardware trades where American implements were eminently suited to factory production. whereas the British consumer appears to have preserved a greater degree of sovereignty, contrasting with the producer initiative apparently dominant in the USA. Rosenberg also argues that the lack of producer initiative was a very important factor in retarding the development of efficient specialisation in capital goods production, citing the proliferation of locomotives of different design in the mid-nineteenth century as evidence of the alleged tendency for British engineers to be preoccupied with purely technical aspects of the final product, rather than with the efficiency of the productive process.

The precise extent of such a lack of standardisation is in dispute, but in those industries where it can be identified the movement towards specialisation by firms was slower than in the USA, notably in the critically important engineering industry where British firms more characteristically produced a wide range of products in comparison with American producers (Rosenberg, 1976, pp. 160–1), though specialisation did increase in the middle decades of the century (Floud, 1976, pp. 10, 15). Indeed, Payne was more impressed by a general trend towards specialisation in those years, a period when he thought 'the majority of British firms became increasingly specialised', especially in the textile, light metal and other consumer goods industries in which special mercantile relationships and highly skilled labour forces were prominent characteristics (Payne, 1974, pp. 43–4). Until we know more about the business sector we are in no position to generalise with confidence either as to whether British manufacturers retained labour-intensive methods for too long and whether they were justified in so doing, or whether the trend during the second and third quarters of the century was towards greater specialisation between producers, and with what effects.

With the extension of steam power and the increase in factory employment, the various forms of the outwork system began to decline, though in some industries, notably textiles and clothing, affecting chiefly women and girls, technology created outwork where hitherto it had not existed. In others, outwork was extended, persisting long after the 1870s (Landes, 1970, p. 119). The size of factories and workshops increased, the average workforce exceeding 200 by 1870, with the largest concentrations of workers, numbered in thousands, to be found in railways and shipbuilding. The increased use of machinery tended to render the number of employees less satisfactory as a criterion of size than hitherto, but because joint stock company formation was in its infancy even at the end of our period, a trend in average company capitalisation would not yield a more reliable indication of changes in size (Jeffreys, 1938, p. 105). The characteristics of British business, then, in the years before the 1870s were those of small, if growing, size, of private ownership, and the combination of management and ownership by a single family.

EFFICIENCY AND ENTERPRISE

Habakkuk has underlined how peculiarly appropriate such a structure was to the economic realities of the mid-nineteenth century, but acknowledging that perhaps within it were to be found the seeds of business atrophy (Habakkuk, 1968, pp. 6, 7, 15). Such a view has been espoused by Payne in a recent review of Victorian business, valuable because it charted our areas of ignorance but vulnerable in its attempt to present an independent interpretation of Victorian business none the less. Payne argued that between 1830 and 1870 an ability on the part of businessmen to earn 'comfortable' profits probably led to an ossification of industrial organisation and structure (Payne, 1974, pp.

42–4). Payne's argument is that they earned adequate profits, often resulting from a protective policy of product differentiation to secure higher profits per unit of output, that this enabled them to shun innovative diversification, and that all too many British entrepreneurs possessed expectations and presumptions relating to ownership and control which limited growth: 'Faced with an apparently limited market for the existing range of products, failure to grow was often incorrectly attributed to demand conditions rather than to the limited nature of entrepreneurial resources' (p. 44). It is true that Payne, like authors of the essays below, points to business failures and provides examples of firms in decline in this period, thus ruling out the most sanguine and unqualified view of the era as a golden age. But focussing upon Victorian expansion on the one hand, and upon the character of, and commitment within, firms on the other, Payne infers that the fruits of economic growth were denied only to those firms which possessed unenterprising leaders. While different in degree, such a view is none the less similar in kind to that which he quotes from Samuel Smiles, who 'not without reason', Payne comments, 'observed that "Anybody who devotes himself to making money, body and soul, can scarcely fail to make himself rich. Very little brains will do." ' Much of Payne's argument is offered in the subjunctive mood, but is congruent with Alfred Marshall's description of the mid-nineteenth century when 'an unprecedented combination of advantages enabled businessmen to make money even when they were not throwing themselves with energy into that creative work by which industrial leadership is made and maintained'. A time when 'in most cases the weak as well as the strong made good profits' and 'were satisfied with themselves' (Marshall, 1919, pp. 87, 92–3).

An important omission from Payne's discussion of the performance and aspirations of British industrialists in the period 1820 to 1870 is a consideration of the level and movement of profitability and profits. He notes that profits were 'relatively high' for some British firms able to secure oligopoly power through product differentiation, while many small firms made 'comfortable profits' (Payne, 1974, p. 42). The acceptance of current profit levels as 'adequate' and the accumulation of sufficient for leisure, he argues, discouraged enterprise, but in the absence of foreign competition in the early and mid-Victorian period did not prevent survival and satisfaction (pp. 43–5). Were British entrepreneurs guilty of protective product differentiation and resistance to 'innovative diversification' at the level of the firm? Product differentiation is essentially a competitive strategy, and as a lever to achieve monopolistic power possesses serious limitations in an industrial context of free entry and intense competition.

It is true that, as in the pioneering phase of industrialisation, several of the best-known names of those captains of industry conducted their operations on the basis of patent exploitation or some unique market advantage, for example, Heathcoat, Lister, Bessemer, Crossley, Macintosh, Salt (*Fortunes Made in Business*, Vols I–III, 1884); but differentiation, especially in the consumer goods industries, was a dynamic process, not impervious to competition in longer than the short run, and dependent for success upon consumer tastes. Differentiation in the engineering industry appears to have resulted from the practice whereby the purchaser provided specifications to suppliers, one effect of which was to hinder the emergence of specialist engineers and to hamper the development of certain kinds of highly efficient machine tools. But the response of British engineering firms to American light engineering competition in the 1850s and 1860s, belies Payne's general claim of gradual ossification of British industrial organisation with a concomitant aversion towards innovative diversification.

Similar contracting relationships prevailing in sections of engineering were characteristic, too, between buyers and sellers in the shipbuilding industry, but Payne's stricture certainly cannot be levelled against an industry whose organisation and production methods were revolutionised, beginning in the 1840s, predominantly by 'new men' on the Clyde. For here, and to a less extent in the north-east, the trend was towards the large establishment linking shipyard and engine-work and which, though as yet untypical, already dominated investment and production in the industry by the 1870s, constructing iron steamships which bore little resemblance to the sailing vessels made of wood which they were superseding (see Slaven, Chapter 5).

As iron was the first major British industry whose output volume was overtaken by foreign competitors the charge of ossification should apply most effectively. Erickson's analysis of the structure and organisation of the closely related steel industry in the 1860s, dominated by well-established family firms (Erickson, 1959, pp. 12–13) certainly supports such a view, as does Hyde's recent claim that productivity in the smelting sector stagnated or declined after the widespread adoption of the hot blast (Hyde, 1977, pp. 162–3). But if Allen's comparisons between British, European and American productivity are valid, they suggest a rising productivity in Britain and Europe from a higher base level between 1840 and 1870, whereas blast furnace productivity in the USA stagnated. Such conclusions warrant a more favourable interpretation of the activities of British ironmasters than is often made (Allen, 1977, pp. 626–32). Riden has criticised Allen's productivity measures (see Riden, Chapter 3), and without commenting on entrepreneurial performance concentrates upon identifying the relevant factors which influenced the course of innovation in the industry, attaching particular importance to differing resource endowments in explaining these comparisons. Riden emphasises not only the relevance of resources in determining the pace and location of technological diffusion, but also the hindrance to more rapid innovation presented by price and piece-rate agreements in the industry which, given the labour-intensive technique characteristic of puddling, limited the opportunities for cost-reducing innovation. Both of the principal technical inventions affecting iron production in this period, the hot blast of the 1830s and the tall blast furnace pioneered in the Cleveland district in the 1860s, were designed to economise fuel consumption. When Bessemer produced steel from the converter in 1858, and Siemens from the open hearth in 1865, the relatively high cost of steel, not unconnected with Bessemer's patent protection to 1870, coupled with the consequent need for demonstrable comparative superiority over iron, produced conditions which were not conducive to the more rapid adoption of the new steel-making process, especially as the 1860s were difficult years for iron producers. Thus, factors other than ossification and entrepreneurial myopia would appear to be of relevance in explaining why the British iron industry had been overtaken by 1870.

The competitive context in which engineering and small metal manufacturers found themselves, though less dramatic than that which faced textile producers in the 1860s, none the less did little to encourage, or allow, the stiffening of industrial sinew. Fluidity and a high turnover of firms characterised engineering, and the considerable degree of specialisation which developed in some sections of the industry between the 1830s and the 1870s, (notably textile machinery and heavy machine tools) seems to have enabled specialised firms to survive almost as successfully as the unspecialised ones (Floud, 1976, pp. 11, 15, 168). Specialisation in this context usually meant specialisation not in a particular product but in a range of technically similar products; specialisation based on other considerations, such as the needs of potential customers, either by individual firms or groups of firms, was less common (p. 14).

Floud's impression of the machine-tool industry, one of the most highly specialised branches of engineering, is that it was neither hidebound nor conservative, and that the responsiveness of manufacturers to the market acquits them of the charge of inefficiency (p. 67). In the west midlands the three decades beginning in 1830 brought the greatest expansion in output of small finished consumer goods and in the number of distinct industries. In part, the growth in demand generated by railway and steamboats, gaslighting and sanitary science, and changing tastes in furniture and domestic ornaments, was met by an increase in the number of producers. But of equal importance was the enterprise demonstrated by men already in business, turning their energies and capital and know-how away from the traditional trades, and in many cases adopting new production methods, for the special skill of the Birmingham manufacturers and artisans could be applied to the production of highly finished goods, irrespective of the material inputs (G. C. Allen, 1929, pp. 32–9, 42–4). A similar process of differentiation, specialisation, and industrial renewal occurred in the light manufacturing trades of the Black Country. Here, as in the Birmingham trades, a similarity in, and divisibility of, technology in the manufacture of hardware and other metal goods produced a high measure of resource mobility, leading to intense competition. Manufacturers introduced additional lines to their existing product range to offset a fall in demand for others, or began to specialise in the production of altogether new items based on new methods (Church, 1969, p. 308). It is precisely this kind of resourcefulness and adaptability which was characteristic of the consumer goods industries of the midlands which suggests that specificity in output in an era preceding mass advertising was neither a barrier to entry, nor as Payne suggests, a one-way process (Payne, 1974, p. 44).

Though far from complete by 1850 the trend towards vertical integration and combination in the cotton industry has been interpreted as a defensive response to competition and depressed profit margins, a strategy which offered maximum flexibility in highly unstable conditions. The reversal towards single-process firms in the 1850s is explained in terms of a more rapidly growing demand for both yarn and cloth, with a greater stability in the markets for yarn, reducing the importance of flexibility and encouraging specialisation as the demand for specific items grew (see Lee, Chapter 8). In the woollen and worsted industry the trend was towards integration in the conversion of wool to cloth, and to specialisation in the main processes of combing, spinning and weaving, the differences in organisation being explained by the greater dependence for profit in woollen manufacture upon the blending of raw materials (see Sigsworth, Chapter 9). Despite the general trend towards greater specialisation, however, the inflation in textile prices during the 1860s as the disruptive effects of the American Civil War made their impact, forced cotton, woollen and worsted manufacturers to experiment and innovate in order to survive.

Whether it is true, as Payne has suggested, that the reliance by manufacturers upon wholesaling factors and merchants tended to encourage the production of an excessively wide range of goods is open to question, a thesis which is at odds with his argument regarding increasing specialisation among manufacturers. The merchant was typically concerned with conducting trade at the same time as maintaining a 'critical balance of liquidity' (see Cottrell, Chapter 12) involving credit from brokers and bankers, a situation which hardly encouraged the acceptance of consignments whose range was 'complete' but not necessarily saleable. Furthermore, the second half of the century saw a greater proportion of business done by merchants on their own account (see Cottrell, Chapter 12). The growth of specialisation in shipowning beginning in the 1840s, and in warehousing by the 1860s, contributed to the greater efficiency of commercial services, though the stability of commercial enterprise was not, on the whole, improved by intense competition in the mercantile sector.

None the less, if we are to believe Joseph Pease, one of the leading industrialists in the north-east, with diversified business interests there and in London, too, it appears that it was in the mercantile, rather than in the manufacturing sector, that fortunes were to be made. He claimed that, perhaps with the exception of the biggest Manchester cotton spinners who did not hold stocks, the great quantity of money made in the cotton, silk, metal and coal trades in the previous ten years was due to fluctuation in the prices of raw materials and exploitation of stock in trade: '. . . the only men who succeeded in making money succeeded in consequence of carrying on a speculative kind of business: that has arisen from the want and regularity in the values of money and produce; the man who did not so speculate, buying largely at one time and selling very freely at another, did not succeed' (*PP*, 1947–8, vol. VIII, q. 4690). The claim that accumulation of immense wealth occurred in trading rather than in manufacturing is strengthened by recent research into the occupational distribution of wealthholders in the nineteenth century. If that was indeed the case, and if we follow Payne's argument, which relates 'a certain conventionally acceptable income level . . . or fortune' to entrepreneurial castration, then it is in the mercantile, rather than the manufacturing sector that we should expect to find a more widespread inducement 'to substitute leisure or political power or prestige from philanthropic works for income maximization[1] (Payne, 1974, pp. 44–5). Payne, however, was referring to the self-imposed limitations to growth in British business in general, though in support of his argument he quoted William Rathbone, the Liverpool merchant and shipowner, who in 1869 observed: 'My feeling with a merchant was that when he got over £200,000 he was too rich for the Kingdom of Heaven' (Marriner, 1961, p. 3). Payne implied that such a figure could be accepted as a 'conventionally acceptable income level' for men of business in our period, presumably beyond which, it is inferred, the marginal utility of monetary income declined rapidly.

But an analysis of wealth and occupations in the nineteenth century suggests that whereas many merchants, bankers, shipowners, merchant bankers and stock and insurance brokers earned substantial fortunes, the typical successful *manufacturer* left an estate amounting to less than £100,000 in the decades before 1850 and only slightly more after that time (Rubenstein, 1977, pp. 605–7, 613). The accumulation of wealth was facilitated, according to Payne, by higher profits per unit of output, achieved by a process of product differentiation, and this in a period when, he suggests, 'many firms would have gone down . . . had they been confronted by the degree of competition encountered by their successors' (pp. 38, 44), an observation which seems to ignore not only the spur of intense competition between firms within the domestic market, but also the pressure on profit margins, to which we shall return.

PERFORMANCE AND PROFIT

Payne's review of British business history between 1830 and 1870 questions the presumption of unqualified strengths and achievements of entrepreneurs in that period compared with their predecessors in the 'heroic' period of the Industrial Revolution; Payne also infers that the pressures and problems in business during the second and third quarters of the century were less intractable than those in preceding, or succeeding, decades. This interpretation is consistent with Deane and Cole's thesis that the growth of the cotton industry in the second quarter of the century, was that it derived from expanding *profit margins* and output (an interpretation from which Lee dissents (see Chapter 8)), while for the third quarter Payne's view is close to a form of the conventional wisdom which has hitherto described these years as the Great Victorian Boom. No such presumption that profits were relatively easy to secure in the third and fourth decades of the century is to be found. In evidence presented to the Select Committee on Manufactures, Commerce and Shipping in 1833 witnesses representing the cotton, wool, iron and shipbuilding industries were unanimous in regarding the period since 1827 as one of severe competition, rising output, falling prices and profits. Not even Thomas Tooke, evidently sceptical of the views expressed by some of the witnesses who appeared before the Select Committee, suggested that trade and manufacturing was being carried on with greater than 'adequate capital and reasonable returns' (Tooke, 1857, pp. 241–2).

He did not define what he meant by 'reasonable returns' (a notion to which we shall return), but a few of the witnesses did, even if they claimed that since the commercial crisis of 1825–6 profit levels had been less than satisfactory until the recent past. Nearly twenty years later, Stephen Moulton, the rubber manufacturer, recorded what he regarded as a 'reasonable degree of profit', in describing a return of 5 per cent on capital (without the interest some other contemporaries expected before 'profit') as 'working against the bone', and that a figure of 20 per cent was the generally acceptable margin on sales for which he strove (Woodruff, 1958, pp. 105, 205).[5] His opinion, however, was that of a quasi-monopolist with patent protection. The evidence offered by Lewis Lloyd, the Manchester banker, Anthony Hill, the Welsh ironmaster, and Henry Nelson, the London shipowner, suggests that contemporaries reckoned a figure somewhere between 10 and 16 per cent on capital employed might be termed reasonable to good, and this appears to have included a notional 4 or 5 per cent interest on partners' and borrowed capital, but made no allowance for depreciation. Joshua Milne, the Oldham cotton spinner, reckoned that after maintenance, depreciation allowance and 5 per cent interest on capital, his profit for 1832 had been 'rather more than 5 per cent', which is an order of magnitude not dissimilar to those referred to above. When Henry Ashworth gave evidence to a House of Lords Committee in 1846 (*PP* [HL], vol. VI, 1846, p. 335), he quoted an 8 or 9 per cent rate of return on capital as 'normal', figures which included a 4 per cent allowance for partners' interest. R. H. Greg was slightly less optimistic, claiming that 'a superior manufacturing firm' would make $7\frac{1}{2}$ per cent over a twenty-year period (pp. 380–2). Nearly twenty years later John Watts, a knowledgeable industrial observer, regarded $12\frac{1}{2}$ per cent as a normal average rate of return in the cotton industry (1868, p. 342).

Empirical evidence on profits is extremely sparse, and even when profit figures do come to light their interpretation is fraught with difficulty and renders meaningful comparisons between series which conceal ambiguities of accounting practice (and not unusually dubious stock and depreciation procedures[6] virtually impossible. This is not the place for a detailed review of the evidence, though it is worth assembling information readily available. Gatrell's examination of the accounts of the Greg, Ashworth and Birley Mills suggests that the rate of profit on capital employed was relatively low, round about 5 per cent (net of interest and allowance for depreciation) in the 1830s, and considerably lower than that in the 1840s (Gatrell, 1972, tables 18 and 19, p. 363). Profit figures in the 1840s for the worsted firms, Barstow and R. V. Marriner, indicate rates of return on net tangible assets of more than 14 per cent and nearly 4 per cent respectively, though Barstow's figures are overstated, and possibly those of Marriner too.[7] These compare with 8 per cent for Barstow in the 1850s (though even more overstated) and 5 per cent for Marriner. Ashworth's New Eagley cotton mill reveals a rate of 9 per cent on a roughly comparable basis, and the same in the 1860s (Boyson, 1970, p. 30). Nine per cent was also Barstow's (overstated) rate for that decade, but Marriner's figure was slightly below 5 per cent. Greg's cotton profits tended to decline in the 1830s and 1840s, moved slightly upwards in the 1850s, only to resume their downward course in the 1860s. But while the highest profits were recorded in particular years in the 1850s and 1860s, these decades also brought the deepest troughs of the entire period between 1830 and 1870 (Gatrell, 1972, pp. 328–63). The return on capital employed at Kenricks, a leading hardware manufacturer, varied between 4 and 15 per cent between 1830 and 1850, before allowances for depreciation and including partners' interest of 5 per cent. Only in five years did the return exceed 10 per cent, and twice fell below 5 per cent (Church, 1969, p. 45).

Profit fluctuations were related to fluctuations in prices which also influenced profit trends. It is impossible to be precise in discussing the relationship, over time, between the prices of raw materials and the prices of manufactured goods, because quality changes were particularly important in the nineteenth century as technology led to product improvement. Moreover, the greater the element of fashion in this or that product, the more difficult it becomes to make any comparison of 'prices' over time. Acknowledging these problems, we have concentrated on those items furthest from fashion and nearest to the intermediate stage of production, for example comparing price movements in a given cotton count, with a specific count of cotton yarn, and a common quality plain cloth. On the basis of observed trends in several price series between 1850 and 1870 (Church, 1975a, table 1), and others discussed by Matthews (1954) in the 1830s we suggest that the trend in industrial profits was strongly influenced by a tendency for the prices of raw materials to rise faster than the prices of manufactured goods, and to fall relatively more slowly. Consequently in those industries where raw materials accounted for a substantial proportion of total costs and the major percentage of variable costs, the squeeze on unit profits was severe.

For example, in the cotton industry raw material costs were estimated at least 50 per cent of variable costs *c*. 1830, and in one firm were as much as 70 per cent early in the 1840s (Church, 1975a, p. 80, fn. 8). It is true, of course, that rising material costs were partly offset by the installation of self-acting mules and power looms, bringing about the operational phase of mechanisation, in which rising labour productivity was accompanied by a reduction in the capital costs per unit of output. Figures quoted by Ellison indicate that the cost of cotton as a percentage of the value of output increased from 20·9 to 36 per cent between 1829–31 and 1880–2, a trend also consistent with the secular decline in the quality of cloth manufactured for export (see Lee, Chapter 8). At the same time, Ellison's data showed that between 1829–31 and 1859–6, payments to labour, including wages, salaries etc., fell as a percentage of the gross receipts in the cotton industry, from 36·2 per cent to 25·8 per cent (Ellison, 1866, p. 69). Deane and Cole (1969) have interpreted this as indicating 'a marked increase in the share of profit in net output', but the remaining column for 'other expenses' in Ellison's table includes the cost of coal, gas, water, oils, dyes, stores, wages paid to mechanics, joiners, builders etc., wear and tear of machinery, interest of capital, in addition to profit. The claim that an increase in profit occurred in the 1830s, 1840s and 1850s, is therefore open to doubt even on Ellison's figures, for 'other expenses' (and one presumes especially those relating to the associated capital expansion of factory production from the 1820s) roughly maintained their percentage importance, until a fall occurred between the mid-1840s and 1859–61. The cost of cotton as a proportion of total costs rose sharply throughout the period.

Matthews's interpretation of the movement of profits in the 1830s, and that of Hughes's in the 1850s, also conflict with Deane and Cole's conclusions which underpin Payne's analysis of Victorian business history. Further doubts are raised by the recent histories of two leading cotton firms, Ashworth Brothers and McConnell & Kennedy, the historian of the latter firm concluding that 'productivity did not increase quick enough . . . to offset the declining cotton/yarn price margin's effects' (Lee, 1972, pp. 142–3). Evidence offered before the Select Committee on Manufactures, Commerce and Shipping in 1833 by Finlay, Houldsworth, Graham, Smith, Greg and Milne, lends further support to this view. Von Tunzelmann's research has also drawn attention to the effects upon cotton manufacturing methods of a particularly severe squeeze on gross margins per pound which resumed in 1845–7, heralding an apparent permanence of reduced gross margins and stimulating the search for improved techniques which would retrieve profitability (von Tunzelmann, 1978, pp. 290–1). A similar mechanism came into operation in the worsted industry, in which the cost structure resembled that of cotton, and by the mid-1850s the ratio of finished products to new wool inputs had fallen from between 3 and 4 to 1, to about 2 to 1, a change attributable, in part, to 'the excess price of wool' but also to the cost reductions in manufacture (von Tunzelmann, 1978, p. 543). Innovations in the quality and style of worsteds were achieved by the introduction of cotton warps, lowering costs, which by making available wool-based products at prices lower than relatively expensive all-woollen worsteds tapped a new and rapidly expanding overseas demand. Woollen manufacturers tackled a similar problem by varying the proportions of virgin wool to shoddy and mungo, developments supported by Lister and Donnisthorpe's wool-combing machine: the lack of progress in dyeing either wool or worsted fabrics was the principal weakness in an industry in which the characteristics of raw materials were crucial in determining success or failure in markets and the profitability of manufacture (see Sigsworth, Chapter 9). Reductions in the cost and price of finished goods thus depended as much upon the purchase and blending of raw materials as upon technical and organisational change. Less is known about the course of industrial change in other textile industries but similarities in cost structures and in relationships between the prices of raw materials and manufactured goods in the leather and rubber industries suggest that developments may have resembled those in the major sections of the textile industry.

A characteristic feature of conditions in the important textile sector was a pull to investment and expanded output, the result, in part, of a growth in the demand for textiles, both in the industrialising and, especially from the 1840s, in the newly developing countries. But there was also an incentive for manufacturers in this highly competitive sector simultaneously to invest and expand output, in order to offset the effects of the growth in demand upon inelastic supplies of textile fibres. Larger output could reduce overheads, a component of capital costs which Ellison's figures show to have been large for the cotton industry (Ellison, 1886, p. 61). Faced with rising prices of their raw materials, manufacturers invested in known innovations and in new technologies, but this increased productive capacity and intensified competitive pressures. This was true for the cotton industry virtually throughout the entire period, for woollen and worsted yarn manufactures in the expansion phases in the 1850s, while for cloth producers expansion continued until the late 1860s. The difference reflected the existence of greater possibilities for technical progress in the manufacture of cloth, which was the process furthest from the raw material. The problems of raw-material supply led to the emergence of associations of merchants and manufacturers anxious to solve them, either through substitutes or by finding alternative supply sources, notably India for cotton and flax. The tentative conclusion may be drawn that the high rate of industrial growth, at least in the most important sector, textiles, was associated not only with expanding markets but also with intense competition which stimulated investment in cost-reducing innovations in the hope of long-run improvements in profitability. The result was an almost perpetual compression of profit margins (Church, 1975a, p. 43). Similar pressure helps to explain the preoccupation of leather manufacturers with splitting machinery in this period (Bevan, 1876, p. 67), while rubber manufacturers able to maintain relatively high profit levels on the basis of patents none the less experienced a squeeze on profit margins as raw-material prices rose at the same time as growing competition led to falling prices of manufactured goods (Woodruff, 1958, pp. 99–102).

The cost structure of the iron and engineering industries contrasted with that of textiles. In 1833 Anthony Hill, an iron producer on a considerable scale in South Wales, employing about 1,500 men and boys in seven blast furnaces and 'mills', reckoned that perhaps three-quarters of the value of bar iron consisted of labour cost, while in engineering the value-added proportion was likely to have been greater, providing even less scope than in the primary processes of economising in the use of raw materials. None the less, the course of pig-iron prices, as estimated by Riden, followed a secular decline from the 1820s to the early 1870s, and relative to prices in general moved in step cyclically but fell further (see Riden, Chapter 3). As in the case of the cotton industry, in each downswing of the trade cycle pig-iron prices did not share in the relatively rapid recovery of output. Riden's review of the evidence on aggregate data prompts the conclusion that when rising, or even stable, output was accompanied by falling prices, the industry was experiencing 'its chronic complaint of overproduction in the face of falling demand, the result of high fixed costs and inelasticity of supply in the short run' (Chapter 3, p. 71). As this describes the general situation, except for brief boom periods, in the late 1820s and mid-1830s, the late 1840s, and from the mid-1850s to the early 1860s the output dynamism of the industry can hardly be attributed to expanding profitability unless drastic production economies were achieved.

Economies of scale should have reduced fixed costs per ton of iron, as coal prices fell steadily and blast furnaces grew in size and contained an increasing amount of ancillary plant (Riden). The hot blast and lesser known innovations reduced coal consumption and lowered smelting costs. In the manufacture of bar iron, after the adoption of puddling completed by 1830, there were no spectacular innovations, in either the forging or rolling of iron comparable with the introduction of the hot blast in smelting, though wet puddling and other minor modifications to plant economised on iron (Riden). Given the limited possibilities of further scale economies, especially in puddling furnaces, so long as labour accounted for the major proportion of variable, if not total, costs, profitability depended much upon labour-saving innovation, which hardly affected the primary process of transforming ore into pig iron. The puddling process, in which the basic technique remained largely unaltered throughout the period, continued to be as labour intensive as when it was first introduced in the eighteenth century. The formal agreement binding the selling price of iron to wage rates between 1848 and the 1860s suggests that little scope existed for cost-reducing innovation here, and this rigid wage structure, taken together with the structure of costs and the implications of heavy fixed investment, prompt scepticism for the view that the 1850s and 1860s was a period of easier profitability and higher unit profits than in the preceding decades. Birch records that between 1854 and 1870 roughly 30 per cent of all furnaces were idle, many awaiting reactivation when induced demand raised prices sufficient to justify temporarily an expanding output, which in turn again depressed prices (Birch, 1967, pp. 124–5, 222–4). A recent study of technological change in the iron industry drew a contrast between the eighteenth and nineteenth century as follows:

'The eighteenth century entrepreneur often made innovations in order to increase output and to earn windfall profits. His nineteenth century counterpart was *forced* to adopt new methods in order to maintain profits threatened by falling price levels and by increased competition. As often as not, the ironmaster of the nineteenth century made innovations to insure his survival in an increasingly competitive industry.' (Hyde, 1977, p. 200)

Much the same can be said about shipbuilding, in which capacity in relation to the level of demand provides the key to understanding the course of industrial change. For whereas there appears to have been no general long-term increase in tonnage rates before the boom of the early 1870s (see Slaven, Chapter 5), the rapid price changes within cycles were most significant in influencing investment decisions of owners and builders. Again, because investment in shipbuilding was 'lumpy', the industry tended to suffer from the effects of prolonged periods of excess capacity. Thus, shipping and shipbuilding were in a generally depressed state throughout the 1820s until the boom beginning in the mid-1830s when investment by shipbuilders was, by their own euphemistic admission, both remunerative and considerably better than for many years (Matthews, 1954, p. 119). Not until the boom of the early 1850s did annual tonnage built exceed that constructed in each of the years 1838–41, and the fifties' boom left the shipbuilding industry with excess capacity until the early 1860s when, as in the case of the iron industry, demand caught up, partly induced by the American Civil War (Matthews, 1954, p. 119; Hughes, 1960, p. 219). Shipbuilders' practice of pricing normally on a cost plus basis did not always prevent losses, due to the intensity of competitive tendering or gains due to special market factors, but Slaven suggests that the 10 per cent commonly employed as the cost plus figure is indicative of what constituted a reasonable profit.

Underpinning the impressive growth in industrial output was the expanding supply of cheap coal, especially after 1850 when the effects of reduced costs of transport, increased competition between coalfields, and higher labour productivity reduced relative coal prices at inland points distant from coalfields and prevented a rise in the price of coal. In common with other primary production, labour was the major cost, representing between 50 and 75 per cent of the cost of coal-getting throughout the nineteenth century (see Taylor, Chapter 2). By reducing the costs of coal-getting and by raising labour productivity through improvements in methods of ventilation and in raising and handling coal some progress was achieved in counteracting the tendency towards diminishing returns. Employment in the industry grew twice as rapidly as population growth between 1841 and 1871, while wage rates and earnings showed little overall movement before 1850 and the 1870s (Taylor). Taylor's suggestions for the notion of normal profitability among colliery owners is the same as those which Slaven suggested for the shipbuilders, 10 per cent. But in the 1850s and 1860s, following

a period in the 1830s and 1840s for which he has found little evidence
of regular profits, knowledgeable contemporaries reckoned that an
average of not more than 5 per cent profit had been earned over the
two decades, a figure confirmed by the taxation data, with the heady
boom of the early seventies bringing to colliery owners an
unaccustomed bonanza. It is hardly surprising that a contemporary
observer commented of coal, 'there are great prizes to be gained . . .
but for every prize that is gained there are a great number of losses'
(quoted by Taylor, p. 59 below). Taylor also raises the interesting
question of whether those who benefited most from the coal industry
were the landowning royalty holders rather than the mining entrepreneurs, a suggestion which parallels the claims by contemporaries
referred to elsewhere that speculation rather than production offered
the greatest opportunities for gain.

Just as the productivity of coal mining depended largely upon the
geological conditions and the efficient utilisation of labour, so in railways, building and shipbuilding, the supply price of the 'goods'
produced was strongly influenced by the mode of industrial organisation adopted and the effective deployment and management of a
heterogeneous workforce. Slaven maintains that managerial and
organisation changes were just as important as the technical innovations reshaping the industry from the 1840s. This may have been even
more true in the case of the building and civil engineering industry,
where before 1850 the cost-reducing effects of mechanisation in cutting
and shaping material inputs were extremely limited and could have
made only a marginal contribution towards the depression of costs
in a period of buoyant demand. Thus, although the price of building
materials fell somewhat before 1850, and the wages of building
workers, too, before 1840, building prices seem to have declined
markedly less than wholesale prices in general. Cooney implies that
had other cost-reducing 'innovations' been introduced, the effects of
a secular growth in demand for all types of construction might have
increased building prices. The innovations which helped to keep prices
down included the growth in the scale of building enterprise, competitive tendering for whole building contracts, and the widespread adoption of the labour-only subcontract – measures which produced
complaints about competition and low wages or intensity of work.
After about 1850 any cost economies due to the intensification of
labour from wage cutting and subcontracting appear to have been at
least temporarily exhausted as resistance to hard driving increased and
wages began to rise. The relative stability of building prices in the
1850s and 1860s, a trend slightly more favourable from the builders'
standpoint, were probably the result of technical advances in the woodworking and brickmaking trades. Meanwhile, even though the large-
scale operator, with relatively high and continuous contract work

making possible fixed plant, efficient estimating and cost control, and the maintenance of a skilled nuclear labour force, could occasionally make a fortune from building, it was the small builder who continued to be the representative figure in a highly competitive trade (see Cooney, Chapter 7).

In an entirely different industrial context, that of the railways, whose 'output' took the form of services, the managerial contribution was necessarily critical to performance. For whereas the early development of the railways in the 1830s and 1840s was to a considerable degree the creature of greedy speculators and unscrupulous contractors in an era when profits were relatively easy to secure, the creditable (if not very profitable) performance of railway companies in the 1850s and 1860s owed much to the achievement of railway managers in maintaining labour productivity at a time when other developments, expanding traffic and improvements in service, otherwise might have pushed it down (see Gourvish, Chapter 6). Expansion of the Clearing House, signifying the progress made in long-distance traffic control; company amalgamation, despite government hostility; the introduction and extension of pooling agreements, traffic divisions and price-fixing arrangements; these were movements towards a rationalisation of railway enterprise achieved from the late 1840s, helping also to shift the competitive area from price to quality of service. This was a development which the incentive structure encouraged, for government encouragement to unplanned competition, supplemented by increasingly strict controls on the companies' pricing freedom which accompanied each new application to Parliament, offered service competition as the major alternative. Gourvish suggests that operating within these constraints, railway managers not only improved the quality of service, without commensurate rate increases, but also successfully sought out low margin traffic.

The implications of this movement towards lower margins in much of manufacturing industry had as its corollary a fall in the rate of return on capital invested in railway companies, reflected in a decline in dividends. Monopoly profits of the cheaply constructed mineral lines of the 1820s were matched by the more successful trunk route companies, such as the London & Birmingham and Grand Junction, which continued to maintain dividends exceeding 6 per cent until the dramatic transformation in profitability which followed the investment mania of 1845–7. Overlaying the cyclical depression in profits was the growth in competition within increasingly severe pricing constraints, the result of government intervention. The combined effect was to reduce dividends of the leading companies below the yield on 3 per cent Consols. in 1849 and 1850, from which low level they rose slowly from 5 to 5½ per cent in the early 1870s, exceeding the yield on Consols. by 70 per cent. After the pioneering phase to 1847, the considerable investment activity centred upon railways produced relatively low rates of return for private investors (Gourvish). Just as in the textile and iron industries the quasi-rent of the relatively large pioneering firms were eroded by competition by the late 1820s (Gatrell, 1972, p. 330; 1977, pp. 104–6, 124–5), so the quasi-rent of the early railway companies began to disappear from the late 1840s.

DYNAMICS OF INDUSTRIAL CAPITALISM

From the standpoint of the old-established firms we may question whether there is substance in Payne's observation that in our period 'the British entrepreneur had no great inducement to alter the basic economic structure painfully evolved in the pioneering period; textiles and iron remained supreme' (Payne, 1974, p. 35). For this overlooks the enormous differentiation in the composition of the output produced by 'textile' manufacturers and 'ironmasters' and 'engineers' for whom market demand was manifest in the form of particular varieties of such broad categories. Payne's comment also disregards the innovations which were necessary preconditions for the success of 'new men' or young firms in shipbuilding (see Slaven, Chapter 5), in textiles, hosiery, footwear and steel, and for the survival of established firms (Gatrell, 1972, pp. 326–30; Erickson, 1959, p. 187; Church, 1970, p. 43; Weir, Chapter 11 below). For those who did not innovate and lacked the private resources required to sustain indifferent profits or losses, bankruptcy was the penalty. 'In nine or ten years', declared Charles Turner, a Liverpool merchant giving evidence to a Select Committee in 1848, 'you get a new race of commercial men; men who have not known 1825' (*PP*, 1847–8, vol. VIII, q. 1016). He was referring to what he considered to be the harmful effects of boom and profit expansion, such as that associated with the mid-1820s, and the intensification of competition which it engendered. The connection between these factors was implicit in Turner's remark, but the relationship had been stated explicitly in evidence offered to an 1833 Select Committee, and was to be repeated twenty years later by merchants and manufacturers of Manchester. Their opinion was that while spectacular profits tended to discourage exertion and economy a further effect was to attract 'adventurers' into the trade (*PP*, 1833, vol. VI, qq. 5111, 5020; Gatrell, 1972, p. 336). Such a fear was implicit, too, in the minutes of the Birmingham Chamber of Commerce in 1868, when reference was made to the depressing effects of the ebb and flow of economic life: 'if we would take wisdom from the past and avoid the trying times of depression in future, we must prevent the previous expansion which causes them' (quoted in Church, 1975a, p. 52).

Such was the mechanism by which the process of industrial growth occurred between the 1820s and the 1870s, and in Manchester, of all places, it was largely because of their inability either to control the trade cycle or to prevent a proliferation of small capitalists, which intensified domestic competition, that Manchester magnates have been described as committing themselves to the search for markets overseas 'with a vehemence enhanced by their relative inability to solve the more pressing problems on their doorstep' (Gatrell, 1972, p. 321). By 1848 a new generation of cotton manufacturers were regretting the erosion of their own positions by continuing competition and excess supplies in markets from yet other small firms. It was because of the encouragement it would give to the small-scale investor to embark upon large-scale enterprise and burden the market further that the Chamber of Commerce opposed the introduction of limited liability. Gatrell concluded that 'fear of fluctuation . . . exacted from cotton men constant vigilance, a preoccupation with the immediate which ruled out all complacency about the achievement in the long run' (p. 364). Sporadic, but widespread investment and innovation accompanied and intensified competition, not only during the well-researched depression of the 1830s but in subsequent decades, too, throughout much of the ambiguously described Great Victorian Boom of the 1850s and 1860s.

The significance for our understanding of the dynamics of Victorian business or a secular pressure on profits, relieved by booms of enormous dimensions, is that it poses an alternative interpretation to that advanced by Deane and Cole (Deane and Cole, 1967, pp. 189–91), and implicit in the writings of Payne and others. Far from the possibility that high unit profits expanding at an unprecedented rate having blunted the edge and weakened the thrust of Victorian entrepreneurs, it becomes plausible to argue that because profit rates were relatively modest and came under almost constant pressure, the spur to profit was at least as important to the growth mechanism as was an expanding world market due to rising population, income and improved transport. Hitherto, historians have stressed the dynamic of market expansion, sometimes overlooking the powerful economic effects of compression, and the stimulus to innovation and investment generated by a highly competitive economy in which the rate of profit in mining and manufacturing was less than in an earlier stage of industrialisation (See below pp. 37–8). Such a model of industrial progress seems to have been in the mind of Sir William Fairbairn, who in 1849 had explained the mechanisms by which steam power became more and more widely applied: 'the subject was never fairly brought home to millowners and steam navigation companies, until an equalization or reduction of profits directed attention to the saving attainable by a different system of operation' (quoted by von Tunzelmann, 1978, p. 218).

For the Victorian businessman profits were the spur, though certainly not the only goal, but the risks of enterprise were considerable, even in a period commonly supposed to mark the climax of British industrial pre-eminence. Contemporaries were well aware of this, as some of our quotations indicate, and Shannon's analysis of the first 5,000 limited liability companies underlines the validity of contemporary observations. The study showed that almost 36 per cent of the ordinary companies formed in the years between 1856 and 1865 ceased to exist in any form within five years of formation, with a further 4·5 per cent sold or reconstructed. Within ten years some 54 per cent had ceased to exist, those having to be sold or reconstructed accounting for an additional 7 per cent (Shannon, 1933, p. 418). The exclusion from Shannon's figures of inoperative formations, reconstructions, and amalgamations provides a clearer picture, though not substantially different from that presented by Shannon. Of those companies formed between 1856 and 1863, fewer than 50 per cent showed a ten-year survival rate and slightly more than 30 per cent survived twenty years. The remainder went into liquidation (Macgregor, 1934, pp. 100–105). Shannon's conclusion remains valid, that whatever production took place under limited liability in its early days occurred at a business loss (Shannon, 1933, p. 419). The fate of the early limited liability companies was probably no less typical of the mortality rates of private enterprises in partnerships and proprietorships. Writing in 1892, by which time he considered the risks of trade to be diminishing, Alfred Marshall reckoned that

'the number of those who succeed in business is but a small percentage of the whole; and in their hands are concentrated the fortunes of others several times as numerous as themselves, who have made savings of their own, or who have inherited the savings of others and lost them all, together with the faults of their own efforts, in unsuccessful business . . . It is probable that the true gross earnings of Management, that is, the excess of profits over interest, is not on the average more than a half, and in some risky trades not more than a tenth part, of what it appears to be to persons who form their estimate of the profitableness of a trade by observation only of those who have secured its prizes.' (Marshall, 1892, p. 314.)

If profit is to be regarded as compensation for risk, the question arises whether profits were commensurate with risk in the nineteenth century. In our period Consol. yields of between 2·5 and 3·5 per cent may be accepted as the highest return on capital available in the long term and without risk; slightly higher returns were available upon good securities with only minimum risk, which makes the return on railway investment of between 5 and 6 per cent at its greatest far from handsome. Certainly it fell far short of the 10 per cent figure which Gladstone evidently considered to constitute something akin to monopoly profit, and which he proposed should, if achieved in three consecutive years, provide justification for automatic nationalisation by the government (see Gourvish, Chapter 6). Whether this also indicated a general presumption that profits in excess of 10 per cent in any sector of the economy were anti-social is open to question, for railway monopoly was a subject which aroused intense interest both inside Parliament and without, besides which there was already a feeling among many politicians that transport should provide a service to the public at reasonable charges.[8]

If, as we suggest, on the admittedly scanty evidence reviewed above, the national 'satisfactory', 'reasonable' or 'normal' profit of 10 or 15 per cent (including the notional 5 per cent interest on capital) was the figure in the minds of nineteenth-century entrepreneurs, then the question of whether it reflected expectations which were unreasonable, given the risk and compared with the yield on Consols. is debatable. It may be significant that entrepreneurs seem to have expected 4 or 5 per cent 'interest' from capital invested in their businesses, sometimes included in the figure they referred to as 'profit' for this, of course, was equivalent to the usury rate of 5 per cent, which was abolished only in 1833. Whether an additional 5 or 10 per cent net profit is to be considered 'usurious' and therefore 'high' in a post-usury society is entirely a matter of judgement. Thomas Culpepper in 1668, Joseph Massie in 1750, and Adam Smith in 1776 seem to have been in agreement that profit from 'trade' should amount to twice the going rate of interest, and that is the approximate order of magnitude (between 6 and 12 per cent) which Grassby's fragmentary evidence suggests may have been the average return obtained by successful traders at the end of the seventeenth century (Grassby, 1969, pp. 733–45), before the Industrial Revolution and the golden age, if it ever existed, of industrial capitalism.

Pollard has quoted one of Robert Owen's many biographers who referred to the pre-1830 heroic age 'when capital had an extraordinary monopoly value, and when enterprising manufacturers were making with ease 20 per cent and more on their capital'. At New Lanark 'the margin of profit was so wide that we need scarcely look for any other explanation of Owen's success as a manufacturer' (Pollard, 1965, p. 246, quoting Podmore, 1923). The quotation proves nothing, but it does betray a notion of what order of magnitude constituted monopoly profit in the mind of Owen's biographer, and it exceeds the figures we have encountered in our admittedly brief and superficial review of the evidence for the second and third quarters of the nineteenth century. When J. R. Ward refers to 'fabulous profits' having been earned by several of the first generation canals by the 1790s, the dividends referred to are in the region of 20 per cent, and during the boom of 1824–5 earnings went much higher for the most profitable canals, notably the Trent and Mersey (75 per cent), the Coventry (44 per cent), the Stafford and Worcester (40 per cent), the Mersey and Irwell (35 per cent) and the Oxford (32 per cent) (Ward, 1974, pp. 87, 177). These historically high returns included in English's analysis of the dividends of 61 canal companies, showed that in 1824–5 33 earned dividends in excess of 10 per cent (mostly between 11 and 25 per cent), that 7 earned between 6 and 10 per cent, 8 earned less than 5 per cent, while 13 declared no dividend at all (English, 1827, appendix). It is relevant to note that the early railways were built in order to destroy the monopoly profits of the canals shortly after this date.

Crouzet has reviewed the evidence on profitability in manufacturing industry roughly between 1770 and 1820, though based, as he readily admitted, on the record of 'progressive firms in particularly profitable industries' (Crouzet, 1972, p. 196). All achieved 'extremely high net profits' which in good years were often in excess of 15 or even 20 per cent return on capital employed after allowing 4 or 5 per cent as interest on capital (p. 195). 'Very high' though Crouzet regarded these figures he did not regard such levels as sufficiently 'exorbitant' in the long run to leave much of a surplus after reinvestment necessary for growth (pp. 63, 202). He also maintains that despite falling unit profits from the early nineteenth century, there is no evidence to suggest that rates of return were noticeably affected, except during the severe postwar depression (pp. 196–7).

Our impression is that in comparison with 'profits' in the 'heroic' period of invention and industrial revolution during the fifty years before 1825, the rate of return in industry and transport between 1825 and 1870 was lower than hitherto and was not excessive. Moreover, we regard the opinion expressed by Samuel Smiles in 1856, that 'Anybody who devotes himself to making money, body and soul, can scarcely fail to make himself rich, very little brains will do' (quoted in Payne, 1974, p. 35), as quite simply untenable. Another contemporary, William Cotton, formerly a governor of the Bank of England and well acquainted with commercial affairs expressed the opposite view: 'I have scarcely known an instance in which parties without experience have commenced business with a large capital and that capital has not in a very few years been lost' (*PP*, 1851, vol. XVIII, p. 574). The accumulation of substantial riches, it seems, was rather more dependent upon speculation, inventive skills, exceptional enterprise, or windfall gains than merely upon honest plodding. A study of the rise of the Foster's industrial dynasty in the midlands from the late eighteenth century concludes that during the nineteenth century untaxed capital gains were the most important single source of growing wealth. Investment in urban property and landed estates accounted for nearly one half of the assets owned by James Foster in 1849. The other half was in the form of collieries, blast furnaces, forges and foundries, which in the 1840s employed about 5,000 people (Mutton, 1976). The growth of Victorian cities offered attractive opportunities for long-term investment.

Of course, serious *caveats* must be made, not only because of the superficiality of our survey of the evidence, but also because the concept of 'profit' in the first three-quarters of the nineteenth century differed from industry to industry, sometimes between one firm and another. 'Profits' were commonly understood to be the surplus after interest on capital was paid, and the capital on which profit was calculated was often the original partnership capital, or the current capital value of the enterprise (Pollard, 1965, pp. 234–5). The exclusion of 'interest' from 'profit' figures meant that profits were probably often understated, and the expression of profit as a rate of return on the original partnership capital would clearly provide an overestimate. Furthermore, the absence for the most part, of any systematic practice of true percentage depreciation was an offsetting deflationary element in contemporary estimates of profits, for if, as was the rule rather than the exception, depreciation was not deducted, and machinery and tools were replaced only when necessary, profits could be over-stated by anything up to 10 per cent (Brief, 1966, pp. 22–3).[9] The problems of identifying profit are compounded even further by the frequent practice of writing off capital expenditure rapidly from 'profits' in good years and when 'profits' were low or losses incurred to carry forward capital expenditure until profits improved and then write it off.

Pollard suggested that before 1830 'selling prices tended to be so far above total costs, no matter how calculated, that almost any pricing policy was bound to show a net surplus, at least among the leaders in their industries', and that such a favourable market position was not conducive to improvements in accounting practice, which awaited a time when 'easy margins' began to disappear (Pollard, 1965, p. 245). We have suggested that there are indications of their disappearance following the boom of 1824–5, but not even the Property and Income Tax Act of 1842 nor certain clauses of the company legislation of 1855–62 did more than marginally affect accounting practices. A systematic examination of business records of the worsted industry, the only British manufacturing industry to have received such scrutiny, reveals that even in the 1860s and 1870s the practice of making allow-ances for overheads and systematic depreciation of machinery was rare (Hudson, 1978, pp. 13–15). Even though fixed capital had become an important component in manufacturing by that time, accounting conventions lagged behind. The persistence of the partnership form of enterprise, even among larger firms, tended to perpetuate the distinction drawn by contemporary businessmen between interest on capital and profits as the reward of enterprise or windfall surplus

(Pollard, 1965, pp. 271–6). The notion of capital as ancillary to, rather than identified with entrepreneurship, discouraged the regular assessment of profits in a consistent fashion. Even the accounting practices of the otherwise managerially advanced railway companies were less helpful to management than was desirable (Pollins, 1969, p. 159).

Pollard's portrayal of the Industrial Revolution before 1830, when he thought total profits to have been very much higher in relation to 'total industrial incomes', i.e. in relation to wages, than they were to become later, suggests an important respect in which the characteristics of business experience may have differed from those which followed in the period beginning in the late 1820s and continuing at least throughout the second and third quarters of the century, namely industrial structure and profitability. Within the business sector most of the major features of the 'heroic' phase of the Industrial Revolution are well known, though to what extent the achievements were the result of entrepreneurial excellence has been questioned recently by Payne. Stressing that the period 1780 to 1830 presented what was in some ways 'a uniquely favourable economic environment' (Payne, 1974, p. 231). Payne has drawn attention to the ease with which large profits could be made, as much by luck as by judgement, due to an extraordinarily buoyant market and monopolistic advantages which the rapidly developing technology of the period made possible. This follows Pollard's analysis emphasising the element of quasi-monopoly profit which enabled most of the 'advanced industrialists' in coal mining, transport, engineering, silk, chemicals, pottery, woollen and even the cotton industries to make abnormally high profits; whereas monopolistic advantages in mining and transport were due to actual market control, (and in distilling to excise legislation (see Weir, Chapter 11))), the monopoly element in the manufacturing industries was due to 'equal advantages by technique or design'. Only 'the bulk of the cotton industry, and certain sections of the iron industry . . . were truly competitive' (Pollard, 1965, p. 246).

Unfortunately we know little about the longevity of firms, and even less about the differential survival rates and comparative profitability of large and small firms, which makes the implied differences in the structure and profitability of business before and after *c.* 1830 difficult to identify. Chapman has argued that by the 1830s the increase in the optimum size of plant was squeezing out the smaller firms (Chapman, 1972, pp. 26–7, 34), a view which was popular among contemporary observers. Gatrell's detailed analysis of the structure and organisation of the cotton industry presents a different picture, in which although the economic advantages were moving in favour of the integrated firm between 1830 and 1870, only the smallest aspirants, working men lacking the cost of a power loom, found their way into the industry barred. He has argued that competition intensified in the cotton industry during the second quarter of the century (Gatrell, 1977, pp. 120, 124–5). Furthermore, on the basis of an analysis of survival rates during the protracted crisis of 1837–42 he concluded that 'the difference between the vulnerability of small firms as against large, of simple process firms as against mixed, was surprisingly slight' (Gatrell, 1977, p. 121). Even in the cotton industry, which before 1860 was best placed to generate scale economies based on steam-powered production, either financial or marketing constraints in effect limited the scope for large scale enterprise accompanied by large profits, except for a handful of well-established or exceptionally talented entrepreneurs. Besides, the stall system enabled the small man to insert himself into the productive network and benefit from the technical advantages of steam power. The worsted industry offers a parallel in that, like the pioneers in the power-based cotton industry, Lister made a fortune, but it was on the basis of growing competition among woolcombers using his patent machinery (*Fortunes Made in Business*, Vol. I, 1884, pp. 50–63). Titus Salt's enormous profits from the alpaca trade in its early stage of development were soon under pressure from competitors, bringing about a decline in the prices of manufactured goods in the middle decades, when alpaca prices were rising (*Fortunes Made in Business*, Vol. I, 1884, pp. 306–9).

In the rubber industry, which was in its pioneering phase in our period, Macintosh earned substantial profits from Hancock's vulcanisation patent between 1823 and 1848, when Moulton challenged the firm's monopoly with his own patent; but less than ten years later the dominant position which he shared with Macintosh was destroyed by the entry of an American company infringing previous patents with impunity under the protection of Scottish law. Between 1849 and 1860 Moulton reckoned the business had made 20 per cent (but excluding allowances for depreciation), the figures of more than 40 and 50 per cent recorded for the mid-1850s falling sharply with the entry of the American North British Rubber Company on the scene (Woodruff, 1958, pp. 92–3, 227).[10] A similar sequence of quasi-rent profits followed by their elimination through competition occurred also in the iron and coal industries, after the expiration of Neilson's patent on the 'hot blast process' followed by the diffusion of this innovation in English furnaces in the 1840s.[11]

The capital costs of this new technology were relatively modest and quickly offset by the financial savings resulting from its adoption. After the 1840s, when its use became widespread, there were no major scale economies available to the ironmasters until the new steelmaking methods appeared in the 1860s. Neither were economies of large scale production available to the coalmasters, competition between the colliery owners outside the North East following the collapse of the Vend (see Taylor, Chapter 2).

In the footwear industry, Clarks of Street experienced increasing pressures on profits after the mid-1850s, the combined result of increasing competition, rising material costs, the introduction of machinery and a growing burden of indirect production costs which eventually brought losses in the 1860s, the first for twenty years (G. B. Sutton, 1959). Distillers also experienced considerable competition, especially after the excise reforms in the early decades, and during the boom and slumps of the 1820s which ushered in a period of low and declining profitability. A growth in industrial concentration occurred following the introduction of the Coffey still during the 1840s and 1850s eliminating competition from many small producers, though even the large patent distillers failed to fix prices and control competition among themselves (see Weir, Chapter 11).

Even supposing foreign competition was not at least a potential threat in the mid-Victorian decades (and not all industrialists would have agreed), in terms of profit opportunity the industrial structure was such as to render abnormal profits of the magnitude sometimes encountered in the early years of industrial revolution highly unlikely. The mere fact that few technical innovations of fundamental importance occurred in manufacturing and mining in the second and third quarters of the nineteenth century provides a further and important reason to expect a tendency for profitability to be lower *ceteris paribus* than in the 'heroic' phase of the Industrial Revolution, for in the long term competition appears to have kept pace with market expansion.

Our protracted discussion of Payne's generalisations on Victorian business is amply justified by his own anodyne, though apposite, caption for the history of entrepreneurship between 1830 and 1870: 'The Early Victorian Decades: The Need for More Information'. Greater space has enabled us to marshal more information on this subject and as a result to modify some of the prevailing hypotheses and assumptions regarding Victorian business. Their foundation is only marginally less flimsy than those they seek to replace, but if debate acts as a stimulant to further research on the major questions at issue, this collection of essays will have been justified. The basis of the chapters presented here shows that British industrial experience in the second and third quarters of the nineteenth century display common characteristics of intersectoral disparities in price movements, producing diverse patterns of investment and profitability. Supplementary evidence suggests that after the boom of 1824–5, when the 'heroic' phase of the Industrial Revolution was ending, relatively high rates of profit based on 'quasi-monopoly' in much of British industry began to disappear, as industry assumed a more competitive structure, in which fluidity and adaptation to changing circumstances, rather than ossification, are the dominant characteristics.

Our evidence is slim and is based, *faute de mieux*, on observations of microeconomic data, the representativeness of which is in doubt. It suggests, however, that there was probably a general fall in the normal rate of return on capital after the mid-1820s to normally expected levels of round about 10 per cent gross, before depreciation. While profits in the 1830s seem likely to have been lower than in succeeding decades, the difference between profitability in the 1840s, 1850s and 1860s does not appear to have been great enough to warrant the assumption that profits were either easy to secure or large. If such tentative conclusions can be supported by further research then it follows that low rather than high unit profits fuelled the engine of industrial growth during the second and third quarters of the century, and that while the economy in the early and mid-Victorian decades offered huge rewards for invention and pioneering innovation, these were speedily eroded by the almost relentless competitive pressure on profitability which followed each major investment boom.

In the 'drive to maturity' the Rostovian phase coinciding with the post 'Industrial Revolution' era, the stimulus to expansion, as distinct from invention and pioneering entrepreneurship, did not derive from very high rewards and easy gains; for this reason, neither can an alleged disincentive to grow, if such a phenomenon can be identified with any confidence, be attributed to the great Victorian boom, whether identified with the period beginning in the 1830s or the 1850s, to 1873. The rate of innovation in the second and third quarters of the century cannot be explained without some emphasis being placed upon the pressure on profit margins, due, we have argued, in large part to the movement in the prices of raw materials relative to the prices of manufactured goods and to increasing competition. The *form* which invention and innovation took was influenced more by the scope for economies in the use of one of the various input factors, influenced by relative costs, but the mechanism which generated rapid industrial growth was that triggered by relatively modest unit profits and less than impressive rates of return on capital within a highly competitive industrial structure. Buttressed by improvements in communications and an agricultural sector able to sustain a growing population without serious deterioration in living standards, such a combination produced a high-compression economy, which induced unprecedented industrial expansion. The Victorian economy is popularly described as an expanding economy, and so it was; but industrial expansion was as much a result of development induced by the compression of profit margins, as by the widening markets and growth in demand which so often have been regarded as providing the key to understanding the mechanism of British industrial growth in the nineteenth century. Such a model was not conducive to a hardening of industrial arteries, signs of which, as we have tried to show, are few before the 1870s.

Our conclusions are tentative, but we hope unambiguous. That such conflicting generalisations can be argued with the conviction which even the flimsy evidence assembled here makes possible is a reflection upon the state of research into the business history of the nineteenth century. It is odd that while the Victorian era probably attracts more research effort than either eighteenth- or twentieth-century history we know less about the industrial history of the period between 1830 and 1870 than we do of the forty years which preceded and followed. This is especially surprising in view of the claim that more books and articles have been published on industry and trade since 1925 than in any other single category (Harte, 1977, p. 36), and that another measure shows historians of business to have been largely preoccupied with the history of manufacturing and mining enterprises roughly between 1750 and 1914 (Church, 1976, p. 217). None of the major industries has been the subject of a comprehensive study, based on extensive use of primary sources, and Beales's complaint of neglect made nearly fifty years ago has been echoed and re-echoed since that time, latterly by Payne in 1974. Within the limits possible, the original chapters comprising this collection are intended to remedy this need, and to signpost those areas in British business history which deserve more attention if we are to improve our understanding of the character of British industrial capitalism at its zenith and to identify the dynamics of Victorian business.

NOTES TO CHAPTER 1

1   Feinstein (1972) has produced a revised Hoffman series in which he uses data assembled by W. A. Lewis, and incorporating weights on a 1907 base. But as the series begins in 1855 it is not helpful in this context. Table 24 shows percentage increases in industrial production at constant factor cost, between successive ten-year periods as follows:

    1855–64 and 1865–74   3·25
    1860–9 and 1870–9   3·06
    1865–74 and 1875–84   2·47
    1870–9 and 1880–9   2·08

2   Wright (1965, p. 406) points to Imlah's (1958) estimates of the terms of trade as suggesting that manufacturers' margins fell by more than the prices of raw materials. Further, less ambiguous evidence is to be found in Matthews (1954), Hughes (1960) and Church (1975a). See also below.

3   In absolute terms, the statement is true, but when the rate of expansion between 1800 and 1870 is compared with that between 1870 and 1907 the earlier period shows a faster increase, largely due to the low base in 1800 (Kanefsky).

4   Even more surprising is the conclusion drawn by Asher in the empirical comparison of efficiency and technical change in the British and American textile industries in the nineteenth century. Using econometric techniques and data of doubtful reliability his research showed that whereas in accord-

ance with the Rothbarth Habakkuk contention the American industries were experiencing a labour-saving bias in technical growth, that bias was even greater in the woollen branch of British textiles, while the British cotton industry indicated a capital-saving bias (Asher, 1972, p. 441).

5 These figures excluded allowances for depreciation and, therefore, over-estimate the real rate of return. Also relevant is the innovative phase of the rubber industry at this time.

6 For an extreme example see the analysis of the accounts in R. H. Campbell (1961, pp. 170–1).

7 I am grateful to Patricia Hudson for supplying relevant data from her own research.

8 Perhaps a clue to what level of return was considered 'reasonable' in the eighteenth century is to be found in the proposal advanced by five of the subscribers of the Birmingham Navigation in 1768, that Commissioners should be appointed to exercise supervision of the company accounts, and for the disposal for the public use of any surplus of profits over a return of 10 per cent to the subscribers on their investment. A. B. DuBois (1938, p. 205, fn. 289).

9 See examples of depreciation allowances for the 1830s in Pollard (1965, p. 244).

10 Note, however, that despite these high profit figures, it was not until the end of the 1860s that his business was earning enough to finance the firm from re-invested profits (Woodruff, 1958, pp. 33).

11 Bessemer, with his 'cent per cent' rate of return from his patent monopoly hardly affected wrought-iron producers in our period, and among steelmakers, too, bulk production was a special case in the early years of the Bessemer process.

2 The Coal Industry

by A. J. Taylor

Coal is unique among nineteenth-century industries. Not only was it a major industry in its own right, by 1875 directly employing over half a million men and boys, but throughout the century it was virtually the sole supplier of energy to Britain's expanding economy. As the principal extractive industry it also occupied a special place in the economy between agriculture and manufacturing industry; and as the progenitor, provider and customer of the emergent railway industry, it linked its fortunes closely with those of this major force in nineteenth-century economic development.

I

No public records exist before 1854 of coal output at the national level and for twenty years thereafter the annual *Mineral Statistics* made by the Geological Survey have the imperfections that attach to figures based on voluntary rather than compulsory returns (Mitchell and Deane, 1962, p. 115; for an alternative series see *PP*, 1873, vol. X, pp. 324–5). For earlier years the evidence is fragmentary and even less reliable; but the estimate of the Royal Commission of 1871 of an output of 10 million tons in 1800 has at least the right order of magnitude. It accords well with the more firmly established figures of exports from the north-eastern coalfields and with estimates of the major coal-consuming industries; and it is also consistent with contemporary estimates of 13 to 15 million tons for output at the end of the Napoleonic Wars. (*PP*, 1871, vol. XVIII, p. 32; Galloway, 1898, pp. 443–4). From these estimates there may be inferred an annual growth rate by the British coal industry of between 3·5 and 4 per cent between 1815 and 1875 and of 3·5 per cent for the shorter period from 1854 to 1875 – rates of increase which can be compared with a growth rate of 2·1 per cent between 1875 and 1913.

For the more detailed analysis of the pattern of growth before 1854 recourse must be made to less direct evidence. A convenient starting point is the series of returns which cover the supply of coal to London by sea before 1845 and by sea and rail thereafter. Table 2.1 shows the rate of growth of coal consumption in London and its immediate vicinity for quinquennial periods between 1815 and 1875.

Table 2.1   *Growth of Coal Consumption in London 1815–75*

	Coal Consumption, Growth/Annual (%)	
1813/17 – 1818/22	2·4	
1818/22 – 1823/7	3·4	
1823/7 – 1828/32	1·7	2·4
1828/32 – 1833/7	2·2	
1833/7 – 1838/42	3·3	
1838/42 – 1843/7	2·0	
1843/7 – 1848/52	3·5	
1848/52 – 1853/7	3·8	
1853/7 – 1858/62	2·9	3·4
1858/62 – 1863/7	3·5	
1863/7 – 1868/72	3·8	
1868/72 – 1873/7	3·6	

Source: Mitchell and Deane (1962, pp. 112–13).

As a pointer to more general trends in consumption and output these figures must obviously be treated with caution but there are grounds for believing that they understate rather than exaggerate the increase in the rate of growth in coal utilisation in the country at large. In 1815 a large part of the coal produced in Britain was taken by the domestic consumer. With the advance of industrialisation this proportion steadily declined and by 1870 it amounted to less than 18 per cent. The major consumers were now the iron and steel industry (30 per cent) and manufacturing industry (with 23 per cent for steam power alone). In both these industries not only had output increased substantially faster than general population growth, but the rate of growth had tended to accelerate with the passing of time. This was most noticeably the case in the textile industries where the total horse-power employed grew by 45 per cent between 1838 and 1850 but multiplied a further three and a half times in the next eleven years (*PP*, 1871, vol. XVIII, pp. 204–5; Mitchell and Deane, 1962, *passim*, citing Factory Returns). It seems, therefore, probable that the rate of growth in coal output was significantly higher after 1845 than before and reached its nineteenth-century peak at some point in the thirty years between 1845 and 1875.

It would be wrong to infer, however, that because the rate of growth was substantial and increasing, it was continuous from year to year. The *Mineral Statistics*, for example, suggest that there were six years between 1854 and 1875 when output actually fell and two others in which growth was minimal. The industry tended to move forward in a series of lurches, each short period of advance being followed by one of relative quiescence and consolidation. The clearest evidence of this is provided by the industry's experience in the early seventies.

The sharp expansion in demand for iron and steel which accompanied and followed in the wake of the Franco–Prussian War brought a concomitant demand for coal which the industry was not immediately equipped to meet. Prices rose as supply failed to keep pace with demand. In a little over eighteen months from the end of 1871 to the autumn of 1873 pithead prices doubled. The emergency brought new capital and labour pouring into the industry. Workings earlier abandoned as no longer economic were reopened and new sinkings begun. Output rose by 10 per cent in two years and supply gradually came to terms with demand. By the end of 1873 the general boom had exhausted itself. Output continued to rise, but now with falling prices, until in 1875 it reached 133 million tons. At this figure production remained firmly stabilised until 1880 when demand again began to move forward.

Many of the collieries projected in the years of high demand had not come into operation by the time the boom was spent. Some never reached maturity, others were kept standing for years until they could be operated at a profit, and some were sold at a price well below the cost of their winning to entrepreneurs who were thus able to write off much of the initial capital cost. Two substantial collieries on the Cannock Chase coalfields, for example – East Cannock and Leighs Wood – having cost £150,000 and £100,000 to win, were sold for £20,000 and £5,000 respectively; and of the Northumberland coalfield it was said that 'nearly everybody who took collieries in 1873–5 failed' (Peel, 1951, p. 331; *PP*, vol. XXXIV, p. 129).

In the mid-nineteenth-century growth of the coal industry the railway had been the industry's essential handmaid. The railway had been created by coalowners in the north-east to serve their own immediate needs. But, Frankenstein-like, it turned on its creators, first intensifying competition within the north-east itself and then depriving the coalfield of the monopoly which it had hitherto enjoyed in supplying coal to the highly prized London market. This, however, was only part of the wide general changes which the new form of transport was effecting in the map of coal distribution in Britain. While coal from the inland fields was penetrating the London market, north-eastern coal was finding new outlets not only in its own local markets but across the Pennines and in the industrial north, and new markets were opening up in the rural areas of southern England and Scotland. Between 1835 and 1870 the price of coal at the quayside in Newcastle increased by 70 per cent while at the ship's side in London it fell by over 18 per cent. The decisive breakthrough had come precisely at the point when competitive railborne coal first entered the London market on an appreciable scale in the mid-fifties (*Colliery Year Book*, 1962, p. 416; Mitchell and Deane, 1962, p. 482). The main beneficiaries of these developments were consumers at a distance from the coalfields but even in Manchester, served by collieries less than two miles from the city centre, the price paid for engine coal was on average 6 per cent lower over the period 1851–70 than it had been between 1831 and 1850. (Knowles, 1890, p. 49).

The railway cheapened coal in a double sense: by reducing the cost of transportation and by increasing the competition between and within the coalfields. It also itself, directly and indirectly, provided a market for coal. By 1869 2 million tons were consumed by Britain's locomotives, almost as much as was needed to provide power for the machines in the cotton industry (*PP*, 1871, vol. XVIII, p. 205). Indirectly, through the use which it made of iron, bricks and other materials, the railway also made great if uneven demands upon coal, and these increased as the tempo of railway building grew not only at home but also overseas.

In marketing terms, coal was basically a passive industry, responding to demands made upon it rather than seeking actively to create them. This is not to say that individual entrepreneurs were lacking in aggression. There was fierce competition within the coalfields, and entry into the London market, in particular, was keenly sought. But the general opinion within the industry, of coalowners and miners alike, was that at any given time the market for coal was limited; and this view became explicit in restrictive institutions and practices like the Limitation of the Vend of the north-eastern coalowners and the stint on output practised intermittently by miners' unions from at least the 1830s. The export trade, however, provided greater scope for initiative. Throughout the nineteenth century export demand was expanding more rapidly than home consumption. Between 1837 when they first reached 1 million tons and 1854, exports quadrupled. In 1854, they constituted 6 per cent of British output and by 1875, at 14 million tons, this proportion had risen to just over 10 per cent. The north-east and south Wales reaped the main benefit from this expansion and by 1875 there were districts in both coalfields which depended on the sea-going trade not only for their prosperity but for their survival; but for the wider British coal industry, as for the economy in general, the significance of this advance in foreign demand lay rather in its promise for the future than in its importance in the coal economy of the 1870s (Mitchell and Deane, 1962, p. 121).

II

Like agriculture, coalmining is an elemental industry, dependent for its success, and indeed its existence, on what nature provides or withholds. The profitability of a colliery is basically determined by the quality of its coal, the depth, inclination and extent of faulting of its seams, the presence or absence of water and gas and the colliery's accessibility to the markets in which its coal can be sold. Because of the great variety which these natural conditions imply, the industry does not encourage easy generalisations.

In institutional terms nineteenth-century agriculture and coalmining also had much in common. Each was based on the landlord–tenant– worker relationship; but whereas the landowner was an active partner in the working of the land, he came to play an altogether more passive role in mining operations. Already by the beginning of the century in many coalfields landowners had retreated from the front line of mineral exploitation, preferring the secure return of the royalty- holder to the more speculative profits of the entrepreneur. Even as landlord, however, the landowner was tending to play a less positive part in the working of his coal than of his farmland. This was, no doubt, in part because, while the soil was rightly seen as a permanent possession, with a value to be maintained and enhanced by the renewal of its fertility, coal was a wasting asset with a once-for-all value extinguished on its sale to a lessee. In consequence the major concern of nineteenth-century landowners was to frame leases in ways intended to maximise their incomes. Though there were notable exceptions, landowners in general no longer took upon themselves the proving of seams and the sinking of shafts, and by the end of the century in the eyes of many the landowner had become a parasitic element in the industry (Ward, 1971, p. 71). The most that could be said in the landlords' favour was that the burden which they laid upon the industry did not increase and perhaps even diminished with the passing of time. Royalties, running on average at 6d per ton in 1890, were at this level little different from what they had been throughout the second half of the century (*PP*, 1893–4, vol. XLI, pp. 5, 10).

Only a small number of landowners were still working their own coal in 1830 and these comprised only a small minority of the nation's colliery owners. Yet their importance was far greater than their mere number might suggest. In Cumberland two landowning families, the Lonsdales and the Curwens, dominated the industry; in Lancashire the Dukes of Bridgewater and the Earls Crawford were equally pre- eminent; in Yorkshire the largest colliery operators were the Fitzwilliams; and the Dudleys were even more powerful in the Black

Country. It was, however, above all in Durham that the role of the great coal-working landowner was most evident. In a district notable for the size of its colliery enterprises none were so large as those of the Earl of Durham and the Marquis of Londonderry, each of whose operations by 1843 involved investments of at least a quarter of a million pounds (*PP*, 1843, vol. XIII, pp. cvii–cviii).

In 1830, as indeed throughout the earlier history of the coal industry, the north-eastern coalfield had been in the forefront of British mining development not only by virtue of the amount of coal which it produced but also in the quality of its mining practices and the size of the operating units. A return covering 31 of the 41 collieries shipping coal on the Tyne in 1828 shows capital investments in the collieries varying between £15,000 and £110,000 and payrolls similarly rising from 118 to 614. The average investment was £38,000 and the average work-force 322. Even larger enterprises were operating on the Wear and here the landowning colliery operator was most in evidence. As early as 1815 the Vane-Tempests (forebears of the Londonderrys) employed over 1,000 workers and the Lambtons 850. By 1843 the Londonderry collieries were employing 1,497 and the Lambtons 1,690 – the latter dispersed among five collieries. (Buddle MSS., North-east Vend Book; *PP*, 1843, vol. XIII, pp. cvii–cviii).

Few if any individual entrepreneurs in 1830 could match the great landowners in the size of their mining operations. Though individual operators were still to be found in the north-east their undertakings were in general small, with capital commitments below rather than above the average for the district. More commonly, the north-eastern collieries were in the hands of partnerships or companies of a basically joint-stock character. The number of shareholders in these enterprises was never large and, though on occasion shares were advertised through the local press, the general practice was to keep ownership in the hands of those known to each other and knowledgeable in the coal trade. Two striking exceptions were the Durham County Coal Company and the Northern Coal Mining Company. Established as broadly based joint-stock companies in the mid-thirties, each came to grief in the following decade (Galloway, 1904, p. 11). They were thereafter held up as a standing warning to strangers not to meddle in an industry whose problems they did not understand.

Outside the north-east, colliery operations in 1830 were in general on a smaller scale. In that year the Lambton collieries, the Londonderry collieries and Hetton Colliery each shipped over 300,000 tons of coal. By comparison the Duke of Bridgewater's Worsley collieries produced 165,000 tons, while Earl Fitzwilliam's South Yorkshire collieries supplied 60,000 tons in 1826 and 225,000 tons in 1838 (Bridgewater MSS., Fitzwilliam MSS.). These were among the most notable of large-scale aristocratic enterprises. Additionally on every major coalfield were to be found coalowners working coal under lease and producing amounts comparable to those mined by the second-grade collieries of the Tyne and Wear, but unlike the north-eastern collieries they were still exceptional in the districts in which they operated. In general the observation of Morris and Williams on the state of the South Wales coal industry in 1840 holds good for most of the British coal industry outside the north-east at this time.

'While at one extreme there were employers like Thomas Powell, already extending his operations from colliery tó colliery and from valley to valley, there were at the other the owners of innumerable tiny levels, employing fewer than a score of workers . . .; in between there was the average Welsh colliery with fewer than 100 workers and the average coal-master owning usually one of these collieries or, at most, two.' (1958, pp. 13–14.)

If enterprises were small, so also were individual collieries. Here again the north-east was untypical. Because the workings were in general deeper, the commitment in capital and manpower was necessarily larger in the north-east than in other coalfields. The proliferation of operating units was most noticeable in districts like the west midlands where coal was worked in thick seams close to the surface by small coalmasters with limited resources, but it was also the case, for example, on the Fitzwilliam estate where the 62,000 tons of coal produced in 1826 came from six separate collieries, none of which supplied more than 20,000 tons (Fitzwilliam MSS.).

By 1875 there were still many collieries in productive existence with workforces to be counted in tens rather than hundreds – though of only a few districts could it be said as of the black country that collieries 'spring up very much like mushrooms: they are here today and gone tomorrow, working in some cases a few weeks, or months at most' (*PP*, 1873, vol. X, p. 471). In general, however, collieries and enterprises had grown in size. What had been exceptional in 1830 was now commonplace. In 1874 in the Rhondda Valley alone there were seven collieries producing more than 100,000 tons of coal each and a further thirteen with outputs of over 50,000 tons (Jones, 1895, pp. 49–51). This growth in size could be paralleled in every major coalfield and it was from such collieries that the nation's coal supplies were now substantially drawn.

There were, nevertheless, still considerable regional and local variations. Whereas in south Durham in 1875, 177 collieries each produced on average 110,000 tons of coal, in Gloucestershire the average output from 90 collieries was 14,000 tons. For the country as a whole the average was 33,500 tons and outside the north-east most of the major coalfields came close to this figure. But this similarity itself concealed substantial variations within the individual coalfields. In west Lancashire, for example, the Wigan Coal & Iron Company, the inheritor of the old Crawford domain, was by the early 1870s producing nearly 2 million tons of coal from thirty-three collieries. These collieries varied greatly in size but their average output at 60,000 tons was twice that for the county as a whole. Further east where Andrew Knowles & Company was the dominant producer, the collieries were even larger, but to the north round Burnley and Haslingden much smaller operating units still survived (*PP*, 1876, vol. XVII, *passim*).

III

The growth in the size of undertakings and collieries was in part the consequence of the demands and opportunities presented to the industry by an expanding market, in part the result of the greater depth of working which increased output necessitated. This in its turn stimulated the technical changes which the industry experienced in the middle decades of the nineteenth century. Until at least 1750 coal had been considered unworkable at depths below 120 yards. The advent of the steam-engine and of cast-iron tubbing, however, made it possible to exploit deeper seams. In 1793 a sinking at Howgill Colliery in Cumberland had reached 330 yards. By 1830 this depth had also been reached in the north-east and shortly afterwards a new winning of 530 yards was made through the magnesian limestone at Monkwearmouth in Durham. Thirty years later coal was being worked at nearly 700 yards at Astley in Lancashire and similar deep winnings had been made in North Staffordshire. Also by 1860 depths of 370 yards were reported in Leicestershire, of 290 yards in Yorkshire, 340 yards in the west of Scotland and 600 yards on the Wear. These, of course, were exceptional cases; but they reflect a general tendency for winnings and workings to deepen in response to the intensifying presures of increasing demand for coal. (Galloway, 1898, p. 355 and 1904, p. 13; Clapham, 1932, p. 101; R. C. Taylor, 1855, p. 95; *Colliery Guardian* 21 September 1861).

Greater depth of working had no fundamental effect on the method of working coal at the pitface, though it necessarily brought in its train improvements in ventilation practices. Pick and shovel mining remained general in Britain throughout the nineteenth century and as late as 1913 eleven out of every twelve tons of coal were still cut by hand. The deepening of shafts, however, not only brought improvements in the construction of the shafts themselves and in the winding machinery which served them but also, by adding substantially to the cost of winning and mining the coal, made it essential to extend the area worked from each pit. This implied an increase in the cost of conveying the coal both below ground and up the shaft. A premium was, therefore, put on innovations which would economise the use of labour in coal haulage below ground and increase the raising capacity of the pit shafts. Thomas Burt who began his pit life as a trapper at Haswell, one of the largest Durham collieries, in 1847, wrote in his autobiography: 'My pit-life began during a period of transition. Great reforms were being made in the method of carrying on colliery operations especially in the transit of the coal from the face of the workings to the surface' (1924, p. 52). The changes to which Burt gave special emphasis were the installation of guide rails in the shafts, the replacement of the hook and corf, hitherto ubiquitous in the collieries of the north-east, by the cage and tub, the use of the haulage-engine instead of the horse on the main underground roads, and the employment of pony-putters rather than hand-putters near to the face. These innovations, together with others like the use of ropes of wire rather than hemp, expedited mining operations and enabled coal and men to be brought to the surface more speedily and with greater safety. At the same time the greater use of gunpowder and the adoption of the long-wall system of coal-getting in all districts except the north-east increased the yields of coal to the benefit of both coal-operators and royalty-owners (Galloway, 1904, p. 328; Griffin, 1977, p. 108).

The innovations originating in the north-east spread with varying degrees of rapidity to other areas. The northern counties had long enjoyed a high reputation for their skill in colliery operations and engineers trained in the north-east were to be found in almost every coalfield. Lancashire, in particular, was quick to follow where the north-east led. In 1861 the Wigan district was said to have 'been completely revolutionized within the last fifteen years' and by this time the collieries of Andrew Knowles at Pendleton and Pendlebury had won a national reputation for their output and efficiency (*Colliery Guardian*, 14 November 1861). By contrast, the Black Country was scarcely touched by the example of the north. As late as 1860 shaft guides and cages were to be found in only a score of the district's 400 collieries and the first underground haulage-engine had only just been installed (Lones, 1898, p. 69; Taylor, 1967, p. 87).

Important as such innovations were they in no sense constituted an 'industrial revolution' in the sense that this term has been applied to manufacturing industry and in particular to cotton at this time. A major consequence of the fundamental technological advances associated with the increasing use of power-driven machinery was an increase in labour productivity which in cotton can be broadly estimated as tenfold between 1815 and 1860 and as more than fourfold between 1830 and 1860 (Mitchell and Deane, 1962, p. 187). These spectacular increases were largely the result of the triumph of factory industry and the final elimination of the domestic worker. No increase of such dimensions was to be expected, or in fact occurred, in mining. From the Census Returns and the *Mineral Statistics* it is possible to infer an increase in labour productivity of perhaps 40 per cent between 1851 and 1871, though some part of this was the result of more regular employment of the industry's labour resources and the bringing to the surface for sale of quantities of small coal which had earlier been left below ground. Nevertheless in an industry in which the operation of diminishing returns became all too evident after 1875, the gains of this earlier period are impressive.

A pointer to the benefits derivable from advances in haulage technique is to be found in a comparison of the disposition of the labour force in thirty-one collieries on the Tyne in 1828 and in 1843. In 1828 38·8 per cent of those employed underground in these collieries – 48·3 per cent if overmen, deputies and wastemen are excluded – were working at the face; by 1843 these proportions had risen to 44·0 and 51·8 per cent. There had also been an economy in surface labour to the extent that in 1843 hewers formed 32·8 per cent of the labour force as against 27·5 per cent fifteen years earlier (Buddle MSS.; *PP*, 1843, vol. XIII, pp. cvii–cviii).

IV

The growth in the size of collieries had obvious implications for levels of investment. There were, of course, at any given time great disparities in the size of investment from colliery to colliery. In south Staffordshire in the 1840s the cost of opening up and equipping a pair of collieries was said rarely to exceed £3,000 to £4,000; it could be much less. With this may be contrasted the investment of £50,000 which was commonplace in north-eastern collieries at this time and the £250,000 expended in a single deep winning at Monkwearmouth by the Pemberton brothers between 1826 and 1843 (*PP*, 1843, vol. XIII, pp. 23, 75; Galloway, 1904, p. 13).

Comparisons between districts and over time are made difficult by the different conventions used in assessing capital commitments. For many colliery owners, particularly those with small enterprises, accounting procedures were of a most rudimentary kind with little attempt made to distinguish between items chargeable to capital account on the one hand and to revenue on the other. In the accountancy field as in other matters, however, practices established initially in the north-east gradually won more general acceptance. In broad terms the convention was to charge to the capital account all those items of expenditure which were necessary to bring a colliery into full commission and to close the account when the colliery was 'sufficiently developed to produce its recouping quantity of coals'

(*Colliery Guardian*, 2 November 1871). Within the capital account, therefore, would be included charges – both in relation to materials and to labour – for the provision of shafts and their equipment, winding gear, engines, ventilation-machinery, underground working stock (including horses and ponies) and surface equipment. In addition, in the north-east at least, it was customary to include the cost of providing houses for the work-force and 'everything requisite for putting [the coal] on board the craft [in the river]'. This would involve payment for varying lengths of private railway line and for the staithes from which the coal was loaded on to sea-going ships, but not the ships themselves (*PP* [HL], 1830, vol. VIII, p. 31).

In 1824 it was estimated that some £2 million was invested in the north-eastern coal industry. A further estimate for 1828 by John Buddle, the distinguished coal-viewer, supported by detailed evidence for the Tyne collieries, suggests an investment of some £2·2 million in the north-eastern collieries then engaged in the London and coasting trades, two-thirds of it in the collieries on the Tyne. Estimates of £9½ million to £10 million exist for the coal trade in the early 1840s, but these are for the *trade* rather than for the *industry* and include investment in ships as well as in collieries. An estimate based on the data for individual collieries suggests a figure close to £4 million for colliery investment alone. When related to employment in the collieries these figures point to an investment per man of £115 in 1828 and of £150 in 1843 (*Statement of the Case of the Northern Coal Owners*, 1824; *PP* [HL], 1830, vol. VIII, pp. 34, 52; *PP*, 1847, vol. XVI, p. 23; *PP*, 1843, vol. XIII, pp. cvii–cviii).

The imprecision of these estimates is self-evident, and, because of this and also of the special circumstances of the north-east, it would obviously be rash to base any national calculation upon them. Fordyce in 1860 provides the first estimate of total investment in the industry. His estimate of £45 million for the industry as a whole and of £14 million for the north-east – £150 per man employed in the one instance and £250 in the other – is possibly too generous but it fairly points the difference between the north-east and other coal-producing districts (Fordyce, 1860, p. 44). Though the evidence is more fragmentary and fragile, estimates of investment and employment in south Staffordshire in the forties and fifties suggest that *per capita* investment in that coalfield may have averaged as little as £50 (Taylor, 1960, p. 217). The Black Country coalfield was notorious for the primitive character of its mining techniques. It patently stood at the opposite pole to Northumberland and Durham, yet it is arguable that, down to 1850 at least, in its *modus operandi* it lay closer to national norms than did the more sophisticated northern coalfield.

In 1867 Henry Briggs, an experienced and knowledgeable Yorkshire coalowner, asserted that 'now at least £100 a man is required as capital in a colliery'. He was speaking primarily of his own county and was quick to concede that other districts might have needs both greater and less than those of the Yorkshire coalfield. But this estimate is not incompatible with that provided four years later by a correspondent in the *Colliery Guardian* who suggested that £50 million was then invested in an industry employing 345,000 men – an investment per man employed approaching £150 (*PP*, 1867–8 vol. XXXIX, p. 58; *Colliery Guardian* 14 April 1871).

Only the most general deductions may be drawn from figures of this kind; but they have sufficient consistency to justify certain broad observations, even though these amount to little more than truisms. It is evident that the capital:labour ratio tended to increase as workings deepened and mining techniques were refined. It would also appear that, as in so much else, what was true of the industry in the north-east in the 1830s had become the general experience of the industry forty years later. But, as in other matters, averages here conceal wide disparities of individual experience.

As the capital requirements of coalmining increased, the methods by which capital had traditionally been drawn into the industry were put under increasing strain. Small single-owner undertakings were still common in many coalfields in 1875 but, where the technology and economics of the industry demanded larger operational units, the public joint-stock company was making headway. In terms of numbers such enterprises were still exceptional. It has been estimated that in 1873 only 10 per cent of collieries in Lancashire and north Staffordshire were owned by public joint-stock companies, in the east midlands only 8 per cent and in Yorkshire 6 per cent. These enterprises, however, included some of the largest producers in their districts like the Chatterley Iron Company in north Staffordshire and the Wigan Coal & Iron Company (Mitchell, 1956, p. 108). More particularly, where coal-working was associated with iron production, the heavy capital requirements of the parent iron industry dictated the adoption of the joint-stock form.

Incorporation, with the limited liability benefits it conferred, would no doubt have come more rapidly in the industry had not early experience cautioned against its general adoption. Shannon has shown for the country at large and Morris and Williams for south Wales in particular how short-lived were many of the early joint-stock enterprises – as also were many undertakings of simpler form. No more than 7 out of 53 joint-stock companies set up between 1856 and 1867 to work coal in Wales were still in existence in 1875 (Morris and Williams, 1958, p. 156). This degree of failure was primarily the result not of inherent weaknesses in the joint-stock form itself, but of the fact that many of the ventures were inspired by the speculative ambitions of the investor rather than by the proven opportunities and needs of the coal-operator. The more enduring companies grew out of concerns which had already proved their viability before adopting the joint-stock form.

The service of capital, though obviously of prime importance to the investor, was never a preponderant element in the cost of working a colliery. It was estimated that on a twenty-one-year lease a return of $7\frac{1}{2}$ per cent was needed to cover the cost of redemption of irrecoverable capital and to meet interest charges on the initial investment. The cost of this in tonnage terms would obviously depend on the yield of the colliery. One somewhat pessimistic computation for a hypothetical deep north-eastern winning put it as high as one-sixth of the getting cost, but in general it was lower than this (Fordyce, 1860, pp. 47–8). Much the largest element in a colliery's working charges in fact was its wage bill. Throughout the nineteenth century coalmining remained a labour-intensive industry. Labour charges invariably accounted for at least 50 per cent and sometimes as much as 75 per cent of a colliery's getting cost, with the variation depending upon the economy of each particular colliery and the short-run movements of prices and wages. Wage rates, like prices, were subject to considerable fluctuation. In the black country, for example, they rose by 40 per cent between 1844 and 1847 and then retreated within two years to their earlier level. Even more vigorous movements accompanied the boom of the early seventies with wage rates through the industry doubling in the course of two years (Clapham, 1926, p. 559; *PP*, 1873, vol. X, *passim*).

The recruitment and effective management of labour was, therefore, of particular importance for successful colliery operation. Employment in coalmining rose twice as fast as the natural growth of population between 1841 and 1871. In part the demand for additional hands was met by the miners themselves. 'Colliers', one perceptive Scottish miner remarked, 'are proverbial for large families, in fact children were and are property' (*PP*, 1842, vol. XVI, p. 452). Nevertheless, there was a continuing need to recruit labour from outside the industry. The Londonderrys imported workers from their Irish estates, stocking weavers were drawn into the east midlands pits and Pennine lead miners migrated into those of Northumberland and Durham. By far the largest supply of labour, however, came from agriculture. Though there were varying opinions about the value of such recruits, particularly for face-work, farm labourers helped greatly to swell the industry's labour force.

Much of this additional labour came into coalmining from declining sectors of the economy. In wage terms, therefore, it offered little competition to the already existing workforce. Nevertheless the industry's need to attract and hold labour found its final expression in the increasing wage rates and earnings of those employed in it. The analysis of wage trends presents its own particular difficulties, in part, because of the uneven availability of data but also on account of the multiplicity of grades of labour, the variation in wage movements not only between but within collieries, and the sharp, short-term fluctuations in wage rates. A broad view of the pattern of wage movements suggests that between *c.* 1830 and *c.* 1850, though there were marked short-run fluctuations in payments corresponding to the general movement of the business cycle, there was little overall movement in wage rates or earnings. Over the next quarter-century the same short-run fluctuations are evident but the long-run trend was decisively upwards. Fluctuations were sharpest in the iron-producing districts where the severe cyclical movements in the consumer industry readily transmitted themselves to coal. There also seems to have been a tendency for wages to rise more strongly in those districts, like Lancashire, where the competition for labour from expanding industry was most in evidence. Yet even in such districts it was not until the late sixties that increases in earnings finally outstripped parallel rises in the cost of living. By the early seventies real wages were significantly higher than they had been in either of the two preceding decades and, though the more substantial gains were trimmed with the passing of the boom by 1875, the miner's living standards were now set firmly on a higher course than that they had run through the mid-century decades (Knowles, 1890, pp. 50–1).

The uncertainties surrounding coalmining inevitably made the industry attractive to the speculator. 'A mine at first opening', Mrs Montague had written in 1765, 'has a prodigious swallow; when it begins to disgorge it makes noble amends' (Blunt, 1923, p. 124). Speculators discounted the risks in hopeful expectation of the great gains to follow. That there were such gains to be made in the industry the careers and legacies of such men as Thomas Powell, John Buddle, Andrew Knowles and George Elliot leave no doubt but it was also true, as a Welsh mining engineer observed in 1857, that 'there are great prizes to be gained . . . but for every prize that is gained there are a great number of losses' (*PP*, 1857 Sess. 2, vol. XI, q. 1570).

It was because of the risks involved in every mining enterprise that John Buddle made seemingly extravagant allowances for profit in his calculations of prospective mining investments. Buddle budgeted for a 14 per cent return on capital as well as providing for interest at 5 per cent and for the redemption of the capital itself (Buddle MSS.). A generation later it was still being asserted that 'a colliery investment should never be entered upon without there is a very reasonable probability of 30 per cent being realised upon the capital invested' (*Colliery Guardian*, 2 June 1871) – 10 per cent of this being normal profit and 20 per cent allowed for the special risks of mining enterprise. Other commentators were more modest. R. W. Brandling, the chairman of the Newcastle Coal Committee in 1830 and a coalowner of long standing, felt that 10 per cent was a fair return on capital but added that few at the time were getting it (*PP*, 1830, vol. VIII, p. 263).

There were undoubtedly at all times some enterprises whose returns measured up to these high expectations. The Hetton Coal Company, for example, was for half a century a byword for success in the north-eastern coal trade and repaid its shareholders many times over for their investment. The Earl of Durham's coal empire had a more chequered history. The collieries were experiencing lean times in the early thirties but in 1837 and 1838 they had profits of £60,000 and £70,000 – a return equivalent to almost 25 per cent on the capital then invested. Subsequently increased investment brought a profit of £84,000 in 1856 and of £380,000 in 1873 and, though these were exceptional returns, set off by others of more modest proportions, they mark out the Lambton collieries as a highly successful enterprise (Spring, 1952, pp. 252–3; 1971, p. 35).

Similar examples of great success can be found on every coalfield, most notably among the larger coalowners. To ride through the years of depression and loss which could overtake any colliery it was advantageous to have the resources and the breadth of coal interests of a Lambton or a Fitzwilliam. The course of the industry's history is strewn with the wreckage of enterprises which lacked the essential reserves to survive through the years of depression. There was inevitably a high rate of mortality among smaller enterprises; the larger undertakings could generally prosper if they came successfully through the shocks of early existence. Few of the north-eastern collieries remained under the same ownership from 1830 to 1875 – partly, of course, because some exhausted their substance – but conspicuous among the survivors were the collieries of the Earls of Durham, the Londonderrys and the Hetton Coal Company.

The story of individual gain and loss merges into a more general picture of the industry's varying profitability. Coalowners, like farmers, were frequently vocal about their misfortunes, more reticent about their successes. When, however, in 1833, Lord Durham said of the industry that 'in no trade is there less regular profit and more steady and permanent expense', he was voicing a complaint which fairly reflected the experience of the north-east coal trade through much of the thirties and forties (*PP*, 1842, vol. XVI, p. 517).

This was also the view expressed by such prominent coalowners as J. W. Pease and George Elliot about conditions in the industry in the fifties and sixties. Both believed that over the two decades profits in mining had not averaged more than 5 per cent and Elliot maintained that his own collieries in Durham and south Wales had cleared no more than 8d per ton in which was included 'interest for money, depreciation of capital and the waste of the corpus of the property' (*PP*, 1873, vol. X, qq. 4453, 7538).

These views can be supported by reference to the returns made by coalowners under Schedule D of the income-tax assessments. These returns present difficulties of interpretation in that they relate to all minerals – of which, however, coal was much the most important – and cover royalties as well as profits. Furthermore, being based on five-year averages, they tend to smooth out the fluctuations which the industry experienced. The figures, however, suggest annual rates of profit for the fifties and sixties varying between 7d and 10d per ton, margins conforming closely to Elliot's declared rate of profit for his own collieries and compatible with the opinion which he and Pease expressed about the general profitability of the trade (Stamp, 1916, p. 220).

Good profits were to be made in 1854–6 and again ten years later, but these were as nothing to those that accompanied the boom of the early seventies. By 1872–3 profits, at 2s per ton, were on average almost three times as high as they had been for most of the previous two decades and those who had endured through leaner years now had the reward for their waiting. A man who had invested in a twenty-one-year lease in 1855 would, if his returns had conformed to the average, have by 1876 received in profit rather less than 1s gross for every ton which his colliery produced. From this he would have had to deduct the amount required to redeem the capital he had sunk in the colliery and to meet the interest charges on the money with which he had embarked on his enterprise.

V

The boom of the early seventies is a climacteric in the history of the nineteenth-century coal industry. From 1875 the rate of growth in output and the level of profit in the industry both fell away sharply. For the twenty-one years between 1875 and 1896 growth averaged less than 2 per cent per annum and, except for five relatively good years around 1890, the industry experienced a dearth of profits unknown in even the worst years of the preceding quarter-century. In most years gross profits, as measured by the income-tax returns, did not on average exceed 6d per ton, no more than the royalty-owner drew without risk to his capital. Not until after 1896 was a higher level of profitability restored and the industry set on a course of sustained prosperity (Stamp, 1916, pp. 220–1).

By comparison with much of the final quarter of the century, therefore, the years between 1850 and 1875 present themselves as a period of relative prosperity for the coal industry. These years saw the industry attain its greatest rate of growth and they culminated in the most spectacular boom it ever experienced. But in relation to profits and wages, the great boom of the early seventies has tended to distort the picture of the industry's progress. Like growth itself, the profits of the expanding industry came irregularly and unevenly, and the rewards in dividends and wages to those who ventured their capital, and still more their lives, in coal might be considered modest. Perhaps indeed the major gainers from the advance of coal in these decades were not those at the centre of the industry but the royalty-holders whose incomes grew in step with the growth of the industry itself and the consumers who, thanks to the mediating influence of the railway, enjoyed through these years the benefits of cheap and abundant energy and fuel.

3 The Iron Industry

by P. J. Riden

In 1810, at the height of the industry's expansion during the war with France, the ironmasters of Great Britain produced about 400,000 tons of pig from some 220 blast furnaces. At the peak of the boom of the early 1870s more than 6·5 million tons was produced from about 700 furnaces. These figures alone indicate the magnitude of the technological and economic changes experienced by one of the leading sectors of manufacturing industry during the first three quarters of the nineteenth century.[1]

There is at present no satisfactory general account of the industry during these years, and coverage of the second half of the period is particularly weak. Whereas interest in the eighteenth-century iron industry and the great technological revolution around 1800 was evident as early as the middle of the nineteenth century and has been sustained to the present day, the same is not true of the period after 1830. Scrivenor (1854) continued his chronicle to his own time at only the simplest level; Ashton (1924) stopped explicitly around 1830; and even Hyde's detailed analysis of technological change in the industry, based on extensive archival research (1971), is thinnest in its final chapter on the years 1830–70. The best overall study is that by Birch (1967) which, although lacking in analysis and badly arranged, at least provides a considerable amount of information from contemporary published material and, if anything, is of more value for the mid-nineteenth century than before. Regional studies of industrialisation also tend to be better on the period around 1800 than the middle of the century.

One probable explanation for this deficiency is the poor survival of business records for the period. Even the largest and best-known accumulations of ironmasters' records are most useful for the early nineteenth century rather than the middle, and extensive enquiries by both Dr Hyde and myself have failed to reveal material of the same wealth and quantity for the period after 1830.[2] Thus detailed cost analysis, such as Hyde undertook for the early period, is hardly possible later on, nor in general can the history of the industry be approached through the records of individual firms. In place of this, a greater wealth of printed sources becomes available after 1830, as the technical press developed, engineering institutions began to publish transactions and official inquiries produced reports and minutes of evidence. Potentially, therefore, there is a good deal more scope for a detailed account of the industry at national, if not local, level than the limited number of studies at present in print might suggest. This, however, would be a major undertaking which can hardly be attempted here. What I have tried to do is offer a largely statistical summary of the main features of the industry, in contrast to Birch's descriptive approach. The aim is to ask questions rather than present answers, to reveal ignorance rather than knowledge and perhaps to suggest lines of enquiry for the future. This chapter may also be of interest as an illustration of how far one can apply quantitative techniques to the history of an industry during this period.

We may begin by considering the output of pig iron, the basic intermediate product from which was manufactured cast iron, wrought iron and, increasingly from the 1860s, mild steel, and the only product for which there are plentiful statistics before the late nineteenth century. Although the government did not collect any iron-trade statistics until 1854, the ironmasters themselves compiled detailed and

Table 3.1   *Pig-iron output in Great Britain, 1815–75*

Year	000 tons	Year	000 tons	Year	000 tons
1815	340	1835	930	1855	3,220
1816	270	1836	970	1856	3,590
1817	260	1837	1,030	1857	3,660
1818	280	1838	1,120	1858	3,460
1819	280	1839	1,250	1859	3,710
1820	320	1840	1,400	1860	3,830
1821	390	1841	1,330	1861	3,710
1822	360	1842	1,080	1862	3,940
1823	450	1843	1,220	1863	4,510
1824	550	1844	1,560	1864	4,770
1825	580	1845	2,200	1865	4,800
1826	520	1846	2,210	1866	4,520
1827	690	1847	2,000	1867	4,760
1828	700	1848	2,090	1868	4,970
1829	690	1849	2,170	1869	5,450
1830	680	1850	2,250	1870	5,960
1831	600	1851	2,500	1871	6,630
1832	630	1852	2,700	1872	6,740
1833	780	1853	2,900	1873	6,570
1834	790	1854	3,070	1874	5,990
				1875	6,370

Note: All figures rounded to nearest 10,000 tons.
Sources: 1815–53: Riden (1977); 1854–75: Mitchell and Deane (1971, pp. 131–2).

apparently reliable estimates at fairly frequent intervals from the 1870s, which may be combined with reasoned guesswork to produce an annual series of pig iron from 1790 (Riden, 1977, p. 455, partly reprinted here as Table 3.1). With figures of this kind it would be foolish to claim great accuracy for every estimate but, taking one year with another, they do provide a more detailed picture of the industry than can be obtained for any earlier period. From 1854 Robert Hunt published annual output estimates based on information supplied voluntarily by the trade, which were probably at first no more accurate than the best unofficial figures. While they presumably improved over time, as late as 1886 Sir Lowthian Bell doubted their reliability. Since, however, the trade did not publish systematic statistics until 1878, with the appearance of the first report of the British Iron Trade Association, one is left with no alternative but to accept the figures in *Mineral Statistics* (Riden, 1977, p. 454).

The general impression conveyed by Table 3.1 is one of rapid and sustained growth throughout most of the period 1815–75, with the industry's output continually reaching new record levels. From the peak of 400,000 tons in 1810 production faltered for a few years and then fell sharply to a trough of 260,000 tons in 1817. An unsteady recovery followed, reaching a new peak of 580,000 tons in 1825. A depression in 1826 was succeeded by a remarkably rapid recovery in the later 1820s, interrupted by the depression of 1831–2 but otherwise extending throughout most of the 1830s. A peak of 1·4 million tons in 1840 was followed by a sharp slump in 1842–3 but in the later years of the decade the industry expanded very fast to reach an output of 2·5 million tons in 1851. The boom of the 1850s rose to a climax in 1857, which was followed by a crash from which output did not fully recover until 1863, when for the first time over 4·5 million tons of pig was produced. At the end of the decade came the short-lived boom of the early 1870s, when output rose to more than 6·5 million tons in 1873.

Such was the national picture, but ironmaking has always been an industry with a high degree of geographical concentration and it is desirable to look at the changing regional pattern of output (Table 3.2). Before 1854 a number of estimates include separate totals for each district; after this date it is probably enough to select every fifth year from the annual totals for each county. Both parts of Table 3.2 reveal the expected high level of concentration, especially the first half, although this may be slightly exaggerated since some early surveys omitted the minor iron-producing areas altogether. At the beginning of the period about 40 per cent of pig was made in south Wales, just under a third in south Staffordshire and the adjoining part of Worcestershire, and a much smaller quantity in Shropshire. These three districts accounted for over 80 per cent of the national total;

Table 3.2   The regional distribution of pig-iron output 1823–75

(a) Before 1854

Year	South Wales		Black Country		Shropshire		Scotland	
	Tons	percent-age	Tons	percent-age	Tons	percent-age	Tons	percent-age
1823	180	40	130	29	60	13	20	4
1830	280	41	210	31	70	10	40	6
1840	500	36	410	29	80	6	240	17
1843	460	38	300	24	80	7	240	20
1847	710	36	320	16	90	5	540	27
1852	670	25	730	27	120	4	780	29

Note: Figures in thousands of tons rounded to nearest 10,000.
Source: Birch (1967, pp. 124–41).

(b) After 1854

Year	South Wales		Black Country		Scotland		North-East		North-West	
	Tons	percent-age	Tons	percent-age	Tons	percent-age	Tons	percent-age	Tons	percent-age
1855	0·8	25	0·8	25	0·8	25	0·3	9	0·1	3
1860	1·0	26	0·5	13	0·9	24	0·7	18	0·2	5
1865	0·8	17	0·7	15	1·2	25	1·0	21	0·4	9
1870	1·0	17	0·6	10	1·2	20	1·6	27	0·7	12
1875	0·5	8	0·5	8	1·0	16	2·0	32	1·1	17

Note: Figures in millions of tons.
Source: Mitchell and Deane (1971, pp. 131–2).

almost all the rest came from Scotland or the coal-measures district of Yorkshire and Derbyshire, the latter with about 9 per cent of the total in the 1820s. After 1830 there was a major shift, with the spectacular growth of the Scottish iron industry, so that by the 1840s a quarter of British pig was made in Scotland. All the other districts lost ground to the Scottish industry in these years.

In the 1850s a much more significant shift became apparent, the rise of the Cleveland district of north Yorkshire, Durham and Northumberland and then, more modestly, the west coast district around Barrow in Furness, both of which had been insignificant ironmaking regions in the early nineteenth century. In 1855 south Wales, the Black Country and Scotland each had almost exactly a quarter of total production and the north-east less than 10 per cent. By 1870 Cleveland's share was over a quarter, the north-west accounted for an eighth, and of the older coalfield districts only Scotland, still with 20 per cent of the market, maintained its position. As large-scale steelmaking got under way later in the decade, the Cleveland district's share rose to a third and that of south Wales in particular collapsed further. The rise of the Jurassic iron-producing district of the south-east midlands, mainly in Northamptonshire and Leicestershire, came only in the 1880s and does not affect the period considered here. Table 3.2 emphasises that throughout the first three quarters of the nineteenth century most British pig was made in three or four well-defined districts and that here detailed regional studies would be most useful.

Out of this continuum of steady change, two marked shifts stand out. One was the rise of the Scottish industry after 1830, attributable in the first instance to the introduction of 'hot blast', an innovation recently re-examined by Hyde (1972–3); the other, more fundamental shift from the ironstone of the coalfields to the non-coal measures ores of the north-east, the north-west, and later the Jurassic belt, was well summed up by a contemporary in 1862:

'Before the railway system was developed to its present extent, it was always considered that the ironstone should be carried to the coal, but partly by increased facilities of communication, and partly by improved manufacture, it has in many cases been found more advantageous to carry the coal as coke to the iron ore'. (Quoted Birch, 1967, p. 331.)

As well as output statistics, price data for pig iron became much more numerous at the end of the eighteenth century. To some extent, a price series for 'pig iron' is an unfortunate simplification. During the nineteenth century several types of pig were distinguished in the trade, each with a different price. For commercial purposes pig was classified by number, ranging from good-quality foundry pig (No. 1) to forge pig (usually No. 4, occasionally as high as No. 6) (Gale, 1971, p. 142). Ideally, we would wish to know how much of each type of iron was produced, together with prices for each category, including such regional variations as there were by this date. In practice we can construct a reasonable series of average prices for each year from 1790, but nothing more ambitious.[3] In Figure 3.1 these prices are presented in index-number form (1815 = 100) alongside the Rousseaux general price index, recalculated from the same base.

In the case of cyclical movements, the iron industry's experience in this period seems to differ little from that of the economy generally. Prices fell with the coming of peace in 1815, recovered around 1820 and then slumped again before the boom of 1824–5. The subsequent trough bottomed out around 1830 and a new upswing reached its peak in 1836. From there until the mid-1840s prices fell once more, peaked again in 1847 and reached a new low in 1851. The early 1850s were years of rising prices, with a peak in the middle of the decade which was followed by ten years of stable prices before the boom of

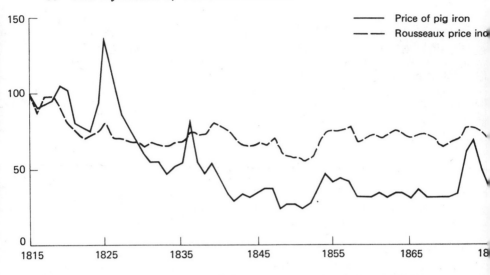

Figure 3.1   *Pig-iron prices and the Rousseaux price index, 1815–75*

the early 1870s. For the most part, this pattern is apparent in both the Rousseaux index and the pig-iron series, although the latter, as one would expect in a capital goods industry, experienced more violent fluctuations. In particular the boom of 1825, in which railway promotion played an important part, and that of 1836, where the same was true again, affected the price of iron much more than the general price level. At the end of the period, the boom which reached its peak in 1873 is much more obvious in the pig-iron index.

What is more important is the sharply different secular trend in pig-iron prices apparent from the graph. Throughout their length the two series largely mirror each other in short-term movements, but only at the beginning of the period are they closely linked in absolute terms. Iron prices rose much faster than prices in general in 1824–5 and then in 1826–7 fell more rapidly. What followed, however, marked the start of a secular fall in the price of iron not shared by other prices. The price of pig continued to fall sharply in the late 1820s after the general series had levelled out and did not reach the bottom of the trough until 1833. The wave of railway promotion around 1835–6 helped to lift prices but again, when the cycle turned, iron prices did not merely fall more sharply but continued to fall for several years more. This pattern was repeated in subsequent cycles so that over the period 1825–75 the two series slowly but surely part company, whereas before then they broadly move together. The Rousseaux index reveals virtually no secular trend between 1825 and 1875; the price of pig, on the other hand, fell quite sharply over the same period or, if one

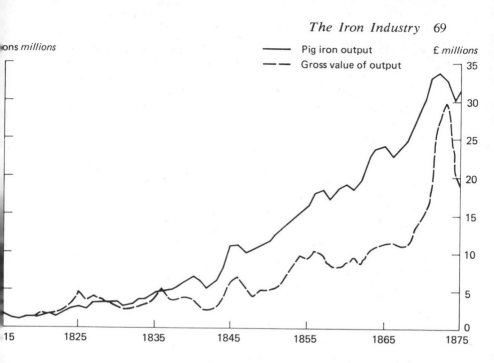

Figure 3.2 *The output and gross value of pig iron, 1815–75*

prefers to omit the boom year of 1825 itself, from the years immediately following 1825 to the early 1870s.

By combining the output estimates with the price series we may look at movements in the gross value of the smelting branch of the industry. This is, of course, very far from a series for the gross value of the industry as a whole, however narrowly one chooses to define it, or a series for the net value of this sector, which would involve considerable problems in estimating input costs. It is merely a convenient means of bringing together output and price estimates. In Figure 3.2 the output estimates from Table 3.1 have been graphed alongside a series of pig-iron prices, which are not the current prices shown in Figure 3.1, but have been deflated by the Rousseaux index in an effort to produce a series for the 'real' price of pig. The resulting graph helps to emphasise the point that in each downswing of the trade cycle the price of iron did not share in the relatively rapid recovery of output, with the result that the gross value of output rose much less fast on trend than output itself. This is particularly apparent in the later 1820s. Between 1827 and 1830 output was higher than it had been at the height of the boom in 1825; prices by contrast fell for several years after 1825 so that the total value of output also fell. The same conditions were repeated on a smaller scale in the mid-1830s, after the boom of 1836; in the late 1840s, after another boom owing much to railway promotion; and in the late 1850s. The fall in gross value after the peak of 1872–3 was the beginning of a more fundamental shift in the industry as wrought iron was superseded by mild steel.

This evidence of prices falling faster than output during downswings in the trade cycle emphasises the particular problems of a capital goods industry, especially one whose fortunes were closely linked to railway building, which appears to have been responsible for a good deal of the upswing in prices and production in 1825, 1835 and 1845. Ironsmelting was in addition an industry with relatively high fixed costs and one in which plant might physically deteriorate when not in use; producers would thus continue in business in the face of falling prices rather than shut down and risk never restarting, aggravating the problem of prices falling because of a drop in demand. These difficulties appear to have been most serious between 1826 and 1831, in the wake of the unprecedented expansion of 1824–5, when demand completely outstripped supply and prices rose to previously unknown levels. Thus the complaints of ironmasters to the 1833 Select Committee on Manufacturers, Commerce and Shipping about the difficulties the industry faced, especially after 1828, appear to be supported by the available statistics.[4] What such experienced ironmasters as Samuel Walker and William Matthews could not foresee was that this slump was not merely a particularly severe cyclical trough but the start of a secular trend in which the price of iron, compared with prices in general, was to fall steadily for a generation.

The output and price of pig iron are almost the only features of the industry in the period 1815–75 for which detailed statistics can be obtained. The output of bar and cast iron, or of different finished products, can only be deduced in general terms. Similarly, there are no connected statistics for the employment of labour or capital or for wages or profits. Because of the diffuse character of the iron industry and the problem of deciding what to include in the way of mining and transport on one side and manufacturing and finishing on the other, it would be difficult to make even rough estimates of employment of capital formation. Isolated estimates of the value of particular ironworks are available for this period but we cannot be sure that the basis on which they were compiled was always consistent and, in any case, they are far too few to enable an estimate to be made of the total capital value of the industry. Much the same is true of profits, for which there are scattered figures in the trade press and company archives but rarely is any indication given of how the figures were determined. We cannot be sure whether fixed as well as variable costs were included or, in the case of the latter, how far the 'cost' of fuel and other raw materials obtained from within the firm was allowed for. Again, detailed manufacturing costs are only available for a handful of not necessarily typical ironworks whose accounting methods may have varied one from another. Hyde's technique of presenting variable costs for a few well-documented ironworks for particular years, adding an estimate of capital costs that is no more than an informed guess, and then comparing the total with the price of pig in that year is not the most convincing basis for generalisations about the profitability or otherwise of the entire ironsmelting industry (Hyde, 1971, pp. 154–8 and 172–6). None the less, his interpretation seems to be consistent with conclusions suggested by the aggregate evidence of output and prices, which is that when both were moving upwards the industry as a whole was profitable, a rare coincidence after 1825. When rising, or even stable, output was accompanied by falling prices the industry was suffering a bout of its chronic complaint of over-production in the face of falling demand, the result of high fixed costs and inelasticity of supply in the short run.

Very little is known in detail of the market in iron in this period. Although the industry was concentrated in three or four main districts, within which, especially in south Wales, a small number of larger firms held a leading position, attempts to secure co-operation over prices or production seem to have been largely unsuccessful (cf. Daunton, 1972, for a recent study of south Wales). It is well known that in each of the main districts ironmasters met quarterly to fix prices for the following three months, but these prices seem to have followed rather than led market forces. In 1842 and possibly at other times of depression there were attempts to organise a reduction in output over the industry as a whole, but it is unclear how far these efforts were successful. The whole question of prices, marketing and co-operation between producers in this period merits detailed examination, a task which would involve not merely an analysis of the trade press but also the voluminous correspondence of the Dowlais Iron Company and smaller accumulations elsewhere. As Ashton observed, trade associations are by their nature elusive; in the absence of records of the organisations themselves one has to seek their echo among the papers of ironmasters who may or may not have co-operated with their fellows. On the slight evidence at present available the impact of quarterly meetings on the market does not seem to have been great.[5]

Although the outstanding feature of pig-iron production between 1815 and 1875 was the growth of output, this was accompanied by few clear-cut innovations comparable with those of the late eighteenth century, which transformed the small charcoal blast furnace blown by water into a much larger structure using coke as fuel and steam blowing equipment. During the nineteenth century furnaces became bigger and more powerfully blown, so that fixed costs per ton of iron probably fell. Although as furnaces grew larger their initial cost became greater and the cost of blowing equipment and ancillary plant also rose, economies of scale should have meant that fixed costs did not rise as fast as output per furnace and even the unit cost of labour may have fallen somewhat. None of this, however, can be demonstrated from business records. Coke ironmasters apparently did not keep the detailed costs accounts for each year's operations that form the basis of so much work on the eighteenth-century iron industry, and it seems to be impossible to construct estimates of input costs, even for individual ironworks, much less for the industry as a whole, over any length of time. Figures are available for a few ironworks for odd years but it is questionable whether the quality or quantity of this material is sufficient to justify the rather elaborate calculations about factor costs and productivity undertaken by Hyde (1971, pp. 155–90) and a very full but not very convincing discussion of smelting between 1790 and 1830. It is arguable whether figures presented entirely as current prices can be compared one with another over a period of forty years, besides which it is by no means clear whether the 'cost' of raw materials produced internally was always calculated precisely or consistently. Apparent changes over time or between different regions may reflect different accounting techniques or shifts in general price levels.

In addition to the problem of input costs, it is difficult to say much about the physical consumption of raw materials. It is important to distinguish between economies possible in the consumption of ore and fuel given greater care at the furnace, economies from specific innovations, and the physical and geological limits beyond which economies in a particular area were not possible. The iron content of ore varied between regions, so that one cannot necessarily deduce much from accounts recording only the weight consumed. It might be that differences in quality would be reflected in different prices but since, with the simple mining techniques of the early nineteenth century, the cost of ore was very largely a labour cost, this difference might not appear in accounts. Poor ore need be no cheaper to mine and transport than richer ore. It is particularly hazardous to take random examples from different regions for different years and try to establish a 'drop' in the consumption of ore per ton of pig over time, since one might be comparing ores of different iron content. The position does not improve after 1855, when Hunt first included estimates of iron-ore production in *Mineral Statistics* (Mitchell and Deane, 1971, p. 129). Until 1872 these were supplied on a voluntary basis and although the figures from some metal-mining districts appear to be reasonably complete, those from the coalfields, which were the more important for most of the period, are merely rough estimates well below the actual level of production. If one take's Hunt's figures and estimates the iron content of the ore, using proportions accepted by contemporaries, the net figure is, in many years, below that of the output of pig iron.

Since there were no significant iron-ore imports before the 1870s and the output estimates for pig iron have always been accepted as reasonably reliable, the conclusion must be that the ore figures are substantial underestimates.

The same is true of attempts to demonstrate fuel economies. Coal varied in character between different ironmaking regions, as did the ratio of coal input to coke output and the amount of coal or coke required to make a ton of pig. For example, fuel inputs in south Wales were generally lower than those in the midland districts, and so a string of estimates arranged chronologically, with an early example from Wales and a later one from Yorkshire or Staffordshire, would give a misleading impression of falling consumption over time. In general, contemporaries reckoned that about three tons of coal were needed to produce a ton of pig, and most estimates of coal consumption by the iron industry before the 1870s prove to be merely the output of pig multiplied by three, perhaps with a rough estimate of coal used for steam raising in the industry added (e.g. Mitchell and Deane, 1971, p. 123).

There appears to have been no innovation in ironsmelting between the end of the eighteenth century and 1830 which substantially altered the cost of making pig. Although the records are inadequate to show the physical consumption of raw materials remaining more or less steady, the lack of major innovation can be established from literary sources and patent records. Ore consumption was largely fixed by geological considerations, while there is no evidence for innovation in fuel consumption until the arrival of hot blast in the 1830s. As for saving resulting from the more careful use of materials, one can turn to a small amount of literary evidence from the end of the period, from which it seems that during the twenty-year spell of high prices, rising output and (one assumes) high profits, which ended about 1810, ironmasters were generally careless in the use of raw materials, especially coal. That this was the case during the Napoleonic War is implied by Matthews's and Walker's comments to the 1833 Select Committee on Manufactures. They both emphasised the lengths to which ironmasters had gone to save money, especially since the boom of 1825, which was followed by several years of overproduction and sagging prices. The fact that there was scope for economy of this kind, despite the absence of formal innovation, suggests that during the period of high war-time profits ironmasters' use of fuel had been less efficient than it might have been. Presumably during the intervening period of acute depression no amount of economy could have avoided losses, and so it was only in the later 1820s that thought was given to the more careful use of fuel. This is probably the explanation for the slight drop in consumption of coal per ton of pig detectable over the period 1790–1830.

The technological history of the iron industry between 1830 and 1870 is well known in outline (Birch, 1967, ch. 9; Gale, 1966, chs. 5–6; Gale, 1967, chs. 4–5). There was a continuing process of plant becoming larger, more powerful and more complicated. Blast furnaces became taller, were built of iron rather than stone, had closed instead of open tops and were blown by more powerful steam engines. The internal lines of new furnaces came to be round rather than square, which improved performance, as did the use of more tuyeres. Exhaust heat from the furnace was no longer allowed to go to waste from the top of the furnace but, with the introduction of the closed top, was recycled with increasing sophistication. All these developments are broadly familiar but less is known of the speed and extent of their adoption and virtually nothing of their economic impact on the industry. Very little cost data have survived for ironworks of this period and virtually none for capital estimates. Hyde concluded a survey of technological change between 1830 and 1870 by claiming that 'There is considerable evidence that productivity in the smelting sector stagnated or declined after the widespread adoption of the hot blast' but his efforts to esimate this stagnation, based on only five observations from various, in some cases unlocated, furnaces, are hardly convincing (Hyde, 1971, pp. 222–3). As he recognised, the one conveniently clear-cut innovation in this period was the introduction of 'hot blast'.

Since the earliest times iron furnaces had been blown with air at atmospheric temperature. In 1828 James Beaumont Neilson of Glasgow patented an invention to supply blast furnaces with hot air, which permitted for the first time the use of 'raw' (i.e. uncoked) coal in the furnace and appreciably reduced the amount of coal required to smelt a ton of iron. The problem of sulphur contamination from the coal producing red-short pig was avoided, since the higher temperature in the furnace enabled the sulphur to be taken out in the slag as calcium sulphate. The installation of hot blast apparatus appears not to have involved great capital expenditure and thus the process should, in a short time, have lowered the cost of pig production, since the physical consumption of the one input where there was scope for economy had been reduced. The introduction of hot blast was re-examined in detail by Hyde (1972–3), who observed that potential fuel-saving was greatest in regions where coal was 'poorest' (i.e. with the lowest carbon content and highest sulphur content) and that potential fuel-saving largely determined the rate at which the innovation was adopted. Scottish ironmasters, whose coal resources were relatively poor, were quick to adopt hot blast, whereas south Wales ironmasters were less enthusiastic. The inland districts of England fell somewhere between these extremes. By the middle of the century, however, most pig was smelted by hot blast and the adoption of the process was no doubt accelerated by the expiry of Neilson's patent in 1842.

The precise economic impact of hot blast on the industry is impossible to measure even approximately. Only for a handful of pioneer, best-practice ironworks is there any detailed information, which even then lacks suitable capital cost estimates, and in any case hot blast was not the only, even if it was the most important, innovation in the industry in the 1830s and 1840s. The general capital deepening we have already mentioned (larger furnaces, use of waste heat, bigger blowing plant) presumably also lowered smelting costs and one can hardly hope to distinguish one innovation from the rest.

It is difficult to establish any means of estimating the productivity of the iron industry in this period and in particular a recent attempt by R. C. Allen (1977) should be viewed with caution. Allen attempts to construct total factor productivity indexes for the iron industries of Great Britain and other countries from 1830 to 1913. The assumptions which he required to make through lack of data to obtain any results at all are so sweeping as to render all the final estimates dubious; his figures for the British industry prior to 1870 are unreliable. Allen seeks to combine data relating to the input of fuel, capital and labour, disregarding the input of ore, since it was largely fixed by geological conditions. As he is forced to admit, there are no British data for the period 1830–70 for capital or labour, while for the consumption of fuel he has only William Jessop's estimate of 1840, which is probably reasonably accurate, and the far less reliable figure printed by Hunt for 1872, which is the product of multiplying the output of pig that year by a single estimate of the consumption of coal per ton of pig (Mitchell and Deane, 1971, p. 123). Intermediate figures between 1840 and 1872 have been supplied by linear interpolation and the resulting hypothetical estimates for every tenth year are related to established pig-iron output data to produce a series which Allen claims, optimistically to represent the total factor productivity of the industry. We regard the figures of doubtful value as a measure of productivity just as his derived data which are employed in a comparison of the British and American industries are equally suspect, certainly down to 1870.

Probably the nearest approximation to a measure of this kind is average blast-furnace output (Table 3.3). This is obviously only a very crude proxy, since increased output was the product of larger furnaces which cost more to build and, presumably, more to operate, even if we are prepared to assume, without direct evidence for or against, increasing economies of scale as plant grew in size. Table 3.3 demonstrates that output per furnace rose from less than 2,000 tons a year in 1810 to about 10,000 tons in 1875. The growth was not entirely smooth, the largest single increase coming between 1828 and 1840, when output rose by about 40 per cent. It would be tempting to attribute this increase to the introduction of hot blast, but there is no definite evidence of a connection between the two. Intuitively it seems

Table 3.3   *Average output of pig iron per furnace 1810–75*

Year	Furnaces in blast	Total output 000 tons	Average per furnace 000 tons
1810	223	400	1·8
1825	259	580	2·2
1828	277	700	2·5
1840	402	1,400	3·5
1843	339	1,220	3·6
1847	433	2,000	4·6
1852	497	2,700	5·4
1855	590	3,220	5·5
1860	577	3,830	6·6
1865	659	4,800	7·3
1870	664	5,960	9·0
1875	629	6,370	10·1

Sources: 1810–52: Riden (1977); 1855–75: Robert Hunt, *Mineral Statistics* (Geological Survey, annually).

likely that this innovation, adopted widely in the 1830s and especially important in Scotland, was responsible for a marked increase in average furnace output, but detailed cost data from which such a connection might be established are lacking. In any case, technological innovation is only one possible cause of increased productivity; factors on the demand side of the equation may also have raised average output. For example, the relatively sharp increase between 1843 and 1847 and between 1865 and 1870 may owe more to shifts in demand than changes in technology, since the 1840s were the period in which domestic railway building was at its height and the later 1860s were years of an expanding export trade in iron.

Pig iron was not exported in great quantity during the nineteenth century and so demand may be discussed mainly in terms of sales to forges for the manufacture of wrought iron and to foundries for casting. In practice, because of the high degree of vertical integration in the iron industry, blast furnaces, forges and, to a lesser extent, foundries, were often owned by the same company and sometimes occupied the same site. Of the two branches of the industry, forging was the more important.

The technological revolution which transformed the iron industry in the second half of the eighteenth century affected the manufacture of bar iron somewhat later than it did either smelting or casting. By 1810, however, Henry Cort's puddling process appears to have become almost universal, since the detailed and apparently reliable output estimates of that year (Riden, 1977, p. 450) make no mention of any other forging process. The output of puddled iron was about 130,000 tons in 1810; assuming the same rather high wastage of pig in early puddling furnaces as contemporary statisticians did (as much as 75 per cent), about half the 400,000 tons of pig produced that year would have gone for conversion into bar and the other half to the manufacture of cast iron. These estimates mark the peak of a trend, which may be traced back to the early eighteenth century and which was greatly accelerated towards the end of the century after the introduction of coke smelting, away from wrought iron towards cast. In the late 1820s it was estimated that about 70 per cent of pig was consumed by the forges (Riden, 1977, p. 452, n. 2); the 'Age of Cast Iron' had passed never to return. Allowing a steady reduction in the quantity of pig required to make a ton of bar, these proportions indicate that by 1830 the output of bar iron was well above 300,000 tons a year, whereas the figure for cast iron was probably no more than about 200,000. By this date cast iron had slipped back to relative unimportance in the market for pig and bar iron, the traditional semi-manufactured product of the industry, had resumed its earlier supremacy.

After 1830 the ratio of 7:3 between sales to forges and foundries seems to have remained roughly steady, as does a wastage of pig in manufacture of about 25 per cent. With these constants in mind it would be easy enough to make rough estimates of bar-iron output from the figures for pig iron and to calculate the output of castings as a residual, although such series would be almost entirely hypothetical. The output of puddled iron was not recorded until 1881, after the decline of the industry had begun. During the period 1830–70, when the wrought-iron trade was at its height, contemporary observers continued to estimate the output of the iron industry in terms of pig, as they had always done, and did not attempt to measure the production of bar iron directly. Nor are there any separate estimates of the output of castings.

Throughout the seventeenth and eighteenth centuries the domestic production of bar iron was overshadowed by imports from the Baltic. The introduction of puddling, however, rapidly brought about an almost complete import substitution, so that whereas in 1790 over half the bar consumed in Great Britain was imported, by 1815 the figure was less than 10 per cent and by 1830 was down to 5 per cent. Similarly the foundry trade had complete control of its own home market and in both branches of the industry imports may be disregarded.[6]

The history of technological change in the wrought-iron trade has yet to be studied in detail, although W. K. V. Gale's work (1966, 1967) provides a useful account of the main innovations. Once puddling had been adopted there were no spectacular innovations in either the forging or rolling of iron comparable with hot blast in smelting. The basic technique of puddling changed little between its introduction in the 1790s and disappearance in the last few years. The falling consumption of pig per ton of bar was presumably partly a case of learning-by-doing in what was always an arduous and skilful craft, whose practitioners remained the accepted *élite* of ironworkers. A more tangible improvement was the introduction of iron bottoms to puddling furnaces in place of sand from about 1820 onwards, which reduced the loss of iron; more important was the modification known as 'wet puddling' or 'pig boiling' introduced in south Staffordshire in the late 1820s, again with the object of economising in the use of iron. The full mechanisation of puddling, however, was never achieved and progress towards this was overtaken in the 1870s by the introduction of large-scale steelmaking, which led to a decline in the industry and a loss of interest in further technological advance. The replacement of wrought iron by mild steel as the main product of the industry did not really begin until after 1870, although once it did the process was rapid and by the 1880s largely complete (Birch, 1967, pp. 352–63). This second revolution in technique marked the start of a new phase in the industry's history.

Although technological change in the wrought-iron industry is well known in outline, it is impossible to measure the impact of the various innovations on the cost of producing wrought iron. If the information on which such calculations might be based does exist, it remains to be laboriously quarried out from the trade press, the transactions of technical institutions and similar sources. In fact, the opportunities for economies of scale seem to have been limited. Puddling furnaces remained small, producing less than 5 cwt per charge, with up to five charges possible in an eight-hour shift. The potential weekly output per furnace was thus strictly limited and any increase in output could only have come from the construction of more, not larger, furnaces. Puddling was also labour intensive, with little scope for substituting capital for highly paid skilled men who, like all ironworkers of the period, were paid by piece-rate. Wages had probably always been tied informally to the price of iron but between 1848 and the 1860s a definite formula, the Thorneycroft scale, was applied in the main ironmaking districts, by which the rate for puddling was determined by the selling price of iron and the rate for other trades calculated from puddlers' wages (Birch, 1967, p. 113; Burn, 1940, p. 13). In these conditions, with labour-intensive techniques applied to small units of production, the opportunity for cost-reducing innovation must have been strictly limited.

If the technology of iron manufacturing in the nineteenth century has been neglected, so for the most part has the history of the iron trade. In this respect, the iron industry is no different from other branches of manufacturing; historians have in general devoted more attention to technology and production than sales and distribution.

Here no attempt is made to do more than provide a simple statistical framework within which more detailed studies of particular branches of the trade might be fitted.

The one source of demand for iron which can be identified fairly precisely is that from overseas, since exports were recorded annually under various heads, themselves a simplification of the wide range of semi- and wholly manufactured goods into which iron was made. It is difficult to establish precisely what proportion of the total output of the industry was sold overseas each year because of the varied composition of iron exports. Clearly, the final tonnage recorded by the customs was appreciably less than the quantity of pig used in the manufacture of the goods, although at the same time there were exports of pig iron itself. In Table 3.4, in order to give a rough indication of the importance of exports to the iron industry, the recorded tonnage has been inflated by 20 per cent, a somewhat arbitrary multiplier intended as a compromise between the 25 per cent conventionally adopted as the wastage in manufacture in the wrought-iron industry and the much lower figure that obtained in the foundry trade. Because this calculation is only a rough estimate, figures have been given for average years within each five-year period between 1815 and 1874 to give a general impression of the role of exports rather than a dubious precision that might be implied by an annual series. Table 3.4

Table 3.4 *The export of iron, by quinquennia, 1815–19 to 1870–4*

	1: *Total exports* 000 tons	2: *Pig equivalent* 000 tons	3: *Pig output* 000 tons	4: *2/3%*
1815–19	60	72	290	21
1920–4	79	95	414	19
1925–9	88	106	640	14
1830–4	142	171	700	24
1835–9	218	262	1,060	25
1840–4	381	458	1,320	35
1845–9	534	641	2,130	30
1850–4	1,039	1,247	2,680	47
1855–9	1,411	1,693	3,530	48
1860–4	1,536	1,843	4,150	44
1865–9	2,027	2,432	4,900	50
1870–4	2,965	3,558	6,378	56

Sources: Mitchell and Deane (1971, pp. 146–7); Table 3.1 above.
Col. 2 = Col. 1 × 1·2; cf. text.

illustrates, none the less, that the proportion of pig exported roughly doubled between the 1820s and the 1870s, rising from about a quarter of the total to roughly half. At a time of rapidly expanding output this represents a massive increase in absolute tonnage and

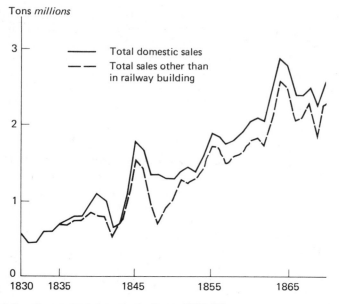

Figure 3.3   *Domestic sales of pig iron, 1830–70*

highlights the role of the industry in Britain's period as the 'workshop of the world'. By far the most dramatic increase came between 1845 and 1850, when exports more than doubled in five years, the largest share of the increase being attributable to rails and other railway iron (Mitchell and Deane, 1971, p. 146).

Although any estimate of the proportion of pig exported during this period can only be approximate, it may be of interest to remove the recorded tonnage of exports (multiplied by 20 per cent) from the annual series for pig output to examine the home market more closely. Figure 3.3 emphasises that, in general, demand from overseas seems to have moved independently of the domestic trade cycle, leaving the familiar peaks and troughs of the latter largely intact. Thus the years of high output, such as 1840, 1855 and 1864–5, stand out clearly and the most striking feature of Figure 3.3 is the much flatter upward trend in domestic sales than that for gross sales shown in Figure 3.2. In each case the rate of growth appears to have been fairly consistent throughout the period, although the subtraction of exports tends to reveal more marked cyclical fluctuations attributable to movements in the domestic economy.

As far as home demand is concerned, most interest has centred on sales to railways, which seem to have become important from about 1835. Several attempts have been made, from the standpoint of the impact of the railway on the economy, to measure sales of iron to main-line railways. B. R. Mitchell's initial foray into this field was followed by G. R. Hawke's more elaborate calculations, distinguishing between rails and other goods, while in Scotland Wray Vamplew has attempted a similar study on a smaller scale (Mitchell, 1964; Hawke, 1970, pp. 213–59; Vamplew, 1969). It must be said that any exercise of this kind can only yield a very approximate result in view of the assumptions required to obtain any estimate at all (the most important being weight of rail per yard, rail life, ratio of route mileage to track mileage and ratio of tonnage of rails to pig-iron equivalent), even if only rails are included. To compute the quantity of iron used elsewhere on railways would be even more difficult.

Hawke's calculations are concluded by tables showing, for each year between 1835 and 1870, the estimated tonnage of pig consumed by the railways in the form of finished goods (1970, pp. 255–9), which, as Rainer Fremdling has recently pointed out (1977, pp. 598–601), compare the consumption of iron by railways in England and Wales with British pig-iron output.

In Table 3.5 Hawke's estimates have been combined with Vamplew's for Scotland (which commence only in 1840; before then Scottish railway mileage was so small that Hawke's estimates can stand without adding greatly to the inaccuracy of the calculation) and then compared with pig-iron output to produce a fuller and more precise picture. Despite this revision, Table 3.5 has been compiled more to satisfy the curiosity of those who believe that one can make realistic estimates of railway consumption of iron, than in the belief that the percentage in the final column is more than a very rough indication of demand. Sales to railways were at their greatest in the late 1840s, when up to a fifth of the industry's output may have been consumed in this way. For the rest of the period the figure was much less and after 1850 did not rise above 8 per cent in any one year, far less than the proportion represented by exports. These are no more than elementary statistical conclusions; we would have to know far more about the detailed working of the market in railway iron before a full picture could be established. Apart from Hawke's tentative conclusion that a disproportionate quantity of iron for rails, but not necessarily for other railway iron, came from south Wales (1970, pp. 215–30), we know little about the geographical distribution of railway demand.

Hawke's estimates compare railway consumption of iron with total British output of pig but, as Fremdling points out (1977, loc. cit.), it may also be of interest to look at the impact of railway procurement on the domestic market alone, in which railways were relatively much more important. If we are prepared to accept the rough estimates of domestic pig consumption shown in Figure 3.3 then we may set them alongside the Hawke–Vamplew figures for railway consumption of iron (Table 3.6) to show that the proportion of domestic sales in the 1830s

Table 3.5   *Estimated sales of iron to railways, 1835–70*

	1. *Pig output* 000 *tons*	Sales to railways 2. *E. & W.* 000 *tons*	3. *Scotland* 000 *tons*	4. *Total* 000 *tons*	5. *4/1%*
1835	930	11	—	11	1·2
1836	970	17	—	17	1·8
1837	1,030	45	—	45	4·4
1838	1,120	67	—	67	6·0
1839	1,250	89	—	89	7·1
1840	1,400	259	32	291	20·8
1841	1,330	104	15	119	8·9
1842	1,080	62	26	88	8·1
1843	1,220	49	4	53	4·3
1844	1,560	126	2	128	8·2
1845	2,200	135	114	249	11·3
1846	2,210	215	42	257	11·6
1847	2,000	312	69	381	19·1
1848	2,090	438	186	624	29·9
1849	2,170	363	58	421	19·4
1850	2,250	249	50	299	13·3
1851	2,500	104	9	113	4·5
1852	2,700	198	15	213	7·9
1853	2,900	101	13	114	3·9
1854	3,070	179	28	207	6·7
1855	3,220	130	34	164	5·1
1856	3,590	94	43	137	3·8
1857	3,660	203	28	231	6·3
1858	3,460	154	44	198	5·7
1859	3,710	199	44	243	6·5
1860	3,830	182	42	224	5·8
1861	3,710	163	82	245	6·6
1862	3,940	226	78	304	7·7
1863	4,510	246	111	357	7·9
1864	4,770	209	82	291	6·1
1865	4,800	231	76	307	6·4
1866	4,520	281	67	348	7·7
1867	4,760	222	63	285	6·0
1868	4,970	131	75	206	4·1
1869	5,450	354	65	419	7·7
1870	5,960	193	111	304	5·1

Sources: Col. 1: Table 3.1 above; col. 2: Hawke (1970, pp. 258–9); col. 3: Vamplew (1969, pp. 72–3, col. 3).

Table 3.6 *Pig-iron output, exports of iron and railway consumption of iron, 1835–70*

	1. Pig output 000 tons	2. Exports 000 tons	3. Home sales 000 tons	4. Railways 000 tons	5. 4/3%
1835	930	240	690	11	1·6
1836	970	230	740	17	2·3
1837	1,030	230	800	45	5·6
1838	1,120	310	810	67	8·3
1839	1,250	300	950	89	9·4
1840	1,400	320	1,080	291	26·9
1841	1,330	430	900	119	13·2
1842	1,080	440	640	88	13·8
1843	1,220	540	680	53	7·8
1844	1,560	550	1,110	128	11·5
1845	2,200	420	1,780	249	14·0
1846	2,210	520	1,690	257	15·2
1847	2,000	660	1,340	381	28·4
1848	2,090	750	1,340	624	46·6
1849	2,170	850	1,320	421	31·9
1850	2,250	940	1,310	299	22·8
1851	2,500	1,100	1,400	113	8·1
1852	2,700	1,240	1,460	213	14·6
1853	2,900	1,510	1,390	114	8·2
1854	3,070	1,440	1,630	207	12·7
1855	3,220	1,310	1,910	164	8·6
1856	3,590	1,730	1,860	137	7·4
1857	3,660	1,910	1,750	231	13·2
1858	3,460	1,680	1,780	198	11·1
1859	3,710	1,830	1,880	243	12·9
1860	3,830	1,800	2,030	224	11·0
1861	3,710	1,630	2,080	245	11·8
1862	3,940	1,870	2,070	304	14·7
1863	4,510	2,040	2,470	357	14·5
1864	4,770	1,870	2,900	291	10·0
1865	4,800	2,020	2,780	307	11·0
1866	4,520	2,110	2,410	348	14·4
1867	4,760	2,360	2,400	285	11·9
1868	4,970	2,450	2,520	206	8·2
1869	5,450	3,210	2,240	419	18·7
1870	5,960	3,390	2,570	304	11·8

Sources: Col. 1: Table 3.1 above; col. 2: Mitchell and Deane (1971, pp. 146), inflated by 20 per cent; col. 3: col. 1 less col. 2; col. 4: Table 3.5 above.

and 1840s, especially the latter, represented by railways was substantial and undoubtedly establishes the industry as the largest single outlet for the iron trade, other than exports, in this period. The railways appear to have accounted for about a quarter of domestic sales during the minor boom around 1840 and possibly as much as half at the peak of railway building in 1848. After 1850 the figures fall to a much lower level but remain slightly above 10 per cent down to 1870.

The important place occupied by domestic railway building in the iron industry between 1835 and 1850 was taken over after the middle of the century by exports of railway goods, which is another aspect of the railway's impact on the industry which Hawke does not consider. Between 1850 and 1870 railway iron represented at least a third and sometimes as much as half the total tonnage of iron exported, so that when these figures are combined with those for domestic railway consumption of iron the total represents a substantial part of the industry's entire output. Unfortunately, exports of railway iron were not separately enumerated until 1856, by which date demand from domestic railways was well past its peak as a percentage of total production. If, however, we add to our previous estimates of domestic consumption those for exports, similarly inflated by 25 per cent to allow for wastage in manufacture, then the importance of railway exports in the 1850s and 1860s becomes clear (Table 3.7). Between 20 and 25 per cent of

Table 3.7   *Foreign and domestic sales of railway iron, 1856–70*

	1. Pig-iron output 000 tons	2. Railway exports 000 tons	3. Home sales 000 tons	$\frac{2+3\%}{1}$
1856	3,590	578	137	20
1857	3,660	573	231	22
1858	3,460	541	198	21
1859	3,710	661	243	24
1860	3,830	566	224	21
1861	3,710	473	245	19
1862	3,940	501	304	20
1863	4,510	558	357	20
1864	4,770	510	291	17
1865	4,800	543	307	18
1866	4,520	623	348	21
1867	4,760	726	285	21
1868	4,970	729	206	19
1869	5,450	1,110	419	28
1870	5,960	1,324	304	27

Sources: Col. 1: Table 3.1 above; col. 2: Mitchell and Deane (1971, p. 147) (inflated by a wastage factor of 1·25); col. 3: Table 3.5 above.

the total output of the iron industry was consumed in the production of goods for railways, mostly by this date for export. For the period between 1844 and 1859 Fremdling, drawing on various foreign sources, suggests that, as a cautious estimate, 30 per cent of British iron exports were consumed by railways (1977, pp. 599–601, 604).

The difficulty of estimating sales to railways should warn against attempting any similar exercise for the rest of the home market. The uses to which iron was put by this date were too numerous and the technology too complicated for even a simple list of outlets to be of much value. Whereas in the eighteenth century the output of the industry can be divided into exports and domestic consumption and the latter roughly apportioned between naval and military sales, nails, castings and other broad categories, this is hardly possible in this period. Except for the few years of the Crimean War military demand during the long peace of the nineteenth century was not of great significance, while the peaceful uses of iron were so numerous that apart from a division of 70 per cent to wrought iron and 30 per cent to castings little more can be said. At the beginning of the nineteenth century the engineering industry was in its infancy and much forging and foundry work, and steam-engine building, was done by ironmasters themselves and may reasonably be regarded as part of the iron industry broadly defined. By 1870 a vast and complex engineering industry had grown up to manufacture cast and wrought iron, a development that is outside the range of this chapter. All that it offered here is a graph (Figure 3.3) showing the steady increase in domestic consumption of iron, other than in railway building, between 1830 and 1870, with fluctuations that seem to correspond fairly closely to movements in the economy as a whole. This may perhaps be taken to indicate that, once one has removed railway demand, there was no one customer of the iron industry whose pattern of demand differed appreciably from the general course of the economy and might thus give some special character to the history of the iron trade. On the contrary, fluctuations in sales of iron in the domestic market appear to reflect fairly closely successive trade cycles between 1830 and 1870.

What conclusions can be drawn from this brief summary of the mid-nineteenth-century iron industry? In the first place, the period has been neglected in comparison with both those before and after, a neglect that may owe something to the apparent paucity of archive material. Because of this it is difficult to build up a picture of the industry as a whole from the history of individual firms, since there are only a few detailed case studies. There is a certain amount of statistical material available, more than in the eighteenth century, but much less, both in quantity and quality, than after 1870. We can establish roughly the output and price of pig iron, from which it appears that rapid growth of production was accompanied from the late 1820s to the early 1870s by a long-term fall in prices, although the cyclical experience of the industry was similar to that of other sectors of the economy. These aggregate figures are the only clear guide to profitability. Apart from production and prices there are few detailed statistics, while literary sources have remained underexploited in attempts to reconstruct the industry's history. The technology of iron-making in the nineteenth century has been less closely studied than in the eighteenth; this is especially true of the forge and foundry branches of the trade. The steady increase in average blast-furnace output is a crude measure of rising productivity, but attempts to calculate a more elaborate total factor productivity index are probably doomed to failure by inadequate data. The demand for iron has similarly been neglected, apart from the attention devoted to consumption in domestic railway building. In fact, throughout the period, the export trade was much more important than sales to railways; indeed after 1850, exports of railway iron alone were more important than sales to British railways. This is yet another topic which would benefit from a much closer examination than has been possible here, a conclusion that may fairly be applied to the entire history of the industry from the end of the Napoleonic War to the dawn of the Steel Age.

NOTES TO CHAPTER 3

1　Because of the strict word limit imposed on contributors to this volume and the fact that my Oxford BLitt thesis 'The Growth of the British Iron Industry 1700–1870' is available for consultation I have kept general references to printed sources to a minimum and assumed others interested in this field are familiar with the work of Charles Hyde and Alan Birch. Although Hyde's published volume on the iron industry (*Technological change and the British iron industry, 1700–1870*, Princeton, 1977) was available at the time of writing I have preferred to quote from his earlier Ph D thesis (1971) since his treatment of the subject there is much fuller.

2　Hyde (1971, pp. 324–7) gives a detailed list of manuscript sources for his thesis. In the autumn of 1976 I circulated all the county record offices to see whether Hyde had missed any large collections or whether anything new had arrived. Neither was the case to any important extent. Both my work and Hyde's was done before the resources of the British Steel Corporation's archives service became fully available.

3　The details of the construction of this index are available on request.

4　Select Committee on Manufactures, Commerce and Shipping, (*PP*, 1833, vol. VI, qq. 9, 506–10, 789) evidence of Walker and Matthews.

5　Apart from Daunton's local study of South Wales (1972) the question of combination among ironmasters in this period has yet to receive the attention it deserves. This paragraph is a tentative comment based on scattered information in Ashton (1924, pp. 162–85) and Birch (1967, pp. 104–18, 366–70).

6　The details of these calculations are set out in my thesis and are available on request.

4 The Engineering Industry

by A. E. Musson

In 1815 the term 'engineering' had only recently come to be applied to the manufacture of industrial 'engines' – prime movers and machinery – as distinct from earlier military engineering, concerned with 'engines' of war and fortifications, and from what became known as 'civil engineering', the building of roads, river navigations, canals, railways, waterworks, docks and harbours. For many years there was no clear differentiation between 'civil' and 'mechanical' engineering, and the foundation of the Institution of Civil Engineers in 1818 was not followed by a separate Institution of Mechanical Engineers until 1847. The two kinds of activity were commonly combined, civil engineering being aided by development of power-driven machinery such as cranes, pile-drivers and pumps, as well as by iron columns, beams and bridges, produced by ironfounding–engineering firms, which also made steam engines, boilers and railway locomotives. Nevertheless, specialisation and differentiation were gradually developing and we shall be primarily concerned with the growth of *mechanical* engineering – with 'engine-making' and 'machine-making' as it was for long more commonly called.

POWER-DRIVEN MECHANISATION AND THE GROWTH OF MECHANICAL ENGINEERING

The millwright was the earliest mechanical engineer, mainly concerned with making and erecting the machinery of watermills and windmills. Many nineteenth-century engineers continued to call themselves millwrights and to be concerned with a similar range of constructional work, while developing iron water-wheels of much greater size and power and also making the transition to 'steam mills'. By 1815 the steam revolution was well under way, based on the earlier engineering achievements of Savery, Newcomen and Watt, but it progressed much more slowly than has been generally realised (Musson, 1976). Its most striking manifestation was in textiles, especially cotton, but the rapid growth of steam-powered textile factories has tended to create a very misleading impression of the pace and extent of mechanisation generally.

Since the development of mechanical engineering was so closely associated with that of power-driven machinery, it is therefore essential to emphasise the very gradual and uneven spread of 'the factory system' in the period up to 1870. The Returns of Factories and Workshops in that year show that it was still largely confined to a few major industries. Over half the total manufacturing horsepower was in textile factories – a third in cotton alone – and nearly another third in iron and engineering works: together these industries accounted for four-fifths of the total, though the Returns do not include coal mines, in which pumping and winding engines had been extensively introduced. In the whole wide range of other industries, steam-powered mechanisation had developed to only a very limited extent. Obviously, therefore, mechanical engineering in this period was concerned predominantly with provision of motive power and machinery for the textiles, coal and iron industries, and also with building railway locomotives, rolling stock and marine engines, as the steam revolution extended to transport on land and sea. Other engineering activities, though varied, were of relatively minor importance.

The steam engine was crucial to the growth of engineering, not only because it provided the main driving force for industrial mechanisation – thus greatly expanding the market for 'machine-making' – but also because of the central role of 'engine-making' itself. For many years, however, development was slow. The early Savery and Newcomen engines were made by blacksmiths, coppersmiths, and iron- and brass-founders. Boulton & Watt similarly had to rely on the casting and cylinder-boring techniques of ironmasters such as the Darbys and John Wilkinson. It was not until 1795–6 that they established their own Soho Foundry, by which time many rival 'engine-makers' had sprung up, either making the older-type engines or 'pirating' Watt's inventions. The expiry of Boulton & Watt's prolonged patent in 1800 threw the field open and 'engine-makers' soon proliferated in the main industrial areas. Throughout the first half of the nineteenth century, however, the great majority of industrial engines remained small, low-pressure, beam engines of the Watt or older 'atmospheric' type. The danger of boiler explosions, which had motivated Watt's opposition to high pressures, continued to restrict progress, but with improvements in boiler-making and design, such as rolled wrought-iron plates, improved riveting and tubular construction, it became feasible to develop high-pressure engines. Most of these, however, remained condensing beam engines, of which the most notable was the Cornish pumping engine pioneered by Trevithick and Woolf, though direct-acting types – with piston and connecting rod acting directly on the crank – were developed, mainly for steamboats, by engineers such as Symington, Maudslay and Penn.

Low-pressure beam engines, however, both reciprocating and rotative, improved by Maudslay, Murray and many later engineers, long continued to be the stock-in-trade of engine-makers, though some of these traditional engines were eventually increased in power by adding a high-pressure cylinder on the other side of the beam, as in McNaught's patent of 1845. Hornblower, Woolf and other engineers had earlier pioneered a more revolutionary 'compound' engine, using steam successively in two high- and low-pressure cylinders, but this type of engine was not successfully developed in this country until the second half of the nineteenth century. In the mid-1850s John Elder applied the principle to the marine engine on Clydeside, and with further improvements in engine- and boiler-making it was gradually introduced over the next twenty years, revolutionising steamship building.

All these engines were of the condensing type, but another revolutionary development was that of the high-pressure, non-condensing engine, pioneered by Trevithick (and by Evans in the USA), in which steam was simply exhausted into the atmosphere. After Trevithick's 1802 patent, his engine was gradually put to various industrial uses, but its most striking application was in the steam railway locomotive, where its compact size and power were of crucial importance. With improvements such as Stephenson's multi-tubular boiler and improved draught from exhausting the steam up the funnel, as in the famous 'Rocket' of 1829, Trevithick's original 'puffer' started a transport revolution, opening an immense new field for mechanical engineering.

THE DEVELOPMENT OF MACHINE-TOOLS

Machinery and millwork in the early Industrial Revolution were largely made of wood, but metal castings were soon introduced, since it was relatively easy to produce parts by pouring molten metal into sand moulds shaped from wooden patterns; increasing employment was thus provided for iron- and brass-founders. There were limitations to the use of the tougher wrought iron, because of the problems of cutting and shaping it. Small parts could be forged and then filed to fit, while bars, rods, sheets and plates were rolled, sheared and slit in water – and later steam-powered mills; steam similarly displaced water in driving tilt-hammers, and eventually Nasmyth's direct-acting steam hammer (invented in 1839) enabled more massive forgings and die-stampings to be produced. Boring engines, improved by Smeaton, Wilkinson and later engineers, also played a vital role in producing accurate cylinders for steam engines; together with drilling machines, they also came to be steam driven.

In all these developments, the importance of advances in heavy iron founding and forging are well known. Many such firms went into the production of engines, boilers and machinery, and this close association between the iron industry and engineering continued throughout our period. Gradually, however, specialist engine- and machine-making firms developed, separate from the ironworks which supplied them with pig and bar iron. In London and Manchester, for example, which became the main centres of engineering, such supplies were brought in from the iron-producing areas: proximity to markets for engines and machinery was clearly the major locational factor. Moreover, early engineering firms were able to draw on existing craft skills and tools in such centres. In fact a medley of wood- and metal-working craftsmen went into mechanical engineering: not only mill-wrights, iron- and brass-founders, but also blacksmiths, coppersmiths and tinsmiths, carpenters, joiners and turners, instrument makers, clockmakers and watchmakers (Musson and Robinson, 1969, ch. 13). In the 1830s Nasmyth was still recruiting such craftsmen, who could soon learn to operate machine-tools (Smiles, 1883, pp. 214–16; Musson and Robinson, 1969, pp. 505–6).

This development of machine-tools was the crucial factor in the growth of mechanical engineering. In such metal-working trades as instrument, clock and watch making, treadle- and pole-operated lathes, drills and 'wheel [gear] -cutting engines' (with milling cutters for shaping teeth in small gear-wheels) had long been used, and were now developed into heavy power-driven machine-tools, which were brought increasingly into use from the late eighteenth century onwards in production of engines and machinery, which could thus be more accurately manufactured with use of gauges. In the second decade of the nineteenth century the metal-planing machine was also developed, making possible the cutting of true-plane metal surfaces without costly and laborious hand chiselling, filing and grinding. To these machine-tools others were soon added, such as slotting or grooving and paring or shaping machines, so that all kinds and shapes of machinery could be mechanically produced, though final filing or fitting was usually required. Such machine-tools were increasingly made 'self-acting' or 'automatic', that is fitted with mechanisms such as the slide-rest, for setting the cutting tools precisely, thus further eliminating manual skills.

The leading pioneer in these developments was Henry Maudslay (1771–1831), of London, whose famous works became a Mecca for aspiring young engineers (including Roberts, Nasmyth and Whitworth) in the early decades of the nineteenth century. Not only did he produce greatly improved lathes and other machine-tools, but he also pioneered precision engineering and mass-production, with his standard true-planes, measuring machines, gauges and screw-making tackle. His achievements at the turn of the century, in collaboration with Bentham and Brunel in block-making machinery, and similarly with Bramah in standardised manufacture of locks, provide the most famous early examples of mass-production engineering (though see references in

Musson, 1975, pp. 111 and 130, for earlier eighteenth-century efforts). But these have generally been regarded as extraordinarily precocious innovations, that were not followed up in Britain until after the mid-nineteenth-century introduction of the so-called 'American system of manufactures'.

This view is largely mistaken. In fact, mechanical engineering particularly the development of machine-tools, originated earlier and spread more extensively in Britain than in the USA, during the late eighteenth and first half of the nineteenth century. This, indeed, is what one would expect, since the Industrial Revolution occurred first in Britain. Maudslay was not the only pioneering engineer in London: in addition to Bramah and Brunel, there were others such as Rennie, Holtzappfel, Clement, Donkin and Penn, who participated in the development of machine-tools and standardised manufacture of screws, machinery, and steam engines (see below, pp. 93–5). In other areas, moreover, engineering was also rapidly developing. By the second quarter of the nineteenth century, if not earlier, Manchester had become the most important centre of engineering in the country (Musson, 1957–8, 1960, 1970, 1972*b*, 1975; Musson and Robinson, 1969). Scores of engineering firms sprang up there in the late eighteenth and early nineteenth centuries, making water-wheels, steam engines, boilers, textile machinery, machine-tools and eventually railway locomotives. Some, such as Bateman & Sherratt, Peel & Williams, Hewes & Wren, and Galloway, Bowman & Glasgow, had already become very large by the 1820s, each employing several hundred workers, and the number and size of Lancashire engineering firms grew considerably thereafter (see below, pp. 94–5).

Some of these later Manchester firms, notably Sharp Roberts, Nasmyth's and Whitworth's, became outstanding as makers of machine-tools, which they advertised in newspapers and printed catalogues – 'ready-made', standardised and mass-produced. They also developed standardised manufacture of other products. Peel, Williams & Company were advertising standard gear-wheels and machinery in the early years of the century. Roberts was similarly selling standard gear-wheels and screws, together with machine-tools, by the early 1820s, and from 1825 onwards he developed standardised production of mules and looms using templates and gauges, and later applied the same techniques to locomotive manufacture. Nasmyth followed in the 1830s with 'ready-made' production on 'the straight-line system', turning out standard machine-tools, pumps, cranes and hydraulic presses, as well as his famous steam hammers and railway locomotives. Most famous of all was Whitworth, with his machine-tools and precision engineering, the supreme practitioner and propagandist of standard measurements, gauges and screw-threads, mass-production and interchangeability, from the late 1830s right on throughout the third quarter of the century. By the late 1850s he was able to claim, and it was generally recognised, that these methods had been widely, indeed almost universally, adopted in heavy engineering, but Whitworth has been given credit for developments originated much earlier by Maudslay, Roberts and other engineers.

Scholars such as Habakkuk and Rosenberg, however, have been misled by his inflated claims and his advocacy of 'the American system of manufactures' in the production of small arms, leading to the establishment of the Enfield Arsenal in 1854 (see below, p. 99). The Americans, it is true, as we shall see, had a lead in light mass-production engineering of this kind, but as Whitworth himself pointed out, from his own observation of American manufactures in 1853, Britain was at that time supreme in the iron industry and heavy engineering, especially in machine-tools. Indeed, Rosenberg has elsewhere recognised that, despite the early achievements of Whitney and North in small-arms manufacture, the development of specialised machine-making and tool-making in the USA dates only from about 1840 (Rosenberg, 1963).

In Britain these developments started much earlier, though the rapid growth of machine-tool making did not begin until after 1815. The Select Committee on Exportation of Machinery reported in 1841 that '[machine-] tools have introduced a revolution in machinery and tool-making has become a distinct branch of mechanics and a very important trade, although twenty years ago it was scarcely known' (*PP*, 1841, vol. VII, *Second Report*, p. vii). Power-driven, 'self-acting', machine-tools, costing from £100 to £2,000 each, could be operated by semi-skilled machine minders and yet achieve a much greater output of more accurately manufactured, standardised machinery at far lower cost than a generation previously. This finding, based on the evidence of reputable engineers, was confirmed by the recollections of others such as Fairbairn and Nasmyth, who both emphasised the comparatively rudimentary state of engineering in about 1815, when there were no planing, slotting or shaping machines, and, except for some primitive lathes and drills, machinery was very largely made by hand. By about 1840, as they and other observers such as Andrew Ure enthused, 'self-acting' machine-tools had brought about a 'revolution' in machine-making, almost entirely displacing handwork and producing precisely engineered, interchangeable parts. These developments, with increasing emphasis on standardisation, were certainly extended by Whitworth, but they had long been under way.

They were stimulated by the rising demand for steam engines and machinery, by the problems of getting precisely manufactured, interchangeable parts, by the scarcity and cost of skilled labour, and by trade-union apprenticeship and manning restrictions. By introducing 'self-acting' machine-tools, employers were able to dispense very largely with the craft skills of millwrights, to recruit relatively unskilled workers at lower wages, and to have more machines manned by a single operative (Musson and Robinson, 1969, ch. 15; Jefferys, 1946, ch. 1; Burgess, 1969 and 1972). These developments were associated with increasing labour specialisation. Thus in large Manchester engineering works in the 1830s there was what a contemporary termed 'the utmost economical sub-division of labour', with many specialised groups of workers: in addition to the more generally skilled engineers and millwrights, there were pattern-makers, moulders, smiths, strikers, turners, borers, fitters and boiler-makers (Musson and Robinson, 1969, pp. 467, 485). Such increasing specialisation was incompatible with traditional craft skills: machine minders could be employed in repetitive production on specialised machine-tools, without any apprenticed training. Trade-union opposition – culminating in the famous 1852 strike, but continuing long after that defeat – could not prevent, though it may have delayed, technological change and gradual labour dilution; there is some evidence, in fact, that it was a direct cause of labour-saving mechanisation.

GENERAL ENGINEERING AND SPECIALISATION UP TO 1850

It was mainly in London and Lancashire that the most remarkable developments occurred. There were considerable differences, however, between the engineering activities of these two areas. In London, steam-powered mechanisation was far less industrially concentrated and there were fewer large factories, so a more diffuse, lighter engineering developed there. John Farey's investigations in the first quarter of the nineteenth century showed steam engines being used for pumping in London waterworks, breweries, distilleries and dyehouses, for grinding operations in flour mills etc. and for a wide variety of other manufactures, including industrial and marine engineering (Musson, 1976, pp. 425–6). Maudslay & Field, in Westminster Road, and John Penn, at Greenwich, became the most renowned metropolitan engineers, particularly in the manufacture of marine engines, but others were also outstanding in particular fields – John Clement and Charles Holtzappfel in machine-tools and precision engineering; Joseph Bramah in hydraulic engineering; Bryan Donkin in paper making and printing machinery – though all these and other firms, such as the Bow Foundry and Alexander Galloway, also carried out a wide range of general engineering. Fairbairn also established a large shipbuilding and marine engineering concern at Millwall, though it failed in the 1850s. The importance of London, however, in early engineering has been very inadequately appreciated.

In Lancashire, Manchester became the centre not only of the revolution in the cotton industry but also of that in engineering associated with it (Musson, 1957–8, 1960, 1970, 1972b, 1975; Musson and Robinson, 1969). We have already seen how Roberts, Fairbairn, Nasmyth and Whitworth had established the city's engineering predominance, especially in machine-tools, in the second quarter of the nineteenth century. At the same time, older firms such as Sherratt's Ormrod's, Hewes & Wren, Peel Williams & Company, and Galloway's continued to be of major importance. (In the late 1830s Sherratt's large works was acquired by Mather & Platt, who were to maintain and develop their established engineering reputation.) In 1837 over three-quarters of the steam power in Manchester and Salford was in the cotton industry (Musson, 1976, p. 430), so engineering there was concerned mainly with textile machinery, water-wheels, steam engines, boilers, millwork, and machine-tools, as well as steam-heating and gas-generating plant, hydraulic presses and weighing machines. Most firms were general engineers, but there was an increasing tendency towards specialisation. Though many large firms made their own machine-tools, some engineers, notably Nasmyth and Whitworth, developed a special reputation in the field. Similarly, while many big cotton-spinning and manufacturing concerns long continued to make their own machinery, specialised textile engineering soon developed. Sharp Roberts, for example, became outstanding as textile machine-makers, together with Parr, Curtis & Madeley, described in 1851 as 'the most extensive makers of cotton spinning machinery in Manchester'. Indeed, an even higher degree of specialisation developed in the manufacture of parts of textile machines, such as spindles, rollers and bobbins (Musson and Robinson, 1969, p. 436).

These tendencies towards specialisation were remarked on in 1841 by William Jenkinson, himself a manufacturer of spinning machinery in Salford, who divided the industry into three sections: 'the manufacture of steam-engines, mill-gearing, hydraulic presses, and such other heavy machinery, I should call one class; the next, and a separate branch, I should say, was tool-making; and the third I should call [textile] machine-making, with its various branches of spindle and fly-making, and roller-making' (Musson and Robinson, 1969, p. 477). By that time, a further class of specialisation was emerging, in the manufacture of railway locomotives, in which Manchester engineering firms played a prominent part from the 1830s onwards, especially Sharp Roberts, Nasmyth's and Fairbairn's, who were among the most important in this field by mid-century.

Such specialisation, however, was never clear-cut, most firms remaining general engineers. Sharp Roberts & Company, for example, the most notable textile machine-makers, also manufactured machine-tools, locomotives and many other products. Parr, Curtis & Madeley, though similarly outstanding as makers of spinning machinery, were also described as 'extensive millwrights and toolmakers'. Nasmyth, as we have seen, had a very varied range of production, in addition to his machine-tools and steam hammers (see above, p. 91), while Whitworth's, though outstanding in machine-tools, were described in the late 1840s as 'machinists, millwrights, iron founders, engineers, and toolmakers', making such diverse products as knitting and street-sweeping machines, and later going into armaments and steel, and also into printing machines.

The extensive development of mechanical engineering in south-east Lancashire was revealed by Returns made to the Select Committee on Exportation of Machinery in 1841, from 115 such firms in Manchester, Salford, Bolton, Rochdale, Bury and other towns, with a combined capital of £1,515,000, employment of 17,382, and steam power of 1,811 horsepower: capital per firm thus averaged £13,174, employment 151, and horsepower 16 (Musson and Robinson, 1969, pp. 479–80). By 1845 there were almost a hundred firms in Manchester and Salford alone, variously described as millwrights, engineers, machine-makers, and iron-founders. The size of the largest firms had also greatly increased: by the early 1840s Fairbairn's were employing a total of between 1,000 and 2,000 men in their Manchester and Millwall works; in the Atlas works of Sharp Roberts & Company there were nearly 1,000 by the early 1850s, while Nasmyth, Wilson & Company were by then employing 1,500 in their Bridgewater Foundry at Patricroft (Musson and Robinson, 1969, pp. 479, 485, 505).

These developments in the Manchester–Salford area may be regarded as typical of what was happening more widely in Lancashire. One need only mention such outstanding firms as those of Asa Lees and Hibbert & Platt of Oldham; Dobson & Barlow and Hick, Rothwell (later Hick, Hargreaves) & Company, of Bolton; Howard & Bullough of Accrington; the Haigh Ironworks of Wigan; Fawcett's of Liverpool, and Laird's of Birkenhead – all originating in the late eighteenth and early nineteenth centuries – to show that engineering was growing with similar vigour in all the chief Lancashire towns. The growth of these well-known firms – of comparable size to those in Manchester – was likewise accompanied by the rise and fall of a multitude of obscure textile machine-makers, engine-makers, millwrights etc. as well as more specialised roller and spindle makers.

Engineering was also developing in other areas, besides Lancashire and London, in similar association with local industries. In the West Riding, it grew more slowly than in neighbouring Lancashire, as the woollen and worsted industries lagged behind cotton in power-driven mechanisation. In the same way, however, numerous small millwrighting and machine-making firms sprang up, alongside larger ironfounding and forging concerns, such as Kirkstall Forge (Leeds) and Bowling Ironworks (Bradford), while famous engineers such as John Smeaton and Matthew Murray were involved in the early development of water-wheels, steam engines, textile machinery and machine-tools in the Leeds area. Murray, who was employing 200 men by 1826, was one of the first to produce machine-tools for sale, early in the nineteenth century, and on the demise of Fenton, Murray & Wood in 1837 this business was further developed by their successors, Smith, Beacock & Tannett. Other Leeds firms specialising in machine-tools, though also general engineers, were those of Maclea & March, Shepherd & Hill, and Joshua Buckton, all founded in the second quarter of the century (Rolt, 1965, pp. 76–82; Saul, 1967, pp. 22, 24–5). Peter Fairbairn, brother of William Fairbairn, similarly carried forward textile machine-making in Leeds, especially the manufacture of machinery for spinning flax and waste-silk yarns; in 1841 his firm employed 550 men and had a capital of £50,000 to £60,000. By that date there were eighteen engineering firms in the city, with a total of 2,950 men and capital of £305,000. But in the West Riding as a whole the industry was much smaller than in Lancashire: in Leeds, Bradford, Bingley and Keighley, the total workforce was 5,000, capital £407,000 and horsepower 442 (*PP*, 1841, vol. VII, *First Report*, p. 208; ibid, *Second Report*, p. 105, appendix; ibid., *First Report*, pp. 95–6).

In the east midlands, textile manufactures similarly stimulated the growth of engineering. The silk and cotton mills of the area, associated with expansion of the hosiery and lace trades, centred on Nottingham, Derby and Leicester, led to the rise of numerous textile machine-makers, millwrights, and makers of water-wheels, steam engines and machine-tools, along with ironfounding, especially in Derbyshire (see, for example, Nixon, 1956). Oustanding as a machine-tool maker was James Fox of Derby, who was among the first to develop a trade in machine-tools, early in the nineteenth century (Roe, 1916, pp. 53–4; Rolt, 1965, pp. 103–5). In the hosiery and lace trades, frame-smiths sprang up, together with more specialised makers of needles, sinkers, bobbins and carriages, but 'machine-making' evolved very slowly (Wells, 1972; Varley, 1959, *passim*). In the hosiery trade, factories with power-driven frames were not built until the 1840s and it was only after Cotton's patent in 1864 that rapid mechanisation occurred and hosiery engineering became fully established. Similarly in lace-making, though factory production began earlier, soon after Heathcoat's bobbin-net machine of 1808–9, and machine-making gradually developed, it was not until the 1850s and 1860s, when standardised leavers machines began to be made in quantity, that machine-making 'moved from forges and smithies into steam-powered factories' (Varley, 1959).

It may seem surprising that the Birmingham and Black Country district, in which Boulton & Watt's famous Soho Foundry had been established, did not play a more prominent role in engineering during this period. But though steam power was important in the primary processes of the iron and brass industries – in smelting, hammering and rolling – it was only very slowly introduced into the innumerable small metal manufactures of that area, producing buttons, small arms, 'toys' (ornaments and jewellery), edge tools, nails and screws, pins and needles, chains and anchors, hinges, locks and keys etc (Musson, 1976, pp. 417–8, 428–9). In these manufactures, even by the 1860s, 'there had been no "industrial revolution" in Birmingham and District' (G. C. Allen, 1929, p. 113). The Soho Foundry had declined in relative importance and there were no other engineering firms of any great significance until later years, though a few were turning out comparatively small numbers of steam engines, pumps, rolling mills, nail-making, coining and weighing machines. It was not until the development of the cycle and motor-car industries in the last quarter of the century that the west midlands became a major engineering area.

In the north-east of England, however, the massive growth of the coal and iron industries, together with railway and early steamship building, brought about a considerable development of heavy engineering. Much the oldest such firm in the area was Hawks, Crawshay & Company, of Gateshead, founded in 1747; engaged in making all kinds of industrial and marine engines, machinery, millwork, bridges etc., they were by the early 1860s employing 1,500 men (British Association, 1863). 'Equally large was the firm founded by George Stephenson, whose son Robert followed in his footsteps, so that by 1863 R. Stephenson & Company of Newcastle, established 1823, had a workforce of 1,500. By that date R. & W. Hawthorn, founded 1817, also at Newcastle, had 1,000 men, similarly specialising in locomotive building, though, like Stephenson's, they also did a great deal of general engineering, including industrial and marine engines and boilers. From the 1830s onwards, there was a development of specialised marine engineering, in which Marshall's (Willington Quay), Richardson's (Hartlepool), and Palmer's (Jarrow) were each employing 600 to 1,000 men by 1863. Meanwhile, several more general-engineering concerns had been established, of which W. G. Armstrong & Company, of Elswick, founded in 1847, was the most famous, for the manufacture of hydraulic machinery (see below, p. 102), stationary and locomotive engines, millwork and general machinery, while in addition to the 800 employed in these works, he had over 3,000 in his great armaments establishment.

Similarly in Scotland, 'coal and iron joined with the skills of engineering to build a complex structure of steam and iron technology on the Clyde in the heart of a new heavy industrial region' (Slaven, 1975, p. 133 and ch. 5 generally). The tremendous growth of the Scottish iron industry in that area, following the introduction of Neilson's hot blast (1828), was accompanied by the rise of steamship building and marine engineering, associated with such pioneers as

Bell, the Napiers, Tod & MacGregor, the Dennys, the Thomsons, and the Elders, who established Scottish predominance in this sphere by the third quarter of the century. Steam engines and boilers were also required for the rising cotton industry, as well as for the collieries and ironworks of the region: in 1825 cotton accounted for over half the steam power in the Glasgow area, where there was a development of textile machine-making and millwrighting similar to that in Manchester (Musson, 1975, pp. 426–8), while machine-tool makers such as Craig & Donald and Shanks, of Johnstone, also emerged.

These revolutionary developments in the major industrial areas of the country had produced an engineering industry of substantial size by the mid-nineteenth century. According to the 1851 Population Census of Great Britain, it consisted predominantly of 'Engine and Machine Makers', of whom there were about 48,000, though there were also about 7,000 'Toolmakers' and 'Others, dealing in Tools and Machines', together with nearly 10,000 millwrights. Many of the toolmakers and millwrights were doubtless of the traditional kind, while some 7,500 boiler-makers were included with the much greater numbers employed in iron foundries, forges and small metal manufactures. The main concentrations of engine- and machine-makers were in Lancashire and Cheshire (over 14,000), the West Riding (nearly 6,000), and London (over 6,500), with smaller numbers in Staffordshire and Warwickshire (nearly 4,000), Northumberland and Durham (nearly (3,000), Lanarkshire and Renfrewshire (over 3,000), and scatterings elsewhere.

The 1851 Census figures also give some indication of the varying sizes of engineering firms. Of the 1,044 engine-, machine-, and tool-making employers who made Returns, over half (588) had less than 10 men, while another 193 either had no men or did not state the number; but at the other end of the scale 35 had over 100, including 14 with 350 and upwards. There was thus a marked contrast between the large number of small firms and the relatively few big concerns, which in aggregate appear to have employed the greater part of the labour force and were coming to dominate the industry.

1850–75: BOOM OR STAGNATION?

In the celebrated article which he wrote in 1931, D. L. Burn located 'the genesis of American engineering competition' in the third quarter of the nineteenth century, a period 'when by text-book tradition England was the workshop of the world' (p. 302). Using evidence mainly of official Commissions to the USA in 1853–4 and of the international industrial exhibitions in London and Paris in 1851, 1856, 1862 and 1867, as well as technical journals, he demonstrated how, in many manufactures – including small arms, woodworking and agricultural machinery, sewing machines, locks, clocks and watches, screws, nuts and bolts, hydraulic pumps, brickmaking machines, printing presses, and even steam engines – the USA was achieving technological leadership, mainly by development of machine-tools for standardised mass-production, thus superseding traditional handicraft methods. It was largely by introduction of these American techniques that advances were made in Britain, while American exports were beginning to challenge British manufactures in overseas markets. Various explanations were put forward for this remarkable American progress, compared with Britain: the more rapidly growing and more homogeneous domestic market for such cheaper, standardised products; the relative scarcity and high cost of labour, especially of skilled labour; weaker trade unions and greater labour mobility; a better system of popular education; a more enterprising spirit, less attached to traditional manufacturing methods.

Later scholars, notably Habakkuk, Ames and Rosenberg, have reiterated and developed these arguments. Habakkuk has placed particular emphasis on the relative supplies and costs of labour, but his arguments are mainly concerned with the preceding half-century, though mass-production methods were not developed to any great extent in the USA until *after* 1850; in the first half of the century Britain led the way. Ames and Rosenberg have tended to stress the drawbacks of Britain's 'early start', without standardised production; it was only in the 1850s, they consider, with the introduction of 'the American system of manufactures', in small arms etc – typified by the Enfield Arsenal – that Britain slowly began to adopt mass-production methods; but they, too, have failed to appreciate the considerable British progress in machine-tools and standardised engineering in the first half of the century.

These and other scholars have been overmuch influenced by the evidence of Whitworth and other observers in the 1850s, especially in regard to armaments manufacture. Whitworth, as we have seen, tended to exaggerate the British lag in adoption of precision engineering, highlighting his own achievements. But even Whitworth, while impressed by American superiority in woodworking machinery and light engineering, especially small-arms manufacture, pointed out that in heavy engineering the British were clearly superior, a view confirmed by the Ordnance Commissioners (Musson, 1975). And as Saul has shown, Britain retained a good deal of this superiority right up to 1914, as well as catching up in other fields where she had been tending to lag (Saul, 1967, 1968a, 1968b, 1972).

The more prolonged British adherence to craft techniques in lighter labour-intensive industries was economically rational, with a relatively abundant supply of cheap skilled labour and more varied markets. Nevertheless, American mass-production methods were in some cases soon introduced into Britain. In small-arms manufacture, for example, not only was the government factory at Enfield equipped with American machinery in the 1850s, but Whitworth also entered this field, while the new Leeds tool-making firm of Greenwood & Batley (established in 1856) soon acquired an outstanding reputation for their manufacture of special machine-tools for making small arms (Floud, 1971 and 1976); even in the conservative Birmingham trades, factory production of military rifles on 'the interchangeable principle' was started by the Birmingham Small Arms Company in the early 1860s and by the National Arms and Ammunition Company in the early seventies (G. C. Allen, 1929, pp. 185–91, 200–1). Traditional handicraft methods long survived in the manufacture of sporting guns, but for these the domestic market was much smaller than in America and mainly for higher-quality products.

In woodworking machinery, the Americans had similarly demonstrated their superiority at the 1851 Exhibition. The early pioneering of Maudslay and Brunel in this field had not been very vigorously followed up in Britain, but during the third quarter of the century considerable progress was made by several British firms, notably Thomas Robinson's of Rochdale, who took first prize at the 1862 and the next four international exhibitions: 'employing 1,200 men in 1877, they claimed to be the largest such firm in the world' (Saul, 1968b, p. 188).

In the associated manufactures of wood-screws and nails, despite early British developments, the USA had similarly gone ahead in mechanised mass-production. But again American methods were soon adopted here, as by Nettlefold & Chamberlain, who introduced Sloan's automatic screw-making machinery in Birmingham in 1854 and soon dominated this sector of the hardware trade; by 1870 they had about 1,000 employees (Burn, 1931, p. 300; G. C. Allen, 1929, pp. 61–2, 109, 140; Saul, 1968b, p. 190). In most other Black Country hardware trades, however, handicraft production prevailed throughout this period (G. C. Allen, 1929, *passim*). In lockmaking, for example, as in blockmaking, the pioneering of Maudslay and Bramah was not followed up, and the London factory of the American, Hobbs, who introduced automatic lockmaking machinery into Britain in 1851, was still apparently unique in this country in 1870.

Another manufacture notable for American mass-production methods, following earlier European pioneering, was the making of sewing machines, for clothing and boot and shoe manufacturers. The USA led the way from the 1850s onwards, Singer's becoming particularly outstanding. Several British firms, such as Bradbury's of Oldham and Jones's of Guide Bridge, adopted similar methods of manufacture on 'the interchangeable system', with special machine-tools, but their production was dwarfed by Singer's, who opened a factory at Glasgow in 1867 which was turning out 5,000 machines a week by 1880 and was soon to surpass the output of the parent factory in New York (Saul, 1968*b*, pp. 189–90, 212). Similarly in the manufacture of boot- and shoe-making machinery – such as the Howe, Thomas and Blake–McKay sewing machines introduced in the fifties and sixties, followed by the Goodyear machines in the early seventies – the USA dominated both technologically and commercially, agencies for these American machines being set up in centres such as Northampton and Leicester (Church, 1970; Head, 1968).

There was similar weakness in British clock- and watch-making technology during this period, when standardised mass-production was rapidly developing in the USA and Switzerland, almost destroying this formerly pre-eminent British industry. Except for one or two efforts in Coventry and Prescot, traditional craft conservatism prevailed (Church, 1975*b*).

In some of the other manufactures referred to by Burn, however, the British lag was less significant or non-existent. In the making of letterpress-printing machines, for example, British engineers such as Cowper, Napier and Applegarth had already developed sheet-fed machines, both flat-bed and rotary, by mid-century, though American Hoe machines – of which Whitworth was the first British manufacturer – proved more successful in large newspaper offices in the fifties and sixties. For general printing, however, British platen and cylinder-printing machines, such as the 'Wharfedale' (made in Otley) were very popular, though later challenged by American Miehles. Reel-fed rotaries were brought out in the mid-sixties in both Britain and America, and though Hoe's soon took the lead, British engineers such as Duncan & Dawson, of Liverpool, also developed a thriving manufacture. Robert Hattersley produced the first type-composing machine to be widely used for newspaper printing from the sixties onwards, though it was later to be superseded by the American linotype and monotype machines (Musson, 1954, chs. 1 and 6, and 1957–8*b*).

In the manufacture of agricultural machinery, including ploughs, seed-drills, reapers, threshers and portable steam engines, British engineering developed strongly during this period. Several firms in the eastern counties – such as Ransome's (Ipswich), Hornsby's (Grantham), Ruston & Procter and Clayton & Shuttleworth (Lincoln), Garret's (Leiston), and Marshall's (Gainsborough) – grew rapidly and built up a flourishing export trade; by 1870 they were all employing 600 to 1,000 men (Saul, 1968*b*, pp. 188, 207, 211). Though Bell's reaper was superseded by those of the Americans Hussey and McCormick, who established factories in Britain, in other products, especially agricultural steam engines, boilers and threshers, British firms established an international predominance.

In hydraulic engineering, Burn simply referred to the American Gwynne's centrifugal pump, exhibited in 1851 and successfully manufactured here thereafter. But Bramah had much earlier fathered hydraulics, followed by other British engineers such as Murray and Nasmyth in the development of hydraulic pumps, presses and jacks. Bessemer had also exhibited a centrifugal pump in 1851 and various British engineering firms took up their manufacture thereafter. The third quarter of the century was the age of William Armstrong, who greatly extended this branch of engineering by manufacturing hydraulic pumps, cranes, lifts, hoists, capstans, swing and draw bridges, dock gates etc., together with the necessary pumping engines and accumulators (McNeil, 1972; British Association, 1863, pp. 109–11; Saul, 1968*b*, p. 189). Other firms, notably Tangye's, of Birmingham – established in 1857 and employing nearly 1,000 people by 1870 – also became outstanding in this field (G. C. Allen, 1929, pp. 62, 181).

Britain's lead in steam engineering, however, as Burn pointed out, was no longer undisputed. The USA had already produced pioneers in high-pressure steam such as Evans and Perkins, and the Corliss engine, with its improved valve-gear (patented 1849), further advanced American engineering in this field (Burn, 1931, p. 301; Dickinson, 1963, pp. 137–9; Saul, 1968*b*, pp. 205–6). Several British firms, however, notably Hick, Hargreaves & Company of Bolton, soon took up its manufacture. Similarly, though two American engineers, Porter and Allen, pioneered the high-speed engine, exhibited in 1862, British firms such as Tangye's and Robey's quickly followed with improved designs (Burn, 1931, p. 301; Dickinson, 1963, p. 142). In marine engineering, Penn's and Maudslay Sons & Field in London, both employing about 1,500 men in the mid-1860s, were still 'easily the foremost in the world in that line', as well as being general engineers (Saul, 1968*b*, p. 188). In the mid-fifties John Elder of Clydeside developed the compound marine engine, whereby engine power and fuel economy were greatly increased, and by the early 1870s Brotherhood's of Chippenham had produced triple-expansion high-speed engines; these were to be further developed by Bellis and Willans in the 1880s for electricity generation, while in 1884 Parsons was to patent his steam turbine and turbo-dynamo. Thus Britain's steam engineering pre-eminence was maintained (Dickinson, 1963, chs 8 and 9; Saul, 1968*b*, pp. 205–6).

In other heavy engineering sectors, not mentioned by Burn, such as the building of railway locomotives and rolling stock, and textile machine-making, British predominance was also maintained. The most striking development was the growth of the railway company workshops from the mid-1840s onwards, at Cowlairs, Crewe, Wolverton, Swindon, Derby, Doncaster, Horwich etc. By the early seventies these were among the largest engineering establishments in the country: Swindon employed 4,000 men by 1875, Crewe 6,000 by 1877, while others had 2,000 to 3,000 (Saul, 1968*b*, pp. 187, 195–6). Private locomotive builders were therefore forced increasingly into overseas markets, though home and export sales were roughly equal until the late seventies; thereafter there was a great upsurge in exports, despite growing foreign competition. Several of the older firms went out of business or dropped locomotive building, and production was concentrated mainly in a few large northern firms, such as Sharp Stewart, formerly Sharp Roberts, Nasmyth Wilson and Beyer Peacock (Manchester), Vulcan Foundry (Newton-le-Willows), Kitson's (Leeds), Stephenson's and Hawthorn's (Newcastle), and Neilson's and Dubs's (Glasgow), all employing well over 1,000 men by 1875, though most of them were also general engineers.

The manufacture of rolling stock was similarly divided between private and company builders, but was an even more specialised business. The railway companies had separate carriage- and wagon-building departments, or separate works such as that of the L. & N. W. Railway at Wolverton, while a number of large specialist private firms also sprang up from among the coach-building and metal-working trades, especially in the Birmingham area, where by the late 1860s five such firms were together employing about 3,000 men; the largest, Wright's Metropolitan Railway Carriage & Wagon Company, had 1,200. There was an even higher degree of specialisation in railway equipment by firms such as the Patent Shaft and Axle-Tree Company, of Wednesbury, which was employing 3,000 men by the early seventies, making axles, wheels, points, turn-tables etc. with integrated coal and iron mines, blast furnaces, foundries, and steel plant, as well as engineering works. Other carriage and wagon companies were established in Manchester (Ashbury's), Gloucester, Lancaster, Bristol, and Sheffield, and a flourishing export as well as home trade was developed (G. C. Allen, 1929, pp. 73–4, 92–3, 135, 193, 259–60; Saul, 1968*b*, pp. 203–4).

The immense international predominance of British textiles, especially cotton, during this period was associated with continued developments in textile engineering, greatly improving the construction, speed and productivity of spinning and weaving machines (Farnie, 1953; Ellison, 1886; Saul, 1968*b*, pp. 191–5). With the final removal of export controls in 1843, British machine-making firms greatly expanded overseas sales, in Europe, India and the USA, as well as having a vastly growing home market. The foundations for this growth, as we have seen, had already been firmly laid by mid-century, and old-established firms continued to expand remarkably. Platt's of Oldham were employing 7,000 men in two works by 1875 – John Platt, indeed, could justifiably claim to be 'the largest mechanical engineer in the world' (Burn, 1931, p. 297, n. 2) – while Dobson & Barlow of Bolton had about 2,000 and Curtis & Madeley of Manchester, 1,400. At the same time, newer firms such as Howard & Bullough (Accrington), Hetherington's and Brooks & Doxey (Manchester) soon established outstanding reputations. Makers of woollen and worsted machinery were similarly progressive; Fairbairn's of Leeds were employing 2,400 men by 1875, mainly on textile machinery (Saul, 1968*b*, p. 194; 1967, p. 25).

As William Fairbairn emphasised in his presidential address to the British Association in 1861, the growth of power-driven mechanisation in textiles etc. was entirely dependent upon 'the exactitude and accuracy of our machine tools' – pioneered especially by Roberts and Whitworth – which had almost entirely displaced handwork in engineering (British Association, 1862, pp. lxiii–lxiv), and which continued to be developed in this period. It is true that some of the early tool-making firms, such as Murray and Fox, went out of existence, while others such as Maudslay & Field, Sharp Stewart and Nasmyth Wilson were tending towards specialisation in other fields. Whitworth, moreover, who dominated the machine-tool section of the 1851 Exhibition, is said to have become unprogressive as a result of 'his growing interest in armaments and his egotistical conservatism' (Saul, 1968*a*, p. 208). It has recently been shown, however, that this judgement, based on the biased reminiscences of the American engineer, Charles T. Porter, is by no means borne out by contemporary evidence on Whitworth's works in 1866, when he was employing 700 men, still mainly engaged in tool-making, and producing not only improved lathes, planers, drills, boring and slotting machines, but also new machine-tools such as milling machines (Musson, 1975, pp. 137–8). Moreover, the machine-tool reputation of Manchester and Salford was also maintained by new firms, such as those of Muir and Hulse, formerly managers at Whitworth's, and even more notably by Craven's and Smith & Coventry, both founded in the 1850s, while Massey's assumed Nasmyth's pre-eminence in steam hammers. In other cities, too, there were newcomers, such as Smith, Beacock & Tannett, Greenwood & Batley, and Shepherd & Hill in Leeds, together with new tool-making firms in Halifax and Keighley, stimulated by the mechanisation of the woollen industry. As Saul has shown, these and other firms maintained 'a machine-tool industry of the highest calibre' in Britain right up to 1914 (Saul, 1968*b*, pp. 208–9, and 1967; see also Floud, 1971 and 1976). Moreover, Floud has demonstrated that American engineering competition in the British home and export markets did not become really significant until the 1890s (Floud, 1974).

It was in the light engineering field – in the manufactures of small arms, sewing machines, clocks and watches etc. – that American superiority in standardised mass-production was established, with extensive utilisation of milling and grinding machines, turret lathes, and many highly specialised machine-tools. And such techniques, transferred from these manufactures, were to be of considerable importance later on in the development of the new and far more important industries of motor and electrical engineering, in which Britain was at first to lag. The newer machine-tools were by no means unknown in this country – indeed milling machines had earlier been pioneered here by several British engineers (Musson, 1975, pp. 137–8) – but they were brought into general use much more slowly than in the USA, especially in light engineering. Nevertheless, there was to be a similar British transfer of technology from the manufacture of clocks and sewing machines, first to the cycle and then to the motor-car industry, especially in the Coventry–Birmingham area (Saul, 1968*b*, pp. 212–6; Church, 1975*b*, pp. 626–30). In 1875, however, these new developments were only just being foreshadowed. The Coventry Machinists Company, for example, founded in 1869, had only recently metamorphosed from sewing-machine to cycle firms in the midlands, including such later-famous names as Rudge (Wolverhampton) and Humber and Raleigh (Nottingham), as yet they were only small, as was the total number employed in the industry: in 1881 only 700 engaged in it in the Coventry–Birmingham area (G. C. Allen, 1929, pp. 293–4).

The internal-combustion engine was likewise in its infancy and the petrol-driven car had not yet been born. Gas engines originated on the Continent, pioneered by Lenoir, Hugon and Otto in the 1860s, and it was Otto's improved four-stroke 'silent engine' of 1876 that achieved the real break-through. But British firms were quick to grasp their possibilities: some of Lenoir's engines were made by Reading Iron Works, while Crossley's of Manchester were very enterprising in production and development of the Otto engine (Saul, 1968*b*, p. 216).

It is thus abundantly clear that during this third quarter-century the British engineering industry continued to progress remarkably, especially in the heavy sectors. It not only sustained industrial growth at home, but also rapidly expanded capital exports. It was mainly under pressure from this industry, as well as from growing free-trade opinion, that the restrictions on exportation of machinery and machine-tools were first relaxed in 1825 and then removed in 1843 (Musson, 1972*b*). Because of widespread smuggling and evasion, there are no reliable figures of exports for the earlier period, but they had reached £1 million by 1850 and rose thereafter to £10 million by 1873, when they formed about 4 per cent of the total value of domestic exports (Mitchell and Deane, 1971, pp. 303–4).

With demand growing so rapidly at home and overseas, the total number of people engaged in the industry trebled in the third quarter of the century. The Population Census of Great Britain in 1871 showed a total of nearly 133,000 engine- and machine-makers (including spinning-machine makers, separately classified), together with nearly 12,000 tool and agricultural-implement makers and just over 9,000 millwrights, the slight fall in whose numbers since 1851 reflected the declining demand for traditional all-round skills, compared with the rapid growth of specialised machine minders. The geographical distribution of the industry was approximately the same as in 1851, with Lancashire and Cheshire still by far the most important area, with over 32,000 engine- and machine-makers, but both the West Riding and Northumberland and Durham were now on a par with London, each having 14,000 to 15,000 in that category, followed by Lanarkshire and Renfrewshire with about 10,500 and Staffordshire and Warwickshire with 8,500.

The factory Returns for 1870 showed an industry of somewhat greater size, with 167,000 engaged in the 'manufacture of machinery' in the United Kingdom (including only 3,400 in Ireland). There were 2,000 works, with steam engines totalling 42,000 horsepower, so that the average works had 84 employees and 21 horsepower. But, as we have seen, the tendency towards dominance by the larger firms, already visible at mid-century, had been strengthened during the third quarter and the biggest were now employing several thousand workers.

These increases in total numbers employed and in the size of firms provide clear evidence of the engineering industry's growth during this period. Unfortunately, it is impossible to provide any more precise measure of its performance in terms of productivity and profitability, because the requisite statistics are not available in the very few business records that have survived. But with demand rising so strongly at home and abroad, and with the rapid development of cost-reducing techniques and specialisation, the industry's efficiency and profitability were certainly increased very considerably, providing the resources for the accompanying investment in plant and machinery, evident from the surviving plans and descriptions of engineering works. The revolutionary economic effects of these technological innovations are strikingly illustrated by the metal-planing machine, which cut the labour cost of this operation from 12s (by hand chipping and filing) to less than 1d per square foot, as Whitworth pointed out in 1856 (Musson, 1975, p. 127). Together with the employment of cheaper, semi-skilled machine minders, these technological advances largely explain the remarkable growth from small beginnings of such great engineering fortunes as those of Fairbairn, Nasmyth, Whitworth, Armstrong and other leading figures of the age. But though these were 'glorious times for the Engineers', as Nasmyth enthused on establishment of the Bridgewater Foundry in the boom year of 1836, technology alone could not ensure business success, as shown by the ultimate fate of such an engineering genius as Richard Roberts. As in other industries, entrepreneurial and managerial skills in marketing, finance, works organisation and labour relations were equally if not more essential for survival and growth, in this era of fierce competition and trade fluctuations.

5   The Shipbuilding Industry

by A. Slaven

Between 1815 and 1875 British shipbuilding was completely refashioned. At the outset it was a craft, at the close it was a heavy engineering industry. This transition involved not only a new technology, but a major shift in the centre of production, a vast increase in scale, and fundamental changes in the operation and organisation of the firms.

THE REGIONAL PATTERN

The changing regional distribution of the industry is not easy to delineate. Employment data are incomplete, inconsistent and of dubious reliability, making comparison over time and among districts a hazardous business. According to the Censuses, male employment in shipbuilding expanded from under 20,000 in 1831 to over 61,000 in 1871. Between these dates the centre of the industry moved steadily away from the south and eastern districts towards the north and west. In 1831, employment along the south coast, the Bristol channel and the Thames accounted for nearly half the total, the Thames alone concentrating about 15 per cent of employment along its banks. The north-eastern rivers from the Tyne to the Humber employed nearly as many men as on the Thames, but only about 8 per cent found employment along the Mersey, Dee and other rivers in the north-west, while Scotland claimed about 12 per cent of the jobs. By 1871 the pattern was very different. The southern districts now employed 22 per cent of the workforce, while the Humber–Tyne district concentrated nearly a quarter of the workers along its rivers. On employment data the north-eastern district had displaced the Thames as the largest centre by 1841, and consolidated its leadership thereafter. But if we concentrate on shipbuilding rivers rather than districts, the Thames maintained its dominance in employment into the 1860s when it was ultimately displaced, not by the Tyne, Wear or Tees, but by the Clyde which had exploded from insignificance with 3 per cent of employment in 1831, to 6 per cent in 1851, but 21 per cent of Britain's total in 1871. It was then the largest concentrated area of shipbuilding employment in Britain, and at that time in the world. By 1871, nearly two-thirds of all employment in shipbuilding was concentrated in the northern districts, 26 per cent in Scotland, 24 per cent on the north-east coast, 13 per cent on the north-western rivers between the Mersey and Barrow.

The pattern seems clear enough, but if one sets census enumerations alongside other information on employment, it would appear that the census was heavily defective in collecting employment data. For example, while the Census enumerated 1,895 men employed in shipbuilding on the Clyde in 1851, John Strang claimed that 10,820 men were at work in the yards and engine shops (Strang, 1853). This latter figure is much more consistent with the then Clyde output of over 60,000 tons per year, than the census data. Equally, in 1871, the Inspectors of Factories in their Return on iron shipyards enumerated 24,000 men employed on the Clyde, while the census of the same year indicated 12,892; the same sources indicated 8,813 men and 6,135 men respectively on the Thames. The discrepancies are so large as to cast serious doubt on the use of the census data for shipbuilding in this period. Fortunately the Factory Inspectors Returns for 1871 do give a check on the distribution of the iron shipyard sector which appears to have employed 51,514 men in 1871, out of the total of 61,316 recorded in the census. Of this total 46·6 per cent worked on the Clyde, 25·8 per cent in the north-east, 17·1 per cent on the Thames and 7·2 per cent in the north-western district. This confirms the pattern outlined from the Censuses, stressing the locational shifts to the north and west, and emphasising the leadership of the Clyde district.

Regional output data are so sparse before 1870 as to be of little help in refining this regional picture further. In 1831 the north-eastern rivers launched 32,000 out of the 84,000 tons built in Britain, 38 per cent of the total, while the census only allocated 14 to 15 per cent of the workforce to this district. This underlines the deficiencies of the census and suggests that the north-east was the major shipbuilding district earlier than would be suggested by employment data. By 1871 with a launching of nearly 400,000 tons, the Clyde led with 48 per cent, the north-east following with 43 per cent, confirming the dominance of these two districts indicated by the employment figures.

This change in regional leadership was accompanied by a vast increase in the scale and capacity of the industry. Capacity is difficult to judge, but is usually reckoned as equivalent to peak output at full employment. On this basis the industry had a capacity in the range of 120,000 to 150,000 tons per year at the end of the Napoleonic Wars, rising sharply to over 600,000 tons by 1874, a four- to five-fold increase over a period in which employment appears to have increased by a factor of three. These are the visible dimensions of the technical and structural changes at work in the industry in these years.

INNOVATION IN WOOD AND SAIL

The witnesses before the Select Committee of 1833 were, with few exceptions, of the mind that their difficulties arose from high duties on imported timber and the loss of orders for British ships, as more of the carrying trade appeared to be being captured by ships from countries given unfair advantages through access to the British market under the series of Reciprocity Treaties signed from 1824 (*PP*, 1833, vol. VI, q. 7483). These were immediate grievances deeply held, but they blinkered contemporaries to the fact that the malaise was more deeply rooted in the structure of shipbuilding itself. More protection was called for and would undoubtedly have helped, but of itself would not have solved the twenty-year stagnation of the trade. The industry was characterised by small yards and customary local demand, both contributing to conservatism in building. Tonnage laws of 1773 and 1775 excluded depth from tonnage calculations and encouraged deep, narrow and unstable box-like vessels to evade duty and port dues (Cormack, 1931, p. 358). In addition, price differentials between British, European and North American tonnage were large. Quotations voiced before the Select Committee claimed Scandinavian and Baltic yards could build at £5 to £8 10s 0d per ton against Thames prices of £13 to £14, and that North American prices were similar to the European figures (*PP*, 1833, vol. VI, q. 5891). Beset by these difficulties British builders floundered in the wake of French superiority in the eighteenth century and were swiftly passed in design by the Americans in the early nineteenth century. A British revival in shipbuilding demanded improvements in design, some answer to high-production costs, and advances in capacity, speed and economy.

The first revision of the tonnage laws in 1835 re-incorporating depth measurements in tonnage calculations, and the rationalisation of registration in the new Lloyds Register of British and Foreign Shipping in 1834 encouraged efforts in these directions. The abandonment of the navigation laws in 1849 increased foreign competition and acted as another stimulus to improvement, while the complete revision of tonnage laws with the Moorsom system in 1854 finally ended any advantage in continuing to build the old narrow and deep types of vessel (Cornewall-Jones, 1898, pp. 240–1). In the framework of these legislative changes the British response to American leadership was initially piecemeal, but gathered cohesion and momentum in the 1840s. Improvements came from a small number of men who led a broader reconstruction of the industry by concentrating variously on the hull shape, the design of the bow, the size of the vessel, and the materials used in construction. Wigram & Green in London innovated the cleaner hull of the Blackwall frigates in the early 1830s

(Banbury, 1971, p. 121); Alexander Hall & Company in Aberdeen introduced the sharp 'Aberdeen bow' in 1839 (W. T. Smith, n.d., p. 7). Together with the more theoretical ideas of John Scott Russell and his 'wave-line' form for hulls, these advances placed British builders in a position to respond to the challenge of the graceful American clippers by 1850, their leadership being finally overtaken by Scott of Greenock's iron-hulled clipper, the *Lord of the Isles*, in 1856 (Lindsay, 1876, Vol. 3, p. 294). This new equality was partially sustained by another innovation, John Jordan of Liverpool's idea of composite construction patented in 1850 (Banbury, 1971, p. 160). Combining iron frames and wooden planking sheathed in copper, it avoided the problem of fouling of hulls by marine growth, the great drawback of iron vessels.

Linking their new designs first to oak, then to iron, and for a time to the composite form, British builders tipped the scales back in their own favour in the twenty years from the mid-1830s. A relatively small group of builders pioneered and many more followed. The long-standing weaknesses in design, size and speed were satisfactorily answered, though British tonnage remained more expensive than the North American soft-wood vessels. The diffusion of these improvements was rapid since they merely employed old skills in new designs and ensured that, by 1855, Britain had re-established herself as a great and successful builder of sailing ships.

INNOVATION AND TECHNICAL CHANGE: STEAM AND IRON

Taming the wind and controlling propulsion was beyond the skills of even the greatest designers of sail vessels, but that was the challenge which attracted the pioneers of steam. The natural level way provided by water encouraged early experimentation, and building on earlier work by William Symington in Scotland and Robert Fulton in America, it was Henry Bell who, on the Clyde in 1812, first demonstrated the passenger potential of steam-powered vessels in Britain. His example was quickly imitated and by 1820, of the major shipbuilding rivers, only the Wear had not built and launched its own version of the new steam vessel (Lindsay, 1876, Vol. 4, p. 72).

Bell and the other assemblers of the early steamships quickly encountered four major types of problem which were to set the field of inquiry for the men who were to create Britain's new shipbuilding industry. These were the devising of appropriate marine engines, the development of complementary boilers; the alliance of these to effective propulsive devices; the re-design and construction of hulls suited to the new machinery.

By the 1840s the initial beam engine had evolved through a side-levered variety to the direct-acting oscillating engine which overcame the problem of connecting rods by linking the piston directly to the crankshaft. Boulton & Watt at Soho, Maudslay & Field, and Penn in London, and David Napier in Glasgow were the main contributors to this improvement. In the same period the Watt land boiler used in the 'Comet' had evolved through the first of the marine 'box-boilers' to the introduction from 1835 of the marine version of the locomotive fire-tube boiler (Singer *et al.*, 1958, Vol. 5, p. 153), by which working pressures were increased from $1\frac{1}{2}$–2 lb to 20–30 lb per square inch. The early engines and boilers were sufficient to capture river and short open-sea routes. The direct-acting engines combined with the water-tube boiler opened the prospect of regular passenger services across the Atlantic, and paved the way for the successful introduction of the screw propeller in place of the paddle. Patents for screws were taken variously by Woodcroft in 1826 and 1832, and by Thomas Smith and John Ericson in 1836. Smith's version was the one finally taken up in Britain, following exhaustive Admiralty trials between 1843–5, and found quick favour with merchant builders. Although first relying on gearing to develop sufficiently high revolutions, marine-engine improvements allowed direct connection by 1850 (*Encyclopaedia Britannica*, 1886, Vol. 22, p. 517). Taken together these innovations improved the economy of steam from about 10 lb of coal per horse-power hour in the earliest steamers, to about 4 to 5 lb by the 1840s, making it a realistic proposition for vessels on routes to America, Europe and the Mediterranean. Further economies demanded still higher boiler pressures and more efficient use of coal and steam.

The significant breakthrough here was by the Clyde engineers, John Elder and Charles Randolph, who patented a marine compound expansion engine in 1853, and fitted out the SS *Brandon* with one in 1854. In letters to shipbuilders they claimed 'our patent double cylinder expansion engines expanding the steam to six volumes . . . [give] a saving of about 40 per cent in the fuel required for the Ordinary Engine' (Stephen Papers, 1859, UGD 4/1/1). However, it was not until 1862 that another Glasgow engineer, James Howden, introduced his 'Scotch' boiler (Ravenhill, 1877, p. 283). It was cylindrical and was strong enough to reliably deliver the pressures of up to 40 lb per square inch required to get the best out of Randolph and Elder's compound engine. Only after that did the new engine make much headway, and by 1871, it supplied one-third of the horse-power employed in the British merchant marine. Five years later its share had risen to about three-quarters (Ravenhill, 1877, pp. 281, 284). The doubling of the cost of fuel in the early 1870s, together with the foreshortening of distance with the Suez canal, provided the environment for the full exploitation of compound expansion. By then, Elder and Randolph's promise of 40 per cent savings in fuel were fully achieved and bettered, engines working at 60 lb pressure and consuming a bare 2·1 lb of coal per horsepower hour being common. Moreover, the power to weight ratio had been reduced from about one ton (5,280 lb) per horsepower in the first steamers, to about 480 lb per horsepower in the 1870s, with dramatic savings in space for cargo and passengers (*Encyclopaedia Britannica*, 1886, Vol. 22, p. 519).

This complicated sequence of invention and innovation answered the questions posed by the first steamers concerning engines, boilers and propulsion. It remained to redesign the hulls to suit the new power. Slow-revolving paddles did not unduly strain wooden hulls on short routes, but when longer distances, larger vessels and greater speeds were contemplated, the limitations of wood were quickly reached. Once over 300 feet in length wooden hulls lost rigidity; with fast-revolving screws they sprung leaks and required heavy maintenance.

To the engineer at least, iron was the answer to size and strength. Incredulity was a serious obstacle to its acceptance right from the launch of John Wilkinson's iron barge in 1787 to the 1840s. Both experimental work like that of William Fairbairn in 1838 (Corlett, 1975, pp. 40–1), and accidents like the grounding of Brunel's *Great Britain* for twelve months in 1846–7 (Corlett, 1975, pp. 40–1; Smith, 1938, p. 101), were necessary to demonstrate the strength of iron plates and iron structures. But once experimentation began seriously in the 1830s, acceptance came quickly, iron achieving A1 classification at Lloyds in 1844, and separate rules for iron construction being accepted in 1855. By this time it was clearly established that an iron vessel could be lighter and stronger, and have a greater carrying capacity than a wooden ship of similar proportions.

While an impressive theoretical and experimental literature was also quickly available, it is clear that many at first contrived to build by eye and error, contributing to 'a strong prejudice against iron . . . which is much increased by the defective construction of those already built' (Stephen Papers, 1856, UGD 4/18/7). It is probable that it was a lack of confidence in quality more than comparative prime unit costs of wood and iron which dictated the speed of acceptance of iron. As early as 1843, John Grantham claimed iron to be no more expensive than wood for vessels up to 300 feet, and steadily cheaper beyond that limit (Grantham, 1842, p. 41). Good workmanship had to be allied with good design and good-quality material before doubt and prejudice could be overcome.

The pioneers of iron shipbuilding were, with few exceptions, engineers with little or no experience of building in wood: John Laird followed by John Vernon on the Mersey from 1829; Maudslay on the Thames in 1832 followed by the incomers Fairbairn from Manchester and David Napier from the Clyde; David Tod and John McGregor on the Clyde from 1835, followed by Robert Napier and

Thomas Wingate (Banbury, 1971, p. 60). On the north-east coast the innovators were T. D. Marshall at South Shields in 1839 and Coutts & Company at Walker in 1840 (Dougan, 1968, p. 38). In all the districts some established builders built iron vessels, and all the iron builders frequently built in wood at the outset. But the new industry was substantially the work of new men previously little connected with shipbuilding. The main centres were the Mersey, Thames and Clyde, the north-east not moving strongly into iron until the 1850s when it was picked up by new builders such as Charles Palmer, John Leslie and John Wigham Richardson. Those who combined iron building with other interests, like Maudslay and Fairbairn, quickly fell by the wayside, and only those committing themselves strongly to the new medium survived.

The interplay of wood, sail, steam and iron is complex, but it is clear that the separate potentials of steam and iron were only fully realised when the two were linked. While iron represented only 9·5 per cent of construction in 1850, its share of steam tonnage was already 61 per cent. Within ten years it totally eclipsed wood in the construction of steamers, and one-third of sail tonnage was also iron-hulled in the 1860s. Iron equalled and then passed wooden tonnage built in 1862, and steam tonnage exceeded sail construction in 1870. Although sail tonnage in total did not lose its ascendancy in the British merchant marine until 1883, steam and iron was already the leading sector in British shipbuilding in the 1860s. Between 1845 and 1865, the old industry was overwhelmed and the modern shipbuilding industry based on metal and steam, and located mainly on Clydeside and the north-east coast, had come into being.

The new location is partly related to the degree of preference exhibited for steam and iron over wood and sail among districts, but although both the Thames and Mersey early specialised in iron they could not sustain their leadership. In the 1830s and 1840s, shipowners adventurous enough to order an iron vessel were conservative enough to specify construction in Shropshire, Derbyshire, or other well-known plates. Every shipbuilding district had to pay similar carriage charges, and as long as the quantity of iron used was small no district was much disadvantaged by its location relative to the iron producers. But when large tonnages were regularly required and the Cleveland iron district and the Scottish malleable iron sector bloomed from the 1850s, the balance of advantage began to change.

In 1860 in quoting to a Liverpool shipper, Alexander Stephen declared 'Staffordshire plates . . . do not stand well in our opinion . . . we consider any additional cost for them thrown away . . . about 12/- per ton is lost on carriage alone' (Stephen Papers, 1860, UGD 4/1/1). This scale of cost differential in favour of locally produced plates seems likely to have been the ultimate influence in favour of the north-east and the Clyde. Yet writing in 1869, John Glover rejected the raw-material costs as significant in the decline of the Thames, stressing rather high wages, union intransigence and high overheads (Glover, 1869, pp. 288–91). Pollard also commented on these features while emphasising the flaws of over specialisation in high-cost ships and government orders (Pollard, 1950–1, pp. 76, 78, 79). However, on balance he, too, favoured the conclusion that 'it was the cheap supplies of iron and steel plates and bars and machinery for the yards, and coal to drive the steam engines which were ultimately at the base of the location of the industry along the Scottish and Northern rivers' (Pollard, 1951, p. 214).

FLUCTUATIONS

Shipbuilding is a classic example of a capital-goods investment industry subject to violent swings in demand. Orders ebb and flow with world trade, the course of freight rates, price relatives between old and new tonnage *vis-à-vis* earning power, and shipowners' ability to defer replacement for lengthy periods. This unpredictability of orders, together with the need for a builder to respond quickly to demand, typically generated a tendency to over-capacity in shipbuilding. This is an inherent tendency separate from and additional to the capacity expansion which regularly accompanied strong upward movements in trade and freights. Capacity in relation to the level of demand is the key to understanding the condition of the industry.

Since shipbuilding provides the carrying capacity for world trade, a similarity of movement between tonnage built and the general trade cycle is to be expected, but the relationship is neither simple nor consistent. Between 1822–79 shipbuilding experienced seven major cycles of seven to nine years' duration on average (Figure 5.1). The general relationship with the trade cycle was a lag of one or two years at the peaks and troughs, though this was reversed when shipbuilding anticipated the general turning points in the cycles of 1830–6 and 1867–79. Some such anticipation of the cycle should be expected since capital-goods activity normally turns down earlier than general activity, but in shipbuildings' case, time taken in construction and orders in the pipeline normally caused peaks and troughs to occur later than in the general cycle. Within these cycles, steam construction evidently was subject to sharper swings than sail tonnage. This is basically a reflection of how willing customers were to bear the extra cost of steam at different stages of the cycle, in relation to anticipated earnings from each type of vessel. Steam and sail do not clearly exhibit separate fluctuations until the 1867–79 cycle when they moved in opposite directions: they were then almost complete alternative preferences, steam in demand in the upswing, cheaper sail tonnage recovering after the peak of 1874.

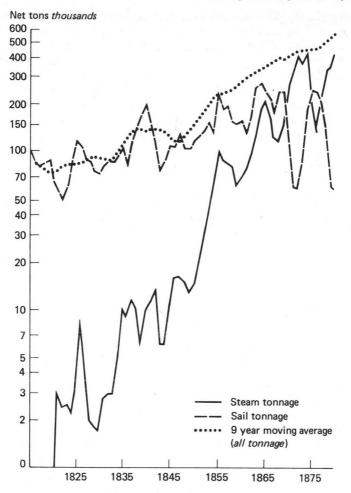

Figure 5.1 *The annual output of sail and steam tonnage, 1815–80*

While the fluctuations were severe, the underlying trend was almost relentlessly upward, checking only briefly between 1842–8, reflecting mainly the capacity-absorption problem created by the surge of new building in the 1830s. The resumption of the upward trend from 1849–50 was strong enough to assimilate the fluctuations of the succeeding cycles almost without trace in an expansion that did not show any significant break until 1882. In the same period Britain's foreign trade expanded three-fold (Imlah, 1958, pp. 96–7) and net credits earned by British shipping jumped from about £13 million per year to £52·5 million in the 1870s (Imlah, 1958, pp. 70–3). The trends are inextricably linked, and Hughes and Reiter postulated that the surge was closely associated with the dramatic increase in carrying capacity made available by the iron-screw steamer from the 1850s (Hughes and Reiter, 1958, pp. 362–5). While new sail tonnage still exceeded steam construction by a factor of three in the 1850s, contemporaries rated one steam ton as equivalent to about four sail tons in carrying capacity (Glover, 1863, p. 26; 1872, p. 35; 1882, p. 45) while Hughes and Reiter's estimates suggest that the effective carrying capacity created by the iron steamer in the 1850s was already equal to that of the larger sail construction.

The major fluctuations around this rising trend involved many influences, yet three recurred with regularity: the effect of war, capacity creation and absorption, and the expansion or slackening of trade. The capacity generated during the Napoleonic Wars held shipbuilding stagnant for two decades while its effects were absorbed. The burst of building between 1836–42 associated with expanding eastern trade and the first China War, saturated the market and kept shipbuilding output down in the succeeding cycle. Similarly the Crimean episode coming on top of the gold discoveries and a consequent heavy emigrant traffic depressed shipbuilding after 1856–7, even though trade continued to expand vigorously both before and after the pause triggered by the financial crisis of 1857. Between 1859 and 1866 war and expanding trade first solved the lingering excess capacity of the 1850s boom, while simultaneously encouraging new construction which, in association with large sales of American tonnage, induced another capacity saturation situation by 1866. The severe financial crisis of that year was a contributory rather than a casual factor in the contraction of output that followed. In the final cycle the Abyssinian campaign and the short Franco-Prussian hostilities contributed to rising freights, but it was a general trade expansion, and the demands for capital goods for American and Russian railways, in particular, which fuelled the great boom of 1868–74. Both the Suez canal and the doubling in coal prices favoured the steamer powered by the compound engine, and a temporary near-abandonment of sail. As in every other major cycle the scale of output generated surplus shipping capacity, and effectively set the level to which production could recover or expand in the next phase (Matthews, 1954, p. 119). Seven years were to elapse before shipbuilding could recover to the level attained in what Disraeli described as the 'great convulsion of prosperity' (Chambers, 1961, p. 169).

PRICES, PRODUCTIVITY AND PROFIT

Price information for tonnage and for labour is plentiful, though its fragmented and inconsistent nature make an overview difficult, especially before 1850. Tonnage rates, quoted in Builders Old Measure from the Stephen diaries, suggest little or no general increase in price between 1824 and 1851, even though fluctuations were substantial between a low of about £7·3 per ton in 1829 and an upper average of £12·2 in 1825 and £11·5 in 1835, 1850 and 1851. (Table 5.1). These are averages and individual vessels did fetch up to £15 in peak years depending on the type of outfit and the class of the vessel. Evidence from the Commissions of 1833 and 1848 suggested prices on the northeast coast were similar to the Stephen figures, though mainly at the upper end of the range, while Thames tonnage was usually as much as a third higher in price, reflecting the higher-rated vessels normally built there (*PP*, 1833, Vol. VI; Pollard, 1951, p. 9).

Table 5.1   *Average Contract Prices per Builders Measurement Ton; wood – sail vessels; Alexander Stephen yards: 1824–51*

Year	£ per ton	Year	£ per ton	Year	£ per ton	Year	£ per ton
1824	11·1	1831	8·5	1838	11.2	1845	8·1
1825	12·2	1832	8·6	1839	10·3	1846	10·0
1826	9·3	1833	8·2	1840	10·1	1847	10·5
1827	8·5	1834	9·9	1841	9·0	1848	11·0
1828	8·3	1835	11·5	1842	—	1849	—
1829	7·3	1836	10·0	1843	8·0	1850	11·5
1830	8·2	1837	10·6	1844	8·4	1851	11·5

Notes: 1824–29 at Aberdeen
1830–42 at Arbroath
1843–51 at Dundee
Source: Alexander Stephen Diaries, University of Glasgow Business History Collection; UGD 4/16/1–3

The situation is less obscure after 1850 when we can compare estimates made by Maywald with contract prices drawn from the Stephen and Denny papers (Table 5.2). Four general points may be made. While all the series point up fluctuations in price, none exhibit any general increase either in sail or steam tonnage rates over the period. Second, the fluctuations are shown more clearly in the yard contract prices than in Maywald's estimates, especially in the Crimean and Civil War episodes when the Denny prices show particularly sharp increments. Third, wood-sail tonnage appears to have been marginally more costly than iron-sail vessels in the 1850s, which supports a common claim of the period. Finally, the ephemerally popular composite vessels were on this evidence up to £2 per ton on average more expensive than simple iron hulls. Although not shown in Table 5.2, composite steamer prices were not significantly different from those of iron steamers in the Stephen's contracts. It is clear that it was the rapid change in price within cycles, rather than

Table 5.2   *Average Price per gross register ton 1850–75 (prices in £ per ton)*

Year	Denny Iron Steamers	Maywald Steamers	Stephen Iron Steamers	Maywald Sail	Wood-Sail	Stephen: Glasgow Iron Sail	Composite Sail
1850	24·0	25·0		16·0			
1851	23·9	25·6		15·9			
1852	21·7	26·2		17·0			
1853	25·2	26·5		18·7			
1854	35·0	25·8		18·3			
1855	33·2	25·1	25·0	18·0	20·4		
1856	37·1	24·5	25·7	17·2	15·7	17·5	
1857	29·3	25·1	—	17·5	17·0		
1858	29·9	25·4	22·3	18·1	16·0	15·5	
1859	28·0	25·1	—	18·1	13·0	15·3	
1860	21·6	26·1	27·2	18·7	—	16·0	
1861	23·9	26·0	32·0	18·5	19·0	16·2	
1862	25·3	26·3	23·8	19·4	18·0	17·2	
1863	27·9	26·8	27·0	19·9		17·5	19·5
1864	29·1	29·2	27·0	22·4		18·4	18·7
1865	29·7	28·6	—	22·1		18·7	17·0
1866	29·1	28·1	24·4	22·1		15·4	17·1
1867	32·4	27·1	22·5	21·4		15·1	17·3
1868	23·8	25·8	20·2	20·3		15·4	17·2
1869	24·4	24·7	21·3	19·4		14·9	16·6
1870	27·7	23·9	28·7	19·2		14·6	17·7
1871	22·1	24·1	29·2	19·3		—	17·0
1872	23·5	28·8	35·2	23·5		19·0	21·0
1873	29·5	32·7	37·0	26·4		20·7	23·5
1874	27·2	33·1	38·5	25·7		19·0	
1875	28·5	31·1	29·2	23·4		16·5	

Note: Maywald's estimates are for steamers, but his hull prices may be taken as equivalent to sail vessels. In his calculations wood is taken as the main construction material to 1862, iron thereafter.

Sources: K. Maywald: "The Construction Costs and the Value of the British Merchant Fleet 1850–1938", *Scottish Journal of Political Economy* Vol 3, 1956. Denny: UGD3/5/1–3, Contracts; and, D. S. Lyon, *The Denny List*, Vol 1, 1975. Stephen: UGD4/8/1–7 and UGD4/18/7.

the general trend in prices, which was significant for the builder. Fluctuations which could increase or decrease tonnage rates by a third, or on occasion by half, typified the unstable and difficult business environment in which the shipbuilder had to work.

If these tonnage prices are linked to production data, the value of ships produced appears to have increased from about £1·7 million per year in the 1820s, to about £4·4 million in the 1850s at Clyde

Table 5.3 Average weekly wages in time work in selected shipbuilding occupations

Period	Carpenter	Joiner	Smith	Fitter	Riveter	Rigger	Blockmaker	Labourer	Boy
[1]									
1826–30	15s 6d – 17s		18s						5s – 7s
1831–5	14s – 17s								4s – 6s
1836–40	17s – 19s								4s – 6s
1841–5	15s – 17s 6d								
1846–50	16s 6d – 19s 6d								
[2]									
1846–50	21s 9d	19s 8d	21s	24s 7d		25s		11s	3s 8d
1851–5	24s 7d	22s 5d	25s 5d	27s 9d		22s 2d		12s	5s 8d
1856–60	26s 5d	24s 5d	27s	29s 5d		22s 9d	22s 8d	13s	5s 8d
1861–5	28s 2d	25s 2d	27s 5d	29s	25s 9d	23s 5d	22s 5d	13s	6s 2d
1866–70	28s 2d	27s 9d	30s 2d	31s 6d	23s 9d	27s	27s	14s	6s
1871–5	30s 11d	29s 2d	30s	31s 6d	28s 5d	27s 5d	27s 9d	15s	7s 5d

[1]Rates from Alexander Stephen's yards for Aberdeen, Arbroath, Dundee. UGD4/16/1–4.
[2]Rates from Wm Denny of Dumbarton Leven yard. University of Glasgow Business History Collection. UGD3/12/6.

Index of Average Wage Rates in Engineering and Shipbuilding: 1860 = 100

	Tyne	Wear	Mersey	London	Clyde	Dundee	Belfast
1850	89	90	—	99	(89)[1]	82	—
1855	104	—	103	100	105	104	96
1860	100	100	100	100	100	100	100
1865	108	109	102	101	116	(115)[2]	(106)[2]
1870	104	—	(102)[3]	103	111	—	—
1874	128	124	116	107	131	135	123

Notes: [1]1851. [2]1866. [3]1869.
Source: Bowley and Wood (1906, table 2, pp. 162–3).

prices, and £4·7 million on the Maywald estimates. During the period 1870–5 the average value per year was £12·4 million on the Stephen–Denny prices, and £12·6 million on Maywald's figures. Over the same period, Deane and Cole estimated that shipbuilding's contribution to national income rose from about 0·5 per cent to around 1·5 per cent (Deane and Cole, 1969, p. 235).

Estimates of the price of labour are complicated by changing job characteristics between the wood- and iron-based industries, and by the intrusion of piece-rates into the more usual time-rate basis of payment; here we assume time-rates as the normal practice. The range of rates seems to have been substantial, especially before 1850. Taking the Stephen rates as a base (Table 5.3), it is clear from Bowley and Wood's compilations that districts varied substantially (Bowley and Wood, 1905, p. 68; 1906, p. 69). In the carpenter–shipwright grades, rates on the Clyde were about 20 per cent higher; the differential increased to about a third in the north-east and two-thirds on the Mersey, while Thames rates were double those in the Stephen yards.

After 1850, the differentials narrowed but remained significant in traditional grades of work. In 1860, shipwrights earned 24s to 26s per week on the Clyde, 30s on the Mersey and north-east coast, but 42s on the Thames. The relative position was unchanged by 1870. But in the new grades of work, near-uniformity was evident. For riveters and platers the range was 30s to 32s in most districts, with London marginally higher at 33s to 38s per week. On the basis of index numbers of average rates calculated by Bowley and Wood for the main districts it seems that rates advanced about 12 per cent between 1850–60 on the Clyde, Tyne, Wear, and the Belfast, while being static on the Thames and Mersey. Between 1860 and 1874, Clyde rates advanced by 31 per cent, and 24 to 25 per cent on the north-east and Belfast, while the Mersey and Thames movements were limited to 16 and 7 per cent respectively. Labour-rate differentials were by then small in the dominant iron sector, certainly less than 10 per cent between districts. Rates were also flexible up and downward with the tonnage rates, making it possible for the wage-cost element to remain roughly constant within the range of 25 to 30 per cent of the total cost of production of a ship (Pollard, 1951, p. 208).

Productivity changes are even more difficult to estimate. Factor cost and man-hour data are sparse, and a sophisticated calculation depends on more detailed work on company papers. Rough, general indications give some clue. The suspect census employment data linked to production suggests an increase in output from 5 to 6 tons per man-year in the 1830s, to 7 to 8 tons in the peak of the 1870s boom. Vessel size also rose sharply, though construction time did not appear to alter significantly, 6 to 9 months being common throughout. The average vessel size was about 100 tons at the end of the

French Wars, while in the 1870s it was 250 tons for sail and 650 tons for steam, though individual vessels were very much larger. On routes where speed mattered, as on the North Atlantic passenger trade, time was cut in half from 15 to 16 days in the 1840s to 8 to 9 days in the early 1870s. In fuel economy, too, we know that the compound engines of the 1870s consumed only one-fifth as much coal as the early steamers. All this suggests substantial productivity gains. In the 1870s a builder could deliver ships which on average were four or five times larger, up to twice as fast on the longer routes, and infinitely stronger and more durable than the average wooden vessel at the beginning of the period.

Among all these advances the question remains, was shipbuilding profitable? Pricing policy was normally on a *cost plus* basis, and unless seriously miscalculated should, in theory, have returned a regular surplus to the builder. In practice, however, the competition for orders frequently caused shipbuilders to quote at cost, or with the slenderest of margins, with the result that delays in construction, changes in specifications, or sudden increases in factor costs could mean a loss being made.

Incomplete information from the Stephen and Denny yards suggests a common practice of adding about 10 per cent to cost estimates for profit, though twice that figure is reached on occasion (Denny Papers, UGD 3; Lyon, 1975, Vol. 1).[1] Actual results, of course, frequently departed from this norm. In the trough of 1843–5 Denny made losses of up to 7 per cent, converting this to 10 to 11 per cent gains in the succeeding recovery. During the Crimean War, profits on Denny contracts ranged from 12 to 27 per cent, running downward to losses of up to 6 per cent between 1859 and 1861. The 10 per cent profit level was again reached in the Civil War boom of 1863–4, while at the same time Stephens made a surplus of £26,000 on contracts valued at £130,000, a return of 20 per cent. A decade later in 1874–5 the Denny contracts averaged 6 to 7 per cent over cost. In terms of a return on capital employed, Stephen's gross surplus was 36 per cent of the £76,000 employed in 1864, and about 10 per cent on the £150,000 capital a decade later.

No generalisation can be made on the basis of these fragments. At most we can say that shipbuilders had an expectation of profit built into contracts, usually about 10 per cent on cost. In good times when shippers were eager to buy, profits of two or three times this level were not uncommon on individual contracts. But in slumps, losses of similar proportions were frequently made.

THE FIRMS

At the end of the Napoleonic Wars shipbuilding was a small-scale craft. Large yards, like Greens on the Thames with upward of 500 men did exist, but the average yard employed twenty men or less (Clapham, 1952, p. 69) and worked with rudimentary slipways, crude scaffolding, perhaps a derrick and some large saws, borers and bolt-cutters. Other working equipment was normally supplied by the journeymen shipwrights and carpenters. Even substantial builders called themselves shipwrights, or master-shipwright, stressing their craft rather than their function as shipbuilder. Capital requirements were also small. Robert Martin's large Dublin yard is reputed to have cost £5,000 in 1812 (Pollard, 1951, p. 51); when Alexander Stephen bought up his deceased brother's yard in Arbroath in 1829, it cost him £505 for all the materials, and a ship on the slipway (Stephen Papers, 1830, UGD 4/16/1). It then employed twenty-seven men, a fairly average establishment according to Clapham.

A yard could operate on such limited capitals owing to a number of features typical of the industry. Yards were normally rented, rarely owned. Timber was purchased by commercial bills or on occasion supplied by the customer. This latter was common practice on the Wear and Tyne, and typical of the floating fringe of smaller builders attracted into the industry in boom conditions. The cash flow for many materials therefore relied on commercial credit, and that for wages and other outlays came from the instalments paid by the customer during construction. These were varied, sometimes purely on a time basis, more usually due as various stages of construction were completed. Three or four instalments were common, though the number could stretch in slack trade, and then rely more heavily on bills than on cash settlements. Payment might also be made in part by the builder accepting an older vessel, normally again when business was slack, and the builder anxious to dispose of new work. While the builder could then resell the vessel to realise his capital, few did not at times find themselves having to operate the vessel, either directly or by charter. Builders could also become shipowners when vessels built on speculation did not find a purchaser. It was in fact common practice throughout this period for builders to commence new tonnage without a definite purchaser in view.

Steam had at first little effect on this pattern of arrangements. The engine and boilers were simply additional parts to be purchased from specialist suppliers and assembled in the yard. The integration of yard, engine works and boiler shops remained untypical of the industry, though by 1870 every district had its examples of large establishments linking a shipyard and engine work, such as Elder,

Napier, and Tod & McGregor on the Clyde, Rennie on the Thames, Laird on the Mersey, Pile and Doxford in the north-east. The more common arrangement, however, was a customary link with an established engine builder in the local area. Hawthorn, Stephenson and Clark were major suppliers in the north-east (Dougan, 1968, pp. 55–6), Caird Kincaid, Elder and Napier on the Clyde (Shields, 1947), Penn and Rennie on the Thames (Banbury, 1971). Such arrangements spread risk and capital requirements in a new industry and at the same time generated a complex of inter-related engineering firms in each of the main districts. When iron was introduced the inter-dependence and spread of capital in specialist firms assumed even greater importance. A very few companies built their own ironworks, such as the Thames Ironworks & Shipbuilding Company in London, and Charles Palmer on the Tyne. But again, customary links were more common, the Clyde not moving into this type of vertical integration until the end of the century.

The new iron shipyards did not immediately impose insuperable capital burdens on prospective entrants to the field. Barry estimated an outlay from £5,000 to £25,000 in the 1850s (Pollard, 1951, p. 55), and when Alexander Stephen moved to the Clyde, his outlay was in this range. By 1857 he and the landowner had each laid out about £9,000 on site and slipway improvements, and the annual rental was £1,224 (Stephen Papers, UGD 4/18/7, 1 September 1847; 1858, UGD 4/1/1, 4 August 1858). An outlay of about £18,000 got the Stephens into iron shipbuilding. At the same time, at Dumbarton the Dennys had £50,000 locked up in their Leven yard and a further £87,000 in shipping interests (Denny Papers, 1859, UGD 3). Meanwhile, on the Thames, C. J. Mare's bankrupt business was refloated as the Thames Ironworks & Shipbuilding Company, with a capital of £150,000 in 1856.

The range of capital outlay was large, but by the 1870s the investment in the largest iron yards was in the order of £200,000 to £300,000. Tod & McGregor's Clyde yard changed hands for £200,000 in 1872[2] and Robert Napier's in 1878 for £270,000 (Pollard, 1951, p. 73). Even then, one estimate suggested a minimum requirement of $160,000 on the Clyde, about £33,000 (Pollard, 1951, p. 73).

While an impression of the range of capitals required can be given in this way, it is extremely difficult to make an estimate for the industry at large, even at the end of the period. If we take the Clyde as an example, we can illuminate the problem. In 1871, the Factory Inspectors' Returns enumerated 90 iron yards in Britain employing some 50,000 men; 27 of these yards and 24,000 of the men were at work on the Clyde. On the basis of known sale values in relation to scale of output, perhaps 6 or 8 of these had capitals in excess of £200,000. Another 4 or 5 may have been in the £100,000 to £150,000 range and the remainder in the £30,000 to £50,000 range. At the upper and lower limits suggested, capital employed in iron yards on the Clyde may have been in the order of £2·4 to £3·4 million. With nearly a third of the iron yards and over 40 per cent of the iron-yard workforce, a proportional estimate would give the capital in Britain's iron shipbuilding industry in the range of £7 to £10 million. But until much work is undertaken in researching yard valuation, this must remain an unsupportable guess. Stretching credibility, we may hazard the view that investment in the industry in 1870–1 was unlikely to be less than £7 million, the average per yard may have been about £80,000, and it is unlikely that any firm had much less than £30,000 involved in the business. The large yards were not numerous, but they already dominated the investment and production in the industry.

The largest yards in 1871 were on the Clyde with an average of 852 employees compared with 400 to 500 on average in the other districts. With few exceptions, the firms in all the districts remained family and partnership in form, only 17 of the 90 iron shipyard companies having taken the public-company status. Continuity of ownership throughout the period could also be found on every river, but most of the leading companies in the 1870s were young, dating from the 1840s and 1850s. All had adopted an organisational structure based on functionally specialised departments, engine shop, boiler shop, shipyard, drawing office, and so on, relying increasingly on specialised departmental management. The managerial and organisational changes were just as important as the technical innovations in reshaping the industry in these years, and were perhaps one further factor pushing the development of the new industry into the hands of mainly new firms.

CONCLUSION

Between 1815 and 1875 British shipbuilding was utterly transformed in scale, location, structure and technology. An initial revival of the traditional industry in wood and sail between 1830 and 1850 was quickly supplemented and then overwhelmed by the revolution in steam and iron that shifted the centres of production to Clydeside and the north-east. The effect was to transform the status of British shipbuilding from one of backwardness to that of world leadership. Where Britain had been a traditional importer of ships, she rapidly became a major exporter, 24 per cent of all steam tonnage constructed between 1856 and 1875 being built for foreign flags (*Statistical Abstracts of the United Kingdom*, 1862; Cormack, 1931, appendix, table 1). By 1870, with 3 million tons of steamships, Britain dominated world trade routes, 59 per cent of world steam tonnage being under the British flag, much of the rest having been constructed in British yards, or at least engined by British marine engineers (Jeula, 1875, pp. 81–3). The root source of the success was the skill in invention and innovation in iron and steam technology, or, as John Glover put it in 1872, 'Iron and Coal have enabled us to recover our place as the greatest among the maritime carriers; and it may be said, without boasting too much, that our engineers and shipbuilders have made such splendid use of these two minerals in the production of carrying machines, as to deserve the preeminence which our flag has won' (Glover, 1872, p. 229).

NOTES TO CHAPTER 5

1 Estimates of profit for Denny of Dumbarton compiled from the Denny Papers, University of Glasgow business history collections, UGD 3.
2 Shortly before the yard was sold to Handyside & Henderson, there was a move to convert it to a public company with £350,000 capital, the purchase price within that set at £250,000 (*Glasgow Herald*, 20 January 1872). The sale at £200,000 is recorded in the *Glasgow Evening Citizen*, 27 September 1872.

6 Railway Enterprise

by T. R. Gourvish

I

Only a brief examination of the railway industry is necessary to uncover its three most striking characteristics – novelty, size and concentration. While some authorities have claimed very early beginnings for this form of transport, the railway *proper*, incorporating the requisite elements of specialised track, mechanical traction, facilities for public traffic and passenger facilities, was essentially a product of the mid-late 1820s. It came with the opening of the Stockton & Darlington (1825) and Liverpool & Manchester (1830) companies. And its basic structure was created in the following half-century. By 1875, over 70 per cent of the ultimate route mileage had been constructed. The scale of this new technology was soon apparent. The capital raised by companies in the United Kingdom amounted to £630 million by 1875, equivalent to an annual rate of £12½ million, dwarfing the fixed-capital formation of basic industries such as cotton, coal, and iron and steel. Gross revenue, running at £19 million a year in the 1850s, rose to £52 million a year in 1870–5, equal to the output value of the woollen industry, and double that of coal. Permanent employment on lines opened for traffic reached 56,000 in 1850. By 1873 the figure had risen to 275,000, or 3·3 per cent of the male labour force. Thus, while recent scholarship has sought to modify some of the more extravagant claims made for the railways in their impact on the economy, there is no doubt that they represented a significant addition to the Victorian industrial structure. A third characteristic, concentration, was also visible at an early stage. The great investment 'mania' of 1845–7 left 61 per cent of UK railway capital and 75 per cent of gross traffic revenue in the hands of 15 major companies, a mere 8 per cent of the total number of 180 concerns (data for 1850). By 1870, the same number of companies, now only 3½ per cent of the total of 430, controlled 80 per cent of the capital and 83 per cent of the revenue. The share of the four largest railways – the London & North Western, Great Western, North Eastern, and Midland – amounted to 38 and 44 per cent respectively.

It is true that attention should also be directed to the more modest, often more speculative, activities of the smaller companies. But railway history in the period to 1875 is very much the history of these large railways and their antecedents, and this will be reflected in the analysis that follows.[1]

II

Railways, unlike several Victorian industries, tend to attract analyses which begin with an assessment of profits and proceed to explanations. Most basic texts, for example, contrast the relatively high rates of return before 1870 with the lower returns that followed, exploring changes in capacity utilisation, the external constraints on commercial freedom imposed by governments, and the quality of management.[2] But the period before c.1875 was not one of uniformly high profits, and the difficulties induced by major trade recessions are only too familiar. It is therefore important to consider the nature of both trend and cycle. Figure 6.1 gives the two most commonly used measures of railway profits – the net rate of return on United Kingdom paid-up capital, 1854–75 (from the *Railway Returns* data collated by Mitchell and Deane, 1962), and the average dividend on the ordinary shares of the leading fifteen British companies, 1840–75 (a weighted average, calculated from the data in Mihill Slaughter's *Railway Intelligence*, 1849–75, adjusted for known overstatements of dividend). As is expected, both measures show a rough correspondence with observed cycles in Hoffman's index of industrial production (excluding building) (see Table 6.1). But the chronology of the turning points is coincident in only half the cycles considered. In 1864 and 1872 railway profits anticipate the peak in industrial production by two years, while the

Table 6.1 *Cyclicity in Ordinary Dividends, Net Rate of Return, and Hoffman's Index of Industrial Production (Excluding Building), 1840–75*

PEAKS			TROUGHS		
Ord. Divs	Net R.R.	Hoffman	Ord. Divs	Net R.R.	Hoffman
1845	—	1845	1843	—	1842
1854	—	1853	1850	—	1847
1857	1857	1857	1855	1855	1855
1860	1860	1860	1858	1858	1858
1864	1864	1866	1862	1862	1862
1872	1872	1874	1868	1867*	1869
			1874	1874	

*No data available for 1868
Source: Figure 6.1, and Aldcroft and Fearon (eds) (1972, p. 12).

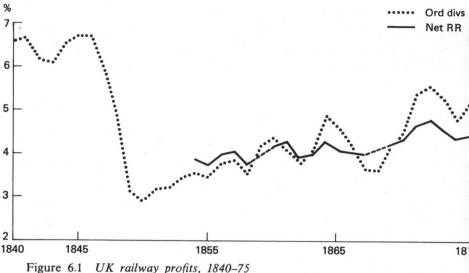

Figure 6.1   *UK railway profits, 1840–75*
Sources: Mitchell and Deane 1962, pp. 255–6; Slaughter (1849–75)

troughs in profits in 1850 and 1874 do not show up in Hoffman at
all (where 1874 appears as a *peak*). A clear-cut explanation for this
variation is hard to find. But the delayed trough in profits of 1850
may be attributed to the rough-and-ready, often fraudulent manipulation of accounts as confidence waned with the passing of the great
investment 'mania' (see Pollins, 1969a, pp. 138–61; Broadbridge, 1970,
pp. 38*ff*).

Business cyclicity also served to increase the disparity between
expected and realised profits. Malcolm Reed, for example, has pointed
out the considerable difference between the estimated returns of six
major companies in 1836 (in excess of 10 per cent) and actual earnings
in 1843 (under 5 per cent), while J. R. T. Hughes contrasted the high
expectations of 1844 with the low earnings of the early 1850s (Reed,
1975, p. 25, unweighted average net returns of 10·6 and 4·7 per cent
calculated from table 2; Hughes, 1960, pp. 184–9). Finally, as is well
known, the Overend, Gurney 'crash' of 1866 helped to send a number
of major companies into bankruptcy and enforced financial reorganisation, among them the Great Eastern, and London Chatham & Dover.
But profit levels were also a function of investment and operating
decisions which influenced the short-run viability of particular routes,
and, consequently, many lines failed to exhibit the distinct cyclical
patterns of the aggregate data. The trough of 1843, for example,
produced a wide range of earnings, and Reed's table of only six
companies gives returns of 2·6 to 9·2 per cent. Equally, the 'crash' of
1866 scarcely disturbed the earning power of companies such as the

Taff Vale and Lancaster & Carlisle, whose ordinary dividends remained in the high 10 to 12 per cent range. Company diversity, then, is an equally important characteristic of railway profitability in the period.

What can be said about the *trend* in profits? First, it does seem that the high rates of return of the cheaply constructed mineral lines of the 1820s were matched by the more successful trunk-route companies such as the London & Birmingham and Grand Junction. These railways maintained high dividends in the 1840s in spite of the escalation of construction costs by concentrating on first-class passengers and high-tariff freight. Before 1846, the average ordinary dividends of the leading companies remained above 6 per cent (see Figure 6.1). The investment 'mania' of 1845–7 brought a dramatic change, however. In the ensuing depression, dividends fell below the yield on 3 per cent Consols – in 1849 and 1850 – and the 1850 'low' of 2·88 per cent was more than 50 per cent lower than the average return for the 1840s as a whole. The break in trend was clearly influenced by the amplitude of the cyclical downswing, but it was also a product of government intervention and, in particular, the encouragement of competition in the industry coupled with tighter controls on the companies' pricing freedom. From 1850, dividends showed a gradual but steady upward trend: a log linear regression line yielded an annual growth rate of 1·91 per cent for the period 1850–75.[3] By the early 1870s shareholders were enjoying the comparatively healthy returns of 5 to 5½ per cent, some 70 per cent above the yield on Consols. This improvement occurred despite a pronounced swing towards geared stocks – notably, the large-scale conversion of debentures into fixed-interest stocks – which reduced the share of ordinary capital in total paid-up capital from 56 per cent in 1858 to 40 per cent in 1875 (*PP*, 1876, *Railway Returns*, vol. LXV).

The net rate of return on United Kingdom paid-up capital follows the ordinary dividend series in showing a gradual upward trend. Returns rose from about 3·75 per cent in the mid-1850s to about 4·5 per cent in the early 1870s, with an annual growth rate of 0·85 per cent over the period 1854–75. And if we accept an estimated return for 1850 of 3·05 per cent, the growth rate for 1850–75 is similar to that for dividends, namely 1·21 per cent.[4] Our findings, then, indicate a steady improvement in profitability after the 'mania', the result partly of increased co-operation in the industry – exemplified by the plethora of traffic-pooling agreements – but principally of a growth in traffic without an immediate threat to the companies' handling capacity (Ashworth, 1960, p. 121).

This being said, it must be admitted that profits after 1850 were on the whole modest. An unweighted average dividend for the leading 15 companies, 1850–75, amounts to only 3·65 per cent. Only 5 companies – the London & North Western, Midland, Great Northern,

Lancashire & Yorkshire, and North Eastern – paid dividends of 5 to 6 per cent, while 4 – the Great Eastern, Manchester Sheffield & Lincolnshire, North British, and London Chatham & Dover – were unable to pay 1½ per cent (the latter paid nothing at all). Ordinary dividends do not necessarily reflect net rates of return on capital spent and earning, of course. Interest payments on lines under construction, commitments to other companies and, in particular, the guarantee of high dividends to subsidiaries, the cost of raising capital in periods of dear money – all are relevant here. The Great Eastern, for example, paid on average only 0·67 per cent in ordinary dividends, 1863–73, while its net rate of return on productive capital was 4·15 per cent. The disparity is to be explained by the commitment of over 40 per cent of paid-up capital to guaranteed interest and dividends of 5 per cent and over (Great Eastern Railway Accounts, RAIL 1110/158). Indeed, given the rudimentary state of accounting practices before the Regulation of Railways Act of 1868, we should expect discrepancies caused by a variety of decisions concerning the use of reserves, and the allocation of expenditure to capital and revenue accounts. Finally, the manipulation of accounts to maintain dividends during times of difficulty in the capital market was generally paid for by low dividends after 'irregularities' had been exposed, neither coinciding with current rates of return. Unfortunately, it is difficult to take this subject much further. The published accounts of important railways such as the Great Western, Midland, and London Brighton & South Coast leave too many important questions unanswered to permit a confident reassessment of profits over the long term. But we can say, from an examination of the records of three companies – the London & North Western, Lancashire & Yorkshire, and South Eastern – that the disparity between ordinary dividends and the net rate of return was relatively small. For 1850–75, dividends understated current returns by only 6 to 13 per cent.[5] This test does little to alter our analysis of the industry's overall profitability.

III

Railway investment is at once a complex and a much-studied subject. The compilation of adequate data has involved a considerable academic effort, and we are fortunate to have access to the results. In Figure 6.2 we present three of the most important series: Mitchell's estimates of UK gross capital formation (including land costs), 1831–75; Kenwood's gross investment series for Britain, 1825–75 (excludes land, and legal and parliamentary costs); and Hawke and Reed's raised capital data (i.e. paid-up capital and loans) for the UK, 1825–75 (Mitchell, 1964 pp. 315–36; Kenwood, 1965, pp. 313–22; Hawke and Reed, 1969, pp. 269–86).

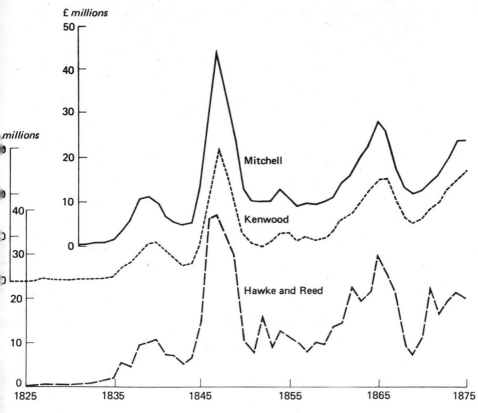

Figure 6.2 *UK railway investment, 1825–75*

Figure 6.2 clearly shows that the pattern of railway investment was dominated by four major 'cycles', peaking in 1840 (1839 [Mitchell]), 1847, 1865 (1866 [Kenwood]), and 1874–5. Indeed, Kenwood was encouraged to assert that investment was characterised by three 'long waves' of thirteen to sixteen years' duration. Nevertheless, interest has centred upon the relationship between fluctuations in investment and the trade cycle, with the aim of exploring the role of railways in the overall process of economic growth. Here, the consensus appears to be that while railway promotion influenced the pattern of economic activity from the 1830s, its role was a supporting, rather than a leading, one. Decisions to undertake investment tended to be concentrated in the expansion phase of the cycle, and the lag between promotion and construction, extended by the nature of parliamentary procedures, meant that the contra-cyclical influence of railway building was dominant.[6]

Before turning to Figure 6.2 for verification of this thesis, it is important to recognise that none of the available series is an ideal aid to cyclical analysis. Mitchell derived his capital-expenditure data by applying the ratio between paid-up capital and capital expenditure for a sample of companies to the whole population, a procedure which Hawke has suggested could lead to margins of error as high as 20 per cent for particular years (Hawke, 1970, pp. 199–203). Mitchell himself was aware that his series could be a misleading indicator of cyclical change in the late 1840s because the cost of services was recorded at the time of entry into company accounts and not necessarily at the time of their performance (Mitchell, 1964, p. 336n.). Kenwood, in measuring 'reproducible capital', excluded a number of items of expenditure – land purchase, legal and parliamentary charges, interest paid out of capital, and 'non-railway' expenditure on docks, steamboats etc. – which were certainly of importance to companies in the early years of their existence, and not without influence outside the industry. Finally, Hawke and Reed's series is a measure of capital *raised*, representing activity that lagged behind promotion and usually anticipated actual expenditure. Although little can be done here to adjust the data, it is necessary to accept the possibility of margins of error in particular years, since timing is of such crucial importance to an assessment of the role of railway investment in economic fluctuations.

What, then, can be said about the customary view of railway investment? First, Figure 6.2 does show a clear lag between peaks of economic activity in 1836 and 1845 and investment peaks in 1839–40 and 1847. But although railways continued to seek capital primarily in boom conditions, and despite the plausible hypothesis that after 1850 the state of the capital market was an increasingly vital determinant of investment decisions (Hughes, 1960, p. 184; and, recently, Cottrell, 1976, p. 20*ff*.) it is more difficult to trace a clear lag relationship for the 1860s and 1870s, whether we use Deane's GNP estimates or Hoffman's index of industrial production.[7] Consequently, the view that railways played a sustaining role in the growth process appears more fragile when applied to the period after the second 'mania', if timing is given a central place in the analysis. It is, therefore, desirable to consider factors influencing investment other than mere boom conditions and general business confidence.

The possibility that factors endogenous to the railway industry affected investment has not escaped attention, of course. Matthews, in his careful dissection of the 1830s and early 1840s, recognised that it was the development of locomotive and engineering technology in the late 1820s and the commercial success of the Liverpool & Manchester Railway, rather than trade fluctuations, that encouraged the promotional activity of the early 1830s, before the speculative stage of the 1835-6 boom. He also suggested that the decline in company promotions in 1838-43 was more the result of caution than business stagnation (Matthews, 1959, pp. 108-13). Reed has recently taken the argument a stage further. Limiting his examination to the period 1820-44, he suggests that railway development had a basic 'rationality', in terms of the geography of the system's expansion, technological factors (including significant shifts in costs in the early 1840s), and the resources available for railway building at the various stages. Cyclical booms, he argues, did not induce the contemporaneous railway booms. Rather, manias emerged out of pre-existing promotional booms, and these were largely the result of endogenous factors. The schemes of 1844, which are customarily associated with 'mania', are here regarded as logical extensions to the network encouraged by the established main-line companies, and speculative influences are accorded a minor role (Reed, 1975, pp. 1-31, 266-72).[8]

That endogenous factors also influenced investment activity is not in doubt. Besides technological development and commercial viability, the promotion process itself was a causal factor. The alterations made to parliamentary standing orders for new schemes, which made promotion more difficult from 1838 and easier again from 1842, certainly contributed to the fall and subsequent rise in activity. Similarly, Gladstone's Act of 1844 which, among other things, provided for the nationalisation after twenty-one years of new companies earning 10 per cent net or more, did much to encourage undue optimism about future profitability during the second 'mania' (Pollins, 1971, pp. 29, 36). But the extent to which the existence of endogenous factors validates the hypothesis of railway development as a self-generating, 'rational' phenomenon must remain a matter for debate. Reed, while arguing that manias did not play a leading role in railway development to 1844, warned against the acceptance of a simple division between endogenous and exogenous variables, and referred to the co-existence of 'rationality' and risk in railway promotion. Thus, while the timing of railway investment and the general business cycle before 1850 suggests that boom conditions encouraged railway promotion – and the importance of speculative elements in the investment activity of the late 1830s and mid-1840s must be admitted – the presence of endogenous factors indicates that promotion was both influenced by and itself influenced the prevailing economic climate.

What, then, are the implications for an analysis of the period after 1850, where the supporting role of railway investment is more difficult to measure with precision? Was there a shift in the balance of forces shaping the investment process, and did the relationship between investment and economic fluctuations alter? These questions are not unimportant in view of the maintenance of fairly high rates of growth in the industry. Indeed, over 60 per cent of total expenditure in the years 1825–75 came *after* 1850.

Hughes, in his account of the 1850s, indicates that the contra-cyclical role of railway construction continued. Investment lagged behind the peak of 1853 by a year, sustained activity after the Crimean War, i.e. in 1856–7, and helped to induce recovery in 1858–9. But the extent of these operations was much more limited than in the 1830s and 1840s (see Figure 6.2). In fact, the industry's impact on trade-cycle behaviour was greatly reduced after the 'mania'. Lower profit levels deterred investors and increased the companies' dependence on favourable market conditions. The minor promotion boom of the early 1850s, for example, was basically the result of low interest rates between 1851 and 1853 (Hughes, 1960, pp. 184, 190–9).

Renewed investment activity was characteristic of the early 1860s and early 1870s. Here, the situation appears to have been rather different from that obtaining before 1850. The timing of investment fluctuations tended to coincide with that of the economy in general, rising to a peak in 1865–6, falling to 1869, then rising again to 1874–5 (Figure 6.2). Why was this so? An explanation is to be found in the nature of new investment and the way in which capital was raised. After 1860 much of the additional construction took the form either of ambitious and, on past experience, risky ventures in the London area or of extensions into the rural periphery of England, Scotland and Ireland, where returns were expected to be lower than for the English main lines. Since profits in the industry remained well below the expectations of the 1840s in spite of a revival after 1850 (Figure 6.1), little was done to alter the cautious attitude of investors. This, together with the diversion of much speculative interest overseas, drove home railways into the arms of contractors and finance companies, notably in the boom of 1863–5. These important intermediaries in the investment process were involved not only in floating new schemes but in sustaining the financing of construction (Pollins, 1969*b*, pp. 212–28; Cottrell, 1976). The fragility of many of these arrangements, however, helps to explain the speedy collapse of the boom in 1866. It does seem that the inability of railways to generate investment activity without help explains the closer correspondence with the trade cycle and the reduction in contra-cyclical influence. To sum up, the greater strength, although by no means total dominance, of endogenous factors in railway investment in the 1830s and 1840s served to influence the course of economic fluctuations and produce a clear contra-cyclical response. But after 1850, and particularly after 1860, such factors were dampened, and railways became much more dependent on the state of the capital market.

Timing is not, of course, the only way to assess the contribution of railways to economic cycles. The share of railway investment in total domestic investment and in national income are clearly significant and have engaged academic attention. Mitchell, one of the first to quantify the relationship between railways and the process of growth, showed that railway investment rapidly became an important component of domestic investment, consuming nearly 2 per cent of the national income by the late 1830s. And the order of magnitude changed dramatically as the 1840s progressed. It is now a matter of cliché that 'railway investment in the second half of the decade leapt ahead to great dominance, taking at its height in 1847 not far short of 7 per cent [6·7] of national income . . . [or] about two thirds of the value of all domestic exports' (Mitchell, 1964, p. 322). Expenditure on railway construction consumed about 4½ per cent of national income between 1845 and 1849, representing as much as half of all domestic capital formation. At these levels, it is easy to agree with Hawke that railway activity must have involved a reduction in consumption as well as a redirection of investment (Hawke, 1970, p. 210; see also Church, 1975a, pp. 33–4).

We should not allow the impressive size of the railway's contribution during the second 'mania' to obscure the impact of investment at other times, however. In the 1850s and early 1870s, for example, annual investment was close to 1·5 per cent of the national income, not far short of the level of 1837–40. And the strength of the activity of the 1860s should be recognised. As Hawke demonstrates, railway investment over the period 1860–6 was more than a quarter of gross domestic capital formation, and over 2 per cent of national income (Hawke, 1970, p. 209).

At company level, the strong secular rise in capital expenditure was a matter of much contemporary criticism. Writers such as Chattaway were quite certain that it was the unexpectedly high cost of construction, much of it avoidable, that had caused the low profit levels of the late 1840s and early 1850s (Chattaway, 1855–6, pp. 3–5).[9] Undoubtedly, increasing capitalisation was a major element in the reduction of net rates of return. But the difficulties that managements faced on this score were established at an early stage. Successful pioneers such as the Liverpool & Manchester and London & Birmingham cost over £50,000 per route-mile, and the average for the United Kingdom was as high as £33,000 in 1844. A relatively high standard of construction, over-optimism about engineering difficulties, and inadequate checks on the expenditure of interest groups such as engineers and lawyers, were all relevant here (Gourvish, 1972, pp. 20*ff*.). Speculative waste, particularly in the second 'mania', was also severely criticised. Of the 9,000 miles sanctioned in the years 1845–8, only 5,000 had been built by 1858 (Pollins, 1971, p. 41). Nevertheless, capital expenditure per route-mile did not increase greatly after 1850: by 1875 some 16,500 miles had been constructed for about £38,000 per mile.

Although the railways' considerable investment activity helped to produce low rates of return for private investors, there seems little doubt that *social* rates of return were impressive. Hawke's calculations, while containing some controversial elements, suggest that returns were of the order of 15 to 20 per cent for England and Wales, 1830–70, and that there was no deterioration after 1840 in spite of the fall in private returns. If investors found the expectations of the early 1840s largely unrealised, the economy certainly gained substantially from the investment process (Hawke, 1970, pp. 405–8).

IV

The major features of railway operation are familiar. GB passenger traffic grew steadily from 21·7 million in 1842–3 to 490·1 million in 1875, an overall growth rate of 8·86 per cent a year. Freight tonnage increased from about 5 million tons in 1842 to 196·2 million in 1875. At the same time, passenger revenue rose from £3·1 million to £24·3 million (5·85 per cent a year), freight revenue from £1·4 million to £32·1 million (8·54 per cent), and total revenue from £4·5 million to £58·6 million (7·22 per cent).[10] The influence of the trade cycle on revenue growth was fairly slight, the only interruptions occurring in 1858 (all three series), 1852 (passenger revenue),[11] and 1862 (freight revenue).

The secular growth in the market for railway services was accompanied by significant changes in the composition of the traffic. The first was the move towards freight (see Table 6.2). In 1845–6 the major

Table 6.2 *Analysis of Traffic of the Major British Railways (percentage distribution)*

Year	Passenger Revenue	Freight Revenue	Passenger Traffic (Numbers)			Passenger Traffic (Revenue)		
			1st	2nd	3rd	1st	2nd	3rd
1845–6	74·1	25·9	16·2	37·9	44·7	38·6	41·1	20·3
1870	43·6	56·4	10·6	24·6	64·8	25·3	30·5	44·2
1875	42·3	57·7	8·2	11·8	79·9	22·4	16·6	60·9

Sources: PP 1847–8, vol. *LXIII*; 1871, vol. *LX*; 1876, vol. *LXV*.

companies derived 74 per cent of their revenue from passenger traffic (including mails and luggage). By 1850, however, the rapid increase in freight had reduced this to 49 per cent (*PP*, 1851, Vol. LI). Thus, the companies very quickly took up a lower margin business where handling costs were higher and general operating costs more unpredictable. Consequently, profit levels were reduced. After 1850, as we have seen, profits began to pick up again, and this coincided with an improvement in managerial expertise and, in particular, with an ability to handle long-distance freight flows, aided by inter-company agreements and the workings of the Railway Clearing House. The passenger–freight ratio also tended to be more stable, with passenger revenue falling to only 44 per cent of the total by 1870 and 42 per cent by 1875.

The second change was the shift within passenger traffic to third class (Table 6.2). In 1845–6 third-class passengers made up under half of total numbers and produced only 20 per cent of revenue. By 1870, the proportions were 65 and 44 per cent respectively. The concentration on low-fare traffic intensified in the next five years. There was a sharp decline in the second class, which was actually abolished by the Midland in 1875, and the major companies were left dependent on third-class passengers for 80 per cent of their traffic and 61 per cent of their revenue. This move down market, accompanied by a general reduction in fares, aggravated the capacity problems facing the industry and had a predictable effect on operating margins. The 'operating ratio', i.e. costs expressed as a percentage of revenue, which remained surprisingly stable at between 47 and 49 from 1855, moved upwards to average 54 in the years 1873–5 (Mitchell and Deane, 1962, pp. 225–6).

At company level diversity remained a dominant characteristic. The major railways included passenger specialists such as the South Eastern (77 per cent of total revenue in 1875) and freight specialists such as the North Eastern (72 per cent of total revenue), and there was a similar disparity in the distribution of passengers among the classes (cf. Hawke, 1970, pp. 37–40). It is also difficult to identify commercial success with any particular form of traffic specialism, or with any region of the UK. Certainly, dividend performance does seem to have been associated with the size of a company's first-class business in the early 1840s. For 1845–6, significant correlation coefficients may be derived for both passenger numbers and revenue.[12] Later on, however, the histories of the companies reveal a greater complexity of operating experience. In 1875, for example, the passenger specialists included the profitable London Brighton & South Coast and the near-bankrupt London Chatham & Dover, both of which were operating in London and the south-east. At the same time, the highly successful Midland and the weak Manchester Sheffield & Lincolnshire companies were freight specialists with operations concentrated in the midlands and the north. They also had the highest levels of third-class traffic. It is not surprising, then, that correlations of performance with types of traffic mix for 1870 and 1875 produce negative results.[13] Companies were subject to a whole range of factors, including differential levels of inter-modal and intra-modal competition, inherited capital difficulties, and increased government interference with the freedom to choose and charge traffic, all of which restricted the ability of managements to select or even locate a recipe for operating success.

Can any valid generalisations be made about the way in which managements responded to the challenges they faced? Can we establish the 'quality' of entrepreneurial response in the industry? Unfortunately, while railway historians such as Hamilton Ellis have often seen railway-company history in terms of heroes and villains, economic historians have been more cautious. They have recognised that the railways brought something new in British business history with their scale and complexity, but have been reluctant to isolate the management variable in their analyses of capital investment and operating trends. The situation, then, is very much the reverse of that facing the historian of other industries, where attention is frequently given to the quality of leadership without relating it to the parameters of economic performance. Here, we are not short of such measures but, with a few exceptions, lack detailed analyses of the contribution of management.[14] It is difficult, therefore, to establish standards by which to assess the adequacy or otherwise of the major companies' operations.

Nevertheless, we can be clear about one thing. Management problems and deficiencies were, ironically, at their worst in the 1830s and early 1840s, when the companies found profits relatively easy to come by. At a time when British industry generally was slow to introduce management 'systems' and professional managers, the practice of the railways, with their special problems of organisation and control, was distinct. As pioneers of 'big business' activity they combined all the now familiar problems of the large-scale company – joint costs, integrated processes, depreciation, obsolescence, and the control of a complex and diffuse organisation. It is scarcely surprising, then, to find that the early companies experienced difficulties in their efforts to forecast capital costs, find suitable managers and professional specialists such as engineers, surveyors and lawyers, and recruit staff experienced in a new and (until 1850 at least) rapidly advancing technology. Consequently, early operation was often haphazard, not to say hazardous, with companies forced to call on the precedents of stage-coach and canal. Organisational procedures were equally uncertain. Control of staff was lax, with the result that minor frauds were commonplace, and it was not until the later 1840s that a fairly uniform executive structure was adopted, with a general manager at the top. But the most significant factor was undoubtedly the over-optimistic forecasting of construction costs and likely traffic flows. Several railways were more the creatures of greedy speculators and unscrupulous contractors than the victims of inexperienced managers. The legacy of the construction stage for companies such as the Eastern Counties was such that no traffic manager could produce satisfactory profits, however gifted he was.[15]

Management after the 'mania' is much harder to assess. Hawke's total productivity series for the railways of England and Wales exhibits an annual growth rate of 3 per cent, 1840–70. This is attributed almost entirely to improved capital utilisation as traffic expanded. Growth was faster in the 1840s, and Hawke does suggest that half of the 15 per cent growth a year, 1842–6, was due to improved technical innovation and improved management. Here he refers to the amalgamation movement, which produced conglomerates such as the Midland and London & North Western, and the decision to take up freight traffic. But after 1850 the managerial response was, apparently, unimportant, particularly since there were only minimal technological developments before the advent of steel rails in the late 1860s. 'Railway management', Hawke suggests, 'has to be credited with some gains in the 1840s but there was no such spectacular management success after 1850' (1970, p. 308).

Leaving aside comments on the necessarily approximate nature of the calculations, it does seem that Hawke's assessment of management is both harsh and incomplete. It is true that technological advance was more limited after 1850, although there was a steady trend to heavier trains and rails and some operational savings were produced by the substitution of coal for coke as locomotive fuel. But other areas of managerial intervention must be explored. After all, Hawke disagrees with Kingsford's view that the railways' use of labour was 'increasingly unsuccessful and unprofitable', suggesting that labour productivity remained fairly stationary after 1850 (Kingsford, 1951, p. 10, cit. Hawke, 1970, p. 285, and see ibid., p. 311). This was surely no mean achievement at a time when the companies were taking on more and more traffic and improving greatly on the primitive service arrangements of the past, and it should be accorded a management contribution given the knowledge that control of labour costs was the most popular area for attention when economy was required.

We should not neglect the possibility that the established companies did a great deal to lessen the effects of the 'mania' and the ensuing intensification of competitive and pricing problems. With so many new entrants in the industry, particularly in the early 1850s, but also in the 1860s, it is to be expected that aggregate figures might mask the success of the established companies in maintaining productivity growth and keeping profits higher than they would have been. The expansion of the Railway Clearing House, for example, illustrates the progress made in traffic management over longer distances. By the early 1870s the House was dealing with 38 per cent of UK freight and 17 per cent of passenger traffic on the 92 per cent of total UK route mileage owned by its members (Bagwell, 1968, pp. 295, 304). The companies also managed to effect amalgamations, in spite of the hostility of the government. Between 1850 and 1875, the London & North Western absorbed no less than thirty-two separate concerns, the Great Western absorbed twenty, and in 1854 the first regional monopoly was established with the creation of the North Eastern. In addition, there was the plethora of pooling agreements, traffic divisions and price-fixing arrangements, which although fragile, particularly in the 1850s, nevertheless influenced the net revenue position of the participating companies and helped to shift the competitive area from price to quality of service.

Railway management had its shortcomings, certainly, and in the early 1870s there was clearly more room for the marketing enterprise displayed by the Midland. While some executives such as Mark Huish wrestled bravely with problems of costing and pricing, it remained true that companies were unable to price effectively due to the difficulty of establishing the costs of particular traffics. It is no surprise to learn that 'a policy of maximizing profit on the existing traffic was not energetically pursued', and that railways sought to encourage regional traffic development without strict reference to cost (Hawke, 1970, p. 360). But the overall evidence about management activities after 1850 must make us wary of reaching hasty conclusions about their effectiveness, until further empirical work is undertaken. Managers were certainly encouraged to follow Edward Watkin's dictum that 'the whole object of the management of a Railway is dividend' (*Railway Official Gazette*, August 1882), but until we know more about the circumstances of the individual companies our judgements must remain tentative.

The key to the relative success of the railways in the 1830s and early 1840s lies in the specialism within the market for transport services at a time when managerial expertise was a rare commodity. The problems which confronted the industry after the burst of promotion in the late 1840s may be attributed in part to prior weaknesses in forecasting, but due attention should also be paid to the unplanned competition encouraged by government and the more severe controls on pricing freedom which accompanied each new application to parliament. The contribution of management after 1850 may have been to respond all too effectively to the challenge by seeking out low-margin traffic and improving greatly the quality of service. It was these factors that were to cause particular headaches in the period after 1875, when government interference became more pronounced.

NOTES TO CHAPTER 6

1   In 1850 the companies were distributed thus:
LONDON–NORTH: London & North Western, Midland, Great Northern

LONDON–SOUTH: South Eastern, London & South Western, London & Brighton

LONDON–EAST: Eastern Counties (from 1862 Great Eastern)

LONDON–WEST: Great Western

NORTH: Lancashire & Yorkshire, Manchester Sheffield & Lincolnshire, York & North Midland, York Newcastle & Berwick

SCOTLAND: Caledonian, Glasgow & South Western, North British.

By 1870 the York & North Midland and York Newcastle & Berwick companies had combined to form the North Eastern (1854), and the London Chatham & Dover had emerged as a major company by virtue of its capital expenditure.

2 See the debate initiated by Ashworth (1960), Aldcroft (1968*b*), Pollins (1971) and Irving (1976).

3 $\log y = a + bt$ (t = time): $y_1 = 1\cdot1717 + 0\cdot019t$ $r^2 = 0\cdot72$
$$(32\cdot80) \quad (7\cdot87)$$
figures in parenthesis = t ratio.

4 Log regressions: 1854–75 $\log Y_2 = 1\cdot342 + 0\cdot00845t$ $r^2 = 0\cdot65$
$$(79\cdot34) \quad (6\cdot13)$$
1850–75 $\log Y_3 = 1\cdot245 + 0\cdot01205t$ $r^2 = 0\cdot75$
$$(59\cdot72) \quad (8\cdot42)$$

5 London & North Western R.R. 6·57 per cent, ord. div. 5·79 per cent; Lancs & Yorks R.R. 5·65 per cent, ord. div. 5·30 per cent; South Eastern R.R. 4·72 per cent. ord. div. 4·11 per cent. Company Accounts, RAIL1110/237, 269–70, 424–5, P.R.O.

6 See the analysis of Matthews (1954, pp. 202*ff*.) for the 1830s and early 1840s; Hughes (1960, pp. 184–206) for the 1850s, echoed by Mitchell (1964, pp. 329–30) and, with some reservations, Hawke (1970, pp. 363–79).

7 The Deane series has peaks in 1856, 1859, 1865, and 1874; the Hoffman index (excluding building) in 1857, 1860, 1866 and 1874 (Aldcroft and Fearon, 1972, pp. 9, 12).

8 I am grateful to Dr Reed for adding to his analysis in a personal communication of 2 October 1977.

9 Chattaway is frequently quoted in the secondary sources.

10 Data from Mitchell and Deane (1962, pp. 225–6), unadjusted for changes in the series, see ibid., p. 227n. Log regressions:

Passenger traffic $\log Y_4 = 3\cdot484 + 0\cdot0886t$ $r^2 = 0\cdot97$
$$(71\cdot43) \quad (33\cdot81)$$
Passenger revenue $\log Y_5 = 1\cdot422 + 0\cdot0585t$ $r^2 = 0\cdot96$
$$(35\cdot34) \quad (27\cdot08)$$
Freight revenue $\log Y_6 = 1\cdot007 + 0\cdot0854t$ $r^2 = 0\cdot91$
$$(11\cdot16) \quad (17\cdot60)$$
Total revenue $\log Y_7 = 1\cdot924 + 0\cdot0722t$ $r^2 = 0\cdot95$
$$(33\cdot71) \quad (23\cdot54)$$

11 The exceptional growth of passenger traffic in 1851, encouraged by the Great Exhibition, helps to explain the interruption of 1852.

12 Dividends/first-class numbers: 0·6194, dividends/first-class revenue: 0·6338. A combination of first-class revenue and freight revenue produces a correlation coefficient of 0·7313 (*PP*, 1847–8, Vol. LXIII).

13 The only exception is a combination of first- and second-class revenue and freight revenue in 1870, with a correlation coefficient of 0·689.

14 Exceptions are Gourvish, (1972) and, for a later period, Irving (1976).

15 For a general survey of early railway management, see Gourvish (1972, pp. 19–45), and Pollins (1971, pp. 55–68).

7 The Building Industry

by E. W. Cooney

'How very little since things were made
Things have altered in the building trade.'
(Kipling, 1910)

Not even the rapid advance of the Industrial Revolution was capable of stimulating changes of technique and organisation in building anything like so deep and extensive as those that marked the progress of the industries which were setting the pace of change. In the first volume of his *Economic History*, written half a century ago, Clapham noted that 'The building trades had gone through no revolution in technique before 1825 . . .' There had been no more than a 'partial change in organisation', imprecisely indicated by the coming into general use between 1750 and 1800 of the term 'builder' to describe the entrepreneur in the industry (1926, pp. 71–2, 162–6). Even more to the point, in his second volume which takes us to 1886 he had nothing revolutionary to record about building; only gradual technical change and continuing advance of the capitalistic master builders, some of whom were large employers (1932, pp. 36, 79, 129–31). Subsequent studies have confirmed Clapham's conclusions. (For instance, Bowley, 1966, ch. 1; Cooney, 1955; Hobhouse, 1971, ch. 1). Yet by that time, or indeed earlier, industrialisation and urbanisation were evidently far advanced in developments which could not have taken place without the close involvement of the building industry. Revolutionary change on the one side and relative stability on the other, point to an underlying question: what processes of change and adjustment united these contrasting features of the economy?

Before turning to these matters there are several observations of a general kind to be made. The first draws attention to those features of building which go far to explain why it was so slow to be 'industrialised' in the manner of an increasing part of the economy for which it provided shelter. Its main products were complex and bulky and each structure had its own particular, topographically often distinctive, location in which it had to be secured. There has not even yet been a rapid, general transfer of the making of such products to factories. Despite advances in technology and considerable interest in innovation and investment, progress in that direction in this country has been limited and unsteady. The nineteenth century saw even smaller changes, so that traditional materials and methods pre-dominated throughout our period (Samuel, 1977, pp. 27–32). Moreover, a good many of such advances as have taken place, giving rise to greater productivity of capital and labour and lower prices, have occurred in kinds of work which are usually distinguished from the building industry as such. Brickmaking, for instance, at one time frequently carried on at the building site or nearby, wherever suitable clay was available, has become a large-scale, mechanised, mass-production process no longer to be seen as part of building. It has been the same with the cement industry. The onset of this differentia-tion can be traced to the period with which we are concerned.

The second general observation is that slow change in the charac-teristics of the building industry is most noticeable if one thinks of it in terms of the traditional 'trades' (as both Kipling and Clapham evidently did). It is rather less so if the view is enlarged to include the newer but closely related work of civil engineering which flourished so greatly during the nineteenth century. In particular, there appeared some firms which were huge by the standards of the building industry in the narrower sense and operated not only nationally – which few builders did – but ranged across the continents in the course of their contracts for railways and other public utilities. Thomas Brassey, a pioneer of these enterprises, is said by Middlemas to have employed nearly 100,000 men at the height of his career (1963, p. 22). But despite the innovations of this period, such as the large-scale use of iron, much civil engineering work continued to consist of 'muck-shifting' by means of pick, shovel and wheelbarrow and of the traditional skills of the bricklayer and stonemason, though steam-powered plant was increasingly used. Since they have so much in common, such as the durability of their products, common methods of work and often a common pool of resources, it can be useful to regard building and civil engineering as one industry, 'construction', and so obtain a category which is particularly serviceable for con-sideration of relations between the economy as a whole and the important proportion of capital formation which it contributes.

The third observation is that although an impressionistic contrast drawn between a rapidly developing economy and urban society, and a building industry in which organisation and techniques changed only slowly suggests a relatively slow growth of productivity in that industry, in practice, as Gould points out, it is difficult to reach con-clusions based on adequate data, particularly in respect of any changes in quality (1972, p. 296). It needs also to be borne in mind that pro-ductivity may have been raised simply by means of a faster pace of work, legitimised by changes in socal attitudes, and effected through competitive market relationships without a proportionate rise in wages. We should note, too, that there is not necessarily a constant relationship between technological advances and hence the capital-output ratio may have varied. Finally, there is the heterogeneous character of the products of building, standing as they did in a variety of functional relationships to the process of economic development, some almost inextricably tied into it as capital goods such as factories were, and others, such as houses and public buildings, more loosely involved. The basic difficulty, as Deane and Cole point out, '. . . is that of defining capital formation so that it bears some relation to productivity, and so that it can provide a meaningful picture of the transition from a pre-industrial to an industrial economy' (1969, p. 276). There appears to be no simple solution. The necessity, for instance, of any particular amount of new housing and other social building in connection with a particular rate and course of industrial development can probably not be established on general grounds. In each case, it is a question of the actual response to a changing situation. In nineteenth-century Britain the gradually rising relative price of building (Maiwald, 1954, *cf*. graph 2, p. 195 and graph 4, p. 200) seems not to have prevented growth of effective demand for country houses and substantial houses for the middle classes, as well as much public and social building in course of time, but it may have been otherwise in the case of part at least of the urban working classes' response to the housing market.

In the face of these uncertainties the building industry can be looked at from a succession of different standpoints to see what conclusions they suggest in connection with the main question. We shall look at building as part of capital formation, at the course of relative prices, at technological advances and organisational developments and the state of attitudes and expectations about the practice of competition, and finally at the bearing of standards and tastes on willingness to spend on building.

Capital formation has of course always had a place in explanations of industrialisation. One view of its importance was foreshadowed two centuries ago in Adam Smith's comment that, 'It is by means of an additional capital only that the undertaker of any work can either provide his workmen with better machinery, or make a more proper distribution of employment among them' (1976 edn, p. 343). However, the difficulties of making estimates of the process are, as we have already noted, so great, particularly for the economy as a whole, that it has been reasonable for conclusions to range widely between, for instance, the suggestion by Deane and Cole that the proportion of national income invested rose quite slowly over a period of sixty to seventy years during the Industrial Revolution down to the railway-building boom of the 1840s (1969, pp. 263–4) and Rostow's much more dramatic judgement that the rise in the investment ratio to the level needed for sustained growth took place in two decades between 1783 and 1802 (1960, pp. 8–9). If Rostow's view is correct it implies greater demand on the responsive capacity of the building industry, requiring a more rapid increase of output in an early period which shows least indication of technological or organisational advances towards economies in capital and labour and consequent increase of productivity. If there really was a take-off into sustained growth in Britain towards the end of the eighteenth century then it came about with a building industry which differed very little in its arrangements from that which had served the needs of a slower-moving age.

The most recent and most comprehensive estimates of capital formation covering this period support the idea of a relatively rapid, substantial rise in the investment ratio. Put forward by Feinstein for the years 1760–1860 – with emphatic warnings about the unavoidable elements of conjecture and arbitrary assumption in such an exercise (1978, p. 28) – they show gross domestic fixed capital formation at 1851–60 prices rising from about 7 per cent of gross domestic product in the 1760s to a peak of 11 per cent in the 1790s, dropping back 'a fraction' during the Napoleonic War years and then remaining 'remarkably steady' at a rate of 10 or 11 per cent of income down to the 1850s (1978, p. 90 and table 28, p. 91). (I am grateful to Professor Feinstein for facilitating use of this work before publication.)

Feinstein's figures confirm expectation that products of building bulked large in this development. The point can be illustrated in several ways, each to be seen as providing only an impression, both because of the statistical uncertainties and because of the uncertain boundaries of building itself, already referred to. Take first a very wide view of building, or 'construction', excluding industrial machinery and equipment, mining and quarrying, carriage and coachmaking and shipbuilding, but including such products of civil engineering as railways, roads and bridges, canals, waterways, docks and harbours, in addition to dwellings, public buildings and works, industrial and commercial buildings, and farm buildings, improvements and equipment. In that case the annual average per decade of capital formation due to building ranged between 81 and 88 per cent during the century-long period. However, this very wide view unavoidably includes some engineering products, notably railway rolling stock, as well as the farm equipment, which do not properly belong in it. If one now takes a much narrower view and considers only a range of products attributable to building in a more traditional or customary sense, such as dwellings, public buildings and works, and industrial and commercial buildings, then the decade annual averages drop greatly to between 32 and 58 per cent and the range of variation from decade to decade is found to be much wider (Feinstein, 1978. Calculated from table 6, p. 40. See also pp. 88–9).

During the late eighteenth century, when the investment ratio was rising, building held its relative position whether viewed widely or narrowly. From the latter standpoint, its place in capital formation is found to increase through the early years of the nineteenth century up to a maximum of 58 per cent in the 1820s. A decline to 35 per cent in the 1840s contrasts with a rapid rise in railway building to 28 per cent of capital formation in that decade. The largest fall was in housebuilding where there was not only relative decline but also an absolute reduction in output of about a quarter (Feinstein, 1978, table 6, p. 40) – and this at a time when population and income were still increasing about as rapidly as earlier in the century.

First impressions, therefore, suggest that the building industry proved least well able to meet the needs of an industrialising society not at their onset but half a century later when the process was already far advanced. If so, that may reflect several factors: the precipitation of the British economy of the eighteenth century into a state of rapid growth and change from an already high level of organisation and income; the comparatively slight capital requirements of the engineering industry in the early decades because growth, though rapid, arose from a very small initial position; and the relative decline of capital formation in agriculture which accommodated other uses of resources. But railway building was different. Its position reminds us of the suggestion by Deane and Cole of its culminating place in the growth of capital formation, though not to the extent of supporting their conclusion that it significantly raised the investment ratio (1969, p. 261). The rise to 28 per cent in the 1840s took place almost entirely after 1830 in the course of only ten to twenty years. The growing concern – mounting to alarm – about bad, overcrowded housing and insanitary towns which marked those years is well known. Undoubted, too, is the continuing growth of both population and income. But none of this sufficed to sustain effective demand for new housing. The network of markets for capital, labour and materials in a society of large extremes of incomes and wealth generated decisions whereby railways were rapidly extended and housebuilding was checked. Another order of things would have been needed to ensure that the benefits of railways could be had without loss of welfare in housing, particularly in the short term. The thrusting aside of housbuilding by railways can be seen as an extreme instance of a process which has been remarked generally about the place of building in capital formation. That is, its relative decline in face of the rise of technologically newer industries (Kuznets, 1966, p. 257; Gould, 1972, p. 146). However, on our wide view of building, this generalisation is not supported by Feinstein's estimates for 1760–1860. But it is when we look at the industry in the narrower way and particularly if housebuilding alone is considered. The relative decline of building appears, too, in Feinstein's estimates for 1856–1913 (not fully comparable with those for the earlier period), from which dwelling and other new buildings and works can be reckoned at 60 per cent of fixed capital formation at 1900 prices in 1856–75 and at 56 per cent in 1894–1913 (1972, table 40, pp. T88–9).

The decade averages of building and of fixed capital formation, as a whole do not reveal the relation of the industry to the trade cycle nor do they show whether there was a distinctive longer cycle in building. Study of the latter is particularly associated with other topics such as urban growth, population growth and internal and international migration, and capital exports. (See, for instance, Dyos, 1968b, pp. 36–7; Lewis, 1965, ch. 1; Thomas, 1973, ch. 7.) But we shall attempt no more here than to consider briefly views of the course of fluctuations in the British economy between 1815 and the 1870s.

Major business cycles, with an average duration of about nine years, have been identified by Rostow with reference to large-scale commitments to long-term investment at home and/or abroad and emergence of relatively full employment at the peak, and by Aldcroft and Fearon in terms of industrial production (excluding building). Comparison of their summary findings (Rostow, 1948, p. 33; Aldcroft and Fearon, 1972, p. 12) with Shannon's graph of brick production (1934, p. 302; also in Cairncross and Weber, 1956, p. 321) suggests that down to the end of the record of brick production in 1849 fluctuations in building activity were broadly part of the general course of business. Shannon notes, too, that brick production was said by Newmarch to have risen in the mid-1850s to the boom of 1857 (1934, p. 316). Comparison can be carried forward to 1870 in a similar way by reference to a particular form of timber, lathwood. Though small in volume and value, it was widely used in building and is likely to be more representative of activity than the railway construction figures which were all that was previously available and which have been seen as showing the first long, twenty-year cycle in building (Thomas, 1973, p. 84 and pp. 175–6). Imports of lathwood from 1830 not only conform well with the course of brick production and the trade cycle, but down to 1870 (when the series ends) continue to show good agreement with the major business cycles after 1849 (Cooney, 1960, pp. 260–1). Rather than the postulated twenty-year cycle, which is not evident, it has been tentatively suggested that there was an even longer fluctuation with peaks in the late thirties and the middle sixties and a trough in the late forties (Hall, 1961–2, pp. 330–1). In the 1870s, when Rostow identifies 1873, and Aldcroft and Fearon 1874, as the peak year of the trade cycle there is a sign of greater divergence of building activity than in previous booms. It can be seen to have continued expanding to 1876, and even later in some places (Cooney, 1960, pp. 262–6; Habakkuk, 1962, p. 210; Lewis, 1965, pp. 194–200). The probability, therefore, is that building, intricately involved in capital formation, moved in step with the major business cycles of the fast-growing economy between 1815 and the 1870s, the divergence towards the end signalling a more complex situation in the later nineteenth century (Williamson, 1964, ch. 6, *passim*). Whether the industry did more than that and also followed its own distinctive course of fluctuation before the 1870s is less evident. Certainly there were regional and local differences, such as Shannon remarked and Lewis traces in greater detail, showing that the local circumstances of building were important (Lewis, 1965, ch. 4, *passim*). But a general twenty-year building cycle in Britain between 1815 and the 1870s would seem to remain conjectural in the face of data which are not only limited but also complex and susceptible to different explanations.

Against a background of evidence of the importance of building in capital formation and of its accelerated growth in line with the faster growth of capital and income, changes in the relative price of building may next be considered for what they can suggest about the industry's adaptive capability. With scanty data and a complex of possibilities, any conclusions must be conjectural but may be still worthwhile as a link between the macro-economic view of building provided by capital formation and details of the industry's organisation and techniques. Given that the rate of capital formation appears to have been increasing quite substantially during the last decades of the eighteenth century, and that the productivity of building is unlikely to have risen much when organisation and methods were changing only very slowly, is there any indication that a rise in relative price was the means whereby larger quantities of resources became available? In a wide view of the economy there is at most a very slight sign of this. Feinstein's index of building prices covering wages, bricks and timber (and iron from 1810) shows a rise of 43 per cent over the last four decades of the century, while a general index of wholesale prices increases by 37·5 per cent (1978, table 5, p. 38). As Deane and Cole remark about wages, the balance of the evidence 'suggests that the purchasing power of an average day's wage for workers in the building-trades changed little in the last forty years of the eighteenth century: if anything the trend may have been slightly downwards' (1969, p. 21). The likely means of adjustment to rising demand was the concurrent rapid increase of population and the labour force, enabling expansion of this labour-intensive industry to go forward quite easily without a relative advance of wages and, therefore, in the circumstances of stable productivity, of prices also. But within the overall national situation there were, as they point out, considerable regional differences. It can be seen, for instance, from their data that by the

1790s there had been a relatively large increase in building craftsmen's wages in Lancashire where industry was, of course, developing most remarkably (1969, p. 19). As to materials, bricks were made by hand with simple equipment from clays which occurred widely. If labour was available, supply could respond quickly to demand. Shannon's index shows, for instance, an output of bricks 40 per cent higher in 1790–4 than in 1785–9 (1934, p. 316, table A). Increasing quantities of timber were imported without any indications of serious difficulties of supply until the period of the Napoleonic Wars after 1800 (Gayer *et al.* 1953, pp. 851–3). Physical inputs for building seem, therefore, not to have placed any exceptional constraint upon the first period of rapid industrial growth. Greater difficulties might arise from time to time when the market rate of interest on mortgages of land and buildings pressed on the limit set by the usury laws, checking the flow of finance – but this was a recurrent, short-term situation arising from a variety of particular circumstances, not an enduring change.

The war years after 1800 saw prices for building materials and labour rising faster than the average of commodities. Timber, in particular, became more expensive. But building continued at a high level, though Feinstein's figures show a slight check, as they do also for capital formation as a whole in relation to gross domestic product (1978, tables 5, p. 38; 28, p. 91; 29, p. 93) Building was favoured, no doubt, by the easier credit situation which followed suspension of cash payments by the Bank of England in 1797, all the more so in view of the constraint of the usury laws (Shannon, 1934, p. 313; Lewis, 1965, pp. 25–8).

In the era of peace and ever freer trade after 1815, there was a marked fall in prices of building materials down to the 1840s, but even so it was less than the decline in wholesale commodity prices generally from the very high levels of 1801–20. Wages of building workers appear to have fallen only slightly in the 1820s and 1830s and then to have risen a little in the 1840s. Consequently the price of building would seem to have fallen less than prices generally between 1815 and 1850: by 23 per cent compared with 40 per cent (Feinstein, 1978, table 5, p. 38). In the following decades, down to the inflationary boom of 1870–3, with prices of materials tending downwards and wages rising a little, there appears to have been an overall stability in the price of building which matched the comparative stability of prices generally in those years (Maiwald, 1954, p. 195 and Church, 1975*a*, p. 25)

Should we conclude that we have found between 1815 and 1850 an episode when growth of demand for building, much of it arising close to the heart of the process of economic growth by then evidently in full swing, was able to overcome supply constraints only by paying a rising relative price for the products of an industry which, as we shall see, was not itself the scene of extensive, cost-reducing mechanisation? The idea is supported by the fact that such advances in mechanisation as can be traced occurred mainly after 1850 rather than before. But it would seem to be somewhat at odds with contemporary complaints about the severity of competition, and about low wages or harder work, made by builders and workmen particularly with reference to the 1830s and 1840s, which may be more than reaction to short-term depressions of trade, and to which we shall refer again later. Two considerations may throw light on this contradiction. The first is that the price of building has been inferred from the prices of inputs, not generalised from actual prices paid by building owners (Feinstein, 1978, pp. 37–8). The second is that there is evidence of developments in organisation which, even without mechanisation, could account both for the complaints about competition and wages or intensity of work, and could also have restrained the price of building below the levels suggested by an index based on input prices. Employers, some of them working on a larger scale than anything previously known in building, were beginning to combine all the 'trades' in single enterprises and engage in open competitive tendering for contracts for whole buildings for fixed sums, the method increasingly favoured by building owners. Such innovations may well have been painful to many in the industry who were not so adaptable or so well placed to take advantage of them. If employers, they would find business harder to win, or less profitable; or if employees, a situation in which wages and work were likely to be the crucial factors in the profitability of a competitively gained contract and hence subject to pressure by the contractor – who might resort to labour-only subcontracts rather than undertake the more complex task of direct employment of a variety of different tradesmen, as well as labourers. We may note, too, that growth of demand, which could have raised the relative price of building, could also have been one of the circumstances which encouraged builders to undertake these innovations, to which we shall refer again later. Meanwhile, it is arguable that they were capable of bringing about a lower level of prices than otherwise would have prevailed. But, as we cannot observe this directly or estimate its magnitude, we are not in a position to dismiss the possibility that there was a relative rise in the price of building.

During the first three decades or so after 1815 there is little in the development of mechanisation to suggest that it could have reduced costs and hence limited a rise in the relative price of building. Advance became effective only after 1850 when, as we have noted, the price of building appears to have moved more nearly in line with the general course of prices. While the building site in all its variety was always likely to be a different setting for reduction of costs by means of labour-saving machinery, there were better prospects for machines to cut and shape stone and wood, and to make bricks, away from the site in specially equipped workshops and yards. An early, impressive instance is provided by the complex woodworking machines proposed by Sir Samuel Bentham (Inspector General of Naval Works and brother of the utilitarian philosopher), designed by the elder Brunel and constructed by Maudslay for use in Portsmouth Dockyard in the mass production of ships' rigging blocks. With these machines the work of 110 skilled men could be done by 10 unskilled labourers, plus a 30 horsepower steam engine, at a saving of £17,000 per year, for a capital outlay of £54,000 (Singer *et al.*, 1958, pp. 426–8). This was as early as 1808 and is testimony not only to the creative imagination and skill of the innovators, but an indication of the importance of large and probably steady demand in making the case for labour-saving investment.

Blockmaking was sophisticated work compared with the sawing of timber into planks and boards, to which the power of horses and water-wheels had already been applied to begin the gradual displacement of the sawyers from their sawpits. Steam-driven machines now began to be used in the manner explained to Mayhew in London in 1850, the first of them being dated to 1806 or 1807, but strong competition with the hand sawyers only to about 1840 (Thompson and Yeo, 1973, pp. 389–91) Powered machinery also began to be applied to the lighter work of the carpenter and joiner and to stonecutting. By the mid-century the majority of modern types of machine tools had been devised (Singer *et al.*, 1958, p. 441). But progress seems not to have been fast. Clapham thought that the brilliant inventions made during the wars had been half forgotten and that there was no mechanical advance from 1810 to 1835 (1926, p. 445). By the early 1840s Thomas Cubitt, already a notable innovator in building, was exciting attention by the elaborate plant he had installed in his new works beside the Thames (Hobhouse, 1971, ch. 14 *passim* and appendix V). Mayhew's intelligent carpenter in 1850 had first heard of planing floorboards by machinery twenty-one years previously, followed by machines to groove and tongue the flooring (Thompson and Yeo, 1973, pp. 415–6). But when Whitworth and other British experts visited the USA in the 1850s much evidently remained to be done, for they received a strong impression of the advanced state of woodworking techniques in the country compared with Britain (Burn, 1931, p. 294; Rosenberg, 1969, pp. 75–7).

The limited extent of mechanisation in building can be inferred from Musson's analysis of Returns made for 1870 under the Factory and Workshop Acts. Average horsepower per employee can be reckoned to have been 0·12 in 'manufactures connected with building etc.', i.e. builders, marble and stonemasons, carpenters, joiners etc., painters, cabinet and furniture makers, and 'not named above'. (For the builders alone it was 0·08 horsepower) This figure, 0·12 horsepower, is less than one-third of the average for all the industries covered in the Returns. Assuming an average of 5 horsepower per steam engine or water-wheel – there was a small amount of water-power in use – then 3,629 out of a total of 21,012 works, or less than one in five, would have had any power at all at that time (Musson, 1976, appendix, p. 439). Such effect as there was in reducing costs must mostly have been felt after 1850 when, as we have seen, there does seem to have been comparative stability in the relative price of building.

Development of machines for brickmaking points in the same direction. Apart from the horsepowered pugmill for breaking and mixing clay, there seems to have been no significant mechanical advance before 1850 (Bowley, 1960, pp. 61–7). An average of 0·44 horsepower per employee in the manufacture of bricks and tiles can be calculated from the 1870 returns (Musson, 1976, p. 439). It must have accrued largely during the previous two decades. Another important invention, the Hoffman kiln of 1858, was first used in Britain in 1862 so that its substantial contribution to reduction of costs evidently must have taken place well after 1850 (Bowley, 1960, pp. 65–6).

If this was the situation in the workshops connected with building and in brickmaking, we may be sure, for reasons already given, that there was even less power per employee in use on the building sites where, it should be noted, most of the industry's workforce was to be found. The Returns for 1870 show 155,519 employees connected with building (as well as 22,907 brickmakers) which can roughly be compared with Feinstein's estimate, based on the 1871 Census of Population, of 660,000 persons in building and contracting (Musson, 1976, p. 439; Feinstein, 1972, p. T131). That is, about a quarter of the workforce was in a situation where powered machinery could most readily be utilised. While steam-powered machinery was certainly in use by then on building and civil engineering sites, particularly the larger projects, there seem to be no grounds for putting it even at the modest level of capacity found in the workshops.

To sum up, while cost-reducing technical improvements in building were slow moving, the evidence of their emergence mainly after 1850 suggests that they contributed to making the relative price of building move a little more favourably from the building owner's point of view in the 1850s and 1860s than it may have been doing previously.

As we have already remarked, there is another aspect of costs which may tell against this conclusion. There are indications that in this very labour-intensive industry, the first half of the nineteenth century saw an increase in the pace and regularity of work and, in some sectors, a decline in quality, as well as wages lower than those regarded as usual. As we have said, the relative price of building may, therefore, not have risen by as much as is suggested by wages and the prices of materials. Mayhew, presenting his views of 'the Labour Question' as he saw it in London, with obvious sympathy for the workingman, records the alleged increase in the pace of work. Particularly worth noting are his accounts, in 1850, of the 'strapping system' in joiners' workshops for getting high output for the usual wages by driving strong, younger men at a very fast pace of work, and the 'slop' system of cut-price subcontracts on the building sites in which low wages went with bad workmanship. Mayhew was told that these methods had developed strongly since the 1820s. He emphasises the numerical weakness of the trade unions and the lowering effect on wages and conditions of work of the countrymen who flocked to London (Thompson and Yeo, 1973, pp. 416–29). Some years earlier the editor of *The Builder*, the architect Joseph Aloysius Hansom, had responded to a correspondent's complaints about 'the present ruinous competition' among builders with the comment that this subject was 'perhaps the most momentous of any that can engage our attention. The question of competition, contracts, and piece-work is one that requires a vigorous handling . . . Competition begets suspicion and fraud . . .' (1843, no. XIII, p. 156). Hansom's concern about these matters went back at least as far as his prominent involvement, together with Robert Owen, in the Builders' Union and its co-operative Builders' Guild a decade earlier (Postgate, 1923, p. 84*ff*.). His criticism of competition was echoed in 1850 by 'some master builders of the "honourable trade" – gentlemen of high character' as well as by 'architects of equally high standing' – upon whom Mayhew had felt it his duty to call in order that 'I might not be misled by the journeymen'. He found 'the same opinion entertained by them all as to the ruinous effects of the kind of competition existing in their trade to a master who strives to be just to his customers, and fair to his men' (Thompson and Yeo, 1973, p. 422).

Mayhew's 'society men', members of the craft unions, naturally stood out in opposition to such conditions, striving to defend the 'honourable' branch of their trades against the 'dishonourable' and to work only for employers who had 'a regard for the welfare and comforts of their men', as Mayhew said (Thompson and Yeo, 1973, p. 416). Of the London journeymen carpenters and joiners, for instance, Mayhew reckoned that only about one in ten were in unions in 1850 (Thompson and Yeo, 1973, p. 410). Even if – as Musson remarks of Mayhew's evidence about men in skilled trades as a whole – the proportion was more likely one in five or six (1972*a*, p. 18), it is beyond doubt that trade union members were very much in a minority, not only in London but throughout the country, a situation that did not change rapidly. Attempting an estimate of aggregate membership of building unions in the whole country in 1885–6, Clapham put their number at 'something like 100,000 out of a body of perhaps 775,000 building craftsmen in Great Britain' (1932, p. 158). What did this minority accomplish in the way of higher wages, shorter hours and better conditions of work? Musson sees them as increasing in strength during the years of mid-Victorian prosperity and able to gain substantial improvements in wages, hours and working conditions (1972*a*, p. 59). No doubt, as he implies, the tide in the economy was flowing their way. How far their example and influence ensured that it reached further into the lives of the non-union majority than it would otherwise have done is matter for conjecture. A good deal should no doubt be allowed to market forces and the long-term implications of economic development. But in view of the indications of intensification of the pace of work in an increasingly competitive environment between the 1820s and the 1850s, the building workers' recurrent campaign for a recognised shorter working day is particularly significant even when, as in 1859–60, the struggle was not immediately successful or, as in 1872, only partly so (Postgate, 1923, p. 113, ch. 8 *passim*, and pp 295–8). A. L. Bowley summarised the long-term change in the second half of the century as follows: Summer hours in London in 1861, 56½; in 1873, 50 (1937, p. 25). To this may be added Clapham's summary of the opinion of the Central Association of Master Builders in the late 1880s. They believed, he wrote, 'that the amount of building work, particularly of bricklaying, done in an hour had been approximately halved during thirty years of fairly effective trade unionism' (1932, p. 159). Since wages had tended to rise, the 'operative builders' could look back to early struggles and feel that they had made progress.

It comes as no surprise to find that employers and workmen alike felt an intensification of competition during the first half of the nineteenth century. Rapidly growing towns and cities were the setting and stimulus to expansion of unregulated – or self-regulating – markets for the products of building, bringing larger numbers of people into the full, open-market relationship in an era of increasingly confident opinion in favour of competition as a source of efficiency, welfare and equity. One expression of this opinion was advocacy of and preference for open competitive tendering for the whole building – contract 'in gross' – instead of separate arrangements with each master tradesman for his work to be paid for at agreed prices, which might be those shown in published builders' current price books (Cooney, 1955, pp. 174–6, and 1969 *passim*). At the same time the architect was being identified as the professional guardian of the client's interest when work was carried out in this new way, his status and functions being clarified by the foundation of the Institute of British Architects in 1834, with its insistence that members must not work as surveyors or obtain any financial benefit from builders whose work they were supervising (F. Jenkins, 1961, pp. 117–18). The small membership of the Institute – a minority of the profession throughout the rest of the century – is one sign that the new system was unattractive to many who styled themselves architect (Kaye, 1960, table III, p. 175). Competition was criticised – not least by architects – because, as Hansom said, it led to fraud and suspicion, the builder being tempted to scamp the work and the building owner and his architect to accept an unrealistically low tender from among the competing contractors who felt pushed in the same direction. Hence effective contract work on this basis required clear and precise specification of what was to be done which, in turn, caused architects to produce much more detailed drawings than had previously been thought necessary, stimulated the emergence of the quantity surveyor from among the building measurers to show precisely the amounts and qualities of materials and labour, and similarly pressed the master builders to strive, with the help of competent clerks and foremen, to estimate realistically and manage contracts efficiently (Cooney, 1955, p. 176). In these ways, Clapham's 'partial change in organisation' was carried forward still further. The Cubitts again were in the lead among the builders, though Thomas Cubitt turned to specialise in large-scale speculative development of housing while his brothers, William and Lewis, kept to contracts (Hobhouse, 1971, pp. 96–8). The pressure of opinion in favour of the new system is to be seen in the record of parliamentary inquiries into the conduct of building work for government, especially the Report on the Office of Works in 1828 which concluded in favour of contract for the whole building on the argument that 'the method which appears the most prudent for individuals to adopt could not prove disadvantageous to the Public . . .' (*PP*, 1828, vol. IV, p. 319). Their judgement was tested only a few years later on a grand scale when the new Houses of Parliament had to be built following the fire of 1834. As Port says, lump-sum contracts were advocated as an economical way of building, so that much of the work was let on that arrangement, principally to the large firm of Grissell & Peto. But not all, for the architect, Barry, sometimes advised in favour of contracts for prices (1976, p. 101). The Select Committee's judgement was tested in another manner, again in the 1830s, when there was an upsurge of feeling and action among workers – and some small employers – which led, as Postgate puts it, to 'a general attack all along the line upon the new system of "general contracting" ' (1923, p. 72). The 'fierce intensity' of the practice later on is remarked on by Summerson in his survey of building in London in the 1860s, in which he gives several examples of contractors' low rates of success in winning tenders (1973, pp. 12–13). At this point we may note Marian Bowley's criticism that the separation of design from construction –

which, as we have said, was advanced by the system – left the architect with no more than a long-term stimulus towards raising his reputation by introducing innovations, thereby hindering reduction of costs (1966, pp. 33–4).

Although it was not the only cause, the system of contracting for the whole building encouraged the spread of the comprehensive master builder at the expense of the master tradesmen whom it outmoded. Required to work on a larger scale in meeting the needs of such contracts he saw – as Thomas Cubitt, for instance, did as early as 1815 when he was awarded the large contract for the London Institution's new building – the advantages of setting up his own permanent workshops and yard and a comprehensive force of tradesmen to ensure completion within the contract price and agreed date (Hobhouse, 1971, pp. 7–8). The workshops, in turn, provided the setting for further economies by means of power-driven machines (Hobhouse, 1971, ch. 14 *passim* and appendix V).

Cubitt was outstanding, the acknowledged pioneer whose work, moreover, was on a vast scale – 'a leviathan among the builders of his generation'. (Dyos, 1968b, p. 649). While few could approach his size of operations, the new methods could be applied on a smaller scale, even down to firms employing a dozen or a score of men. The supersession of the traditional master craftsmen by the master builders has not been traced closely, but it is evident that in course of time the comprehensive or general builder became the commonest kind of firm in most parts of the country (Ministry of Works, 1950, pp. 3–6 and table III). It is evident, too, that change was gradual. The *Dictionary of Architecture* remarked in 1852 that 'the system of combining all the trades does not seem to have existed much before the commencement of the present century, and has been perfectly carried out only by a few capitalists, as is evinced by the anxiety displayed at present to guard against the evils of sub-letting' (Cotes, 1852, 'Builder'). Throughout the country development was uneven; apparently slowest in small towns and rural areas, as one would expect, but also less extensive in Scotland and in parts of the north of England where contracting with separate tradesmen is said to have continued well into the present century (Ministry of Works, 1950, p. 4). It is perhaps surprising that the innovation occurred at all, given the weakness of the technological stimulus, particularly at first, and the slightness of advantage over the older organisation which is suggested by the latter's slow retreat and long survival in some places. Rapid growth of the housing market clearly favoured such speculators as Thomas Cubitt. Contractors were apparently also stimulated towards change by the preference of building owners for a single contract, and by the disapproval of subcontracting other than such as might be thought necessary by the architect.

While large size is not of the essence of the master builder's comprehensive organisation, there are indications that the supersession of the master craftsman was accompanied by the appearance of firms which were large by the standards of early and mid-Victorian industrial experience. The Census of 1851 provides a view – though one flawed by incomplete Returns – of the scale of employment by builders. In England and Wales there were 5 firms in the largest class, 350 employees and over, of whom 3 were in London. At the lower level of 200 and over there were 19 firms, with 9 in London (Census, 1851, XXX, p. cclxxvi). These small numbers of larger firms should be viewed in the setting of 3,614 employers in England and Wales and 739 in London who described themselves as builders. (That the older order of master craftsmen could also work on a large scale is a possible inference from the fact that there were four employers, described as carpenter or joiner, who employed 200 or more men. One of them was in London. But they may, of course, have employed other craftsmen besides carpenters or joiners.) An impression of the further advance of the large firm can be gained from the membership of the Central Association of the Master Builders of London in 1873, among which there were 6 firms who had more than 800 employees and 41 who had more than 200 (Dyos, 1968*b*, p. 653). But 168 firms had less than 50 employees. It is evident that small businesses and traditional methods were far from being extinguished by the progress of innovations and by such increase as there was in the numbers of large firms in early and mid-Victorian building. Small firms seem to have flourished, particularly in speculative housebuilding, to judge by studies of suburban London and Sheffield, but even in that branch the later part of the century saw a tendency towards the larger firm (Dyos, 1968*b*, pp. 659–60; Aspinall, 1977, pp. 9–11). And, of course, they had a large field of work in maintenance, repairs and alterations, then as now. Their importance is not to be found simply, or even primarily, in their contribution to total output of building – since the much smaller number of large and medium-sized firms was likely to surpass them in total output – but in their functions as a source of fresh enterprise and as a nursery in which larger firms originated. It is clear, therefore, that full appreciation of the dynamics of the building industry's organisation and growth should embrace both the many small firms and the comparatively few large ones, the latter drawing our attention to innovations in this period, the former reminding us of the industry's continuity with earlier times (Cooney, 1970, pp. 355–7).

This evidence, limited though it is, of the response of builders to the growing demands of the market, the new conditions of contract, and opportunities for technical advances, suggests that any effect on costs before 1850 may have come mainly from intensification of labour and from wage cutting in subcontracts, the other influences producing their results to any significant extent only in the second half of the century. If so, the relative price of building may, as we have already suggested, have moved less unfavourably to the consumer than is indicated by input prices. Thereafter, while the other influences towards lower costs were no doubt diffusing through the industry, we may note Maiwald's support for Jones's estimate that although efficiency increased after 1850, mainly because of advances in the woodworking trades, gains in other branches were offset by 'diseconomies associated perhaps with growing discontent among the workmen leading to increased cost of supervision . . .' (1954, p. 189). In the industrialising, urbanising society, restraint on the long-run relative price of building was not likely to come very readily.

The question also arises why some builders thought it worth while to operate on such a large scale that they could undertake a number of substantial contracts or speculative works at the same time. No doubt part of the answer lies in the economies of the larger, more sophisticated fixed plant they were thereby able to afford which gave a better chance of reducing costs and so competing more effectively. But, given the limited extent of mechanisation, perhaps even more important was the need to operate continuously at a level of work which could cover the expense of maintaining a permanent staff of experienced clerks and foremen and at least a nucleus of skilled, reliable workmen as a means towards the efficient estimation and control of costs (Cooney, 1955, p. 172). Important, too, no doubt, was the prospect of the larger personal fortune which would accrue to the successful builder – whether contractor or speculator – from applying his entrepreneurial and managerial talents to a larger amount of work. Although detailed studies are not numerous, the process can be followed closely in Thomas Cubitt's advance from the modest livelihood of a journeyman carpenter in London at the beginning of the century, mainly by way of speculative housebuilding, to 'his million pounds' at his death in 1855 (Hobhouse, 1971, p. xix). The enterprising building and the financial acumen of another millionaire, Edward Yates, in speculative housing in the London suburbs in the second half of the century have also been traced (Dyos, 1968*b*, pp. 669–73). Both men's success depended considerably upon borrowing, well judged by them of course, but a source for lesser men of the frequent bankruptcies for which the industry was notable. A view of the financial rewards of heading a sizeable firm of contractors is provided by the partnership of William Higgs and Joseph Hill in London during the twenty years from 1877 to 1896. Beginning with a capital of £30,000, equally shared (about £15,000 consisting of plant, machinery and stock), their profits averaged £10,460 a year (though subject to quite wide fluctuations) from which they drew an average of £9,135 a year, thereby ending the period with an enlarged capital of £56,500. They had constructed a great variety of public, social and commercial buildings and some private houses, usually undertaking between half a dozen and a score of contracts at the one time and employing a labour force which can be very roughly estimated at upwards of 500 men in summer, rather less in winter. (Judged by the weekly wage bills in the light of current wage rates and summer hours of work for bricklayers and labourers and assuming a proportion of 60 skilled men to 40 unskilled.) (I am indebted to Higgs & Hill Ltd for access to the account books on which these observations are based. See also Higgs & Hill Ltd, 1948, pp. 4–10 for the firm's early history.) Evidently the partners were unlikely to become millionaires by means of this high-class contract work, but the return on their capital, though variable, was far more than they could have obtained as rentiers from secure, fixed-interest investment. The difference – the reward of skilled enterprise, risk taking and managerial effort – placed them comfortably in the ranks of the affluent businessmen of their time.

There is more to the demand for building than is suggested by the functional concept of shelter for the increasing quantity and widening range of specialised activities of the developing economy and society. Questions of style and taste in building – the aspect of 'delight' in Sir Thomas Wotton's phrase from an earlier age – are not necessarily reducible to the needs of economic progress. For all their penny-pinching, or prudent thrift, or concern for public economy, people were clearly interested – sometimes intensely so – in the form and appearance of their buildings (Durant, 1976, pp. 139–43). Such attention, amounting sometimes to enthusiasm, probably raised the cost of buildings above what was strictly necessary from a narrowly functional point of view. It encouraged spending on ornamentation – sometimes very costly – and may have inhibited resort to innovation of cheaper materials and methods, though such innovations were not absent from the building scene. But, as Marian Bowley has remarked, 'Aesthetic innovations and technical innovations in the nineteenth century were completely out of step with each other' (1966, p. 32). An extreme illustration of the cost of ornamentation and the economy of functionally based innovation is to be found by comparing the expense of that small, traditionally made and lavishly ornamented structure, the memorial to Prince Albert, with the cost of the radically original and immense building of iron, wood and glass, the 'Crystal Palace' for the Great Exhibition of 1851. The Memorial cost over £120,000 (Summerson, 1973, plate no. 53) and the Exhibition building not so much more at £185,000 (Hitchcock, 1954, p. 537). But the former was closer to the mainstream of Victorian feeling and practice than the latter, at least over a wide range of public, social and commercial buildings, and houses. Current preference no doubt supported Lord Melbourne's complaint that the temporary accommodation which had been speedily built for Parliament after the fire of 1834 seemed like 'a Primitive Methodist Chapel' (Rorabaugh, 1973–4, p. 162). So, members proceeded to shelter themselves in one of the most expensive, lavishly decorated buildings of the age at a cost of several millions of pounds, though not without some grumbling (Port, 1976, ch. VIII *passim*). Perhaps the spirit of the majority is exemplified in Disraeli's advice that 'We all eat quite enough, and some of us drink a great deal too much, but this I will venture to say, that no man can be too well housed' (Hole, 1866, p. 1). Whatever may have been their frame of mind, the more prosperous among the people of the age evidently housed themselves very well, sometimes sumptuously, and increasingly so, not only in their domestic accommodation, the finest of which Girouard has described and analysed so perceptively (Girouard, 1971, *passim*), but also in their business, social and public lives, and now and then in the accommodation of their factory work (as at Sir Titus Salt's great mill and its dependent community beside the Aire). The histories of architecture, such as Hitchcock's comprehensive study (1954), and our surviving inheritance, show us what they wanted and were willing to pay the master builders to provide. What was not in evidence, even at the end of our period, in the 1870s, was adequate housing for all the families of the working classes. Market relationships, however much their competitive efficiency may have improved, could not achieve that: 'the Housing Question' was being posed.

A summary of what has itself been a summary would be out of place. As our opening question indicated, while so much else was changing the building industry itself was slow to change. But its output increased greatly, fulfilling one of the essential conditions of economic development, and in terms of its own history the changes that did take place were noteworthy. And now and again an event such as the design and construction of the Crystal Palace suggests the potentialities of cost-reducing innovation. However, as Hitchcock remarked, even by the middle of the present century most kinds of building contained a lower proportion of factory-made parts than went into the Crystal Palace (1954, p. 542).

8   The Cotton Textile Industry

by C. H. Lee

I

In the second and third quarters of the nineteenth century the cotton industry entered the second major phase of its development, having played a leading and well-known role in the British industrialisation in the half century prior to 1825. During this earlier phase of growth, the characteristic feature of the industry had been the rapid growth of factory-based spinning, with an extensive accumulation of plant and capital equipment. The weaving section of the industry still retained the organisation and technology of pre-industrial days founded upon the handloom. While exports had not been negligible, even in the difficult and hazardous days of the French Wars which spanned, almost without a break, the two decades before 1815, the home market generated the main stimulus to growth in that period. During the period which provides the context for this chapter, one of the prime features of the development of the cotton industry was the integration of weaving into the new industrial order of factory production, and the consequent decline and disappearance of the oft-lamented handloom weaver. Furthermore, exports provided an increasing share of rising returns from business and were important in stimulating significant and permanent structural changes in the organisation of the industry.

By most conventional indices of growth measurement, the cotton industry expanded rapidly and continuously between 1825 and 1875. Factory employment increased from 237,000 in 1834 to 331,000 in mid-century and to 483,000 by 1878 (Blaug, 1961, p. 379). This was not all newly created employment since the numbers of handloom weavers declined and, of course, some of the new factory workers were trans-formed handloom weavers. This increased labour was required to operate a greatly increased capital output capacity. The number of spindles increased from 7·0 million in 1819–21 to 21·0 million in 1850, and 44·2 million in 1878, while the number of powerlooms grew from 14,000 to 250,000 and then to 515,000 between the same dates (Deane and Cole, 1969, p. 191). There was a related expansion of factory

building installed with steam power to drive the new machinery, so
that the total capital invested in cotton increased from £22 million in
1834 to £83 million half a century later (Blaug, 1961, p. 359). In
response to this massive increase in productive capacity manufacture
expanded, reflected most obviously in the growth of raw cotton
consumed from 119 million lb annually in 1819–21 to 628 million lb
in 1849–51, and to 1,262 million lb in 1874–6 (Mitchell, 1971, p. 179).

The focus of this chapter is firstly upon the nature of the demand
which produced such an impressive response in human and capital
investment and in output, and this problem forms the substance of
Section II. The following two sections seek to evaluate the impact
of this demand upon the structural development of the cotton industry,
and to sustain the argument that the middle of the nineteenth century
marked a significant turning point in that process, releasing forces
and beginning trends which formed the character of the industry
throughout the rest of the century.

II

The growth of demand for cotton goods, divided into the two main
branches of manufacture, namely yarn and cloth or piece goods, must
be inferred from the volume and value of production, and throughout the middle decades of the nineteenth century such data showed
continuous, although unsteady, increase. Between 1829–31 and 1849–
51 yarn output is estimated to have increased from 217 million lb to
557 million lb, and then to 1,009 million lb by 1869–71. Cloth output
rose from 153 million lb to 457 million lb and then to 828 million lb
over the same period (Blaug, 1961, p. 379). Since prices in all sectors
of the cotton industry fell over this period, output growth in value
terms was less great than in volume. The data in Table 8.1 show,
however, the strong upward pressure of demand for both yarn and
cloth, and further that the middle of the century marked a shift to
higher rates of production growth in both sectors.

Clear differences are also indicated between the yarn and cloth
markets, and the growth rate of the former remained higher throughout the period. Yarn enjoyed a number of possible outlets, most
obviously it supplied the domestic cloth trade, and the export market
for yarn, but cotton yarn also comprised a basic input for lace,
thread and hosiery. These latter markets were the preserve of the
fine spinners. Although the export market grew at a faster rate than
the domestic market for yarn prior to 1850, it took a minor share of
the total output. According to Ellison's estimates the proportion of
yarn output which was exported varied around 25 to 30 per cent of
total output up to 1850, and thereafter declined to about 20 per cent

Table 8.1 Sales of Cotton Goods (£m.)

	Trend Equation	Rate of Growth (per cent per annum)	Mean Deviation (per cent)	No. Years M.D. over 10%	No. Years M.D. over 20%
1827–49					
Yarn: Domestic	– log Y = 1·2991 + 0·0124 X	2·9	10·213	10	2
Export	– log Y = 0·7418 + 0·0148 X	3·5	12·148	14	4
Cloth: Domestic	– log Y = 1·2597 + 0·0004 X	0·1	13·322	13	6
Export	– log Y = 1·1602 + 0·0070 X	1·6	8·592	6	1
Yarn TOTAL	– log Y = 1·4099 + 0·0127 X	3·0	10·235	11	2
Cloth TOTAL	– log Y = 1·5192 + 0·0036 X	0·8	8·287	8	2
1850–74					
Yarn: Domestic	– log Y = 1·6949 + 0·0249 X	5·9	10·440	9	5
Export	– log Y = 0·9986 + 0·0182 X	4·2	9·608	9	3
Cloth: Domestic	– log Y = 1·3502 + 0·0099 X	2·3	26·728	19	13
Export	– log Y = 1·5679 + 0·0197 X	4·7	7·820	7	1
Yarn TOTAL	– log Y = 1·7755 + 0·0238 X	5·6	9·492	7	4
Cloth TOTAL	– log Y = 1·7867 + 0·0156 X	3·6	10·816	8	5

Sources: Ellison (1886, appendix, tables 1, 2); Blaug (1961, pp. 376–9).

over the next quarter century (Ellison, 1886, table 2). The increased growth rate after 1850 reflects the strength of home demand for yarn. A further change of trend between the two periods is the decline of instability. This is measured by deriving the growth trend equation by linear regression, and then calculating the deviations from trend for each year in the series, as shown in Table 8.1. There is a small reduction in the mean deviation from trend in the latter period, but this is probably rather misleading. In the earlier period yearly deviations exceeded 10 per cent on 11/23 years while for the later period this occurred only in 7/25 years, and most of these years were affected by the cotton shortage occasioned by the American Civil War in the early 1860s. By contrast the decade of the 1850s and the years 1868–73 were very stable. The second quarter of the nineteenth century was characterised by a continuous series of fluctuations reflecting the effects of the trade cycle. Matthew's close analysis of much of this period illustrated this pattern which is further indicated by the pattern of trend deviations in the yarn market. Overall the yarn market increased both more rapidly and with less short-term instability after 1850 than had been the case during the previous twenty-five years.

The cloth market exhibited different characteristics from this in a number of important respects. It was much more export oriented than yarn. Prior to 1850 the trend for growth of cloth in value terms is almost static in the domestic market. While there was a marked increase in this growth rate after 1850, throughout the period 1825–75 the domestic cloth market exhibited extremely high variations shown in the high mean deviation for domestic cloth sales and in the large number of years in which a deviation over 10 per cent was recorded. After 1850 the instability in this market was even greater than in the earlier years. The effect of this was dampened by the growth and stability of the export market for cloth. The stabilising effect is clear, especially in the earlier period where the total mean deviation for cloth was less than either the domestic market or the export market figure. This indicates that the two trends were working in opposite directions and modifying their separate effects. After 1850 with much higher growth rates in both markets, the increasing export stability was not sufficiently powerful to offset the greater instability of the home market. But, although the mean deviation for the total cloth market was greater after 1850 than it had been before that date, there was some slight fall in the number of years in which extreme deviations were recorded. Since the value of goods sold in the home market have been generally assumed to be more expensive than exports, estimates vary from 14 per cent more to twice as expensive, this instability in the home market must have severely inhibited the weaving production.

The increasing importance of the export market for cloth was attended by changes both in the destination of such goods and of their quality and value. With regard to cloth exports between 1820 and 1850, South America, and particularly Brazil, accounted for 27·5 per cent of the increase by weight, while Asia accounted for 36·5 per cent. In the following three decades all markets showed a decreasing share of the increase except those in Asia, which together took 64·6 per cent of the increase which was three times that recorded in the earlier period. When the Asian market is further analysed, India alone is shown to have taken 47·8 per cent of the increase in cloth exports from Britain (Ellison, 1886, p. 63). Asia also took a preponderant share of the increase in yarn exports, while China and Japan took over half and India accounted for 31·0 per cent. Before 1850, Europe had been the destination of almost two-thirds of increased yarn exports. This geographical pattern of shift away from the European and United States markets which were so important at the beginning of the century to South America and then Asia embodied another significant trend change, related to a secular decline in the quality of British cotton exports. Sandberg's analysis explains this trend as being an effect of the constant reorientation of trade away from markets in which indigenous infant industries were being fostered by tariff protection (Sandberg, 1968*b*, pp. 1–27). British exporters turned towards other low-income countries where such protection was not evident or effective, and especially towards India where British influence was paramount. While lower-quality cloth, and thus cheaper cloth, became increasingly more important in the composition of exports in the course of the century, finer goods were not excluded. Competition from domestic producers in British export markets were usually in the lower-quality ranges leaving, prior to 1875, ample scope for British cottons in the higher-quality markets where they retained superiority.

During the second and third quarters of the nineteenth century, therefore, the British cotton industry enjoyed an ever-increasing demand for its product. It has been suggested that this demand was highly elastic, and that manufacturers were able to move to succeedingly higher levels of output at lower prevailing prices because their costs diminished. A recent study has shown, however, that a more realistic explanation is provided in terms of a series of inelastic demand and supply curves moving together to provide higher levels of output. Such an explanation is quite consistent with a lower prevailing equilibrium price level. The basis for this explanation of growing demand is that an increase in world-wide demand for cotton goods occurred not in response to a fall in the price of the product, or even through the medium of reduced costs by way of a reduction in the price of raw cotton, but rather in response to a general increase in world demand as populations and national incomes increased, and more countries moved into the market economy for what was a simple, cheap and basic commodity (G. Wright, 1973, p. 79).

While a linear regression equation explaining cloth exports (C) as a function of cloth prices (P_c) for Britain gave the following result:

$$C = 17\cdot8 - 2\cdot32 \; P_c \qquad R^2 = 0\cdot59$$
$$(0\cdot34)$$

Wright found that if demand was allowed to shift with time (t) and quality of cloth (Q), the price coefficient became statistically insignificant (G. Wright, 1973, p. 77).

$$C = 7\cdot39 + 0\cdot10 \; P_c - 0\cdot52 \; Q + 0\cdot06 \; t \qquad R^2 = 0\cdot99$$
$$(0\cdot17) \qquad (0\cdot33) \qquad (0\cdot007)$$

In this case only the factor of time is significant as forming an explanation of changes in cloth exports, suggesting the paramount influence of demand factors. It is not possible, unfortunately, to devise a meaningful set of data to represent world demand for cotton goods, so that direct estimation is not possible. Other aspects of the same analysis conducted by Wright did, however, also produce insignificant values for price coefficients in all cases. Finally, the elasticity of demand for raw cotton in both Britain and the USA was found to be inelastic, with a value between 0·31 and 0·65 (G. Wright, 1973, p. 78).

Thus the growth in demand for cotton goods was due primarily to the growth in world demand in the middle decades of the nineteenth century, although Hobsbawm's judgement that the South American market saved the cotton industry in the first half of the century is an overstatement (Hobsbawm, 1969, pp. 146–7). The growth of production was a direct response to this growing demand, involving an increasing dependency on the export market directly for cloth and indirectly for yarn. In value terms the share of cloth exports increased from 43·2 per cent in 1829–31 to 55·1 per cent in 1849–51 and 61·8 per cent in 1869–71. While the share of yarn exported directly fell from 22·6 per cent to 20·2 per cent and then to 15·2 per cent over the same period, obviously a large share of the yarn sold in the British market was ultimately destined for export as cloth. Major changes in trend appear to divide the period 1825–75 about the middle of the century. In the earlier period, exports were less important, growth was slower and there was less stability in the pattern of growth as indicated by deviations from trend. In the latter period, growth in both spinning and weaving was considerably faster than hitherto and, with the exception of the shock effect of the impact of the American Civil War on cotton supplies in the early 1860s, a greater degree of stability seems to have been achieved in most markets.

III

The rapid growth of the cotton industry in the middle decades of the nineteenth century was characterised by marked changes in the structure of production, as well as in the size of productive capacity. The principal feature of this change was the growth of vertical integration prior to 1850, in the combination of spinning and weaving processes within one firm and usually within one factory, and after mid-century the relative and then absolute decline of the combined firm in favour of specialisation of production in firms which either spun yarn or wove cloth. In 1850 combined firms, which were on average larger than single-process firms, contained more spindles than did the larger number of spinning firms, the ratio was 11·1 million to 9·9 million spindles. The same combined firms operated 199,000 powerlooms compared to 51,000 in the hands of single-process weaving firms (Ellison, 1886, pp. 72–3). The powerloom was, of course, one of the foremost technical developments of the first half of the nineteenth century, during the course of which period it replaced the handloom and transferred the weaving section of the industry from the cottage to the factory. In 1819 there were estimated to be only some 14,000 to 15,000 powerlooms, a total which grew to over 100,000 by the middle 1830s, and further to 250,000 by 1850 (Taylor, 1949, p. 117). Thus over 75 per cent of the powerlooms installed between 1819 and 1850 were set to work in combined factories. Similarly, since few of the 7 million spindles in use at the former date could have been in integrated firms, about 75 to 80 per cent of spindle capacity added between 1820 and 1850 must also have been within combined firms. This strong trend to vertical integration between the Napoleonic Wars and 1850 reached its peak around, or a little after, mid-century. In the following decade the number of combined mills increased from 573 to 698, but the rate of addition of capital and labour was slowing down and was not as rapid as the growth of single-process firms. After 1860 the combined firm declined in numbers, falling to 597 by 1878. By the latter date combined firms accounted for 15·5 million spindles and were far exceeded in capacity by the single-process spinners who operated 28·7 million spindles. While the combined firms still retained the dominant share of weaving capacity, 280,000 powerlooms compared to 235,000 in single-process firms, their share of that form of productive capacity was falling (Ellison, 1886, pp. 72–3). Throughout the rest of the century this trend towards the specialised separation of spinning from weaving continued.

The alternative production strategies of vertical integration and specialisation obviously offer different advantages and entail different problems. Within the context of the cotton industry, integration means the combination of spinning with weaving. The preparatory processes of cleaning and combing were always associated with spinning from the first days of mechanisation, while the final processes of dyeing and finishing were always traditionally isolated. The principal advantage to be gained from integration of production processes is usually assumed to be reduction of costs by eliminating payments to middlemen and transport dues. It can also provide a certain kind of product flexibility in that the firm has the alternative of selling both yarn and cloth and thus taking best advantage of either market. This flexibility is gained at the cost of another form of flexibility obtained by a specialised firm. The latter is confined to the yarn or cloth market, but will be able, more easily than the combined firm, to adjust to a different quality or type of yarn or cloth, thus obtaining flexibility within the specific product. Such adjustments are difficult for combined firms which need to maintain a fixed yarn/cloth ratio within the plant unless productive capacity is to become idle. Most integrated textile firms are found to produce a narrow range of commodity. The need to integrate processes calls for more careful management of the production line than is the case in specialisation and a larger-scale operation. It may seem, therefore, that the advantages of integration lay in stability and cost minimisation, while the attractions of specialisation lay in the flexibility of operation within a specific sector.

While the years prior to 1850 did see the establishment of single-process firms for spinning and weaving, the main trend, as has been indicated above, was the growth of combined firms. Since spinning was a factory-based manufacture of long establishment by 1815, the problem may be rephrased to inquire why spinning firms not only expanded their capacity in the following decades, but added power-looms to extend business into weaving. The possible explanations may be gathered under two general headings as being stimulated by expanding trade and profit, that is by attraction of opportunities or alternatively as a defensive mechanism under less happy business conditions.

The basis for the former line of argument may be found in the thesis advanced by Deane and Cole that this period witnessed rapid growth and expanding profit margins in the cotton industry. This provides a necessary corollary to the expanding market demand conditions already established, since even strong demand must be supplemented by the attraction of advantage to the supplier. The case for a growing profit margin is based on aggregate data for the value of final output and raw materials. The difference between these values is the value added, and when the cost of wages and salaries is subtracted from the value added, the residual sum represents profit and other costs of production. This residual figure, for the industry as a whole, did increase during the 1830s and 1840s as the calculations of Deane and Cole (1969, p. 187) show. Hence their conclusion that

'however generously we allow for factors of technical change or fashion in determining the size of the gap, there seems little doubt that its increase in the 1830s and 1840s reflects a marked increase in the share of profit in net output. It is significant, moreover, that this coincided with the period of maximum growth in the cotton industry.' (Deane and Cole, 1969, pp. 188–9.)

A number of reservations may be expressed about this conclusion. The large increase in machinery and power must have contributed significantly to the miscellaneous cost part of the residual, in the form of coal supplies and water supplies, costs of additional machinery and spare parts, all of which diminish the profit share in the residual. But even if the residual figure is accepted as comprising wholly of profit returns to the industry, it does not substantiate the theory for growth via profits, either as incentive to expand or as capital if ploughed back into the business, unless one can know the distribution of that bulk profit between the firms in the industry. Such evidence is, of course, unavailable. Thus a high aggregate profit for the entire industry may be extremely misleading if the true distribution of profit between firms is very unequal and where a small number of firms make very large profits while the majority struggle to break even and cover their costs. It seems not unreasonable to assume that the growth via profit theory requires that a substantial number of firms should at least have good prospects of future profit and the comfort of some past profit.

The argument and evidence for high profits runs counter to the prevailing view of contemporaries who, in unison, bewailed the low level of profits at this time. There are two related dangers inherent in accepting these views. First, businessmen are prone to characterise business as bad, especially when they are in the public eye, and the evidence given to the 1833 Select Committee must be regarded in such a context. Further, many of those who did testify to low profit in 1833 referred back to the really good and profitable days before 1815. During the exceptional circumstances of the years of the Napoleonic Wars large profits could be obtained at some risk, and hindsight must have made any modest profit seem poor in contrast to those halcyon days (Lee, 1972, ch. 4). Thus the word of contemporaries must be accepted rather tentatively. The picture of low profits painted by the witnesses to the 1833 Select Committee was explained as resulting from both increasing demand and high profits obtained in earlier days. As a result, production increased rapidly in relation to the growth of demand with the effect of intensifying competition, forcing down prices and cutting profit margins. The evidence found by Matthew's study on the period 1825–42 does confirm this view, and provides an explanation. During boom years, such as 1825–6, there were bursts of factory construction and the size of factories was such that it often took several years for a firm to be able to afford sufficient machinery to fill the building. One solution was to let part of a mill to other firms. The time lag between the construction of a mill and its operation at full capacity was often long enough to witness the passing of bouyant trade conditions and the onset of a slump. Even so, it remained sensible to complete installation of as much plant as possible and to run a factory at full production even if trade prospects were poor. Hence the increase of capacity and production is consistent with poor levels of profit. The reason for this apparent contradictory behaviour lay in the fact that the cotton industry was such that the share of fixed costs in total costs was relatively high. This was noted by Matthews as being true in the 1820s and 1830s (Matthews, 1954, p. 130). In 1842, Henry Ashworth of Bolton, himself a manufacturer, made the same point. His figures related to a spinning firm with a capital stock of 52,000 spindles which, at full capacity, could produce 12,000 lb of yarn annually at a cost of 8·25d per lb (Ashworth, 1842, pp. 74–5). Within total costs involved, fixed costs including rent on capital, repairs and maintenance, insurance, rates, and wages for staff who were essential at all levels of production, amounted to 29·4 per cent of the total outlay. The variable costs of spinners' wages, fuel and 'contingencies' could be varied with the level of output. Ashworth estimated that to cut production by half and thereby cut variable costs by half would increase the cost of the yarn that was spun by 2·5d per lb to 10·75d per lb, because of the fixed-costs effect.

'To those who will duly weigh the above calculations, made by practical men, it will no longer be difficult to understand why an undiminished, or even increased, production goes on contemporaneously with losing prices. The manufacturer and spinner have only a choice of evils, and they choose the least. If the loss upon a full production be found, upon calculation, to be less than that incurred by working short time, they prefer the smaller sacrifice. And the Directors (of the Manchester Chamber of Commerce), unhesitatingly declare their conviction, that it is upon the latter principle that a great proportion of establishments in this district have been carried on at a loss during the last years.' (Ashworth, 1842, pp. 74–5.)

Ashworth's calculation is for the extreme example of a 50 per cent cut in output. Even with the high fixed-cost requirement, some modest reduction in output and variable costs was compatible with a smaller increase in unit costs. If the calculation is repeated on the assumption of a 90 per cent output, the cost per lb of yarn increases from 8·25d to 8·55d. Indeed by 1841-2 short-time working was prevalent in the industry since, according to Matthews, many firms had already exhausted their reserves under the stress of earlier trade crises (Matthews, 1954, p. 142). Since there were many firms in the industry, it seems likely that few, if any, had control over the price of their sales, then maximisation of production and also of productive capacity represented an appropriate business strategy for most firms, and was also compatible with either 'high' or 'low' profits, however they be defined.

A related point to the high fixed-cost situation was the fact that production maximisation helped to spread necessary overheads over as large a volume of output as possible. Hence expansion of capacity was justified even during trade recession, and indeed it could represent an appropriate risk-avoiding strategy. This might well provide the main explanation for the inclination of spinning firms to add powerlooms to their capacity during this period. Furthermore, power-looms were relatively cheap both to purchase and to house. If there was spare-mill capacity and a shortage of cash, this represented a more feasible form of expansion than the acquisition of additional spinning machinery. It also offered the cost-saving advantages of integration noted above. One witness to the 1833 Select Committee explained the addition of weaving plant to spinning concerns as being the result of falling profits in the latter sector from the mid-1820s (Select Committee on Manufacturers, Commerce and Shipping, 1833, Q.9420). The Ashworth spinning firm of Bolton began to weave in 1841 when 96 powerlooms were installed, a stock which had increased to 290 by 1853. The firm's chronicler explained this development only in that it was common practice amongst spinners in time of depression (Boyson, 1970, p. 60). A survey taken in Stockport and Hyde in 1833 found that almost every spinning mill in the district had an adjacent weaving shed (Taylor, 269 p. 120). While the expansion of spinning firms to encompass weaving can be explained within the context of a high-profit situation, a more plausible thesis is that it represented, for most firms, a defensive strategy in which overheads were spread over a greater volume and type of output, and in which a wider range of markets were accessible and a market guaranteed for at least a part of the yarn output of the firm, and at a modest additional capital outlay.

While the combination of weaving with spinning was the principal structural trend in the industry prior to 1850, the number of separate spinning firms and power-weaving firms also increased. Such firms were smaller, on average, than combined firms, although there were notable exceptions such as the fine spinners who had been amongst the industry leaders in the pre-1815 years. They remained amongst the largest firms in the 1830s (Gatrell, 1977, Vol. XXX). This branch of the industry produced for specialised markets for lace and hosiery production, and for thread. Integration with the weaving section was neither possible nor appropriate for such firms. Other specialised firms may have lacked capital for integration, or may well have chosen to survive without it, and powerloom weaving firms were often very small in scale. As Gatrell has shown, the diversity of firm size remained through the first half of the century with the continued existence of small firms side by side with the great concerns (Gatrell, 1977, Vol. XXX). By 1850 the trend towards vertical integration appeared to be long and firmly established, the reasons for its reversal and disappearance have never been fully explained.

IV

While the growth of separate spinning and weaving firms, and the relative and eventual absolute shift away from vertically integrated firms in the cotton industry were obviously related phenomena, it will clarify explanation to consider each development separately. The growth of the single-process spinning firm, as indicated in Table 8.2, can be partly explained by the great increase in demand for yarn in the third quarter of the nineteenth century. While this is often associated with the appearance of the Oldham Limited spinning firms in the 1860s and 1870s, it is pertinent to observe that the relative shift to spinning only was marked in the first half of the 1850s when, for a short period, the Factory Inspectorate collated data on the addition of factories and power supply in the different branches of the industry. Between 1851 and 1856, almost half of the additional power installed in the entire industry was accounted for by single-process spinning firms in extensions to existing plant and in the servicing of 240 new factories (*Reports of the Factory Inspectorate, 1850–6*). This increased demand has been depicted as a function primarily of a greatly revived export trade for yarn after 1865, and Hughes further suggested that this is the key to the shift away from vertical integration (Hughes, 1960, p. 99). But the evidence does not sustain this hypothesis. While yarn exports increased in value and volume, the share of yarn exported was a declining proportion of the total production, and the yarn export market grew at a slower rate than the home market as shown in Table 8.1.

While the great increase in demand provided the stimulus for the expansion of yarn production, technical innovation made a significant contribution. This took the form of a self-acting mule, developed by Roberts in the 1830s but adopted only slowly.

Table 8.2 *Capital and Labour in the British Cotton Industry*

Spinning Only	1850	1856	1861	1878
No. Mills	834	986	1,142	1,159
No. Spindles	9,912,767	16,820,518	16,308,959	28,671,423
No. Employed	95,239	114,336	125,907	155,615
Spindles/Mill	11,886	17,059	14,281	24,738
Employees/Mill	114	116	110	134
Spindles/Employee	104	147	130	184
Weaving Only				
No. Mills	278	460	779	765
No. Powerlooms	50,935	78,555	148,646	234,503
No. Employees	31,565	50,206	75,175	111,664
Looms/Mill	183	171	191	307
Employees/Mill	114	109	97	146
Looms/Employee	1·6	1·6	2·0	2·1
Combined Mills				
No. Mills	573	652	698	597
No. Spindles	11,064,250	11,189,699	14,008,316	15,535,267
No. Looms	198,692	220,191	250,043	280,408
No. Employees	190,287	209,857	231,646	211,183
Spindles/Mill	19,309	17,162	20,069	26,022
Spindles/Employee[1]	167	155	131	200
Looms/Mill	347	338	358	469
Looms/Employee[1]	2·4	1·7	2·0	2·2
Employee/Mill	332	322	332	354

[1]Spindles/Employee on assumption that Loom/Employee ratio is same as in weaving firms, and Loom/Employee ratio on assumption that Spindle/Employee ratio is same as in spinning firms.
Sources: Ellison (1886, pp. 72–3), Hughes (1960, p. 98).

'Before the cotton famine some hesitancy existed in people's minds as to whether the self-actor mule was a complete success, and it was only the more adventurous spinners who would order a complete concern of self-actors, some having a lingering notion for the old hand mule.' (Andrew, 1887, p. 6.)

Its contribution was considerable when adopted, mills could be twice the width than hitherto, and one man with two boys could operate 1,600 spindles on a self-acting mule compared to 600 hand spindles (Farnie, 1953, p. 15). This machine increased output by 15 to 20 per cent over the hand mule, and by the 1870s it was extending its capability from the coarse yarn to produce medium and fine yarns up to counts of ninety. There were significant increases in labour productivity.

'The number of hanks of 32's yarn produced per spindle rose from 22½ (in 1866) per week of 60 hours to 27 (in 1880) per week of 56½ hours . . . it signified an actual increase in production of 22 per cent and the quality of yarn spun had increased 8 to 10 per cent in strength.' (Farnie, 1953, p. 42.)

The Oldham Limiteds, which became the symbol and wonder of the new order because of the scale of their operations in spinning, emerged mainly after the mid-1860s, and some of the explanation for their advent has been attributed to the innovation of limited liability in the early 1860s. This was the view of Andrew, and one which he directly related to the widespread adoption of the self-actor mule. He further suggested that many old mills closed during the cotton famine years were not reopened and that the new joint stock firms had the capital to build very large factories with the newest machinery (Andrew, 1887, p. 6). This development put increasing pressure on smaller firms with less resources available to keep up with technical developments, and the intense competition which came from Oldham.

'The main force which brought about the decline of spinning in the north (of Lancashire) was the competition of the Oldham Limiteds from the 1870s onwards, cutting yarn prices by 1½d per lb. because of their new machinery' (Farnie, 1953, p. 162.)

Such expansion of output and capital investment could only emerge within the context of a greatly expanded demand for yarn.

Given that there was good reasons for the emergence of the Oldham Limiteds as spinners, it might be wondered why they did not follow the earlier tradition of expanding from spinning into weaving, and thus become vertically integrated concerns. To answer this type of question, business biographies are needed. The only study to date in this particular area concerns the Sun Mill, founded in 1858 and the pioneer of the Oldham Limiteds. It was, in fact, founded as a co-operative weaving venture, but within two years it was decided to increase the capital of the firm and build a spinning mill. This course of action appears to have been stimulated by complaints about yarn bought and worries about unsold stocks of cloth (Tyson, 1962, pp. 77–8). The initial intention was that the firm should provide yarn both for its own weavers and for the market, but by the time that spinning commenced in 1863, the orientation away from weaving was such that discussions were held to decide whether or not the stock of eighty powerlooms should be sold off. This course of action was not followed, but the firm appears to have undertaken only a modest amount of weaving during the 1860s, and that without realising a profit. After 1867 there is no indication of any further weaving (Tyson, 1962, pp. 121, 146, 160). While the unattractiveness of weaving might have been a general deterrent from vertical integration after mid-century, it seems probable that the main weight of explanation must be placed on the vastly expanded demand for yarn which permitted a level of specialised and increased production well above the effective demand prevailing before 1850. It might be also that the greater stability of that demand, except during the cotton famine, gave further encouragement to specialisation.

The separate weaving enterprise, while also pre-dating mid-century, became much more numerous in the following quarter century. Its growth was, of course, related to that of the separate spinning firm and constituted its main market. The development of the separate weaving firm was also a function of the great increase in effective demand, although in this case it was the export market which predominated, and especially the Asian and more specifically the Indian market for cheap, low-quality cloth. This provided opportunities for both growth and reorientation of business, as in the case of John Lean & Sons of Glasgow (Slaven, 1969, p. 496). This firm began as a cloth trading business, first buying from weavers and then employing handloom weavers direct in 1845 to ensure more regular supplies of cloth. By 1854 they had invested in powerloom equipment in rented premises, and three years later this equipment and more was established in the firm's own factory and the transformation of the business was complete. As the firm's biographer observed, 'Between the first and third decades [of the firm's existence] the average annual gross turnover increased more than eight-fold, and the main market switched from the domestic trade to that of India.' (Slaven, 1969, p. 500.) This firm, like most weaving businesses, was relatively small. But Slaven concluded that small firms could both survive and prosper in the expansive Indian market if they could endure the wait between production and sales in a market characterised by rapid changes in taste, temporary gluts and price falls, and stock accumulations.

Capital availability and even technical innovation were less important to the growth of the single-process weaving firm than was the case in spinning, although there were technical developments which speeded up powerloom machinery. Since weaving machinery was cheaper, more enduring and more adaptable than spinning machinery, and easily housed, it was open to those with little capital and could be conducted on a modest scale. The number of firms increased markedly from mid-century and, although the average size increased from 163 powerlooms and 100 employees in 1850 to occupy 398 powerlooms and 188 employees by 1890, they remained much smaller than firms in other branches of the industry (Farnie, 1953, p. 197). Furthermore, even by the late 1870s when the spinners had passed the combined firms in share of total spindleage, the weavers accounted for less powerlooms than the vertically integrated firms.

One of the most obvious features of the growth of the separate weaving firms was its locational concentration. The cotton industry as a whole was heavily concentrated in Lancashire and Cheshire by 1825 and this aspect of the industry became increasingly pronounced as time passed. The concentration of weaving represented further local specialisation within Lancashire. While the first half of the century had seen the bulk of growth concentrated in the south-east Lancashire and north Cheshire area, the separate weaving firms became strongly associated with north-east Lancashire, in the towns of Burnley, Nelson and Colne, and Blackburn. This locational shift has been incorporated as a major explanation for the decline of vertical integration. Jewkes argued that there was a greater demand for weavers than for spinners after 1850 because spinning enjoyed greater labour-saving economies than weaving. This resulted in a search for cheap labour which was found in north-east Lancashire where wage levels were distinctly lower than in the south of the county. This location also offered a tradition of handloom weaving and surplus agricultural labour as further attractions to potential weaving firms (Jewkes, 1892, p. 98). This certainly provides an adequate explanation for the growth of specialised weaving, although not necessarily for the decline of vertical integration. Even within the weaving area there was considerable local specialisation of production: coarse and plain cloth being produced in Rossendale and Rochdale, medium plain goods in Blackburn and Bury, and light fancy goods in Preston, Chorley and Ashton, while Bolton and Bury specialised in the heavy fancy trade. This list indicates that while north-east Lancashire was a growth point for specialised weaving, it did not preclude the development of weaving elsewhere. Indeed, in Bolton, usually associated with spinning, the number of powerlooms increased from 2,131 to 17,680 between 1850 and 1890 (Farnie, 1953, p. 167). Thus while the locational attraction of north-east Lancashire shaped and facilitated the growth of separate weaving, its prime determinant must be seen to be the rise in demand abroad for cheap cloth after mid-century and especially with the growth of the Indian market from the late 1850s onwards. Low capital requirements and ease of entry were further permissive factors.

The growth of separate spinning and weaving can thus be partly explained by the increased demand for cotton goods after 1850. But this does not answer the question as to why the combined firm played a decreasingly important role in this expansion, rather than dominating the industry as before 1850, and why such firms did not limit or even squeeze the small specialised firms from the market. One of the reasons for the slower growth of the combined firm in the growth after 1850 may lie in the fact that economies of scale were not great in cotton. In the case of a combined firm greater scale, and these firms were already considerably larger than single-process firms by mid-century, imposed increased organisational pressures, especially with regard to the co-ordination of the production process.

'This implies a minute knowledge of machinery and hands, of what they can do, and of the stage to which the work in hand has progressed; a knowledge of which is seldom consistent with the management of very large works . . . And when goods cannot be produced for stock it requires very clever marketing indeed to keep the productive capacity of the weaving shed and the order book in such close and continuous contact that the machinery standing idle is a minimum and the time of its idleness a minimum.' (Chapman, 1904, p. 163.)

This may stand both as an argument in favour of specialised small-scale weaving and against large-scale integrated production. The growth of organisational problems in relation to scale and the lack of substantial economies to scale suggest that the characterisation of growing integration as a continuing process of production rationalisation on the basis of internal economies may have little validity in this industry (Hughes, 1960, p. 99). It was argued earlier that the principal benefit afforded by vertical integration prior to 1850 was the flexibility offered in unstable market conditions in that market outlets were multiplied. Such a factor was less significant after mid-century when demand grew more rapidly and when market situations were more stable. Under such conditions the impetus towards integration would diminish. The problems of integrated production lead to the question as to how fully integrated were the combined firms. Such evidence as does exist suggests that the extent of integrated production was considerably less than the total capacity of the combined firms. Data relating to the capacity of spindles and powerlooms of a number of combined firms in Oldham in 1846 showed a ratio of spindles per powerloom ranging from 18·2 to 150·0 (Butterworth, 1856, pp. 179–82, 192, 212). Later estimates suggest that it took about 55 spindles to occupy one powerloom which indicates that the above sample of combined firms included those who sold surplus yarn and those who had to buy yarn to feed their powerlooms. In 1884 the ratio varied between 57·1 and 66·7 spindles per powerloom in combined firms (Chapman and Ashton, 1914, p. 493). This tends to lend support to the view often expressed by contemporaries in the first half of the century that integration was primarily a defensive extension into weaving when spinning profits were low. It also suggests a situation in which the full-cost savings of vertical integration were often not realised, and that the combined firm was often little more than the housing of two distinct and separate manufacturing processes within the same premises. One of the few business biographies about cotton in this period is the story of the Ashworth mills near Bolton. They were spinners who incorporated weaving into their business in 1841, and continued to expand this side of the business through to the 1870s (Boyson, 1970, pp. 77–8). Increasingly during that decade the two sides of the business became divorced as the spinning section made fine yarn which was sold for sewing cotton, while the weaving section was supplied by yarn bought from other firms. In 1880 the spinning section was closed and the firm had passed from spinning through integration to become a weaving business. Factors in producing the latter situation included the interests and personal background in weaving of the new master who took over in 1880, and that the spinning section, which had been losing money through the 1870s, needed to be extensively re-equipped (Boyson, 1970, p. 82).

If the advantages which had been provided by integration were diminishing in the market situation of the third quarter of the century, the pressures on this type of firm were increasing. One powerful source of this was the competition of the Oldham Limited spinners. In the 1860s and 1870s such firms had the most modern technology, and competition involved re-equipment for many others besides the Ashworth mills. For some firms this represented an appropriate time to switch to single-process manufacture, and usually meant the abandonment of the spinning section. Between 1866 and 1886, thirty combined firms in Burnley alone closed their spinning sections (Farnie, 1953, p. 164). Such a trend was marked throughout northeast Lancashire and was aided, doubtless, by the increasing concentration on weaving in the area. The spinning sections which were closed were usually small in size, from 5,000 to 15,000 spindles, and producing coarse yarn up to counts forty and fifty (Farnie, 1953, p. 136). Abandonment of weaving sections by combined firms was less common. There was not the same kind of competition offered here as in spinning, the machinery was cheap, adaptable and lasted longer. Even so, and despite some addition of weaving capacity to spinning firms in the 1880s, the number of combined firms fell absolutely in the last quarter of the century.

Productivity is rather difficult to measure and compare between the different branches of the cotton industry, but the data in Table 8.2 suggest that while the combined firm might have had a comparative advantage in this regard in 1850 in terms of labour/machine ratios in spinning, this seems to have considerably diminished by the late 1870s. It may also be that the combined firm had reached its maximum size by mid-century, given the preference of Victorian businessmen to run their own concerns personally and their reluctance to delegate authority. The private combined firm may also have reached the extent of its capital availability.

The decline of the combined firm has been explained in terms of the decline of its comparative advantage in a rapidly expanding market where defensive commercial strategy was less vital than before 1850. It remains to discuss those reasons which have most often been advanced to explain this phenomena, namely improved transport communications and changes in market organisation. While transport development clearly improved linkages between different branches in the industry, it is difficult to explain why it should have caused structural change. Even if growth had been inhibited in less accessible locations such as Burnley, an independent weaving section could have developed closer to the Manchester area, and indeed some of the combined firms of that area might have switched from spinning more quickly. Transport change had an obvious locational influence on the development of the industry but probably only a small effect on structural change. Many writers have suggested that divergence of markets was crucial after 1850.

'In general we may say that, largely because the markets for which spinning and weaving were respectively connected were roughly of the same form in the first half of this century, it was then economical for the two processes to be carried out under the same management, as the cost of marketing and transporting a great deal of yarn was thereby saved; but that when the common market (that for yarns) and the market peculiar to spinning (that of raw cotton) developed, while the one peculiar to weaving (that of cloth, which is a compound of a greater number of markets than are united in those of cotton and yarn) failed to develop, the two processes, spinning and weaving, required in some cases different kinds of organising capacity and so tended to drift apart.' (Chapman, 1904, pp. 163–4.)

He further argued that marketing was a more important quality in weaving, since there was a great variation in the range of finished product and specialised knowledge was required for success. This is not borne out by Slaven's description of Lean & Sons who appear to have been rather ignorant, necessarily, of their market (Slaven, 1969, p. 496). More generally, Chapman does not show how the cloth market became more diverse than the yarn market. Ellison, by contrast, extols the advantages of spinning over weaving in terms of a more diverse market for yarn in exports, lace and thread, as a partial input in Yorkshire woollens, as well as the cotton weaver himself. There seems some discrepancy with Chapman's own description of the separation of finishing from weaving because the finishers had to adapt a standard product to the requirements of the particular customer. It seems most probable that the separation of markets was an effect of the growth of the industry to considerably higher levels of output. It is not easy to see how market diversification should lead to structural specialisation. A combined firm could continue to operate in both yarn and cloth markets or, if fully integrated, in the latter market only, as indeed such firms had done prior to 1850. It is hard to imagine that, if other factors had favoured integration, market organisation changes would have impelled specialisation in manufacturing process.

V

The conclusion of this chapter is that changed market conditions, and especially the great increase in export demand for cheap cloth, was primarily responsible for the structural changes in the cotton industry after mid-century. The advantages of combined production were diminished by the massive increase in the market, but the advantages of specialisation were magnified, and the successful competition of large-scale and technically advanced spinning firms further diminished the attractions of integration. The pattern of growth of the British cotton industry in the second half of the nineteenth century was marked by a degree of specialisation of function not matched in any other country, because no other nation was able to take advantage as fully as Britain of the growth in world demand. In the long run, the preference for specialisation against flexibility produced an industrial structure which had difficulty in adapting to diminished markets in the twentieth century. The specialisation born of the buoyant markets in mid-century laid the foundations for the problems of overcommitment of resources familiar to students of the twentieth century.

9 The Woollen Textile Industry

by E. M. Sigsworth

Generalisations about the behaviour of businessmen in the wool textile industry during the nineteenth century must necessarily reflect the industry's complex structure. Its various sections posed at any time different problems and opportunities for entrepreneurs. The profit-maximising calculations of the dyer, comber or spinner on commission work were distinct from those of the manufacturer buying raw materials for conversion into finished products. Indeed, their interests were often opposed to each other. Similarly, the business stratagems of the mercantile sections of the industry, whether involved in specialist dealings in raw wool, yarns, tops or cloth, diverged from those pursued by the manufacturer, and each type of merchant, though performing similar basic functions, faced different markets and, therefore, opportunities. Buying, holding and selling the commodity in which he traded, his economic function was further differentiated clearly from that of the commission agent with whom he competed but who did not finance the holding of stocks, whether they were in transit to more or less distant markets or whether they were being held speculatively.

Within the manufacturing industry producing cloth and yarn for sale to the merchants there was, throughout, a clear distinction between the woollen and worsted branches, so clear indeed that they can virtually be regarded as separate industries. Though each used wool to make cloth, the types of wool and other materials used, the nature of the cloth produced and the markets catered for; the pace and timing of technological changes and the structure of the two branches differed radically.

Thus, during the nineteenth century there was a distinction, varying in degree in different periods of time, it is true, between the woollen industry in which, increasingly during the period under consideration, all the processes needed to convert wool into cloth were performed by the same firm, and the worsted industry in which the main processes of combing, spinning and weaving tended to be organised horizontally with firms specialising in each process.[1] The diminishing extent of horizontality in the Yorkshire woollen industry is shown in Table 9.1.[2]

Table 9.1   *Functions of Firms in the Yorkshire Woollen Industry*

	1849	%	1861	%	1867	%	1874	%
Spinning only	532	60·4	422	44·4	263	31·9	199	20·0
Weaving only	9	1·0	28	3·0	35	4·2	35	3·5
Spinning and Weaving	180	20·5	275	29·8	382	46·7	567	56·8
Not known	159	18·0	199	21·5	138	16·8	197	19·7

The problems of organisation of productive factors and those posed by technological change which were faced by the 'average' worsted producer were correspondingly less extensive than those of the woollen manufacturer. From a different viewpoint, the range of opportunities open to the latter for substitution between raw materials arising from differential changes in their relative prices was much wider than that available to the worsted manufacturer. Whether wholly dependent upon supplies from other firms or spinning part of his own requirements, the worsted cloth producer bought yarns in a competitive market which dealt in standardised types, qualities and counts of yarn, just as the specialist spinner, in turn, bought standard tops from the comber or topmaker. The main innovation in worsted raw materials was the increasing use of cotton warps combined with a wool weft from the late 1830s onwards, in order to keep down the price of the product woven by the Bradford section of the worsted industry which catered for the lower-priced worsteds for mass consumption. In addition to using cotton warps and with the same end in view, the woollen manufacturer also had available the wide range of types and colours of 'shoddy' or 'mungo' without which, as Clapham wrote, 'the nineteenth century would have been chillier or dirtier or both' (Clapham, 1952, p. 39). The producer of these unglamorous raw materials and the specialist dealer in the wool rags from which they were derived were themselves a thriving subsection of the industry. The market for rags was established at Dewsbury after 1860[3] and the rag-wool industry was concentrated in the Spen and lower Calder valleys.

The complications of product specialisation, both in whole sections of the wool textile industry and in individual firms comprising those sections, must be added to these examples of organisational distinctions which make generalisation difficult. Thus there was, within the woollen industry, an important difference between the 'white' and 'mixed' cloth manufacturers. The former sold undyed cloth to the merchant who either had it dyed in his own dyehouse or on commission by specialist firms located mainly in the industry's market centres such as Leeds or Huddersfield,[4] thus creating a specialised class of dyeing entrepreneurs and subdividing the woollen merchants into those who did and those who did not organise the dyeing processes on their own premises, employing labour and capital.

Superimposed upon these divisions of the woollen industry were differences arising from specialisation in products of various qualities catering for differing markets. These were also reflected in geographical diversity. Thus, the west of England woollen industry produced high-quality cloths, and the contraction of the industry during the nineteenth century was due in part to a failure to compete successfully with the West Riding woollen manufacturers in the production of the coarse and medium types of cloth and the gradual erosion by Yorkshire competition of its share of the market for higher qualities (Beckinsale, 1951; Tann, 1967; Mann, 1971; Ponting 1971; Ponting, 1972, pp. 235–47; Ponting, 1973). The Scottish industry of the border country specialised in making woollen tweeds (Martindale, 1972) and the relatively small Welsh woollen industry made flannels in Montgomeryshire, and webs in Merioneth during the first half of the century, with these local areas of product specialisation fading as the Welsh industry shifted westward during the second half (J. G. Jenkins, 1969). In Yorkshire, where entrepreneurial success was a reason for the decline of woollen manufacturing elsewhere, there were again important local differences in the qualities and types of cloth produced. The woollen manufacturers of the lower Calder and Spen valleys, centred upon Batley, Morley, Dewsbury, Heckmondwike and Ossett specialised in blanketmaking and in the 'low' end of the market for woollen cloths, with dominance in blanketmaking being achieved between 1820 and 1860 (Jubb, 1860; Glover, 1961–2). Finer qualities of woollen cloth were made in Leeds and more especially in the villages adjacent to the west. In the Huddersfield district the emphasis was upon fine-quality 'fancy' woollens.

Similarly in worsted production, although the decline and fall of the East Anglian industry during the late eighteenth and early nineteenth centuries[5] meant a much higher degree of concentration in the West Riding than was the case in the woollen industry,[6] there were important distinctions in the qualities of cloth being made within the region. In and around Huddersfield, fine qualities of worsted were produced, especially apt for men's suitings (Crump and Ghorbal, 1935, pp. 120–6), whereas the Bradford and district trade had thrown everything into achieving cheapness, and produced cotton warp mixture catering above all for the ladies' dress trade.

Distinctions in product both nationally and within the West Riding textile area meant, as Clapham long ago observed, that there was often little community of interest between cloth manufacturers:

'Woollen and worsted men, whether employers or employed are often unconscious of common interests and indeed their interests are very frequently opposed to one another. This cleavage . . . is repeated within the trades. The outsider does well to avoid confusing the woollen trade of Huddersfield with that of Batley. He must understand that the Leeds trade is not as the trade of Morley, which is five miles away or as that of Guiseley which is nine miles away. The worsted stuff trade of Bradford is distinct from the worsted coating trade of Huddersfield and Halifax carpet making has little in common with either . . . cleavage . . . (is) accentuated by that local feeling which is perhaps the strongest force in the life of the West Riding and thanks to which places but a few miles apart each work out their own salvation in their own way.' (Clapham, 1907, p. 206.)

Such distinctions, even at the broadest level so far indicated, were a major factor inhibiting the ability to create common wage scales for weaving which would have facilitated collective bargaining. The woollen and worsted industries displayed the weakest trade union organisation of any major British industry, with just under 3 per cent of its workers being unionised in 1904 (Clapham, 1907, p. 204). Whether in woollen or worsted, the wool textile manufacturer performed his business functions free from the constraints of well-organised labour unions and had effectively done so since the last major strike in the industry which had occurred in 1825 amongst the Bradford and district wool combers and weavers. The small trade unions which did exist were amongst skilled workers such as spinning and weaving overlookers and wool sorters, but their organisation, too, reflected the industry's geographical and product specialisations since local divisions over-rode what might, at first sight, have seemed to have been a common interest inherent in the type and status of the work. Whether as cause or effect, the wool textile industry was characterised by 'what are frequently called patriarchal relations between masters and men',[7] and its leaders in public orations frequently prided themselves upon the harmony of their relations with labour. Thus, John Crossley of the Halifax carpet-making firm could say in 1879 that 'no dispute or misunderstanding has ever occurred but such as was there and then by mutual compromise, adjusted, with one single exception, nearly forty years ago. We had then . . . a strike of some ten days' duration'. Fosters of Queensbury had their mill defended by their workers, against passing Chartist demonstrators and enjoyed a strike-free history throughout the period 1819 to 1890.[8]

More difficult to assess because of its very nature, there was, however, another divisive factor at work which further fragmented the interests of the wool textile business community. There were two main avenues down which the cloth producer drove in search of profit. On the one hand, there was the trade in 'bread and butter cloths', highly standardised products, usually in single colours, meeting a demand which fashion altered little from season to season supplying, for example, the subfusc cloths favoured by the Victorian male. The dictates of mourning customs in an age of high rates of mortality, guaranteed for the manufacturer a heavy concentration of demand for black fabrics ranging from serge to the light alpaca and mohair fabrics for women's dresses.[9] Such cloths were produced for a highly competitive market with little scope for product differentiation within grades of cloth. Their makers were 'price-takers' working to finely calculated profit margins and who, if successful, became rich by selling large quantities of cloth at low unit profit rates. For the woollen manufacturer especially, the profitability of such cloths derived largely from the skill with which he blended raw materials to ensure the least-cost input consistent with maintaining a reputation for the quality of his output. The blend constituents were kept highly secret and the blend books in which details were recorded were often kept in code. It was this, of course, which helps to explain why no market for woollen yarns emerged comparable to that, which was an important feature of the worsted industry. It may also help to explain why the woollen industry was slower to mechanise than the worsted industry and why the size of individual concerns remained generally smaller. In 1870, the average British woollen factory employed 70 workers compared with 175 for the average worsted factory.[10]

To polarise the alternatives in order to illustrate the point more fully, the other *extreme* production possibility open to the cloth manufacturer, especially in the ladies dress trades,[11] was to vary output seasonally in order to try to reap the profits from short-run imperfections in the market. The over-riding stratagem was to try successfully to anticipate, months ahead, next season's fashions, producing in advance, colours and designs which would hopefully capture the market, until competition from less perceptive imitators reduced profit margins. The biggest worsted producers not only employed their own cloth designers but sought advance information from Paris correspondents in order to keep ahead of their competitors. As S. Smith, the president of the Bradford Chamber of Commerce, put it in 1856:

'Every person connected with this market was aware that no sooner was a new article produced and brought into the market than, before it had been out for three months, a similar looking article was produced with a few picks less and a little lighter.' *Bradford Observer*, 31 January 1856.)

More vividly, the situation was outlined by a correspondent to the Bradford newspaper in 1852:

'My friend D [merchant], has secured to himself a style of goods which will create a profit and a sensation during the approaching season.

He takes good care to impress upon his manufacturer not to let others see his goods until this order is executed. The result is that D is well stocked before his competitors know about it.' (*Bradford Observer*, 11 March 1852.)

In this case the initiative was from the worsted merchant. Whether, however, merchant or manufacturer took the lead, the effect was the same – an expression of the search for short-run quasi-monopolistic profit. Although both the woollen and worsted industries in Yorkshire were said to have been dominated by the aim of producing large quantities of cloth at small unit profits, and by implication to have been highly competitive, it is noticeable that the search for a niche in which the rigours of competition could be evaded expressed itself in a variety of ways, long before the industry evolved combinations of dyeing firms and of commission wool combers. In the blanket trade, Hague Cook & Wormald of Dewsbury, though characterised by 'small unit profits' in their American trade (Glover, 1961) managed also to participate in the oligopolistic structure of the market catering for the Navy and Ordinance Board's demand for blankets (Glover, 1963–4; Plummer and Early, 1969, pp. 64–5). In the alpaca and mohair cloth-producing sections of the worsted industry, the purchase of the raw materials was arranged in collusion between the few firms which dominated the trade, Fosters of Queensbury, Titus Salt and Mitchell Brothers (Sigsworth, 1958, pp. 243–70). In the production of combing machines, Lister enjoyed (for several years) an outright monopoly and charged would-be purchasers of the machine accordingly:

'. . . it was the largest patent right that was ever paid for a machine . . . the trade was well satisfied to give me what otherwise would have appeared to be an outrageous price, the sum of £1,200 A MACHINE OR £1,000 PATENT RIGHT, the machine itself costing about £200. But even at that price it was highly profitable and for years I sold a large number.' (Masham, 1904, pp. 438–46.)

Similarly, J. Crossley & Sons, the Halifax carpet firm, monopolised the sales of George Collier's carpet loom and also his loom for weaving velvet, having financed the experimental stage of their development:

'Messrs. J. Crossley and Sons thus became the proprietors of a series of patent rights which were of great value and for many years yielded them an immense revenue. Every carpet manufacturer in the kingdom found it necessary to adopt Mr. Collier's loom . . . so that for a time, the Crossleys enjoyed a practical monopoly of the trade.' (*Fortunes Made in Business*, 1884, vol. III, p. 273).

Such devices as the exercise of monopoly pricing through the use of patent law far exceeded in duration and effect for the firm, of course, the type of short-run profit-maximising exercise of the merchant or manufacturer exploiting the temporary advantage of having created for himself an imperfectly competitive position in the market. Furthermore, whilst success had its obvious rewards, the risk of failure was correspondingly evident. For wool textile entrepreneurs engaged in this type of trading, the degree of risk was thus much higher than that facing the 'bread and butter' cloth producer. To be sure, individual producers doubtless varied their production in order to meet both types of demand and therefore spread their market risks associated with fashion, just as they spread those involved in catering for different geographical markets. Again, however, what is important in trying to understand the businessmen of the wool textile industry in the nineteenth century, is to appreciate those differences between them and the different nature of the demands upon their expertise arising from the type of markets which they served.

Whatever those markets for the product may have been, however, wool textile entrepreneurs found that the characteristics of their raw-material supplies were crucial in determining success or failure. Once more, however, the complexities of the situation require recognition. To begin with there were broad differences between the types of wool used by woollen and worsted manufacturers, the former using relatively short and the latter relatively long fibres. Within these broad classifications, however, there was a variety of wools which was rooted not only in fibre length, but in quality – the varying thicknesses and degrees of elasticity of fibres, the amount of hair or 'kemp' in the wool and its degree of cleanliness which varied with pasturing practices. Selection of the wools most suited for the intended product called for the exercise of fine judgement in balancing quality with price. It was here, of course, that the tactile skills of the wool sorter were essential and the familiarity which the sorter acquired with the intricacies of the wool market and the importance of the price of wool in costing the final product[12] explains, no doubt, why this relatively well-paid occupation which was an important element in the wool textile industry's 'aristocracy of labour', was a well-known source of recruitment into the entrepreneurial ranks of the industry. For the woollen manufacturer, the availability of a similarly wide range of types of shoddies and mungoes was an added field for the exercise of judgement denied to the worsted manufacturer, since the short-staple lengths of grand wool fibres made them entirely inappropriate for worsted processing. For a small section of the worsted industry, however, alpaca and mohair were used as well as wool fibres.

The market for raw wool, however, to take its most aggravating economic characteristic, was very volatile with understandably sharp price fluctuations, given the high degree of short-run inelasticity of supply. An increase in demand, especially in the short-run, could not easily produce a corresponding increase in supply, for this could only arise from an increase in the number of sheep.[13] It is not surprising, therefore, to find that anxieties were being expressed about wool supplies during the 1850s, culminating in the establishment of the Wool Supply Association in 1859, and the encouragement in the 1860s by the Bradford Chamber of Commerce of cross-breeding in New Zealand which increased the supply of long wools as well as carcase weights (Clapham, 1907, pp. 80–1.). Such measures, however, sought to alleviate the problems of the industry arising from an increase in the long-term demand for its products not being matched by a corresponding increase in raw-material supplies and resulting in a secular increase in wool prices. This, of course, meant difficulty in competing with other textile products, especially cottons, for it must be remembered that wool textile manufacturers competed not only with each other but with other textile producers.

The elasticity of substitution between wool textiles, cottons and, to a less extent, linen was always in the forefront when the price of raw wool was under discussion, and it was this which explains the economic significance of the use of adulterants such as cotton warps and rag wools (Baines, 1859, p. 6; Baines, 1875; Clapham, 1907, pp. 80–1; Sigsworth, 1958, pp. 48–9, 70–1). Again, however, the situation varied between different wool textile producers. Those selling high-quality woollen or worsted cloths were insulated to a much greater degree from the competition of cloths made from other fibres. Shoddy and mungo, for example, seem hardly to have been used in the west of England woollen industry.[14] At this level of quality there was no room for the use of these adulterants or of cotton warps. It was overwhelmingly in the Yorkshire wool textile industry searching for mass production at low unit profits that costs needed to be cut to ensure not only that the profit margin on a piece of cloth should be as wide as possible, but that the product should be competitive with cotton fabrics. The price of wool was, therefore, a crucial matter and it is not surprising that it was the Bradford trade from which the impetus came to establish the Wool Supply Association and the Bradford Chamber of Commerce which listened attentively to the prospects of establishing flocks of long-woolled sheep in Tibet.[15]

The relative price movements of textile fibres, therefore, affected different sections of the wool textile industry in differing degrees. The situation arising as a result of long-term price changes was, however, more complex in its effects.

First, there were the effects of changes in sheep-breeding practices originating in the eighteenth century and still being worked out in 1850 (Hartwell, 1973, p. 335). These had the effect of increasing the length of staple in the home-produced fleece so that British wools became increasingly less relevant to woollen production and were eventually of use only to worsted, flannel or hosiery manufactures. Even so, and in spite of the increasing use of cotton warps to the point where Baines estimated in 1858 that 95 per cent of worsteds incorporated them (Baines, 1859, p. 7), and notwithstanding the spread of mechanical combing in the late 1840s and 1850s which enabled shorter stapled wools to be combed, the worsted industry's demand for raw material was, in the 1860s, outstripping supply. Thus, the price of combing wools in the mid-1860s was higher than at any time during the previous half-century,[16] the easing of prices after the 1860s being partly a result of the extensions of cross-breeding of merinos with long-woolled Leicesters in New Zealand.

The diminishing relevance of British wools to woollen manufacturers was offset by greatly increased imports of short-stapled wool, the use of cotton warps in the lower qualities of cloth and, of course, the ever-increasing supplies of shoddy and mungo. The domestic clip was, in any case, fairly static in supply, according to contemporary estimates which are, admittedly, of dubious provenance. Imports of merino wool came first from Spain and then from Germany which, by 1824–5 accounted for two-thirds of wool imports. By 1830 imports of German wool were running at 24·6 million lb, Spanish wools 1·6 million lb and a small supply of 1·9 million tons was imported from Australia. Twenty years later the sources of importation had undergone great changes: Australian supplies were now 38 million lb, and those from Germany had dwindled to about 9 million lb and those from Spain had almost vanished. By 1870, out of a vastly increased total of imported wool which had reached 263·3 million lb, Australia supplied 175·1 million lb, British South Africa 32·8 million lb and South America 12·7 million lb. These greatly increased supplies of wool, as yet suited mainly for woollen processing help, no doubt, to explain the changed tone of Baines's supplementary chapter, surveying progress between 1858 and 1870, when he is dealing with sources of raw material.[17] Additionally, the use of shoddy had greatly increased. Imports of woollen rags which had measured 6·7 million lb in 1858 had increased to 72·5 million lb in 1878 – a source of supply second only to Australian raw-wool imports (Sigsworth, 1949, p. 984).

Thus the woollen and worsted sections of the industry faced differing situations – both, it is true, saw the price of their main raw materials rise but the increase was far greater for long wools than that for short staples. Thus the average price of Lincoln Half Hoggs, suitable for combing, rose by some 96 per cent, comparing the years 1846–50 with 1871–5, while that of Port Philip merinos over the same period increased by only 46 per cent (Mitchell and Deane, 1971, p. 496).

Each branch of the industry faced other problems arising from their sources of raw material. First, as had been seen, the supplies for the woollen industry came increasingly from overseas and from ever more distant pastures. The growing importance of Australian supplies was recognised with the beginning of regular colonial wool sales in London in 1835 (Clapham, 1907, p. 317). Intelligence about the prospects for the market must thus have been increasingly difficult to obtain as sources of supply shifted to the opposite side of the world and this added to the problems of uncertainty affecting entrepreneurial decision making in an industry which, in any case, disposed of the biggest proportion of its output to the USA and depended again upon slow channels of communication for the feedback of information about market conditions affecting sales. This extra difficulty due to the increasing amount of colonial wool affected the woollen industry more than the worsted branch during the period under consideration, though of course it was being increasingly mitigated in the 1850s and 1860s as electric telegraph connections were established between London – or more relevantly, the West Riding – and the rest of the world.[18]

Price fluctuations in a raw material which was a large determinant of the price of the product, accounted for the importance of success or failure in wool buying for the wool textile producer. A decision to buy or sell wool at the correct time could do more to enhance the overall profitability of a firm than was possible by assiduous attention to details of technology or business organisation.[19] The penalties for an incorrect decision were correspondingly hazardous.

The implications of fluctuations in wool prices varied, of course, according to the type of productive activity in which a firm was engaged. It depended, amongst other things, on the extent to which the manufacturer bought his own wool. This was generally the case in woollen manufacturing, but less so in the worsted industry. Here, the wool merchant's customer was either the comber or the topmaker, both producing tops for sale, or the comber, spinner, or the manufacturer who had integrated all the manufacturing processes and entered the raw-wool market – sometimes, indeed, bidding directly at the auctions and thus by-passing the wool merchant. Spinners and specialist manufacturers need not buy raw wool at all except, as on occasion they did so, on a speculative venture. They purchased not wool, but tops and yarns and the relationships between the prices of and credit terms upon which wool, tops and yarn were available is a complex matter which has received, as yet, only partial attention.[20] That they did not move together proportionately is, however, clear, and discrepancies between their respective rates of change gave rise to another source of profit to the astute entrepreneur who could buy his materials on more favourable credit terms than those on which he sold the product which he made.

In what has so far been said, the distinction has been made throughout between the two main branches of the industry and, where appropriate, attention has been drawn to the superimposition upon each branch of other divisions. Inevitably these differences were also reflected in the nature, timing and pace of technological change.

In general, the woollen industry was slower than worsted to achieve the complete transformation from domestically organised production using handicraft methods.[21] The worsted industry had completely mechanised the spinning process by about 1820. Handloom worsted weaving was virtually extinct by the late 1850s, the full mechanical reproduction of the fancy weaver's art having been achieved with the introduction of the multiple-box loom and Jacquard looms in the early 1830s. There had, in fact, been little left a decade earlier and all that had remained in the 1850s were small pockets of worsted handloom weavers clinging in poverty and obstinacy to their vanishing occupation.[22] Whereas, however, the decline of worsted handloom weaving had been relatively gradual,[23] the replacement of hand combing by machine had been swift. Lister, with the mechanical aid of Donnisthorpe, had solved the vexatious problem of achieving a successful combing machine in 1845. Within six years the number of hand combers in Bradford had fallen from 10,000 to 5,600 and by 1857 they were extinct as an industrial class (James, 1857, p. 548). Full mechanisation of the worsted industry can, therefore, be said to have been completed by the mid-1850s and it was this which accounted for the most palpably changed characteristic of the entrepreneur in that industry. With the exception of spinning, the typical worsted entrepreneur at the end of the Napoleonic Wars had been much the same as ever, an organiser of domestic textile production taking place in the scattered cottages and small workshops of the West Riding pennines.[24] Forty years later all this had vanished, the handlooms were silent and the formidable steel-toothed handcomb was fast becoming a curiosity which would survive only in firms' waiting rooms or in museums. Production now, was not only completely mechanised but it was centralised in factories, some of which were already impressive in their size; none more so than at Saltaire.[25] Titus Salt's mill was, however, exceptional. The national average size of worsted factory housed 160 employees in 1850 and 169 in 1856.[26] The later stages of mechanisation had been accompanied by a sharp increase in the average size of factory. This had been 76 employees in 1838 rising to 160 in 1850.[27] Thereafter, the average size fluctuated somewhat above the level reached at mid-century.[28] This increase in average factory size between 1838 and 1850, points to the period as being one in which the industry's needs for capital investment rose sharply.[29] In any case, there was a marked distinction between the capital needs of the erstwhile 'domestic' manufacturer and the new factory master. The former had financed circulating capital in the form of stocks of goods in course of manufacture, raw materials and completed products awaiting sale. The interval between outlay in stocks and receipts from the sales obviously varied between the entrepreneur who organised all the successive stages in production and the specialist comber, spinner or weaver.[30]

These differences in time intervals still applied but now, of course, the producer, whatever the degree to which he specialised, was involved in investment in fixed capital. The difficulties of establishing a ratio between the amounts required for investment in circulating and fixed capital respectively between 1770 and 1835 (D. T. Jenkins, 1975, pp. 188–9) remain as insuperable in the succeeding period. All that one can do is to re-iterate the obvious point that fixed-capital investment for worsted manufacturers increased as the industry turned increasingly to factory organisation, and that this increase must have been especially marked during the late 1830s and the 1840s, though falling with differing emphases upon different types of producer.

The woollen industry mechanised more gradually, even in those processes such as spinning and weaving where the adaption of machines introduced into other branches of textile manufacture might seem to have offered an easy mechanical solution. There were, in all, thirty-four separate processes listed by Baines as being performed at Benjamin Gott's Woollen Mill in Leeds in 1858 to transform raw wool into finally finished cloth, so that the mechanical ingenuity required successfully to imitate hand skills was wide ranging with 'proportionate difficulty in effecting improvement' (Baines, 1875, p. 665). The breadth of expertise which was required of the woollen manufacture was much wider than that of the specialised worsted producer. It is impossible to cover comprehensively the course of change in all these processes. Of the most apparent, handloom weaving was slow to be replaced by the power loom. Baines was still writing in 1870 that 'the hand loom has long been giving way to the power loom and the process is now well nigh complete . . . the old domestic manufacture which characterized the woollen more than most other trades, is not far from its end' (Baines, 1875, p. 110). There were, to be sure small surviving strongholds of handloom weaving as at Farsley[31] and Calverly near Leeds and in the Huddersfield fancy woollen trade, but after 1870 they were quite exceptional and accounted for a mere 'fraction of output, even of those types of cloth which had proved least amenable to mechanical weaving. The important[32] machine condenser which pieced together the slivers of carded wool preparatory to spinning, had appeared first in the Scottish border woollen industry, in imitation of American example, but had made little impact elsewhere before 1850. Its more general use came in the 1850s and 1860s (Baines, 1875, p. 665), probably after 1858, when

Baines referred to the condenser as a 'new machine'. It bridged the mechanical gap between the carding machine and spinning on the mule, which Roberts had made fully automatic with two patented inventions in 1825 and 1830. In backward areas of the west of England however mule spinning was still done by hand and had only begun to replace jenny spinning in 1828 (Clapham, 1907, p. 144). Even in the West Riding the introduction of the self-acting mule was relatively slow if the implications of Baines's remarks in 1870 are true that 'self-acting mules have become common: and as existing mules require replacing, self-acting mules will soon become universal' (Baines, 1875, p. 110).

There thus appears to have been about a twenty-year difference between the full mechanisation of the worsted and woollen branches of the industry. Not only did the much smaller average size of the woollen factory make smaller demands upon capital investment, but the slower pace of mechanisation imposed such demands more gradually and placed the two industries in different positions with regard to capital supplies.[33]

For both, however, there was one important process in which, by 1875, no significant progress seems to have occurred. The dyeing of wool textile fabrics in Britain remained wholly an art and still showed few signs of applied science. Lecturing on wool dyeing in 1876, Jarmain regretted that woollen manufacturers

'should have so long submitted to have such a very important branch of their manufacturers carried out by men who, for the most part, work by purely rule of thumb processes . . . The dyer has, in fact, received so many helps from the hands of the chemist that it is difficult to understand why he does not more frequently endeavour to make himself acquainted with the principles of the science . . . were his practice and observation combined with correct scientific knowledge, the British working dyer need fear no rival which any country could produce.'

Though noting some use of aniline dyes developed since Perkin had discovered them in 1856, his account of the properties of the dyestuffs in use in the wool textile industry is still overwhelmingly concerned with the traditional and sometimes bizarre natural products, the supply of some of which must have been extraordinarily inelastic such as that 'found on the surface of the small twigs of trees of the genus *Ficus* on the banks of the Ganges, being deposited there by a small insect called *Coccus lacca*' (Jarmain, 1876, p. 53).

The timing of the use of aniline dyestuffs in a Leeds dyehouse was recalled by Waddington in 1953:

'There are still dyers who remember and often used the old methods of producing dyes from wood, woad, weld, herbs, plants and other vegetable sources . . . These were used by Brayshays and for many years by Waddingtons after taking over their business in 1869 and even later when . . . although Perkin's discovery was made in 1856, many years elapsed before any aniline dyes were being made on a commercial basis to sell to the dyers. There were none being sold in Brayshay's time and only few in the 1890s during the Waddington regime, but the climax was reached in 1897 when the Germans marketed in England a substitute for indigo.'[34]

It was not, of course, simply the slowness to introduce aniline dyes, for which there were several reasons connected with the inadequate provision of scientific and technical education, but the 'rule of thumb' methods of British wool textile (and doubtless other) dyers which were the subject of complaint, as indeed the relatively unsatisfactory results of wool textile dyers had been at least since the Great Exhibition.[35]

Some of the differences between woollen and worsted manufacturers relating to capital-investment requirements have already been noted. It is, in general, a topic which still requires a great deal of investigation. An important difference, however, had its roots in the pre-factory organisation of the two industries. The domestic worsted producer had generally operated on a larger scale than his counterpart in the woollen industry, so that the two were in different positions when the need arose to mechanise production. The difference is nowhere better illustrated than in the emergence in the West Riding woollen industry of the 'company mill' organisation, whereby individual manufacturers possessing insufficient capital to invest in building their own power-driven mills, joined together locally to subscribe shares in order to build mills in which they could avail themselves of the benefits of mechanisation for the processes affected without themselves becoming mill owners.[36] It was a device suited to the essentially small producer which, by enabling him to run with the hounds who were building woollen factories, prolonged his life well into the third quarter of the nineteenth century. It had no counterpart in the emerging organisation of the mechanised worsted industry. Here – though the same was also true in woollen manufacturing – the small man with Smilesian aspirations to become great, could begin the upward ascent by renting 'room and power' in a mill, in the hope that success would enable him to accumulate out of his profits at least part of the capital needed in order to become himself a fully fledged mill owner.

Whether large-scale or small-scale, in woollen or in worsted, and in whatever branch of either industry, the wool textile entrepreneur between 1815 and 1875 was subject to high rates of business mortality. The massive turnover of firms after 1875 has been studied elsewhere

(Sigsworth and Blackman in Aldcroft, 1968a), and there is no reason to suppose that it was any the less before this date. Trading risks which, as has been seen, were inherent in the entrepreneur's market situation, both in the supply of his raw materials and the sale of his product, could be diminished a little by privately acquiring information relating to the credit-worthiness of other traders through the services of the West Riding Trade Protection Association founded in 1848 (Heaton, 1932), or even more specifically the Woollen Manufacturers' and Merchants' Association for the Protection of Trade and Commerce formed under the presidency of the Leeds woollen merchant, Darnton Lupton, in 1856.[37] In the end, however, one is forced to conclude that the typical firm in the wool textile industry during this period, as indeed before and since, was not one which has survived down to the present day, let alone a firm combining longevity with the preservation of some, at least, of its archives,[38] but one which perished, usually through bankruptcy.[39] The implications of this for the history of the industry and the interpretation of the records of surviving businesses have yet to be explored fully. At a different level they were well understood by a contemporary commentator on businessman's behaviour in 1875:

'Small expenditure and a good balance to the reserve fund – that was the policy adopted by our fathers year by year and when a flat-time came, they could afford to do less and do it safely. Things are altered now-a-days. Fast living and high expenditure are now the rule. A large proportion of the profits of a concern is absorbed by household or personal expenses . . . The corollary is simple. Trade is dull, profits are small, expenses are heavy, minds uneasy. Possible consequences – forced business, risky credits. A word to the wise is sufficient.' (*Bradford Observer*, 16 December 1875.)

NOTES TO CHAPTER 9

1 See Clapham (1907, p. 136) for a statement of the position about the turn of the century.
2 From Glover (1961–2, p. 13). In the worsted industry the rise in importance of the single-process firm is dealt with by Sigsworth: '. . . from 1856 onwards, whether one takes spindles, power looms, or employment as a standard of judgement, there was a decline in the relative importance of the combined spinning and weaving mill' (1958, pp. 119–23).
3 Jubb (1860, p. 34). See also Thornton & Sons (1960) for the origins of a firm of auctioneers established at the beginning of the Dewsbury sales.
4 Heaton (1915) is still the best account of the white-cloth area and trade. The similarly organised Leeds Coloured Cloth Hall was the Infirmary Street.
5 The timing and extent of the decline has been a matter for dispute. See Clapham (1910, pp. 195–210); Lloyd-Pritchard (1950); Edwards (1963); Wilson, in Harte and Ponting (1973, pp. 225–46).

6 In 1850 according to the Factory Inspectors' Returns, 86 per cent of worsted spindles and 94 per cent of worsted powerlooms were located in an area bound roughly by Halifax, Keighley, Otley and Leeds (*PP*, 1850, vol. XLII, p. 460). On the other hand, the 1851 Census recorded only 40 per cent of persons employed in woollen production as living in the West Riding (*Census of 1851, Ages and Occupations*). Factory Returns are not a reliable guide to the distribution of woollen manufacturing since a large proportion of woollen production (unlike worsted) was still outside the factories.

7 Clapham (1907, p. 207). See also Hirst (1942). Of the employees of this firm of 'fancy' woollen manufacturers it was written 'there are many families living near the mills of which members for several generations have all been employed by the firm' (p. 23).

8 Sigsworth (1958, pp. xi–xii). The clock over the main gateway to Black Dyke Mills was presented to the firm by its workers ten days after the Chartist meeting on Kennington Common in April 1848 'in gratitude for the Regular Employment their business talents have procured for all employed at Black Dyke Mills of late years and particularly during the Panic of 1847'.

9 For the influence of mourning upon another branch of the textile industries see Coleman (1969).

10 Clapham (1907, p. 117). For woollens, the national average is, of course, reduced by the inclusion of very small units in Wales and Scotland, but even for the West Riding it was still only 74.

11 And to a less extent in the Huddersfield 'fancy' trades in men's fabrics.

12 It is difficult to assemble data relating the cost of wool used to the price of cloth, given the enormous varieties of cloth produced at any one time and changes over time in the proportions of manufacturing costs attributable to different items, as the uses of machinery changes the importance of labour costs. Above all, of course, such information has only survived fragmentarily. Miss Mann's observations for the west of England trade shows that in the early nineteenth century, wool, which had accounted for 47 per cent of the costs of producing cloth in 1786 had risen to 65 per cent by 1859. As she writes, 'After the introduction of machinery, the relation of the different factors in production altered. Wool grew more expensive in proportion, labour less' (Mann, 1971, pp. 320–1). In the worsted industry, raw-material costs accounted for between 43 and 56 per cent of the costs of producing alpaca and mohair cloth by handloom in the early 1840s. Powerlooms cut the cost of weaving by about half and increased the proportionate importance of raw-material costs accordingly (Sigsworth, 1958, pp. 241–3).

13 Except when stocks had been held on speculation against an anticipated rise in wool prices, giving a temporary margin above the season's clip.

14 I can find no mention of either raw material in Miss Mann's authoritative account of the west of England cloth industry between 1640 and 1880. According to Ponting, 'As far as the low woollen manufacture is concerned [the use of shoddy and mungo] several firms in the West did try but their hearts were never in the business' (Jenkins, 1969, p. 242; 1971, p. 123).

15 The Association was, in fact, the child of the Bradford Chamber of Commerce (*Bradford Chamber of Commerce Minute Books*, 1859).

16 Baines (1875, p. 107). The price of Lincoln half-hogg wool reached 27¾d per lb in 1864. Its highest previous recorded price was 22d in 1815 and 1818 (Mitchell and Deane, 1971, pp. 495–6). The price in 1864 was in fact the highest paid during the entire period 1814–1938.

17 Baines (1875, pp. 73–4, 108). In the former he is writing of the high price of wool as retarding 'the advance of the woollen manufacture'. In the latter, he notes that in raw-material supplies, 'our woollen manufacture possesses in our colonies a power of production which seems to have no limit'.

18 Clapham (1952, p. 217) appears to date the linking of Australia via India at about 1870.

19 'Sell and Repent' is the caption of a cartoon still evident in the offices of wool textile concerns.

20 See especially Topham (1953), which is, however, mainly concerned with the worsted industry.

21 With the important exception of cloth-fulling which had been a water-powered process for centuries.

22 See, for example Baker (1858, p. 437) where worsted handloom weavers were still engaging 'in a competition with the power loom which seems all but futile'.

23 It took about twenty-five to thirty years.

24 See Sigsworth (1951-2), for examples of this form of organisation.

25 See Holroyd (1871) for a contemporary view of this manufacturing village.

26 For the West Riding the figures were 170 and 177.

27 For the West Riding the figures were 84 and 170.

28 The figures are:

	1850	1856	1861	1868	1870
England	160	169	162	187	175
West Riding	170	177	172	193	–

Though exceeded in average size by the factories in the flax and jute industries in 1870-1, the worsted factory was almost the same as the cotton factory (Clapham, 1952, p. 117).

29 As such it unfortunately falls outside the period covered by D. T. Jenkins (1975).

30 The commission working comber or spinner, of course, was even less involved in investment in circulating capital.

31 Mrs P. Gaunt of Harrogate can recall handloom weavers still at work here in the early 1890s.

32 Rated as of almost equal importance with the spinning jenny (Clapham, 1952, p. 12).

33 See Pankhurst (1955) for a general discussion based upon surviving business records. The sharply increased size of worsted factories between 1838 and 1850 was unmatched in the woollen industry. Over the whole period 1838 to 1871, the average number of persons employed in woollen factories rose from 46 to 70 (Clapham, 1907, p. 117). Between 1838 and 1856, the *percentage* increases in various measures of size of factories was as follows:

	Woollen	Worsted
Employees	44	177
Horsepower	25	108
Powerlooms	572	1,212

34 Waddington (1953, pp. 9-10). This little-known business history deserves wider circulation.

35 See, for example, Forbes (1853). Forbes, mayor of Bradford, 1849-50, was particularly concerned with the Bradford worsted trade. The same critical comments relating to dyeing were still being made about Bradford worsteds following the exhibition of 1862 (*Bradford Observer*, 18 September 1863). For the woollen industry, see Bousfield (1878) surveying progress since 1851.

36 The West Riding Company mill received attention from the Select Committee on Joint Stock Companies (*PP*, 1844, vol. VII, p. 348; see also Clapham, 1952, pp. 194-6). For recent studies of the evolution of individual mills, see Goodchild (1968) and Sharpe (1968, pp. 14-18) dealing with Gillroyd Mills. See also D. T. Jenkins (1975, pp. 200-1).

37 See 'Rules and Regulations of the Woollen Manufacturers' and Merchants' Association for the Protection of Trade and Commerce' (30 June, 1856), in Leeds Reference Library.

38 For a comprehensive account of such surviving achives, see Hudson (1975).
39 Thus, between 1873 and 1881, admittedly a trying period for businessmen, 2,362 bankruptcies and liquidations of all types were filed in Bradford court (*Bradford Observer*, 31 December 1883).

10   The Shoe and Leather Industries

by R. A. Church

I

At the beginning of the nineteenth century, the manufacture of leather and leather goods constituted, by value, the second or third largest manufacturing industry in Britain, with an output valued at between £10·5 million and £12 million. In 1837, McCulloch ranked leather still below only cotton, wool and possibly iron, but the rapid growth of other industries during the third quarter of the century began to reduce the relative importance of the leather industry (D. Macpherson, 1805, p. 15; McCulloch, 1837, p. 118). Even in 1881 one knowledgeable tanner reckoned that leather manufacturing was 'fifth in importance among the trades of this Kingdom' (Rimmer, 1960, p. 119). Perhaps the industry's relative decline explains why historians have neglected its history, for not until the second half of the century did technical and organisational developments bring about a transformation in any way comparable with the Industrial Revolution as it affected other major British industries. None the less, the preceding decades witnessed growth and some development in response to changes in the size and character of the market for final products, as well as to pressures which stimulated the search for cost-reducing innovations.

A division of the leather trades into leather and leather goods manufacture is complemented by further differentiation on the basis of both products and of raw material. The thicker and heavier the leather required, the lengthier is the tanning process of manufacture, while at the opposite extreme the lightest leathers, often made from sheep or goat skins, were treated with oil or alum, 'tawed' rather than tanned. In between these two extremes existed a wide range of possibilities, depending upon the uses to which the leather was to be put. The main items requiring heavy leathers were the soles of boots and shoes, harness and saddlery, and industrial belting, while light leather made of calf, sheep, goat, and occasionally more exotic skins was employed in the manufacture of shoe uppers, shoe linings, gloves, upholstery, light luggage, roller leather, clothing and novelties. The two branches were distinct and their progress was not necessarily interdependent (Church, 1971, p. 544). Throughout the century, boot and shoemakers and the makers of saddlery and harness provided the major demand for leather. Contemporary estimates for the second and third quarters of the century suggest that between 50 and 70 per cent of the total value of leather output was used in the manufacture of boots and shoes (McCulloch, 1837, p. 703; Poole, 1852, p. 35). The demand for leather was a derived demand, the character and chronology of which depended upon the course of development in the finished goods branches of the industry, but the speed of and manner in which leather manufacturers responded was also determined by the peculiarities of leather manufacture.

The manufacture of leather can be divided roughly into three stages. First, beamhouse work, where the hides and skins were sorted, washed, soaked, depilated and fleshed. Second, tanning, in which the animal pelts were treated so as to become imputrescible and water-resistant. Third, currying, or dressing and finishing, to impart character and appearance. The purpose of currying is to render leather intended for such purposes as harness, belting and certain kinds of footwear uppers flexible and waterproof, by first smoothing the surface and then working in a mixture of cod oil and tallow called 'dubbin'. Finishing includes colouring, providing the surface with a grain pattern, and in other ways making it suitable for its purpose. Raising productivity in the first process meant improving the handling and removal of hides and skins and the reduction in the time it took to dehair and prepare the hides for tanning. The second stage likewise depended much upon the time taken by the tanning liquors to work, and improved handling was again important. The third stage was very much a craft and least likely to benefit from technical improvements.

The reasons why mechanisation proceeded relatively late and slowly include the uneven substance and irregularities of hides and leather which demanded versatile and, therefore, fairly complex machinery, yet to be devised. At the beginning of the nineteenth century, tanning methods had remained fundamentally unaltered since ancient times, the removal of hair and flesh from the hides and the conversion of pelts into leather commonly taking longer than twelve months for the heaviest kinds of leather (Dodd, 1843, pp. 166–84). This was because the only known techniques relied on immersion in water, natural rates of fermentation and lime for dehairing, and vegetable tanning agents, principally oak bark. The search for rapid tanning methods, which can be traced back into the eighteenth century (Clarkson, 1974), met with some success after the Napoleonic Wars. Imported barks with high tannin content, notably valonia, sumach and divi-divi, were partially substituted for increasingly scarce and expensive oak bark which in 1816 had contributed between 25 and 35 per cent of current production costs (Church, 1971, p. 550).

Indeed, a reduced tanning time was an objective included in many of the attempts to improve tanning methods in the early nineteenth century, as rapidly rising bark prices (Clarkson, 1974, pp. 142–3) stimulated experimentation with alternative vegetable materials possessing higher tannin contents and with heating tanning liquors to achieve faster action. By 1850 perhaps 25 or 30 per cent of light leather was tanned with extracts other than oak bark, mainly with sumach, valonia, gambier catechu and other imported plants (Clarkson). Hides accounted for between 35 and 45 per cent of total costs, which helps to explain why in the period of rapidly rising hide prices during the Napoleonic Wars some tanners devoted effort not only to accelerating the tanning process but also to economising on hide inputs. The introduction of machinery to split hides and skins into more than a single thickness reflected this concern, and Bevington's patent of 1806 was designed to hasten and achieve greater control over the cumbersome and time-consuming splitting process at a time when hide prices were rising rapidly under pressure of demand from the army and navy.

After the war, splitting machinery stimulated less interest, as hide prices fell and with it the strong incentive to economise. None the less, by 1851 the jury of the Great Exhibition remarked on the progress towards mechanisation in leather manufacture, notably the 'most important results' arising 'from the invention of very ingenious machinery for splitting hides and skins' (Clarkson, unpublished). Patents for splitting machinery were taken out in 1828, 1841 and 1845, but during the early nineteenth century successful innovation in leather manufacture was almost exclusively attributable to Bevington's, the large Bermondsey tanning firm specialising in the production of light leathers from hides and skins (Hartridge, 1955, pp. 49–50). Bevington's was also responsible for mechanising the tawing process in alum-tawed leather made from sheep skin, sometime before 1830, employing a hydraulic press to squeeze tallow out of the skins before tawing. By the 1840s this firm was also using fulling stocks, or 'drivers', to turn and beat the skins in order to accelerate oil penetration.

It was not until the 1840s, however, that such innovations were being taken up by more than a handful of the larger tanners, and only then was steam power beginning to be applied, even by the large tanners, to splitting machinery (Hartridge, 1955, p. 58). By 1870 the large leading tanners in London and Leeds employed steam pumps for transferring tanning liquor from one pit or vat to another, splitting machinery for shaving hides to the desired thickness, eliminating waste and producing several 'splits' for use in making light luggage and upholstery, fulling stocks for softening hides, rollers for imparting firmness to leather, and rotating barrels for grinding and mixing

202   *The Dynamics of Victorian Business*

tanning extract. By 1870 the use of tannage extracts applied in covered vats had reduced the time taken in tanning from between twelve and eighteen to about four months, though heavy leather tanning in Britain was hardly affected until the introduction of quebracho and chestnut extracts towards the end of the century. More rapid tanning transformed the cost structure of leather production, and by facilitating fuller utilisation of plant and equipment tanners were enabled to increase the rate of turnover and thus protect the rate of return on capital. Hitherto, a considerable proportion of a tanner's resources was tied up in the form of work in progress through the pits, and this rather than the size of initial investment outlay explains why contemporaries considered the trade to be capital-intensive. It may also explain the predominance, until the middle of the nineteenth century, of the wealthy, old-established London tanners (Church, 1971, p. 550).

The industry's structure in 1870 differed in some respects from that existing half a century earlier, for while the general picture is still one of an industry consisting for the most part of many small and almost ubiquitous units, owned or rented by family firms or partnerships and worked by a handful of people, trends were already discernible which, in the fifty years before 1914, were to become the main features of development. By the middle decades of the century a handful of leather manufacturers in Leeds were each employing more than a hundred workers in this newly developing centre of the light leather branch, and London, too, possessed a few large firms (Rimmer, 1960, pp. 142–4; Hartridge, 1955, p. 23). None the less, even in tanning and currying, which possessed the largest production units throughout the entire leather trades, the average size of the unit, in terms of numbers employed, was less than twenty in 1871, the many small tanneries and curriers' shops each employing no more than a handful of people in businesses conducted, with few exceptions, along traditional lines.

Rimmer has explained the predominance of small-scale units in terms of variety of product and the limited extent of the market. Size of market is undoubtedly important, but the significance of the variety of product can be exaggerated. Apart from the broad division between heavy and light leathers in this period before mechanisation, leather, as distinct from leather goods, was a reasonably homogeneous product and the heterogeneity which did exist where one piece of leather differed from another was unavoidably due to the differences between hides and the difficulties of exercising control over a process which depended so much upon 'natural' elements, such as putrefaction. In any case, a single tannery could, and the largest did, comprise several pits each producing leather differing in quality, in so far as was possible, as required. It was on this basis that the large firms of the mid-century had grown up, manufacturing a wide range of leathers. More important in explaining the predominance of small units is the orientation of tanning to raw materials, particularly to hides and oak bark. For a fairly ubiquitous, though dwindling, supply of oak bark had perpetuated the scattered location of small units outside the main centres, which in turn must have retarded the introduction of such machinery as was applicable to the manufacture of leather down to the third quarter of the nineteenth century (Church, 1971, p. 548).

During the early years of the century, legislation appears to have hampered the growth of larger firms, and with the possible additional effect of inhibiting improvements in organisation and technical progress. We have observed that the larger leather manufacturers were principally responsible for leading the industry by inventing, or introducing, machinery for splitting, rolling and handling hides and skins, and by experimenting with improved tannages. Size, therefore, seems to have been an important influence upon innovation, yet for various reasons growth had been unlikely to occur as a result of integration hitherto, except in the light leather craft industries. In the latter branches, glovemaking and leatherdressing were simple operations and well suited to a putting-out system, whereas the heavy leather crafts were occupations requiring skills of a different kind and not readily combined (Clarkson, 1960, pp. 252–3). In 1816, however, some contemporaries suggested other reasons why integration between tanning and currying had not taken place, and to the detriment of the industry. Vertical integration of tanning with currying had been prevented by statute law since 1603, for the purpose of facilitating the collection of excise. By the nineteenth century, separation was no longer complete, for whereas most tanners remained independent, passing on tanned leather to the curriers for dressing and finishing, many curriers dressed leather which was actually owned by merchants, shoemakers and other users, becoming subcontractors (Hartridge, 1955, pp. 22, 63–4). The practice adopted by Walter Wearmouth, a dealer in leather who purchased from tanners directly and sent it to be worked upon by curriers, demonstrates the existence of two sets of intermediaries between tanner and currier. The degree of vertical integration in the 1820s was low, for on the occasion when curriers set up as tanners by deputy, 'so as to carry on the two trades, though not jointly', the possibility of legal proceedings was real and could be effective. Despite such a threat, however, some curriers had ventured into tanning by various discreet arrangements in order to conceal the true ownership (Hartridge, 1955, p. 67).

In 1826 London tanner Francis Brewin, a perpetual experimenter, drew attention to the ways in which the legislation impeded the development of leather manufacture, both by lengthening the period taken due to the roundabout system of making finished leather and by the employment of unnecessary labour and materials involved in transport and handling. He also maintained that such arrangements tended to deter improvements. Sympathetic to this general view, another London tanner, Robert Wearmouth, offered a slightly more analytical explanation for the apparent reluctance of tanners to improve production methods. As leather was taxed and sold by weight, tanners lacked the incentive to remove superfluous matter from hides before tanning. Had he been a currier as well as a tanner, he reckoned he would cut off those parts which cost so much in tax and duty in order to reduce the cost of manufacture by reducing the inputs needed in the tannage process (Hartridge, 1955, p. 70). Witnesses differed in their opinions as to how far the regulations actually prevented integration, but some time after integration became legal in 1830 Wearmouth combined with Roberts to carry on both tanning and leather dressing, with dyeing and finishing departments integrated within the factory. Hepburn's, too, was an integrated enterprise before the mid-century, as was Bevington's (p. 71). These were the leaders of the industry throughout the period during which the good years might bring a rate of return estimated by one contemporary at between 13 and 20 per cent (Burridge, 1824, p. 41), though in 1874 another knowledgeable observer writing in the *Leather Trades Review* reckoned that the wealthy, old-established tanners had received a steady 5 or 6 per cent on capital (Church, 1971, p. 550).

The dominance of the London leather manufacturers was diminished from the second quarter of the century as other centres began to develop. By 1871 the Census figures showed London to have employed 33 per cent of the total numbers employed in the establishments of curriers, leather dressers and dealers in England and Wales, and 16 per cent of those employed by tanners and fellmongers. These figures compared with 17 per cent and 18 per cent for Yorkshire (mainly Leeds), and 7 and 13 per cent for the north-western counties (mainly Liverpool and Warrington). This trend was to strengthen even further after 1871, as the tanning of heavy leather concentrated increasingly in the northern locations (Church, 1971, pp. 546–7).

London continued to dominate the fancy branch of the leather trade while three of the largest leading firms, Bevington's, Hepburn's and Barrow's, each pursued expansionist policies in the middle decades of the century. The factors which explain the relative decline of London as a tanning centre from about 1870 would seem to have had little to do with lack of entrepreneurial vigour, for those tanners who removed their base of operations from the south to one of the 'new' areas were, it seems, responding to circumstances which were altering the economics of tanning. Already in the 1850s, two of the leading London leather merchants had opened branches in Liverpool, the centre of a region which by 1914 was to become first in heavy leather tanning. This was the result of two related developments. One was the growth in the demand for leather, and the necessity to import more and more hides from South America; the second was the port charge differential that existed between Liverpool and London. Bristol tanners, who had hitherto imported hides through the Port of London, claimed to have saved nearly 1 per cent in brokerage and wharf dues by switching to Liverpool, and other tanners also complained of the inferior discount terms offered by the London merchants. In the 1860s, cash purchases of leather would merit a discount equal to two months' interest, whereas merchants in Liverpool offered 2·5 per cent discount of credit for four months. The growth in hide imports and the added significance because of this of transport, handling and credit terms, were factors helping to stimulate relocation of activity, but the drift away from London was intensified by the rise in other components of tanners' production costs. One was rent: tanning, especially of heavy leathers, required considerable space for vats, drying rooms and storage. Another was the cost of transporting oak bark: most sole-leather tanners continued to employ traditional methods throughout the century (Church, 1971, p. 559). Finally, the need for huge volumes of water in the tanning process grew so rapidly during the later decades of the century that serious pressures were imposed on London's water supplies for industrial purposes (Statham, p. 135).

The principal determinant of alternative areas for expansion, however, was the immense growth in imported hides, for they under-line the importance of locating tanneries in, or within easy access to, a port. Second in importance to this was the location of tanneries in areas where, as in London, a large meat-consuming population was accompanied by a concentration of butchers and hide factors. Pro-bably of equal importance was the availability of oak bark. Even in the last quarter of the century advertisements for the sale of tanneries point to those factors which tanners themselves considered to be important for location: ready availability of water, raw materials and good communications. For these reasons – as well as the existence of a relatively large market for leather from the growing population – Leeds began to develop as a leather centre before the large-scale import of hides (and later tanning extract) became a feature of the trade. Then the situation of Leeds as an inland port at the terminal of the Liverpool Canal and the Aire Navigation strengthened its position in competition with London (Rimmer, 1960, pp. 126–31). The rise of the Lancashire industry can be similarly explained. The Merseyside towns, where tanning developed from the early nineteenth century, experienced the stimulating effect of population growth, expanding hide supplies, oak bark from the forests south of the Mersey, and unrivalled water or rail access to the port of Liverpool and to Manchester. The foundations of one of the large Warrington tanning firms was laid in the 1830s by the Reynolds brothers who migrated from the south, as did the Smyths and the Gales, who came from the west country. This relocation of the industry was, as we have seen, partly due to various economic factors operating to the disadvantage of London as a tanning centre, but it was accelerated by the external pressures resulting from the reduction in transport costs and the emergence of serious foreign competition (Church, 1971, p. 552).

The enterprise shown by the owners of these northern firms enabled them to consolidate the regions' position by the growth of the large tanneries built up mainly during the second and third quarters of the century: by Wilson & Walker, by Conyers, by the Kitchen family, by Jackson, and by the Nichols family whose Joppa Tannery at Leeds was the most renowned in the 1850s and 1860s, the period when these firms reached their maximum size after a generation of investment and expansion (Rimmer, 1960, pp. 143–5). 'All utilized whatever machines became available. All operated on a scale larger than more technical considerations dictated, and included currying amongst their processes. Nearly all encountered difficulties when the first generation handed over to its successors' (Rimmer, 1960, p. 145). One of the keys to survival was the command of adequate financial resources to finance investment associated with the installation of pumps, presses, mills, cranes, handling equipment and splitting machinery, the laying out of extensive modern tanyards with high throughput and to bridge the tanning period. By such methods the enterprising tanners speeded turnover and spread overheads; they also economised on the major cost element by reducing waste and by splitting hides and skins, the stimulus for which in the 1850s and early 1860s, as in the Napoleonic War period, was the rapid rise in hide prices, unmatched by a compensating increase in the price of leather (Church, 1975, p. 15).

Except in handling materials the urge to economise labour by mechanisation seems to have been a relatively minor force for progress in the industry. Even in the USA, in contrast with their counterparts in other industries, leather manufacturers showed little interest in substituting machinery for manual labour until the 1860s, but at the Centennial Exhibition in Chicago in 1876, it was clear that the Americans led in the mechanisation of leather production. Not until the last quarter of the century, however, was the technical lag between the two countries to cause concern among British manufacturers, for until then the high bulk and low value of leather, with a resulting high incidence of unit transport costs, effectively impeded imports of leather (Chuch, 1971, p. 545). Furthermore, the simple methods of leather manufacturing generally employed until that period offered minimal scope for manufacturers in one leather-producing country to develop an industry with comparative costs low enough to be able to cover transport and handling costs, and still earn a satisfactory rate of return. Thus, before 1870 the existence of a demand for special kinds of light leather for high-quality uppers and fancy goods explains the predominance of French and German imports, for imported leather was small in volume and complementary to, rather than competitive with, leather produced by British manufacturers (Church, 1971, p. 552).

II

Much the same can be said in comparing the British with European manufacturers of leather goods in 1870, although annual average exports in this category, but mainly boots and shoes, increased in volume and doubled in value in the 1850s compared with the 1840s, and doubled again in the 1860s, when the average was round about £2 million per annum. The main stimulus for the growth of the leather footwear industry, and in turn the derived expansion of leather manufacturing, continued to be the home market. If we may assume a low price and income elasticity for boots and shoes during a period when fashion changes tended to be uncharacteristic of the market for items of basic apparel, the rise in population may be regarded as the most important single determinant of the demand for leather footwear, and consequently for leather.

By the beginning of the century the production of ready-made footwear had developed outside London, hitherto the major centre for the wholesale manufacture of boots and shoes. Northampton, Stafford, and a handful of Northamptonshire villages became subcontracting outposts of the London trade, but the pressure of war-time demand brought about a rapid expansion and greater independence of these new provincial centres of production (Church, 1966, p. 144; 1970, pp. 26–7). Improvements in communuications and greater urbanisation explain the growth of certain centres where boot and shoe production became localised, as an expanding market encouraged specialisation of function and by region, and by the mid-nineteenth century Leicester, Leeds and Street had joined London, the Northamptonshire towns and villages, and Norwich as the important wholesale producers of ready-made footwear (Church, 1970, p. 28). Between the French and Crimean Wars, Northamptonshire manufacturers were able to expand output without difficulty by recruiting from an abundant labour supply released from the county's declining craft industries, in particular silk, woollens and lace. The movement of shoemakers from London in the early years also helped to relieve any serious shortage of skilled shoemakers. Even from the beginning of the century, manufacturers in Northampton and in the larger villages met a growth in demand by putting out work further afield to people in

other villages whose expansion, especially from the 1850s, is attributable to this process of rural colonisation in the lower wage areas,
which enabled manufacturers to secure orders from the public contractors committed to a policy of accepting the lowest tender for
certain types of footwear.

Rural industrial expansion was possible because throughout the
period the wholesale production of footwear was based entirely on
hand methods, and such central supervision as existed was to be
found only at the cutting-out stage, for 'clicking' determined the basic
shape of the shoe. 'Clickers' and the 'rough-stuff' men who cut out the
bottom leather, were the only classes of workers to be employed on
the warehouse premises of a manufacturer. Except in the clicking
process and in the production of the highest quality footwear, the
skills of the ready-made shoemaker were not difficult to learn, though
skilled makers-up usually served a full apprenticeship. It is not surprising, therefore, that the rise of wholesale manufacturing was not
accompanied by the appearance of typically large units of production.
Of the 17,665 master manufacturers making Returns in 1851, 6 per
cent employed more than 10 men while only 31 employed more than
100, though each probably gave out work to as many women and
children in addition (Clapham, 1932, p. 35). Given abundant labour
and the need for only a small minority of skilled shoemakers the
reason why few technical improvements affected the industry before
1840 seems to be self-evident, but it is significant that the first step
towards the application of machinery to footwear production was
taken on the initiative of Thomas Crick, a shoe repairer who remade
shoes for sale from his home in Leicester, hitherto a major centre
of the hosiery trade, but by the 1830s in decline. In the 1830s Crick
revived a method of attaching sole to upper by using French rivets,
a method first invented by a London manufacturer to mass produce
army boots during the Napoleonic Wars, but long since forgotten
(Mounfield, 1966, p. 10). Offering a speedier and cheaper rate of
production, despite its dependence still on manual operation, riveting
made it possible to substitute unskilled for the skilled labour necessary
in making hand-sewn welted footwear. Its advantages are obvious, for
an aspiring manufacturer located in a district where the potential
labour force was totally unfamiliar with shoemaking and which
lacked a tradition and reputation for making and selling boots and
shoes.

Crick's innovation proved to be the progenitor not only of
Leicester's footwear industry, but of others too. For the need for a
machine which could utilise unskilled labour in making boots and
shoes was important if Leicester or Leeds or Bristol was to become a
footwear centre, for these towns lacked an abundant supply of craft
labour. In 1853 the son and cousin of Thomas Crick, who by that time

described himself as a master shoe manufacturer employing more than thirty people, took out a patent for inside riveting and before long a riveting machine which pierced the sole and drove the rivets mechanically established machine riveting as a successful method for manufacturing certain kinds of cheap footwear. This was the basis for the development of the trade of Leeds and Kingswood, near Bristol (Church, 1970, p. 30). A similar stimulus to the more widespread production of cheap, stout footwear in districts not hitherto associated with the production of boots and shoes was the introduction into England in 1847 of a method by which soles were attached to the upper by using wooden pegs, an innovation which affected the growing development of the heavy boot industry in Leeds in the 1850s (Rimmer, 1960, pp. 138–9). The rise of shoemaking in Street was based upon high-quality footwear, as an extension of the Clarks's slipper-manufacturing activities, and the course of the firm's development underlines the pressures which faced manufacturers outside the traditional centres of the industry. The initial success, especially in the early 1850s, necessitated substantial recruitment of labour which the Street employers found 'less tractable' as they cast their net wider throughout the Somerset countryside, and which threatened to jeopardise the Clarks's reputation for high-quality footwear (Sutton, 1959). The introduction of Cricks's riveting method in 1858 helped to solve the problems presented by the demand for heavy boots in Australia, while the substitution of iron for wooden lasts was a step aimed at securing greater standardisation in riveted footwear. That was also, in part, the purpose of introducing machinery for building up heels and attaching to the sole, and why in the same decade the Clarks installed a treadle machine for cutting sole leather and another for stamping soles (Sutton, 1959). Such innovations promoted standardisation, reduced waste, and raised labour productivity, at the same time reducing the potential for labour militancy, and enabling Clarks to introduce a wider range of cheaper 'commoner' footwear.

These innovations occurred after a period between 1851 and 1858 when under the pressure of rising demand raw materials accounted for a rising proportion of the total production costs. As a result, not only had profit margins fallen but net profit also fell. Largely due to inept stocking policy in a period of fluctuating raw-material prices Clarks sustained losses in the early 1860s (Sutton, 1959). The firm's technical policy was beyond criticism, for as well as moving ahead through the introduction of riveting and ancillary machinery, in 1856 Clarks adopted the 'Thomas' closing machine for sewing welted footwear, two years after Crick had introduced it into his Leicester factory and three years before the manufacturers of Northampton and Stafford succeeded in doing so (Sutton, 1959; Head, 1960, p. 136). Away from the major shoemaking towns, in Leicester, Street and

Norwich, where sewing machinery was introduced without difficulty, labour hostility forced the manufacturers of Northampton and Stafford to postpone its introduction until the summer of 1859, after a protracted strike and an exodus of shoemakers from Northampton to Leicester (Church, 1970, p. 36).

Leicester's reputation as a rapidly developing footwear town was almost entirely due to the innovations introduced by Thomas Crick, whose machinery for rolling, cutting and sewing leather were taken up by others, though steam power was only adopted slowly. In 1846 Leicester possessed two footwear manufacturers; by 1870 this figure had risen to 117 (Head, 1960, p. 198). In 1862 he introduced a sole sewer of French design adopting the American Blake sole sewer which would sew 300 stitches per minute, compared with the 10 to 20 stitches of the skilled hand sewer, a few years later. Crick's was possibly the first British firm to experiment with sole-sewing machinery, which in 1864 was housed in a factory driven by steam (Head, 1960, pp. 138–9). Some of his 720 employees, among whom were 420 women and 300 men and boys, were employed as outworkers, but even so, with regard to technical equipment, organisation and size Crick's enterprise was exceptional and perhaps the most advanced firm of footwear manufacturers in the country.

Not until the appearance of the improved American Blake sole sewer in 1867, shortly followed by the rapid welt sewing machine in 1872–3, did steam-power factory production begin to be at all widely adopted (Head, 1960, pp. 29, 139; 1968, p. 163), and most 'factories', so described, in the 1860s were in effect warehouses which contained no steam-powered machinery. One of the most important reasons explaining the tardy adoption of factory organisation is that legislation relating to factories and workshops applied laxer employment regulations to workshops than to factories, with the unintended result that the employment of women and children continued to be possible in workshops, but not in factories. As women and children comprised a major proportion of the industry's labour force, and as sewing machinery was suited to workshop or even home use, the trend towards the concentration of production in factories remained weak. Not until the Education Acts of 1870 and 1876 was the anomaly removed and the employment of young persons significantly reduced and controlled (Head, 1960, pp. 158–9, 287, 291).

Our review of the boot and shoe industry during the second and third quarters of the century reveals that the expansion which occurred was stimulated principally by population growth, urbanisation, trade, and the development of wholesale production. While the technical changes introduced into the trade were not revolutionary in their effects upon industrial organisation and structure they were necessary for those firms who wished to survive in an industry in which high mortality rates were characteristic, though even technical success could not always guarantee commercial viability, as Clarks's bankruptcy in 1862 showed (Sutton, 1959). Labour militancy, rather than finance, provided the major obstacle to rapid innovation in the traditional shoemaking centres. For the impulse to respond to buoyant markets at home and overseas, and simultaneously to escape from the pressure of profit margins due to rising raw-material prices, together with the need to solve the problem of 'green' labour, stimulated invention and innovation outside the major boot and shoemaking districts. In all regions of footwear production, however, abundant labour in these essentially rural areas undoubtedly dampened the incentive even for some of the larger firms to proceed with mechanisation based on steam power and to reorganise production in factories.

11 The Drink Trades

by R. B. Weir

A REVIEW OF SECONDARY SOURCES

In a substantial bibliographical essay on 'Drink and Sobriety in England, 1815–1872', Brian Harrison amassed no fewer than 841 references (1967). Of this impressive total a mere eleven items dealt with the drink industries. By comparison with other aspects of the nineteenth-century drink problem it could well be argued that the drink industries have been afflicted with that curious historical malady known as neglect. The work of recent students of the temperance movement has greatly augmented historical understanding of the extensive social functions performed by drink and drink sellers, but it has scarcely been matched by comparable investigation of drink producers (Harrison, 1967; Lambert, 1975).

This historical imbalance between the social consequences of drink consumption and the changing economics of drink production has survived despite the widespread recognition by economic historians that in early industrial society a high proportion of income was devoted to food and drink expenditure. It raises formidable problems in presenting a re-examination of the course of industrial change in the drink trades, for a re-examination implies the existence of a substantial body of secondary literature to support some general propositions. It will be worth beginning by considering how the different sections of the drink trades fare in this respect.

The drink trades may be defined as including brewing, distilling, cider making, wine and spirit importing, as well as wholesale and retail distribution: a bill of fare sufficient to blunt the most gargantuan appetite. The extent to which these different trades have been subject to historical scrutiny varies considerably.

There has been no major study of the wine trade during the nineteenth century, though Francis (1972) has examined some of its features, mainly from the standpoint of Anglo-Portugese trade, between the end of the Napoleonic Wars and the Gladstonian reforms of the early 1860s. Using G. B. Wilson's estimates of wine consumption (1940, pp. 331–3), it can be seen (Fig. 11.1) that after an initial upsurge

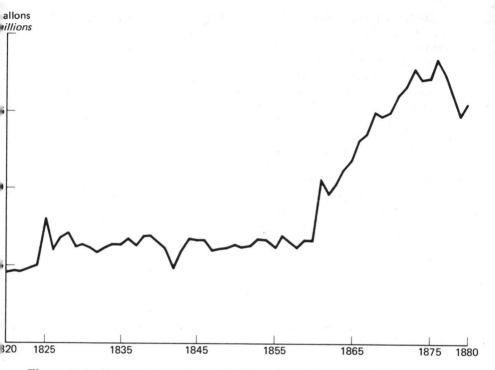

Figure 11.1   *Wine consumption in the United Kingdom, 1820–80*
Source: Wilson 1940, pp. 331–3

in the 1820s, the market stagnated between 6 and 7 million gallons
until 1860. Wine was, as Francis has argued, 'in the last resort a
luxury trade' where merchants aimed at 'limited sales of expensive
wines to the upper classes' (Francis, 1972, pp. 298, 314). Encased in a
complex structure of mercantilist duties – there were five different
rates in 1817 according to the country of origin – real growth only
appeared after 1860 with Gladstone's 'limited but adventurous and
imaginative scheme to open up the wine trade' (Harrison, 1971, p. 248).
This lowered the rate of duty, particularly on light wines, and introduced virtual free trade into wine retailing. Wine consumption rose
from 6·7 million gallons in 1860 to 18·5 in 1876, the peak year for
total and *per capita* consumption in the nineteenth century. The *Wine
Trade Review*, first published in 1863, was sufficiently persuaded by
liberalisation to announce (vol 2, 20 February 1964, p. 8): 'The field
that we take possession of is extensive, and, thanks to the operation of
free-trade principles, is still extending'. By 1886, with a decade of
falling wine consumption behind it, its opinion had altered. 'The
future of the wine trade', it told its readers, 'is whisky'.

If the reforms failed to achieve their weighty social objective of converting the British working class into temperate wine drinkers, it remains true, nevertheless, that they provided a commercial environment in which the more enterprising firms in the wine trade were able to pioneer new methods of marketing wine. Thus Gilbeys, founded in 1857, sought to overcome consumer ignorance of the relative merits of the low-priced wines through advertising and brand names. Their aim was not merely to persuade the consumer that he 'could learn to rely on a Gilbey's label', but also to remove the prejudice that 'cheapness . . . was synonymous with inferiority' (Waugh, 1957). In short, to chip away at the social exclusivity which had hitherto characterised the consumption of wine. Behind their brands lay large bulk purchases made directly from French wine growers so as to exclude the middleman, and by 1872 the firm was financing a chain of licensed grocery shops, 'the first multiple company in this line'. In many respects, particularly the emphasis on brands, the use of advertising, and the direct purchases from the producer, the short-lived expansion of the wine trade foreshadowed the features of the later upsurge in the popularity of Scotch whisky.

Cider making has only recently attracted historical interest with attention concentrated post-1870 due to the greater availability of statistical evidence after that date. Not until the 1880s did cider makers begin to adopt factory methods of production. Before then cider was 'a small-scale farm product, untaxed, and consumed to a substantial extent on the farms themselves' (Minchinton, 1970, p. 60). In other words, a product of local significance only, subordinate to beer even within the five 'cider counties' (Mathias, 1959, p. xxi). With wines and cider accounting for only an estimated 10 per cent and 1 per cent respectively of consumer spending on alcoholic drinks in 1870 (Prest, 1954, p. 85), it can be argued that these gaps in the history of the drink trades are not too important.

By contrast, the dominant products were beer and spirits with an estimated 57 per cent and 32 per cent of the drink market in 1870; even so, the literature on these industries remains far from complete. For the English brewing industry a major gap in secondary sources occurs between 1830, the terminal date of Mathias's major work (Mathias, 1959), and 1886, the starting point for Vaizey's study (Vaizey, 1960). Nor does there seem to be much prospect of the gap being adequately filled in view of the absence of business records for the major breweries of Burton on Trent, from where so much of the impetus for change in the industry came after 1839 (Sigsworth, 1965, p. 545). Business records widen the scope of any investigation but, as Sigsworth has demonstrated with his work on brewing in Yorkshire, other sources such as Excise records, local directories, and the trade press can be utilised to establish the pattern of change at a regional level (Sigsworth, 1967).

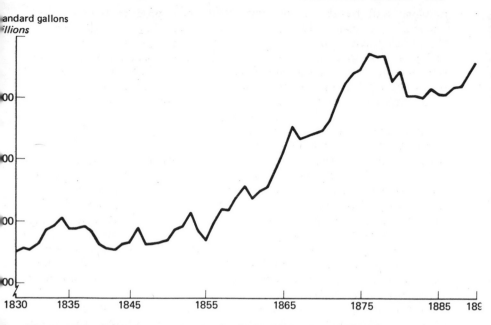

andard gallons
llions

Figure 11.2   *Beer consumption in the United Kingdom, 1820–90*
Source: Wilson 1940, pp. 331–3

So far as other parts of the United Kingdom are concerned, the
history of the Scottish brewing industry is at present being investigated
by Dr Ian Donnachie (1979; see also Donnachie, 1977) whilst, for
Ireland, Lynch and Vaizey have offered an interpretation of the
brewing industry and, much more controversially, of the development of the Irish economy as a whole, from the experience of
Guinness, the dominant firm in the industry (1960).

Certain major interpretative themes are apparent in the literature.
The demand for beer was dominated by two major features. One
was the mid-Victorian rise in consumption from 541 million standard
gallons in 1855 to 1,145 million standard gallons in 1876, the year of
peak *per capita* (but not total) consumption in the nineteenth century
(Fig. 11.2). The other was gradual modification of a varied regional
pattern of beer tastes in response to the growing popularity of Burton
pale ales – 'a change in taste as fundamental as had been the growth
in the popularity of London porter during the second half of the
previous century' (Sigsworth, 1965, p. 544). The extension of the
railway from Derby to Buxton in 1839 freed 'a great industrial potential [that] had been imprisoned in a narrow overland marketing area
by high transport costs' (Mathias, 1959, p. xxvii). Gradually, the
Burton brewers extended their market via the expanding railway

network and by the 1860s and 1870s their product had acquired national significance. The output of Bass's brewery, a crude index of this development, increased from 130,000 barrels in 1853 to 900,000 in 1876, easily outpacing the general growth in the beer market. London brewers met the competition from pale ale by establishing branch breweries in Burton. In other parts of the country, brewers altered their traditional products 'as far as the nature of their local waters would allow before chemical techniques enabled the modification of natural waters to meet brewing requirements' (Sigsworth, 1965, p. 545).

Against this background of rapidly altering consumer tastes a noteworthy feature of the literature is the emphasis laid on the changing structure of the industry. As the producers of a relatively cheap and bulky product, in the pre-railway age brewers were greatly limited in their economical marketing area by high overland transport charges. For example, Mathias estimated that in the eighteenth century the effective market within the reach of a single brewery for mass distribution by drays was only four to six miles (1959, p. xxii). Consequently the scale of production was limited, except in very special circumstances of which London with its unique market conditions provided the prime instance. By 1831 the common or wholesale brewer – the 'power loom' brewer of the Industrial Revolution – accounted for 95·4 per cent of the malt brewed in London. By contrast, the shares of the licensed victuallers and beerhouse keepers were 1·0 per cent and 3·6 per cent respectively. In most other parts of the country the displacement of these 'handicraft' brewers was far less advanced: for England and Wales as a whole the comparable proportions were 54·4 per cent, 34·3 per cent and 11·3 per cent (Sigsworth, 1967, p. 6). However, as densely packed urban markets developed and as the railways carried the country, in Clapham's phrase, into 'an age of easy communications' the brewing process proved highly suited to large-scale production. Table 11.1 traces the broad outlines of the spread of industrialised brewing. The table deserves to be interpreted with caution for, as Sigworth's study of the Yorkshire brewing trade showed, there were substantial local variations in the timing of the common brewer's rise to ascendancy. For example, neither rapid urbanisation nor improved communications transformed the Leeds brewing trade which displayed one of the slowest rates of displacement of the 'handicraft' brewer in the country. In 1872, common brewers in the Leeds excise collection accounted for only 49·4 per cent of the malt brewed. Moreover, the rise of the common brewer in Yorkshire did not involve the emergence of productive units comparable with those which dominated the industry in London and Burton. In Yorkshire, at mid-century a few stable firms were surrounded 'by a constantly changing small flock of ephemeral firms which left no enduring mark'. Not until the last quarter of the nineteenth century, under the impetus of competition

Table 11.1 *Proportions of Malt Brewed by Different Catagories of Brewer (Decennial Averages)*

Years	Wholesale Brewers percentage	Licensed Victuallers percentage	Persons Licensed to Sell Beer (Beerhouse Keepers) percentage
1831–40	56	31	13
1841–50	61	27	12
1851–60	67	22	11
1861–70	73	18	9
1971–80	80	13	7
1881–90	88	7	5

Source: Calculated from Wilson (1940, Table 13, p. 368).

from the Burton brewers and the race for tied houses, was output increasingly concentrated in large productive units (Sigsworth, 1967, pp. 12–16). Whether these same features were evident in other less important brewing areas only further local research will tell.

One other point may be made in relation to Table 11.1. For all the contemporary controversy over the introduction of free licensing in the Beerhouse Act of 1830 it scarcely appears to have impeded the inexorable trend towards the concentration of output in the hands of the common brewers. Very little research has been done into the economic consequences of the Act, but the excise statistics suggest that only in London, where the tied house had developed furthest before 1830, was there a temporary reduction in the common brewers' share of the market. In the London collection the percentage of malt brewed by the new beerhouse keepers rose from 3·6 per cent in 1831, to a peak of 4·9 per cent in 1845.[1] As the great London brewers had always argued, it was their capital resources rather than any licensing monopoly which underwrote their success (Harrison, 1971, p. 86).

Finally, and in contrast to the history of the brewing industry in the eighteenth century, what is striking about the literature for this period is the very limited amount of information on the behaviour of individual firms. Accordingly, there is a great deal of ignorance about issues such as profitability, pricing, investment and organisation; all of which are best studied in the context of the firm rather than the industry and rely on the survival of business records.

Extending this review of secondary material to the distilling industry a rather different pattern emerges. Unlike the brewing industry, the gin distilling trade in England has attracted minimal attention apart from a single article on a London firm of still makers (Slater, Vols 7 and 8, 1965–6). The Irish whiskey industry, in line with its importance in the second half of the nineteenth century as one of the few successful industries in a predominantly agrarian economy has been the subject of a specialised study (McGuire, 1973) and of considerable commentary in the textbooks on Irish economic history (Cullen, 1972, p. 145). In particular, the industry's response to competition brought about by transport improvements and to a contracting home market during the 1860s now forms a significant part of the interpretation of Irish economic development.

Before the middle of the nineteenth century licensed distillers faced considerable competition from illicit producers and income generated from the sale of illegal spirits played an important part in sustaining the peasant economy. Connell's study of the illicit trade in Ireland (1961) has recently been complemented with an account of illicit distilling in Northern Scotland (Devine, 1975, pp. 156–77). If the prominence given to the distilling industry in Ireland reflects that country's narrow manufacturing base in the nineteenth century, then, conversely, it may be argued that the absence of commentary on the Scottish distilling industry, despite its size as the largest in the United Kingdom from the 1840s, owes much to Scottish economic historians' preoccupation with the flourishing heavy industry sector that emerged in Lowland Scotland (Weir, 1977). Indeed, that point may, with the exception of Ireland, be generalised and applied to the drink trades as a whole: the advent of widespread industrial change in the course of the nineteenth century not only offered a greatly increased supply of alternative products to tempt consumers away from alcoholic drinks, it also diminished the relative importance of the drink industries in the economy as a whole.

'UNIVERSAL AND GENERAL COMPETITION' –
SCOTTISH DISTILLERS AND THE EXCISE

Secondary sources provide only a patchy coverage of the drink trades during the period under review, and if the discussion is to reach beoynd the superficial examination of trends it will be necessary to concentrate on one industry. We have chosen to consider the Scottish distilling industry as a case study, but because important developments occurred during the first quarter of the century it would be impossible to understand the subsequent history without first reviewing the legislative changes affecting the trade and considering their effects.

Excise duties in Great Britain raised over £8·5 million in 1793, and provided 47 per cent of the government's income. Although by 1815 the share of total revenue collected by the excise in the United Kingdom had fallen to 37 per cent, the actual sum raised, £29·5 million, was over three times larger than in 1793. More than two-thirds of this sum came from taxation on alcoholic drinks and their raw materials. Taxation on this scale 'to support the enormous expenses occasioned by our wars on the Continent' drove the hand of the exciseman into the furthest recesses of the drink trades (*PP*, 1834, vol. XXV, Parts I and II).

Peace relaxed the fiscal strains of the Napoleonic Wars, but the effects of the postwar depression, particularly in Ireland and Scotland, raised illicit trading to new heights; in 1822 there were 6,278 prosecutions for illicit distilling alone (*PP*, 1823, vol. VII, p. 240). An opportunity for reform of the excise system was thereby transformed into an urgent necessity and with spirit duty 'the most important of all duties under charge of the Excise' it was on the distilling industry that the main focus of reform concentrated (*PP*, 1834, vol. XXV, p. 3).

Following a long tradition going back at least to Sidney Buxton's study of *Finance and Politics* of 1888 (Buxton, 1966, p. 20), historians have customarily attributed the excise reforms to Huskisson during his period of office at the Board of Trade between 1823 and 1827. It has been argued that in implementing the recommendations of the Wallace Commission which investigated the excise system, by lowering spirit duty, between 1823 and 1825 Huskisson effected the first application of free-trade principles. Whilst the new low duty made an important contribution to curbing illicit distilling, it was not the first postwar reduction nor the first experiment with free trade. Rather, it merely marked another step along a reforming path which began in Scotland in 1816 and of which the guiding principle, as explained by the main architect of the reforms, Woodbine Parish, the Chairman of the Scottish Board of Excise, was 'universal and general competition, to prevent monopoly and combination' (*PP*, 1823, vol. VII, p. 252). This principle, initially aimed at problems originating in 'the Celtic fringe', was subsequently extended to other sections of the drink trades, including beer retailing in 1830 and wine and spirit importing from the 1840s.

The precocious application of free-trade principles was designed to solve the practical difficulties of levying taxation on spirits. The growing consumption of whisky in late-eighteenth-century Scotland exposed its potential for revenue raising, but it also revealed a fundamental problem: how to tax spirits when the trade and the economy were jointly characterised by widely differing degrees of development. How, in other words, to design an excise system which would embrace both the small-scale peasant distillers of the Highlands, each individually producing a trifling quantity of spirits but together accounting for a significant volume of output, and the industrialising distillers of the Lowlands, serving an expanding urban market.

None of the different excise systems that operated in Scotland from 1781 (when private distilling was finally outlawed) to 1816 had solved this fundamental problem. All were torn between two major and conflicting objectives. One was the need to safeguard the revenue which, given the small staff establishment of the Excise and its responsibility for administering a wide range of duties, indicated the centralisation of production in a few large, easily policed units. The other, urged by the landed interest and dictated by the sturdy tradition of peasant distilling, was the desire for a widespread licensed distilling industry which would create a market for grain, much of it of low quality, thereby aiding agricultural improvement. Failing to solve this problem, they created instead chaotic fiscal disunity both within Scotland, where there were three major taxation districts by 1797 (Highland, Lowland and Intermediate), and in the regulation of the Anglo-Scottish spirit trade. By 1815 the legislative framework had become 'so blended and mixed, so difficult of comprehension, either by traders or excise officers', that reform demanded bold initiatives (*PP*, 1821, vol. VIII, p. 60). Complexity was not the only problem: the method of levying the duty made it exceptionally difficult for the licensed distiller to produce a good-quality product, and, as in Ireland, the low reputation of 'Parliament whisky' generated a buoyant demand for the output of illicit stills.

In the seven years after 1816 the reformers set out to create a stable excise system which would encourage 'men of little capital to set up small distilleries' (*PP*, 1834, vol. XXV, p. 56). The reforming Acts of 1816, 1818, 1820 and 1823 sought to achieve this by lowering the costs of entry to the trade, by enabling the licensed distiller to produce a good-quality spirit, and by reducing the taxation on spirits and their raw materials. In view of the discussion on the structure of the brewing industry after 1830, it is this policy objective, basically one of trying to make competition safe for the small-scale distiller, that gives the free-trade reforms much of their interest.

THE MARKETS FOR SPIRITS

The consumption of legally produced spirits in Scotland rose markedly after 1823. In 1799, total Scottish spirit consumption was estimated at 3·6 million gallons. If this estimate was anywhere near correct then *per capita* consumption would have been about 2·22 gallons. Following what temperance advocates labelled 'the fatal year' (Mechie, 1960, p. 82) when duty was reduced, *per capita* consumption rose to 2·71 gallons in 1825. No doubt much of this increase was more apparent than real, simply being a diversion of spirit from illegal to licit channels, but the lower duty still held something of a windfall gain for whisky drinkers, especially in the cities where there was keen competition amongst spirit dealers. (*PP*, 1834, vol. VIII, p. 138). By 1836 (Fig 11.3) spirit consumption in Scotland was 287 per cent higher than in 1823, despite additions to duty in 1825 and 1830. Much the

oof gallons
llions

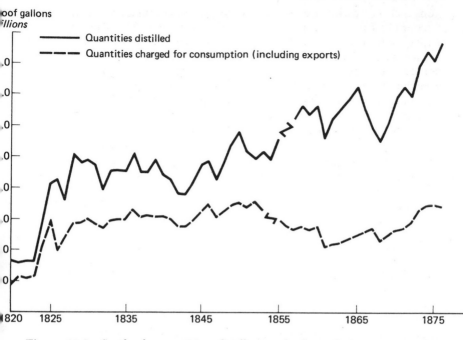

Figure 11.3 *Scotland: quantities distilled and charged for consumption, 1820–76*
Source: Wilson 1940, pp. 336–9

same response was evident elsewhere; in Ireland legal consumption rose from 3·59 to 12·249 million proof gallons whilst in England, following the duty reduction there in 1825, consumption grew from 3·68 to 7·876 million proof gallons.

Reform also opened up two other markets for Scottish distillers. The first and more important was the English market. By bringing England under similar distillery regulations to those in Ireland and Scotland in 1825, reform broke 'the destructive monopoly of the English market' (*PP*, 1823, vol. VII p. 241). Before reform, the Scottish spirit trade to England was the exclusive province of five Lowland distilling firms, all owned by members of two great distilling families, the Haigs and the Steins. In 1820 these five firms shared a trade with sales of 1·3 million gallons, whilst in the home market no fewer than 131 licensed distillers scrambled for a legal market of only 1·8 million gallons. They enjoyed this exalted and enrichening position in the sale of grain spirits for rectification (i.e. redistillation of the spirit and the addition of flavouring from juniper berries and herbs), into gin mainly because of the high fixed and working-capital requirements of the English excise system. They also abused it. Acting in conjunction with the seven great London distilling firms, who accounted for 76 per cent of English output in 1820, they restricted supply and raised prices such that in November 1821 when grain spirits might be had in Scotland for 2s 3d per gallon (duty free), raw spirits could not be bought in England for less than 4s 6d. As the Wallace Commission pointed out, on the prevailing level of spirit consumption in England of 5 million gallons, this differential meant that more than £500,000 was being paid for grain spirits by English consumers than would have been the case in Scotland.

Monopoly profits were anathema to free traders; even more damning was the way these profits had been safeguarded. By 1817 several Lowland distillers were operating on a scale which was not far removed from that necessary to enter for the English trade. To ensure that this latent competition did not materialise, the five export firms took collusive action to undercut them in the home market. This lowered profit margins and prevented possible new entrants from accumulating sufficient capital to establish large distilleries for the English market. Together with the London distillers, the five firms had also bought off intending entrants. In addition to bribery, the export firms had purchased or secured the leases of distilleries capable of working for the English market and closed them down.

Much of the evidence of these tactics was marshalled by aggrieved Lowland distillers. Beneficiaries of the reforms since 1816 they had themselves become ardent free traders. Their's was not the only pressure for reform. The Scottish landed interest mounted a propaganda campaign in Parliament. For example, in May 1822 Captain Wemyss presented a petition from 2,000 barley growers in Fife requesting unrestricted access for Scottish spirits to the English market, estimating that this would raise the annual consumption of barley by 500,000 quarters; another of the many signs of the close relations between land and drink (*Scotsman*, 1 May 1822, p. 147).

In the short run the lowering of the barriers to the English market, the legendary profits of the monopolists, and the great surge in English spirit consumption after the reduction of duty in 1825 sparked off a wildly overoptimistic investment boom in Scotland. Despite 'the intrinsic excellence' (*Scotsman*, 20 May 1826, p. 318) of Scottish spirits, malt whisky was not yet in great demand in England and the existing Lowland distilleries, including the old monopolists, were quite capable of increasing their output to meet the rather different demand for spirit for rectification. The sharp trade recession of 1826 in England, as in Scotland, pulled spirit consumption down. As stocks of Scottish spirits mounted in London, many newly founded distilleries collapsed. This setback precipitated the first post-reform fall in the number of licensed distilleries (Fig. 11.4).

The subsequent development of the Scottish spirit trade with

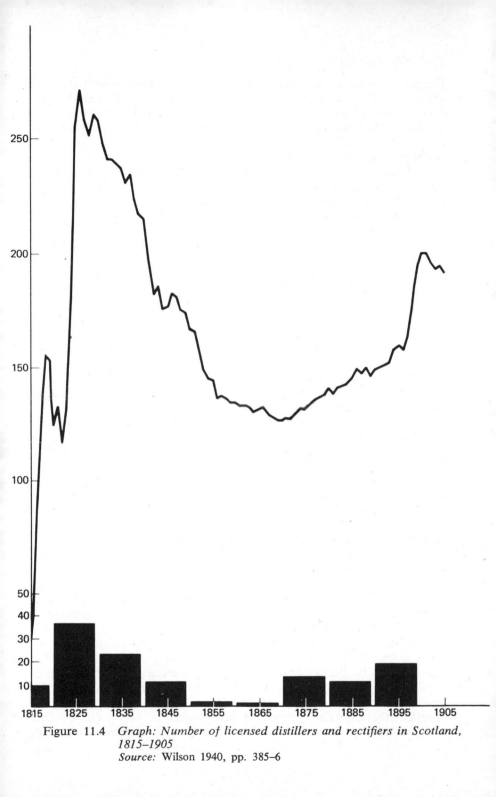

Figure 11.4   *Graph: Number of licensed distillers and rectifiers in Scotland, 1815–1905*
Source: Wilson 1940, pp. 385–6

England is unclear. It was not recorded on a regular basis until after 1860 but the occasional statistics that exist suggest that Scottish distillers gained the lion's share. In 1834, for example, English distillers produced 4·653 million proof gallons. Imports from Scotland were 2·575 million proof gallons, a sizeable improvement on the pre-reform situation and equal to 28 per cent of Scottish output, whilst only 400,000 gallons came from Ireland. With 'scarcely any demand for whisky in the purer state in which it is prepared for consumption in Scotland and Ireland', the bulk of these imports, all but 279,000 gallons, were grain spirits for rectification (*PP*, 1834, vol. XXV, p. 30).

Even without statistics of the trade it is clear that the English market became increasingly attractive to Scottish and Irish distillers by the 1850s. Because the reformed excise system operated with different levels of duty in Scotland, Ireland and England, a major policy aim, the creation of 'a free intercourse in spirits within the United Kingdom', remained unfulfilled (*PP*, 1823, vol. VII, p. 10). Remarkable as it may seem – or perhaps maybe not so remarkable in these devolutionary days – railway travellers still suffered the indignity of an excise search at the border as late as 1849 (Customs and Excise records, 1849). More serious than that curious anachronism, the difference in duty afforded the English distiller a slight degree of protection because of the greater credit requirements for financing a higher duty and without full internal free trade, the customs tariff on imported spirits could not easily be liberalised (Customs and Excise records, c. 1839). The pace at which duty harmonisation could proceed was determined by the campaign against the illicit distiller. Scottish spirit duty was gradually increased from 2s 4¾d to the English level of 8s between 1823 and 1856, the figure adopted in Ireland in 1858. From 1860, brandy, rum and geneva, hitherto the most expensive of all spirits, were free to compete on the same terms as home-produced spirits.

A further increase of 2s per proof gallon in 1860 made the free-trading environment a dismal one for British distillers. Falling spirit consumption occurred throughout the UK, but the depression was deepest in Ireland and Scotland where the increase in duty had been greatest. The position can be summarised by comparing spirit consumption in each national market for the year of peak consumption after 1823 with the position in 1860–4 (Table 11.2).

Ireland, which in the 1830s had been the largest spirit market in the UK was, by the early 1860s the smallest: a result of the activities of the energetic Father Mathew, duty increases, a resurgence of illicit distilling, and loss of population. The Scottish spirit market was also much reduced and only marginally larger than the Irish market. By contrast, the English market was only slightly down: a consequence of the duty increase in 1860 and not fiscal harmonisation. From being

Table 11.2 *Spirit Consumption (Million Proof Gallons)*

	England	*Scotland*	*Ireland*
Excise Duty in 1823	7s[1]	2s 4¾d	2s 4¾d
Year of Peak Consumption	1860	1852	1838
Consumption in Peak Year	12·904	7·172	12·296
Average Spirit Consumption 1860–4	11·207	4·706	4·432

[1]For England, 1825.
Source: G. B. Wilson (1940, pp. 318, 336–9).

the smallest market in the 1820s, consumption had grown and by the early 1860s is was the largest and most buoyant market in the UK.

With permission to bond spirits, an export trade began to be created mainly centred on Glasgow and mainly in malt as opposed to grain whisky, but throughout our period exports remained an insignificant proportion of production. By 1875, 1,097 million proof gallons were exported, accounting for 3 per cent of output. Like the brewing industry, distilling was predominantly reliant on home demand.

THE STRUCTURE OF THE SCOTTISH DISTILLING INDUSTRY

Excise reform set out to make licensed distilling more accessible to the small-scale producer. It did this at a time when, particularly in the Lowlands, mechanisation, the application of steam power, and large-scale fixed investment in distilling plant appeared to be putting competitive power into the hands of the large capitalist distillers. The structure of the licensed industry after reform is thus one of considerable interest, for it provides an opportunity to examine the position of the small-scale producer in a competitive environment.

At first, reform was most successful in the Lowlands, though the widespread movement into licensed production in Perthshire suggests that even some Highland distillers found encouragement in the new legislation. Further north, the few licensed distilleries in operation by 1822 were mainly the result of stubborn, often unprofitable, perseverance by the landed gentry: men like the Duke of Sutherland and William Fraser of Brackla who wanted to find legitimate outlets for grain and to show tenants that licensed production was not impossible under Highland conditions. Until 1823 they remained prophets without honour in their own country, their distilleries isolated islands in a sea of illicit spirit. By 1833 the implementation of the Wallace Commission's Report resulted in them being joined by a host of new licensed producers.

For the Excise, the most gratifying result of the 1823 reforms was the large increase in licensed distilling in areas such as Campbeltown, Islay, Banffshire and Inverness-shire which had formerly been the province of the smuggler. Nor was the influx confined to areas once dominated by illicit distillers. In Perthshire, the continuing benefit of reform was seen in a further increase in the number of licensed distilleries. The same was true of relatively much better policed areas in Lowland Scotland; in the Haddington collection, which covered the fertile East Lothian farming area and in the Glasgow and Ayr collections in the west.

The scale of production in the reformed industry ranged from the very small to the exceptionally large. In Table 11.3 the licensed producers in the Highlands and the Lowlands have been grouped according to the size of their outputs in 1822 and 1833. The table shows the number of distilleries in each output range, the percentage that this constituted of the total number of distilleries, the total amount produced by each group and the percentage that this contributed to the total industry output in the Highlands and Lowlands.

Taking an output of 25,000 gallons per annum as covering small-scale production, a figure which best accords with the distillers' own descriptions of their outputs, it can be seen that the aim of encouraging men of little capital to set up small distilleries was, indeed, remarkably successful. In both the Highlands and the Lowlands the number of small distilleries increased after 1823. Whilst this result was intended in the Highlands, the concurrent increase in the Lowlands reversed after 1823 the previous trend towards the elimination of the small-scale producer. Despite this revival it was in the Highlands that small-scale production predominated. In 1822, when there were 58 Highland distilleries, only one distilled over 25,000 gallons. Small-scale production remained the dominant characteristic of the Highlands in 1833, accounting for 64 per cent of output, but with 18 distilleries producing more than 25,000 gallons an increasing proportion was coming from larger distilleries.

The contrast between the Highlands and Lowlands could not have been greater. In the Lowlands, the number of small-scale distilleries increased between 1822 and 1833, but by the latter date they no longer constituted a majority, and in terms of total industry output they were a much less significant section than in the Highlands, producing a mere 8 per cent of total output in 1833. From 1822 to 1833 the number of very large producers (over 100,000 gallons) in the Lowlands increased and by 1833 they turned out over 58 per cent of total output. The statistics for 1822 do not distinguish between malt and grain whisky distillers but in 1833 there were at least eleven grain distilleries. The smallest grain distiller, Thomas Spears of Leith, produced 36,157 gallons and the largest, James Haig of Lochrin, 514,042 gallons. Their exclusion from the 1833 column in the table means that the role of the large-scale distiller in the Lowlands is accordingly understood.

Table 11.3 Distillers and Output 1822, 1833

HIGHLANDS

Scale of Output in Gallons	Number of Distilleries in the Range and (as percentage of total)		Amount Produced in the Range and (as percentage of total)	
	1822	1833	1822	1833
0–24,999	57 (98)	130 (88)	356,369 (89)	1,264,368 (64)
25,000–49,999	1 (2)	16 (10)	43,581 (11)	562,140 (29)
50,000–74,999	—	1 (1)	—	61,820 (3)
75,000–99,999	—	1 (1)	—	87,042 (4)
100,000 and over	—	—	—	—
	58 (100)	148 (100)	399,950 (100)	1,975,370 (100)

LOWLANDS

Scale of Output in Gallons	Number of Distilleries in the Range and (as percentage of total)		Amount Produced in the Range and (as percentage of total)	
	1822	1833	1822	1833
0–24,999	24 (51)	34 (48)	275,789 (13)	304,166 (8)
25,000–49,999	8 (17)	12 (17)	304,225 (15)	438,994 (11)
50,000–74,999	5 (11)	9 (13)	305,108 (15)	529,775 (14)
75,000–99,999	4 (8)	4 (5)	347,970 (17)	334,581 (9)
100,000 and over	6 (13)	12 (17)	817,828 (40)	2,204,634 (58)
	47 (100)	71 (100)	2,050,920 (100)	3,812,150 (100)

Limits of Range	Highlands		Lowlands	
	1822	1833	1822	1833
Upper	43,581	87,042	185,491	395,763
Lower	632	166	646	617

Sources: 1822: *PP*, 1823, VII, pp. 337–9; 1823: *PP*, 1834, XXV, pp. 229–32.

Notes:
1 The figures for 1822 are for the production of malt and grain whisky. Those for 1833 are for malt whisky only. In 1833 there were at least another 11 grain distilleries. All were located in the Lowlands and 8 of them had outputs over 100,000 gallons in a range from 106,154 gallons to 514,042 gallons.
2 In 1822 the range of output for the 6 Lowland distilleries over 100,000 gallons was from 101,217 to 185,491 gallons. In 1833 for 12 Lowland distilleries it was 101,994 to 395,763 gallons.

Reform produced a stable excise system but not a stable industrial structure. Even before 1833 (Fig. 4), the number of licensed distillers had begun to fall and from 1826 to 1869 an unremitting decline in the number of producers occurred. But which producers?

In the absence of detailed excise returns it is not possible to establish the distribution of the industry in each decade down to 1870. However, in 1864, almost at the nadir of the long-term fall, Charles Tovey in his book, *British and Foreign Spirits* listed the distilleries in Scotland by their excise collections (Tovey, 1864, p. 358).[2] Table 11.4 utilises this information to show the decline in the number of distilleries in each excise collection between 1833 and 1863.

Table 11.4   *Decline in the Number of Distilleries Between 1833 and 1863*

Collection	Numbers	Collection	Numbers
Aberdeen	16	Elgin	10
Argyll		Glasgow	13
(North and South)	15	Haddington	16
Ayr	5	Inverness	5
Caithness	5	Linlithgow	5
Dumfries	0	Perth	26
Edinburgh	2	Stirling	5

Argyllshire still contained the largest number of distilleries as in 1833, but it had lost 15 of its distilleries. Perth, a collection which like Argyll had seemed such an impressive example of the beneficial effects of the reforms, had lost most. Twenty-six of its forty distilleries had gone by 1863. After Perth, Aberdeen and Haddington witnessed the next largest fall. Two-thirds of the distilleries in Aberdeen had disappeared and in Haddington only 1 of the 17 distilleries in 1833 remained. Predominantly urban collections had fared little better. Edinburgh had lost 2 of its 4 distilleries and Glasgow 13 of its 24.

For four collections – Aberdeen, Elgin, Inverness and Perth – the nature of decline can be made a little more specific. By comparing the scale of output in 1833 of the distilleries surviving in 1863, with the scale of output of all distilleries in the collection of 1833, an indication can be given of the type of distillery which survived.

Table 11.5 shows that in these four collections the heaviest casualties were amongst the small-scale distilleries, and in general the chances of survival increased with size. Not always though, for there were some notable exceptions. For example, in the Perth collection neither of the two distilleries with outputs of over 25,000 gallons survived. The casualties included Tullibardine distillery which had produced more

Table 11.5   *Scale of Output in 1833 of Malt Distilleries Surviving in 1863–4: Compared to all Distilleries in the Collection*

Scale of Output in Gallons	Number of Distilleries in the Range							
	Aberdeen		Elgin		Inverness		Perthshire	
	All	Survivors	All	Survivors	All	Survivors	All	Survivors
0– 4,999	7	1	9	2	5	2	6	1
5,000– 9,999	7	2	11	4	1	1	12	2
10,000–14,999	2	1	4	3	1	0	7	1
15,000–19,999	2	1	2	0	0	0	4	1
20,000–24,999	2	1	1	0	2	1	3	2
25,000 and over	0	—	2	1	3	2	2	0

Sources: 1833: *PP* 1834, XXV, pp. 229–32
1863/64: Tovey, 1964, p. 358

malt whisky than any other in the Highlands in 1833. Although the same comparison cannot be made for other collections, it is clear that whilst size may have enhanced the chances of survival, it did not guarantee success. Some of the largest malt and grain distilleries in Scotland in the 1820s and 1830s were located in the Haddington collection, but by 1863 it contained only one distillery.

Even if size did not guarantee success there is no doubt that as the number of distilleries declined, the average size of output increased (Table 11.6).

Table 11.6   *Average Quantity Distilled in Scotland 1825–65*

Year	Number of[1] Distilleries	Total Quantity Distilled (000 proof gallons)	Average Quantity Distilled (proof gallons)
1825	255	8,225	32,255
1830	258	9,883	38,306
1840	215	8,822	41,032
1850	167	11,638	69,688
1860	134	13,312	99,343
1865	131	14,503	110,709

[1] Includes rectifiers as well as distillers which has the effect of understating the increase in the average quantity distilled.
Source: Wilson (1940, pp. 336–7, 386–7).

Excise statistics of the number of licensed distilleries are the net result of movement into and out of the industry, therefore they provide no information about the way the total was composed. Thus, for example, a reduction in the number of licensed distilleries by two might have come about from four new entrants and six failures or no new entrants and two failures. The figures in Fig 4 do not, therefore, represent a fixed 'stock' of distilleries founded after reform and subsequently depleted. The bar chart at the foot of Graph 4 provides a partial indication of the movement into the industry by using the foundation dates of all distilleries which were in existence in 1900 to show the average number of distilleries founded in each decade from 1810–19 to 1890–9. It provides only a partial indication of new entrants because many distilleries had sunk without trace in the intervening period. Nevertheless it displays two significant features. Despite the overall fall in the number of distilleries, new distilleries were being created throughout the period. Even in the 1850s and 1860s when fiscal harmonisation severely depressed Scottish whisky consumption, there were still people prepared to invest in the industry. In a background of widespread distillery failures the other striking feature is the longevity of many distilleries.

In the half century after reform, substantial change occurred in the structure of the Scottish distilling industry. The number of producers dropped sharply whilst output rose, but even so, distilleries, though not output, remained geographically dispersed. The development of the so-called 'golden triangle' around Speyside awaited the construction boom after 1870. Despite the high casualty rate amongst the new distilleries after reform there were some remarkable cases of longevity.

'A COMPETITION IN THE TRADE'

In the early 1830s, contemporary opinion offered two explanations for the reduction in the ranks of the licensed distillers. The first placed responsibility on an upsurge in illicit distilling following the additions to spirit duty in 1826 and 1830. Given the significance of taxation to the balance between licensed and unlicensed distilling, there was something in this; detections of illicit distilling rose from 392 in 1830 to 754 in 1835 (*PP*, 1870, vol. XX). But this was far below pre-reform levels and despite the subsequent succession of duty increases, detections fell continuously with as few as 9 being recorded in 1865. The greatly strengthened protective service meant that competition from illicit distillers was not the main cause of failure amongst licensed distillers. It merely emphasised that smuggling had become a weak argument in the distillers' campaigns against extra spirit duty (*PP*, 1865, vol. XXXI). Poverty had swelled the number engaged in illicit distilling before 1823, after reform it remained a major handicap to the successful pursuit of licensed distilling. For the small farmer–distiller, whisky was a cash crop whose immediate sale was essential to his survival. Lacking trade credit the small distiller could not hold back from the market when spirit prices fell. As a result:

'I do not think the profit is very great, there are so many of them in the business, and so many of them poor, that they are obliged to come into the market to raise money, and perhaps sell their goods cheaper than they can afford: but if they escape bad debts, . . . the price they get for their spirits just now may pay them, but only a bare trade.' (*PP*, 1834, vol. XXV p. 302).

The duty increases exacerbated this situation, for they were levied on a falling spirits market. Between 1826 and 1831, the duty-free price of malt spirits fell from 3s 9d to 2s 8d per proof gallon. Duty rose from 2s 10d to 3s 4d p.p.g., or from 43 per cent to 55 per cent of the wholesale price, more than absorbing a slight fall in barley prices. The distillers' inability to pass on the full amount of the increase in spirit duty emphasised the second explanation. The belief that 'the improved system raised a competition in the trade that has not allowed it to be so profitable to the manufacturer . . .and which has not yet subsided' (*PP*, 1834, vol. XXV, p. 302).

Reform produced a highly competitive spirit market which weeded out many small producers. Adaptation to licensed distilling demanded new skills in production and marketing. Former illicit distillers found the acquisition of these an uphill struggle, for their method of production included features which could prove fatal in a commercial environment, such as the uneven quality of the product, the poor-quality distilling equipment, the waste of spent grains and, above all, the low yield of spirits. Illicit distillers' yields were seldom more than 8 gallons per quarter. In the 1830s small still operators were producing 10 to 12 gallons but large-scale distillers between 14 and 18 gallons. Such differences were not explained by any greater understanding of the nature of fermentation. Robert More of Bonytown, near Linlithgow, told the Wallace Commission:

'We uniformly fill two tuns from one brewing; and so minute are the circumstances on which fermentation depends, and so much does the science of fermentation appear to me to be in its infancy, that those tuns in all circumstances similarly conducted will produce a different result, which we cannot account for; generally speaking it is not the case but I mean to say sometimes it is.' (*PP*, 1823, vol. VII, p. 208).

The distilling industry, like the brewing industry, was still in 'the dark ages' in this pre-Pasteur period. As in brewing, the distiller's response to poor fermentation was cleanliness and more cleanliness 'because if there is the least acidity in our tuns, it destroys our fermentation' (*PP*, 1823, vol. VII, p. 204). The cause of differences in yields must be sought in the greater mechanisation of the large distillery, particularly in milling and mashing, and in the attention to the quality of the raw material. Nothing underlined the difference between large- and small-scale distillers quite so much as the growing trek to East Anglia for good malting barley, in which distillers located in Scotland's best barley-growing areas even participated. Nothing exposed the gulf between distilling and farming more than sentiments like: 'I hold a different opinion from my neighbours about corn; I do not care how cheap corn is . . .' (*PP*, 1831, vol. VII, p. 84). It was this sort of attitude which explained the rapidity with which grain distillers switched to imported supplies in the 1860s; a practice which brewers adopted in the 1880s (G. B. Wilson, 1940, p. 220).

Whilst the pressure to reduce costs strained the old alliance between land and drink, it also led some distillers to renew their efforts to find a method of distilling continuously. The traditional pot still, the common technology of all distillers, had a major limitation for the ambitious, cost-cutting distiller: it was, and is, a discontinuous or batch process. To concentrate the spirit, two or even three distillations were needed which increased the cost of fuel and labour (Customs and Excise records, *c*. 1839).

In 1828, Robert Stein carried out successful experiments with a continuous still at Kirkliston distillery but the design which offered the greatest practical advance was patented in 1830 by Aeneas Coffey, a retired Irish exciseman (Nettleton, 1898, p. 19). Coffey's still broke away entirely from the traditional design. It was heated by steam, and the exchange of heat within the still between steam and wash cut the cost of fuel. With extraordinary efficiency the still produced a concentrated spirit containing between 86 per cent and 96 per cent alcohol (Slater, Vols 7 and 8, 1965–76). The spirit was relatively low in secondary constituents and, therefore, quite unlike malt whisky but a cheaper substitute for pot-still grain whisky. Unlike the pot still, where the quality of spirit could vary widely not only between different distilleries but even within the same distillery from one season to another, the quality of patent still spirit was much more uniform. It came close to being a homogenous commodity, with the result that as fiscal barriers were relaxed and transport improvements widened the market, the potential for severe competition in patent still distilling was very high.

The benefits of the Coffey still: its prodigious output and its lower variable costs, required a sizeable fixed-capital investment. Its diffusion, therefore, followed a familiar pattern: the distilleries which adopted it were the largest producers serving urban markets. In Scotland, the production of grain whisky from pot stills had ceased by 1860, whilst between 1840 and 1850 the proportion of total output coming from patent still distilleries rose from 7·5 per cent to 45·3 per cent. By 1860, the 12 patent still distilleries in Scotland had a combined output of 6·9 million proof gallons. Pot-still distilleries numbered 111, a fall of 57 in the past fifteen years, and they shared an output of 5·7 million proof gallons. In the UK as a whole, 27 million proof gallons were distilled; 63 per cent from patent stills and these were concentrated in a mere 28 distilleries (Weir, 1977).

The patent still radically altered the economics of spirit production, profoundly changing competitive relationships within the UK distilling industry and creating a sharp divide between the patent still distillers and those who continued with the pot still. The high capital cost of the process limited its use to the large-scale distillers, but its greatly enhanced productive capacity meant that unit costs of production and the capital/output ratio were lower than in pot-still distilling. In other words, high costs of entry restricted the number of patent-still distillers, but those who could afford the entry fee gained a lower cost of production. The lower cost of production and the lower price of grain spirit (in 1855, for example, Scottish malt whisky prices ranged from 3s 9d to 4s 6d per proof gallon; the price of grain spirit was 2s 6d) explain the dramatic rise in patent-still output at the expense of the pot still.

The price-reducing effects of the Coffey still were offset by increases in spirit duty, but the competitive position of the pot-still distillers was more seriously affected. After Coffey, pot-still producers stood out as high-cost producers. On the other hand, the prospects for patent-still distillers were by no means trouble free. Between 1840 and 1850 the number of patent-still distillers in Scotland rose from two to twelve. Growing numbers during a period when consumption was being depressed by fiscal harmonisation posed a serious threat. One additional Coffey still meant a larger proportional increase in output than one additional pot still. Attempts to control the output of patent-still spirit therefore became crucial to the grain distillers, and because the high costs of entry kept the number of patent-still distillers relatively small, combination was a more feasible proposition. In October, 1856, six Lowland grain distillers agreed to restrict sales. The agreement only lasted for a year, and it was not until the depression of the early 1860s, after a period of intense competition during which six of Scotland's seventeen patent-still distilleries went out of business, that combination was again attempted. The resulting Scotch Distillers' Association (1856–76) formed the matrix of the Distillers Company Limited (1877), an amalgamation of six Lowland grain distilleries, and the United Kingdom Distillers' Association (1878–88) (Weir, 1974a, p. 289).

One last question remains: Why, given the efficiency of the Coffey still did the pot-still distiller survive at all? In 1816, Woodbine Parish wrote: 'Quality is the first recommendation of whiskey, price the second' (*PP*, 1816, vol. VIII, p. 2). This dictum held good after reform. Because the pot-still process produced a much less pure form of alcohol, the character of the raw materials, the water and the shape of the still determined the flavour of the product. This, in turn, determined the distiller's reputation in the spirit market. What characterised the whisky market was not one single price for malt whisky, but a spectrum of prices for different whiskies. If the malt distiller could establish a reputation for his product a premium price helped to offset his higher cost of production and offered a degree of protection from competition.

In the Highlands, where the bulk of pot stills were located, a local market whose dominant characteristics were poverty and declining population, created great pressure to seek sales in 'the South Country'. The best way to achieve this was through an agent in the major distributing centres of Edinburgh, Leith and Glasgow. Some Highland distilling firms, like the Beauly Distillery Company, exchanged good spirits for bad debts and worthless whisky bills, bankrupting themselves as surely as if they had stuck to their local market (Scottish Record Office, RH 15, 207/9). Others, like George and John Smith of the Glenlivet distillery made an agency agreement with a reputable firm like Andrew Usher & Company, which lasted to their mutual enrichment from 1844 to 1919.

The Spirits Act of 1860 gave permission to mix spirits in bond free from duty and greatly encouraged what Tovey noted as 'the prevalent notion amongst whisky drinkers, especially in Scotland . . . that several varieties of whisky blended is superior to that of any one kind . . .' (Tovey, 1864, p. 150). A specialist whisky merchant, the blender bought direct from the distillers and created out of the heterogenous range of malt whiskies a more uniform product (Weir, 1974*b*, p. 20). Malt whisky, because of the high proportion of secondary constituents it contained, required time to mature before it became fit for consumption. Time and storage required capital and added to the cost of producing malt whisky, much more so than was the case with grain whisky which, although undergoing change during maturation, could be sold at a much earlier age. The blender provided working capital to finance stocks and became a major holder of mature whisky. So, too, did a purely financial intermediary, the spirit broker. In theory the broker's role was to equilibrate the supply of particular types and ages of whisky with demand, but the growing volume of stocks effectively divorced production from consumption. Stocks became more, rather than less, important in the whisky trade and inventory fluctuations a major source of instability. With the addition of grain spirit to the blend, a process assisted by the duty increases up to 1860 and reinforced by the increasing burden of duty as the general price level fell in the 1870s, the blender produced a cheaper whisky. In the last quarter of the nineteenth century, it was the blender, rather than the distiller, who unseated gin and brandy in the English market, laid the foundation for worldwide export sales and created modern 'Scotch whisky'.

NOTES TO CHAPTER 11

1 I am grateful to Professor E. M. Sigsworth for making available some unpublished work on the brewing industry during this period.

2 Tovey's figures are not unambiguous. He mentions, for example, that in 1863, 128 distilleries were entered for production but actually includes 136 in his list. Also, the excise collections in 1863 were not contiguous with those of 1833. Stirling seems to have become the main collection point for those distilleries in Fife, whilst Dundee and Brechin had replaced Montrose.

12   Commercial Enterprise

by P. L. Cottrell

The main focus of this chapter is the activity of mercantile firms in the overseas trade sector during the fifty years or so before 1870. This is a very large topic, and in order to get beyond the level of very broad generalisations within the confines of a single chapter it is necessary to examine either a limited number of trades or the activities of the mercantile community of a single port. Here the second approach will be adopted, the main analysis being the structure of the merchanting firms of Liverpool during the early 1820s and the early 1860s, based upon data drawn from their fire-insurance policies. Special attention will be directed towards the level of capital invested, its profitability, and secular trends in commercial organisation, both before and during 'the great Victorian boom'.

I

The organisation of the overseas merchanting sector was shaped by the geographical structure of trade undertaken, especially the amount carried on with distant countries. British overseas trade has been broken down into its basic geographical components in Table 12.1 with a division into an 'old' area – the countries on the littoral of the North Atlantic, Mediterranean and Baltic, and a 'new' area – that is elsewhere in the world. Such a breakdown is artificial, but the table does demonstrate that before 1815 trade was heavily oriented towards the 'old' area, particularly with regard to exports and re-exports, and consequently involved only short sea passages. Thereafter, the geographical pattern changed, especially in the case of exports, with the 'new' area growing in importance as a result of two spurts, the first in the 1820s and the second from the 1840s. This was due primarily to the growth of new markets for textiles, particularly cotton yarns and piece goods. Markets for these products in the 'old' area, especially the USA and north-western Europe, lost their dynamism with the growth of domestic supplies which were often shielded by high tariff barriers. Accordingly, merchants and manufacturers were forced to

Table 12.1   *Geographical Structure of British Overseas Trade*
             (percentage of total value)

	Exports		Exports and Re-exports		Imports	
	'Old' %	'New' %	'Old' %	'New' %	'Old' %	'New' %
1784–6	81·3	18·6	82·9	17·0	73·6	26·4
1814–16	86·9	13·1	89·2	10·8	70·4	29·6
1824–6	71·9	28·0	74·5	25·5	71·7	28·3
1834–6	72·1	27·9	74·6	25·3	72·3	27·7
1844–6	64·3	35·7	66·9	33·0	68·0	32·0
1854–6	59·7	40·1	64·1	35·8	65·5	34·5
1864–6	52·6	47·4	61·9	38·1	54·4	45·6
1874–6	57·3	42·6	59·8	40·2	66·1	33·9

Note: 'Old' – Europe, USA, Canada and West Indies
           'New' – elsewhere.
Sources: 1784 to 1856: Davis (1979); 1864 to 1876: Mitchell and Deane (1971,
           pp. 315–27). For the period 1784 to 1826 trade with Ireland has been
           excluded while in the period 1864 to 1876 because of the nature of the
           source, North Africa has been included in the 'Old' area.

look further afield and became more deeply involved in long-distance
trades – Latin America in the 1820s and India from the 1830s. The
resultant change in market importance was considerable; Asia in the
mid-1840s absorbed a quarter of the total value of cottons exported,
nearly as much as northern and north-western Europe, whereas in
the 1820s the Orient had taken only 6·6 per cent and north Europe
a third of cotton exports by value (Davis, 1979).

   The fundamental problem posed by trading over increasing distances
was greater uncertainty and consequently higher risks. Before the full
development of the steamship and the oceanic cable in the 1860s and
1870s, knowledge of cargoes, markets and prices and political disturb-
ance depended upon the vagaries of nature, especially the strength
and direction of the wind. The difficulties that could arise even in the
'old' area can be illustrated readily; Liverpool merchants heard no
news from the USA for one and half months during the late summer
of 1822 because of the prevalence of easterly winds. The round
voyage to the east coast took normally fifty-five days but the new
voyages to the Orient were far longer. The *Kingsmill*, the first
Liverpool ship to go to India, took fifteen months, whereas the *Jumna*,
the first from the port to go to Canton, took ten (T. Baines, 1852,
pp. 569, 572, 587, 637, 654). Such long voyages rendered the capital
of either the exporting merchant or manufacturer illiquid. Estimates
made in the early 1830s indicate that returns from such cargoes could
take as long as fifteen or eighteen months to arrive in the hands of
the manufacturer, whereas the 'nicety of the operation of apportion-

ing the supply to the demand is so great that it frequently leads to an oversupply' (Larpent, *PP*, 1833, vol. VI, qq. 2151, 2155). Voyage times were so unpredictable that goods could simply miss the seasonal market for which they were intended (Hunt, 1951, p. 24).

Risks were increased further in the 'new' area of trade because frequently, as on the Pacific coast of Latin America, there were no harbours, and cargoes had to be discharged at sea, a perilous situation should the weather change. In addition, problems arose out of the generally unbalanced nature of trade in the 'new' area. The Latin American republics did provide something of a market for British cottons, despite locally produced goods; however, before the 1850s there was often no return cargo, while some, like Brazilian coffee, could not be shipped because of colonial preferences (Platt, 1973, pp. 79, 81). In the case of China the problem was reversed, and consisted of finding suitable trade goods with which to obtain silk and tea. Initially specie and bullion had been used and from the 1820s cottons began to find a market at Canton, but it took opium, grown in India and smuggled into China, to solve the problem finally (Greenberg, 1951, pp. 94–102, 161–3). The shortage of return cargoes, or where they existed, their frequent bulk compared with exports, caused in turn yet another difficulty, the problem of obtaining the necessary shipping space at an economic rate. Before the steam-shipping conferences of the 1880s, homeward freights, with the exception of bullion, were set by market forces and consequently could vary greatly. During one shipping season in the 1840s they ranged at Calcutta from £2·50 to £10 and at Bombay from £0·75 to £7, the floor being set by the undesirability of sailing in ballast to shipowners, and the ceiling by the amount of pressure upon shippers to despatch cargoes (Broeze, 1975).

II

The changes in the direction of trade led to both the rise of new home ports and the development of new forms of mercantile undertakings, designed to overcome the risks inherent in the longer passage times. The growing importance of the North Atlantic axis in trade during the eighteenth century had led to the emergence of three important western outports – Liverpool, Bristol and Glasgow. Merseyside's commercial expansion received further momentum from the industrialisation of the port's potential hinterland from the 1770s and the tapping of its traffic through the completion of a range of transport improvements – roads, canals and later railways. Consequently, by the 1820s, Liverpool was primarily a commercial centre with very little manufacturing employment besides that related to shipping and the processing of imports (Baines, 1824, p. 195). The port continued to grow rapidly throughout the half century after 1815 and by the 1850s in terms of volume of trade was rivalling London as the nation's premier port for overseas trade. Part of the growth of the port's traffic was caused by a widening of the foreign markets served by its mercantile community. The opportunity to ship to the Orient was seized as soon as the East India Company's monopoly was abolished, and trade with Latin America grew from the beginning of the nineteenth century. The Mediterranean trade began to shift from the metropolis to Liverpool in the 1830s, while imports from the west coast of America and Australia became substantial during the 1850s. According to official statistics, Liverpool's export trade in 1850 amounted to £34·9 million whereas London's was only £14·1 million; Baines has estimated the value of London's imports at £43·2 million compared with £37·4 million at Liverpool.

From 1815 until the 1870s mercantile houses reacted to the increasing risks caused by longer voyage times and the opening of new markets by attempting to trade on behalf of others for a commission, instead of their own account. The main problem for a mercantile house acting as a factor was the inducement of consignments for sale on commission, and John Ewart, speaking of Liverpool's trade in the 1830s, pointed out the critical role of connections, whether with the source of imports or in the British manufacturing districts (*PP*, 1833, vol. VI, qq. 4086, 4096, 4100). These very necessary connections could be obtained in a variety of ways. One was by an apprenticeship in a different mercantile house, the usual form of training before the 1820s, another was by a 'grand tour', the finishing touch to the education of a son of a rising mercantile family, in the course of which visits could be made to other houses to lay the foundation for mutual confidence. But the most usual was through the correspondent network, consisting of closely allied firms scattered along a trade route, which kept in touch by letter, conducted business mutually, and were often linked by filial, nuptial and religious ties, the firmest of connections. Most commission merchants had many correspondents, but generally each had two, perhaps three, principal ones who were given a priority with regard to market information, who were charged lower commissions, and who were assisted during times of financial difficulty. The correspondent system in practice took on a variety of forms, of which the most developed was 'the international house', a concern which usually had its head office in a British port, but was linked to branch houses overseas through resident partners. The worldwide multi-branch commercial house was a feature almost unique to British trading activity during the first three-quarters of the nineteenth century. Some continental firms possessed such networks but they were usually restricted to Europe, while American houses tended to rely on visiting agents and in the east continued to use the supercargo, as did Indian Parsee country traders. In the late 1840s there were about 1,500 British mercantile houses overseas, compared with 150 American and 500 French, with about half the latter being located in the Mediterranean and the Near East (S. D. Chapman, 1976).

Various methods were used to obtain consignments from producers, or from factors acting for them, such as the offer of a complete range of necessary ancillary services – shipping, insurance and warehousing – but the most important was to provide an advance on the bill of lading cost of the goods involved. Ewart thought that a Liverpool merchant would only obtain a consignment from the USA by making an advance (*PP*, 1833, vol. VI, qq. 4109, 4142). The rate at which advances were made varied considerably from 50 per cent up to full cost, and probably the most critical decision that a commission merchant had to make was the determination of the rate at which to give an advance. If pitched too low, then there was a risk of losing the consignment and perhaps the connection; if too high, say above 75 per cent, then the advance might not be covered subsequently by the sale receipts and might give rise to the problem of how any short-fall could be recovered. Such advances committed a firm's capital, but in home ports at least a merchant could obtain credit from brokers.

Brokers acted on behalf of commission merchants but, unlike their principals, they did not obtain the bill of lading and so neither took formal possession of the goods involved, nor easily established a lien on them; it was also unusual to possess the right to sell in their own name. The practice of brokers making advances to factors did frequently blur the *de facto* ownership of the goods involved, but in both Britain and the USA the different legal positions of commission merchants and their agents had been made clear by the 1830s. The interlacing of commercial credit did not stop at the broker because he could obtain advances from a banker (Buck, 1925, pp. 17–24). The financial stability of the economy was therefore threatened when advances on traded goods were not covered when they were sold to the consumer. The consequent liquidity panics, such as those of 1836 and 1857, were compounded by a further development in overseas trade finance – the acceptance credit.

During the first quarter of the nineteenth century, a small number of mercantile firms took on the function of providing credit, through accepting bills of exchange drawn on them on behalf of other parties involved in overseas trade (e.g. *PP*, 1833, vol. VI, qq. 1926, 1928, 1930, 1938–9, 1941, 1944–5). The major innovation in this sphere was the issue of letters of credit which enlarged markets for their carriers, as purchases could be made based upon the creditworthiness of the acceptor who issued them rather than that of the buyer. By the mid-1830s there were five other main providers of such finance, of whom the most important were Wiggin & Company, W. & J. Brown who had a branch at Liverpool, Wildes & Company, and Morrison, Cryder & Company (Perkins, 1975, pp. 6, 10–11, 117–41). Some of the new joint-stock banks entered the letter of credit business in Liverpool during the 1830s boom (Collins, 1972, p. 110). It was a highly risky business if not undertaken with considerable circumspection; Wildes, Wiggins and Wilsons, the terrible three Ws, failed in the 1836 crisis while Browns had to obtain major assistance from the Bank of England as a result of the load of 'bills on exports to America' that they were carrying.

Letters of credit allowed foreign buyers to go direct to British manufacturers and by paying with bills drawn on London were able to obtain a keener price. Americans made an increasing use of letter of credit arrangements in Manchester from the 1820s, while Europeans, initially Germans followed by Greeks, set up branch houses in the City in order to buy direct from the cotton manufacturers' sale rooms. Nathan Meyer Rothschild had established an office in Manchester as early as August 1800 in order to by-pass English agents on the continent (B. Williams, 1976, pp. 17–19). In the 1830s both Browns and Jardine, Matheson, the Indo-Chinese firm, appointed buying agents in Manchester (Perkins, 1975, pp. 32, 87, 91; Greenberg, 1951, pp. 101–2). Some of the larger cotton manufacturers conversely established links with commission houses overseas, particularly in India and Latin America, to which they consigned the ends of long production runs, as speculations, in order to reap the full economies of scale that their manufacturing plants could yield (Shaw, *PP*, 1833, vol. VI, pp. 11, 1,510–11, 1,519, 1,521, 1,525). Such direct links with and by manufacturers resulted in an increasing number of export consignments from the 1830s by-passing the growing number of mercantile houses in Liverpool.

III

The size and composition of Liverpool's mercantile sector in the mid-1820s is shown in Table 12.2. While the directories on which the table is based categorised firms as either merchants, agents or brokers, many in practice acted to varying degree under all such heads and when called upon to describe themselves as in insurance policies, chose the general label of 'merchant'. The most important feature that the table shows, even when due allowance is made for the element of double counting contained within it, is the large number of firms active within the commercial sector. However, what of their relative sizes, in terms of either the volume of turnover or the amount of capital invested? Some contemporary evidence points to a state of

Table 12.2 Liverpool's Mercantile Sector in the mid-1820s

	Number of firms		Number of firms
Merchants (unspecified)	475	Cotton Dealers	17
[of which 10 West Indian		General and Commercial Brokers	101
10 American]		Commission Brokers	16
Coal Merchants	32	Corn Brokers	6
Copper Merchants and Agents	5	Cotton Brokers	56
Corn Factors and Merchants	51	Insurance Brokers	12
Fruit Merchants	5	Ship Brokers	78
Lead Merchants	5	Tobacco Brokers	19
Leather Merchants	5	Wool Brokers	2
Linen Merchants	5	Agents	165
Salt Merchants	13	[of which 33 general	
Slate Merchants	4	55 commercial	
Timber and Ruff Merchants	86	20 shipping	
Wine and Spirit Merchants	122	2 coal]	
Woollen Cloth Merchants	11	Marine Stores Dealers	34
		Fire and Life Offices	21

Source: E. Baines (1824, Vol. 1).

almost perfect competition, of firms roughly equal in size, each undertaking a relatively small amount of business, compared with the total trade of the port in a particular commodity. Ewart stated in 1833 that capital was 'generally diffused' and not concentrated in the hands of a 'few wealthy merchants' (*PP*, 1833, vol. VI q. 4131).

In order to try and answer these questions regarding the degree of concentration, details of Liverpool mercantile fire-insurance policies were abstracted from the 'county' registers of the Sun Fire Office for two periods, 1821 to 1823 and 1860 to 1862.[2] These two triennia were chosen as suitable benchmarks for comparative purposes as a result of a number of factors, both analytical and practical. The first was decided upon as the initial base because trade 'stability' did not return after the Napoleonic Wars until the early 1820s. The second triennium was chosen to avoid the most serious effects of the Civil War and was dictated by the source which ceases in 1863. Neither can be described as 'normal', if such years exist in economic and social history; 1821 to 1823 were the early years of a national boom in overseas trade, while 1860 to 1862 were years of a declining trade from a peak in a minor cycle. For each of these triennia benchmarks sample policies were taken for analysis.[3] Unlike other studies which have used fire-insurance data as a main source, this is concerned principally not with fixed capital but the value of stocks held, for which, with one major exception, there exists at present little corroborative evidence. Further difficulties arise over the reliability of the fire-policy valuations and any conclusions drawn from individual policies should be regarded as highly tentative, particularly where they are not supported by other evidence.

The picture suggested by the data from the fire-insurance policies and supported by Williams's analysis of the bills of entry is of a mercantile community consisting predominantly of small- to medium-sized firms. However, there was a separate stratum of a few very large firms who dominated the cotton and timber import trades. A large number of firms owned or rented a warehouse and had equity interests in shipping, primarily to secure cargo space. As a result of the trades in which they were involved, a few firms owned sizeable processing plants such as sugar houses. Entry into this community does not appear to have been difficult, although to be profitable a firm had to have solid connections with the sources of either imports or exports. Office accommodation could be rented, as could warehouse and shipping space, the latter through specialist brokers. After 1805 duties on imported goods could be deferred while credit to finance transactions could be obtained from both brokers and bankers, although accommodation from the former could limit the subsequent flexibility of a firm in the market place. Analysis of policy data at later benchmarks reveals a structural pattern very similar to that shown by the data for the 1820s.

IV

The existence of a large number of firms, most of which were roughly equal in size, made for a highly competitive environment. The effects of this intensive competition coupled with the world transport revolution of the third quarter of the nineteenth century led to the gradual decline of the consignment/advance system of merchanting. There were two main ways in which factors could compete, either by cutting the levels of commissions charged or by increasing the rate at which advances were given. In order to obtain consignments, but at the same time avoiding the potential dangers of excessive advances, the Liverpool firm of Rathbone's adopted a policy of returning part of the commission. These rebates, which varied from one-third to one-fifth, were naturally resented by other merchants when they became known. Other stratagems that Rathbone's used to retain consignment accounts were a willingness to handle small packets of goods, including those in which they normally did not deal, and the provision of financial assistance to correspondents at times of stringency and crisis. However, these policies proved to be of limited value and consequently the firm turned to transacting a considerable amount of its business on a joint-account basis after 1855 (Marriner, 1961, pp. 54–68). Competition and its dangers in the form of excessive advances caused different reactions in other firms. Brown's in the 1830s found that it could take as long as eight months to collect debts arising from the sale of textiles in America, and consequently decided to abandon export consignments, using the capital released to expand their banking operations. Baring's took a different view, arguing that if 'full' advances were required to obtain consignments of raw cotton thus immobilising capital for a considerable length of time, then the risks involved were no different from outright ownership, while the profits arising from the latter were probably higher than the commissions charged on consignments, commonly 2 or 5 per cent in the 1840s. Accordingly, Barings, together with most other larger mercantile houses, began to conduct a much larger proportion of their business on their account (Perkins, 1975, pp. 92, 101–3).

Increases in the speed of international communications were also leading to a decline in the consignment system established during the first quarter of the nineteenth century. Historians have often stressed this particular relationship and consequently have pinpointed the end of the consignment system in the 1870s, caused by the full development of steam shipping and the linking of world markets by oceanic cables. However, the reduction of oceanic voyage times was a cumulative process which had begun with the growth of subsidised liner traffic in the 1840s. Although the early steam packets could not convey cargoes, they did carry letters and samples which affected the marketing of some products. Selling cotton in transit became established in the 1850s and was taking place on a large scale by the end of the decade. Buyers in New Orleans and Mobile, acting under orders of northern American and European parties, from the early 1850s shipped the staple direct to the Old World and sent only samples to New York, thus omitting the previous first leg in the bulk movement of cotton (Woodman, 1968, pp. 27–9). These changes are confirmed in one aspect by Williams's study of the Liverpool cotton trade. By 1850, 60 per cent of cotton imported through Liverpool was consigned to 'order', whereas the proportion in the 1820s and 1830s had been under 20 per cent. Williams was unable to discern any specific reason for this major change, but suggests that it is connected with the appearance of the steam packet, which allowed information to travel more swiftly than goods, thus permitting the sale of cotton afloat (Williams, 1969). What effects, if any, did these changes in selling methods have upon the structure of the Liverpool mercantile community?

The composition of Liverpool's commercial sector in the late 1850s is shown in Table 12.3. The number of mercantile firms had grown considerably during the second quarter of the nineteenth century with the expansion of the volume of trade handled by the port, while shifts in the direction and composition of trade are reflected in the appearance of new specialist firms, such as iron merchants. None of these developments altered the basic structure.

Warehousing was probably a separate service industry by the 1860s, as was shipowning, although merchanting firms which owned both their own wharves and ships could still be found even at the turn of the century. According to official Returns and business histories, shipowning in Liverpool began to emerge as a distinct occupation in the 1840s. Although the general pattern of shipowning in the port remained unchanged, with each vessel generally belonging to only a few shareholders, an increasing proportion of investment came to have a 'rentier' character, while its management was being given over to either an individual shareholder, not entirely a new development, or managing agents. Fleets or lines of ships, especially passenger carriers, were becoming more common, often established by entrepreneurs who had entered the industry in the 1840s and 1850s as shipbrokers (Davis, 1978). The adoption of steam power appears initially to have had little effect upon the structure of shipowning in Liverpool, as in 1869 only 40·5 per cent of steam tonnage was owned by joint-stock companies, while 17·6 per cent was in the hands of 'single' owners.

There had been some change in the structure of Liverpool's mercantile community during the half century after 1820, but it consisted mainly of the splitting off of shipowning and warehousing

Table 12.3 Liverpool's Mercantile Sector in the late 1850s

	Number of firms		Number of firms
General Merchants	887	Cotton Dealers	30
[of which 157 Commission Merchants]		General Brokers	50
Bullion Merchants	8	Corn Brokers	48
Cider Merchants	2	Cotton Brokers	137
Coal Merchants	132	Insurance Brokers	53
Copper Merchants	18	Ship Brokers	175
Corn Merchants	79	Tea Brokers	9
Fruit Merchants	18	Wool Brokers	22
Hide Merchants	16	Miscellaneous Brokers	81
Iron Merchants	59	Commission Agents	197
Lead Merchants	14	Coal Agents	63
Linen Merchants	5	Passenger Agents	17
Salt Merchants	20	Salt Agents	17
Slate Merchants	12	Steam Packet Agents	36
Tea and Coffee		Miscellaneous Agents	271
Merchants and Dealers	46	Master Porters	17
Timber Merchants	68	Stevedores	53
Tin Merchants	15	Ship Store Dealers	45
Wine and Spirit Merchants	11	Fire and Life Insurance Companies	
		having offices	143

Source: Gore's Directory for 1859 (Liverpool)

into separate service industries. The structure of the buying and selling of goods in the 1860s was very similar to that pertaining in the 1820s, when these functions were undertaken by a large number of small firms, although a limited number of very large firms dominated at least some of the bulk import trades such as cotton and timber. Changes in the speed of international communications and competition between firms had brought about some changes in marketing methods by the 1850s, the development of selling goods in transit and a shift, by the larger firms at least, to conducting a much greater proportion of business either on their own account or on a joint account. The main feature to be explained is continuing numbers of small- and medium-sized firms throughout this period. One factor was the continuing growth in the volume of trade handled by the port which created opportunities for new entrants, particularly if they were prepared to take up one of the newly developing trades. Gaps were not only created by the expansion of trade, but also by the continuous process of attrition caused by recurrent commercial and financial crises, which winnowed out the chaff and made room for new entrants.

V

One of the distinguishing characteristics of Liverpool's commercial community before the 1870s was its vulnerability during liquidity shortages. In the 1847 crisis, 54 failures occurred in Liverpool as opposed to 108 in London, 30 in Manchester, 35 in Glasgow, and 38 throughout the rest of the British Isles (Evans, 1849, pp. 67–113). Such a high failure rate was the product of many factors, not least competitive pressures which pushed firms into undertaking highly risky business in order to obtain consignments, such as making advances upon goods before they were either manufactured or shipped, which led to the downfall of one broking firm. The need to make liberal advances to producers made firms vulnerable, and this vulnerability was increased by shortages of liquidity developing within the local formal financial sector during the upswing of a boom. Increased activity could only be sustained by the local banks rediscounting bills on the London market, and when panic did strike, for whatever reason, then Liverpool's mercantile sector and the banks which served it were forced to look immediately to metropolitan institutions for assistance. This situation had developed from the last quarter of the eighteenth century and continued until the 1870s, with Liverpool being one of the first, if not *the* first, provincial centre to call for aid in each of the great crises of the first three quarters of the nineteenth century.

Mismanagement apart, there were two main factors which account for the weakness of Liverpool's financial institutions: first, inadequate capital bases, and second, a severe imbalance in the term structure of the banks' assets and liabilities. The new joint-stock banks of the 1830s and 1860s proved to be as vulnerable as their private counterparts, readily falling prey to either a panic in the London discount market or a local run on deposits (Anderson and Cottrell, 1975). This situation arose because their capitals were generally small while current accounts made up a large part of their liabilities. In the case of two banks in the late 1840s, current deposits ranged between 20·3 per cent and 36·9 per cent of their liabilities while they maintained cash ratios in the range 1·8 per cent to 6·5 per cent (Collins, 1972, p. 195). Such proportions ensured profitability but not stability and could only be maintained by a heavy reliance on rediscounting. This situation continued until the late 1860s when deposits began to increase at a faster rate than discounts and advances. Consequently, the banks became more liquid and they were able to hold more bills until maturity. The volume of bills coming forward for discount was declining after the early 1870s as a result of telegraphic transfers and the gradual disappearance of the consignment with advance system of merchanting (Nishimura, 1971, pp. 44–54, 57, 97–102). The banks' positions were also eased by term deposits coming to make up an increasing proportion of total deposits from the mid-1870s. Such factors led to the Liverpool area becoming self-sufficient for its credit needs, and so less vulnerable to financial stringency.

In this chapter elements of continuity and discontinuity during the half century after 1820 have been stressed, the largest element of continuity being the persistence of large numbers of small- to medium-sized firms within Liverpool's mercantile sector. It has been argued that such a structure was produced by both an overall increase in the port's activities and recurrent financial crises which decennially removed the weak. But what of the strong: how did some firms manage to survive throughout the period, to insulate themselves against the working of the riddle, in fact to grow? Capital accummulation, as in manufacturing industry, primarily resulted from the ploughing back of profits. The sources and level of profitability is extremely difficult to establish for mercantile firms. Marriner in her study of the Rathbones has been able to reconstitute some of the firm's accounts to show their earnings from various sources, but unfortunately without being able to indicate the amount of capital involved in each of the firm's activities. However, what Marriner has been able to reveal is the sources of strength which enabled this Liverpool firm not only to survive but grow from a capital of £40,000 in 1842 to £600,000 in 1870. It would appear that these characteristics were common to other concerns which had similar rates of growth of resources during the second and third quarters of the nineteenth century. There were three responsible factors. First, diversification of trades so that one compensated for the other, in the case of Rathbone's America and

China. Second, the conscious pursuit of a contra-cyclical policy – crises were expected and firms not only trimmed their sails accordingly, sometimes two or three years in advance, but also they took advantage of the low prices and absence of competition in the wake of a panic. Third, diversification of function in order to spread risk and committed capital. The model life path of a mercantile firm was a start in trading, usually on a commission basis, followed by an increasing element of trading either on its own capital or on a joint-account basis, a shift which sometimes was not desired but forced by competition. Then there was a move into 'foreign banking', foreign-exchange dealing and the provision of acceptance credits, followed finally by a complete shift from trading into merchant banking. Rathbones fought shy of the last step. Barings took it because some of its partners thought that it was an easier way of earning a living than the daily grind of supervising trading in commodities. Brown's, between the 1840s and the 1870s, acted mainly as exchange bankers, though they did retain a strong interest in the movement of cotton to Liverpool, a trade which dovetailed with their acceptance and exchange business. However, firms which developed large banking functions were the exception rather than the rule; most mercantile houses remained essentially trading concerns, though they usually acquired an interest in shipping if they grew to any size. However, if a firm was a new entrant, with few connections through which to obtain consignments, and it took one risk too many when expectations were buoyed up by the euphoria of a boom, then it was liable to be a victim of the next panic, which, although nearly always forgotten, in reality before 1875 was never far away.

NOTES TO CHAPTER 12

1 This essay incorporates some of the findings of research undertaken as part of an SSRC financed project 'The Supply of Capital and the Economic Development of Merseyside, 1680–1880', under the direction of Professor J. R. Harris, B. L. Anderson and the author. I wish to acknowledge the generous financial assistance of both the SSRC and the Research Board of the University of Leicester. The monotonous task of transcribing fire-insurance policies from a source which is unindexed, discontinuous, and varies considerably in presentation was carried out largely by two research assistants, Miss C. Woodhead and A. Gibbons. The views expressed here are those of the author alone, but he is grateful to the editor, Dr Joyce Ellis and Dr P. Musgrave for their advice and comments on earlier drafts. Professor R. Davis kindly allowed the author to read parts of his forthcoming book on overseas trade.

2 The Sun Fire Policy Registers, County Series, MS 11,937 are held at the Guildhall Library, London. The 1820s sample was obtained from vols 132 to 146 and the 1860s sample from vols 485 and 489 to 527. Entries are now on a card index and information on particular firms can be obtained from the author.

3 The author will supply details of the entire statistical exercise on request.

Bibliography

Adams, D. R. Jr (1970). 'English and American Wage Rates 1790–1830', *Journal of Economic History*, vol. XXX.

Aldcroft, D. H. (ed.) (1968a). *The Development of British Industry and Foreign Competition, 1875–1914* (London).

Aldcroft, D. H. (1968b). *British Railways in Transition* (London).

Aldcroft, D. H., and Fearson, P. (eds) (1972). *British Economic Fluctuations, 1790–1939* (London).

Allen, G. C. (1929). *The Industrial Development of Birmingham and the Black Country 1860–1927* (London).

Allen, R. C. (1977). 'The Peculiar Productivity History of American Blast Furnaces, 1840–1913', *Journal of Economic History*, vol. XXXVII.

Ames, E., and Rosenberg, N. (1963). 'Changing Technological Leadership and Industrial Growth', *Economic Journal*, vol. LXXIII. Reprinted in N. Rosenberg (ed.), (1971) *The Economics of Technological Change* (Harmondsworth).

Ames, E. and Rosenberg, N. (1968). 'The Enfield Arsenal in Theory and History', *Economic Journal*, vol. LXXVIII. Reprinted in S. B. Saul (ed.), (1972). *Technological Change* (London).

Anderson, B. L., and Cottrell, P. L. (1975). 'Another Victorian Capital Market: A Study of Banking and Bank Investors on Merseyside', *Economic History Review*, 2nd series, vol. XXVIII.

Andrew, S. (1887). *50 Years' Cotton Trade* (Oldham).

Armstrong, W. A. (1972). 'The Use of Information about Occupation', in E. A. Wrigley (ed.), *Nineteenth Century Society* (Cambridge).

Asher, E. (1972). 'Industrial Efficiency and Biased Technical Change in American and British Manufacturing: The Case of Textiles in the Nineteenth Century', *Journal of Economic History*, vol. XXXII.

Ashton, T. S. (1924). *Iron and Steel in the Industrial Revolution* (Manchester).

Ashworth, H. (1842). 'Statistics of the Present Depression of Trade at Bolton', *Journal of the Statistical Society* (London).

Ashworth, W. (1960). *An Economic History of England 1870–1939*.

Aspinall, P. J. (1977). *The Size Structure of the House-Building Industry in Victorian Sheffield*. Working Paper no. 49, Centre for Urban and Regional Studies, University of Birmingham.

Bagwell, P. S. (1968). *The Railway Clearing House in the British Economy 1842–1922* (London).

Bagwell, P. S. (1974). *The Transport Revolution from 1770* (London).

Baines, E. (1824). *History, Directory and Gazetteer of the County Palatine of Lancaster*. Reprinted in 1968 (Liverpool).

Baines, E. (1859). 'On the Woollen Manufacture of England, with Special Reference to the Leeds Clothing District', *Journal of the Statistical Society*, vol. XXII.

Baines, E. (1875) (ed. K. G. Panting). 'Account of the Woollen Manufacture of England'. Reprinted from E. Baines, *Yorkshire, Past and Present* (Newton Abbott, 1970).

Baines, T. (1852). *History of the Commerce and Town of Liverpool* (London).

Baker, R. (1858). 'On the Industrial and Sanitary Economy of the Borough of Leeds', *Journal of the Royal Statistical Society*, vol. XXI.

Banbury, P. (1971). *Shipbuilders of the Thames and Medway* (Newton Abbot).

Barker, T. C., and Savage, C. I. (1974). *An Economic History of Transport in Britain* (London).

Barry, P. (1864). *The Dockyards, Shipyards and Marine of France* (London).

Beales, H. L. (1934). 'The Great Depression in Industry and Trade', *Economic History Review*, V.

Beckinsale, R. P. (1951). *The Trowbridge Woollen Industry* (Devizes).

Bevan, G. P. (ed.) (1876). *British Manufacturing Industries* (London).

Birch, A. (1967). *The Economic History of the British Iron and Steel Industry 1784–1879. Essays in Industrial and Economic History with Special Reference to the Development of Technology* (London).

Blackmore, H. L. (1972). 'Colt's London Armoury', *Gun Digest* (1958). Reprinted in S. B. Saul (ed.) (1972). *Technological Change: The United States and Britain in the Nineteenth Century* (London).

Blaug, M. (1961). 'Productivity of Capital in the Lancashire Cotton Industry during the Nineteenth Century', *Economic History Review*, 2nd series, vol. XIII.

Blunt, R. (ed.). *Mrs Montagu, 'Queen of the Blues'* (London).

Booth, W. (1886). 'On Occupations of the People of the U.K. 1801–1881', *Journal of the Royal Statistical Society*, vol. XLIX.

Bousfield, C. E. (1878). *Woollens at the Paris Exhibition* (London).

Bowley, A. L. (1937). *Wages and Income in the United Kingdom since 1860* (Cambridge).

Bowley, A. L., and Wood, H. L. (1905). 'Statistics of Wages in the United Kingdom during the Last Hundred Years, Part X, Engineering and Shipbuilding.' *Journal of the Royal Statistical Society*, vol. 68.

Bowley, A. L., and Wood, H. L. (1906). 'Statistics of Wages in the United Kingdom during the Nineteenth Century, Part XIV Engineering and Shipbuilding.' *Journal of the Royal Statistical Society*, vol. 69.

Bowley, M. (1960). *Innovations in Building Materials* (Cambridge).

Bowley, M. (1966). *The British Building Industry* (Cambridge).

Boyson, R. (1970). *The Ashworth Cotton Enterprise: The Rise and Fall of a Family Firm 1818–80* (London).

Bradford Chamber of Commerce Minute Books (1859).

Bridgewater MSS., National Coal Board.

Brief, R. P. (1966). 'The Origin and Evolution of Nineteenth Century Asset Accounting', *Business History Review*, vol. 40.

British Association (1862). *Report*.

British Association (1863). *A History of the Trade and Manufactures of the Tyne, Wear and Tees*, 2nd edn (Newcastle-on-Tyne).

Brito, D. L., and Williamson, J. G. (1973). 'Skilled Labour and Nineteenth Century Anglo–American Managerial Behaviour', *Explorations in Economic History*, vol. X. no. 3.

Broadbridge, S. (1970). *Studies in Railway Expansion and the Capital Market in England 1825–1873*.

Broeze, F. Y. A. (1975). 'The Cost of Distance: Shipping and the Early Australian Economy, 1788–1850', *Economic History Review*, 2nd series, vol. XXVIII.

Brown, P. C. (1926). 'Fire Insurance in Liverpool', *Transactions of the Historic Society of Lancashire and Cheshire*, vol. LXXVIII.

Buck, N. S. (1925). *The Development of the Organisation of Anglo-American Trade, 1800–1850*. Reprinted in 1969 (New Haven).

Buddle MSS., North-east Venal Book.

Buddle MSS., North of England Institute of Mining Engineers, Newcastle.
The Builder (1842–3).

Burgess, K. (1969). 'Technological Change and the 1852 Lock-out in the British Engineering Industry', *International Review of Social History*, vol. XIV.

Burgess, K. (1972). 'Trade Union Policy and the 1852 Lock-out in the British Engineering Industry', *International Review of Social History*, vol. XVII.

Burn, D. L. (1931). 'The Genesis of American Engineering Competition, 1850–1870', *Economic History*, vol. II, no. 6, January.

Burn, D. L. (1940). *The Economic History of Steelmaking 1867–1940: A Study in Competition* (Cambridge).

Burridge, John (1824). *The Tanner's Key* (London).

Burstall, A. F. (1963). *History of Mechanical Engineering* (London).

Burt, T. (1924). *Thomas Burt, Pitman and Privy Councillor: An Autobiography* (London).

Butterworth, E. (1856). *Historical Sketches of Oldham* (Oldham).

Buxton, S. (1888). *Finance and Politics, an Historical Study 1783–1885* (London, reprinted New York, 1966).

Cairncross, A. K., and Weber, B. (1956). 'Fluctuations in Building in Great Britain, 1785–1849', *Economic History Review*, 2nd series, vol. IX.

Campbell, R. H. (1961). *Carron Company* (Edinburgh).

Census of England and Wales (1851). *Report*.

Census of 1851, Ages and Occupations (1852–53). vol. LXXXVIII, parts I and II.

Chaloner, W. H. (1954). 'John Galloway (1804–94), Engineer of Manchester and his "Reminiscences" ', *Lancashire and Cheshire Antiquarian Society Transactions*, vol. LXIV.

Chambers, J. D. (1961). *The Workshop of the World* (London).

Chapman, S. D. (1972). *The Cotton Industry in the Industrial Revolution* (London).

Chapman, S. D. (1976). 'The International Houses; the Continental Contribution to British Commerce in the Industrial Revolution Period.' Read as a paper at the Midlands Economic History Conference, University of Leicester, November.

Chapman, S. J. (1904). *The Lancashire Cotton Industry* (Manchester).
Chapman, S. J., and Ashton, T. S. (1914). 'The Size of Businesses, Mainly in the Textile Industries', *Journal of the Royal Statistical Society*, LXXVII.
Chattaway, E. D. (1855–6). *Railways, their Capital and Dividends* (London).
Checkland, S. G. (unpublished). 'Cultural Factors and British Business Men 1815–1914.'
Church, R. A. (1966). 'Messrs Gotch and Sons and the Rise of the Kettering Footwear Industry', *Business History*, vol. VIII.
Church, R. A. (1969). *Kenricks in Hardware, A Family Business 1791–1966* (Newton Abbot).
Church, R. A. (1970). 'Labour Supply and Innovation 1800–1860: The Boot and Shoe Industry', *Business History*, vol. XII.
Church, R. A. (1971). 'The British Leather Industry and Foreign Competition, 1870–1914', *Economic History Review*, 2nd series, vol. XXIV.
Church, R. A. (1975a). *The Great Victorian Boom, 1850–1873* (Studies in Economic and Social History, 1975). (London).
Church, R. A. (1975b). 'Nineteenth-Century Clock Technology in Britain, the United States, and Switzerland', *Economic History Review*, 2nd series, vol. XXVIII.
Church, R. A. (1976). 'Business History in Britain', *Journal of European Economic History*. vol. 5.
Church, R. A., and Smith, Barbara M. D. (1966). 'Competition and Monopoly in the Coffin Furniture Industry, 1870–1915', *Economic History Review*, 2nd series, vol. XIX.
Clapham, J. H. (1907). *The Woollen and Worsted Industries* (London).
Clapham, J. H. (1910). 'The Transference of the Worsted Industry from Norfolk to the West Riding', *Economic Journal*, vol. XX.
Clapham, J. H. (1926). *An Economic History of Modern Britain*, vol. I (Cambridge).
Clapham, J. H. (1932). *An Economic History of Modern Britain*, vol. II (Cambridge).
Clarkson, L. A. (1960). 'The Organisation of the English Leather Industry in the Late Sixteenth and Seventeenth Centuries', *Economic History Review*, vol. XIII.
Clarkson, L. A. (1974). 'The English Bark Trade, 1660–1830', *Agricultural History Review*, vol. 22.
Clarkson, L. A. (unpublished). 'Tanning 1750–1850', *Cambridge Agrarian History of England and Wales 1750–1850*, vol. IV (forthcoming).
Cole, W. A. (1958). 'The Measurement of Industrial Growth', *Economic History Review*, 2nd series, vol. XI.
Coleman, D. C. (1969). *Courtaulds: An Economic and Social History* (Oxford).
Colliery Guardian (Weekly).
Colliery Year Book and Coal Trades Directory (Annual).
Collins, M. (1972). 'The Bank of England and the Liverpool Money Market 1825–1850'. PhD thesis, University of London.
Connell, K. H. (1961). 'Illicit Distillation: An Irish Peasant Industry', *Historical Studies*, vol. III (Cork).

Cooney, E. W. (1955). 'The Origins of the Victorian Master Builders', *Economic History Review*, 2nd series, vol. VIII.

Cooney, E. W. (1960). 'Long Waves in Building in the British Economy of the Nineteenth Century', *Economic History Review*, 2nd series, vol. XIII.

Cooney, E. W. (1969). 'Public Opinion and Government Policy in Nineteenth Century British Economic History: A Review and a Study of the Building Industry', *Yorkshire Bulletin of Economic and Social Research*, vol. 21.

Cooney, E. W. (1970). 'The Speculative Builders and Developers of Victorian London: A Comment', *Victorian Studies*, vol. XIII.

Corlett, E. (1975). *The Iron Ship: the History and Significance of Brunel's Great Britain* (Bradford on Avon).

Cormack, W. S. (1931). 'An Economic History of Shipbuilding and Marine Engineering, with Special Reference to the West of Scotland'. PhD thesis, University of Glasgow.

Cornewall-Jones, R. J. (1898). *The British Merchant Service* (London).

Cotes, A. (ed.) (1852). *The Dictionary of Architecture*, Vol. I.

Cottrell, P. L. (1976). 'Railway Finance and the Crisis of 1866: Contractors' Bills of Exchange and the Finance Companies', *Journal of Transport History*, new series, vol. III.

Crouzet, F. (1972). *Capital Formation in the Industrial Revolution* (London).

Crump, W. B., and Ghorbal, G. (1935). *History of the Huddersfield Woollen Industry* (Huddersfield).

Cullen, L. M. (1972). *An Economic History of Ireland since 1660.*

Customs and Excise records (c. 1839). M.B. no. 56, 'Deputations of Scottish and Irish Distillers and Observations of the English relative to the System of Warehousing Home made Spirits'.

Customs and Excise records (1849). M.B., 'Suppression by Border Officers of Smuggling between England and Scotland'.

Daunton, M. J. (1972). 'The Dowlais Iron Company in the Iron Industry, 1800–1850', *Welsh History Review*, vol. VI.

David, P. A. (1975). 'Technical Choice, Innovation and Economic Growth', in *Essays on American and British Experiences in the Nineteenth Century* (London).

Davis, R. (1978). 'Maritime History', in Sheila Marriner (ed.), *Business and Businessmen* (Liverpool).

Davis, R. (1979). *The Industrial Revolution and Overseas Trade* (Leicester).

Deane, P. and Cole, W. A. (1969). *British Economic Growth 1688–1959*, 2nd edn (Cambridge).

Denny (1859). UGD3, Journal (University of Glasgow).

Devine, T. M. (1975). 'The Rise and Fall of Illicit Whisky Distilling in Northern Scotland, c. 1780–1840', *Scottish Historical Review*, vol. LIV.

Dickinson, H. W. (1963). *A Short History of the Steam Engine*, 2nd edn, with Introduction by A. E. Musson (Cambridge).

Dodd, George (1843). *Days at the Factories* (London).

Donnachie, Ian (1977). 'Sources of Capital and Capitalisation in the Scottish Brewing Industry, c. 1750–1830', *Economic History Review*, vol. XXX.

Donnachie, Ian (1979). *A History of the Brewing Industry in Scotland* (Edinburgh).

Dougan, D. (1968). *The History of North East Shipbuilding* (London).

Dubois, A. B. (1938). *The English Business Company after the Bubble Act, 1720–1800* (New York).

Durant, S. (1976). 'Ornament in an Industrial Civilisation', *Architectural Review*, vol. CLX.

Dyos, H. J. (1968a). 'The Speculative Builders and Developers of Victorian London', *Victorian Studies*, vol. XI, Supplement.

Dyos, H. J. (ed.) (1968b). *The Study of Urban History* (London).

Dyos, H. J., and Aldcroft, D. H. (1969). *British Transport* (Leicester).

Edwards, J. K. (1963). 'Economic Development of Norwich, 1750–1850, with special reference to the worsted industry', PhD thesis, University of Leeds.

Ellison, T. (1886). *The Cotton Trade of Great Britain*, appendix, table 2 (London).

Encyclopaedia Britannica (1886). 9th edn, vol. XXII.

English, H. (1827). *A Complete View of the Joint Stock Companies formed during the Years 1824 and 1825* (London).

Erickson, C. (1959). *British Industrialists: Steel and Hosiery 1850–1950* (Cambridge).

Evans, D. Morier (1849). *The Commercial Crisis 1847–1848*, reprinted 1969 (Newton Abbot).

Farnie, D. A. (1953). 'The English Cotton Industry 1850–96'. MA thesis, University of Manchester.

Feinstein, C. H. (1972). *National Income, Expenditure and Output of the United Kingdom 1855–1965* (Cambridge).

Feinstein, C. H. (1978). 'Capital Formation in Great Britain', in Peter Mathias and M. M. Postan (eds), *The Cambridge Economic History of Europe*, vol. VII (Cambridge).

Fitzwilliam MSS. Sheffield City Library.

Floud, R. C. (1971). 'Changes in the Productivity of Labour in the British Machine Tool Industry, 1856–1900', in D. N. McCloskey (ed.), *Essays on a Mature Economy: Britain after 1840* (Princeton).

Floud, R. C. (1974). 'The Adolescence of American Engineering Competition, 1860–1900', *Economic History Review*, 2nd series, vol. XXVII.

Floud, R. C. (1976). *The British Machine-Tool Industry, 1850–1914* (Cambridge).

Forbes, H. (1853). *Lectures on the Results of the Great Exhibition of 1851*, 2nd series, no. XXI.

Fordyce, W. (1860). *A History of Coal, Coke and Coalfields* (Newcastle upon Tyne).

Forrest, T., and Gibson, E. (1833). *Report from the Select Committee on Manufacturers, Commerce and Shipping.*

Fortunes Made in Business, Vols. I–III (1884).

Fortunes Made in Business, 'Crossleys of Halifax (1884)', Vol. III (London).

Francis, A. D. (1972). *The Wine Trade* (London).

Fremdling, R. (1977). 'Railroads and German Economic Growth: a leading sector analysis with a comparison to the United States and Great Britain', *Journal of Economic History*, vol. XXXVII.

256   *The Dynamics of Victorian Business*

Gale, W. K. V. (1966). *The Black Country Iron Industry. A Technical History* (London).
Gale, W. K. V. (1967). *The British Iron and Steel Industry. A Technical History* (Newton Abbot).
Gale, W. K. V. (1971). *The Iron and Steel Industry. A Dictionary of Terms* (Newton Abbot).
Galloway, R. L. (1898). *Annals of Coal Mining and the Coal Trade*, Vol. I; (1904) Vol. II (London).
Gatrell, V. A. C. (1972). 'The Commercial Middle Class in Manchester 1820–1857'. PhD thesis, University of Cambridge.
Gatrell, V. A. C. (1977). 'Labour, Power and the Size of Firms in the Lancashire Cotton Industry in the Second Quarter of the Nineteenth Century', *Economic History Review*, 2nd series, vol. XXX.
Gayer, A. D., *et al.* (1975). *The Growth and Fluctuation of the British Economy, 1790–1850* (Oxford, 1953; New York, 1975).
Gilbert, K. R. (1971–2). 'Henry Maudslay 1771–1831', *Newcomen Society Transactions*, vol. XLIV.
Girouard, Mark (1977). *The Victorian Country House* (Oxford).
Glover, J. (1869). 'The Decline of Shipbuilding on the Thames', 'Statistics of Tonnage' and 'Tonnage Statistics of the Decade 1860–70', *Journal of the Statistical Society*, vol. 32.
Glover, F. J. (1961). 'Thomas Cook and the American Blanket Trade in the Nineteenth Century', *Business History Review*, vol. XXXV.
Glover, F. J. (1961–2). 'The Rise of the Heavy Woollen Industry of the West Riding of Yorkshire in the Nineteenth Century', *Business History*, vol. V.
Glover, F. J. (1963–4). 'Government Contracting, Competition and Growth in the Heavy Woollen Industry', *Economic History Review*, 2nd series, vol. XVI.
Glover, J. (1863). 'On the Statistics of Tonnage during the first decade under the Navigation Law of 1849', *Journal of the Statistical Society*, vol. 26.
Glover, J. (1872). 'Tonnage Statistics of the Decade 1860–70, *Journal of the Statistical Society*, vol. 35.
Glover, J. (1882). 'Tonnage Statistics of the Decade 1870–80, *Journal of the Statistical Society*, vol. 45.
Goodchild, J. (1968). 'The Ossett Mill Company', *Textile History*, vol. I.
Gould, J. D. (1972). *Economic Growth in History* (London).
Gourvish, T. R. (1972). *Mark Huish and the London & North Western Railway* (Leicester).
Grantham, J. (1842). *Iron as a Material for Shipbuilding* (London).
Grassby, R. (1969). 'The Rate of Profit in Seventeenth Century England', *English Historical Review*, vol. 84.
Great Eastern Railway Accounts, RAIL 1110/158, Public Record Office.
Greenberg, M. (1951). *British Trade and the Opening of China 1800–42* (Cambridge).
Griffin, A. R. (1977). *The British Coalmining Industry, Retrospect and Prospect* (Buxton).
Habakkuk, H. J. (1962a). *American and British Technology in the Nineteenth Century* (Cambridge).

Habakkuk, H. J. (1962b). 'Fluctuations in House-Building in Britain and the United States in the Nineteenth Century', *Journal of Economic History*, vol. XXII.

Habakkuk, H. J. (1968). *Industrial Organisation Since the Industrial Revolution* (Southampton).

Haigh MSS., Manchester University Library.

Hall, A. R. (1961–2). 'Long Waves in Building in the British Economy of the Nineteenth Century: A Comment', *The Economic History Review*, 2nd series, vol. XIV.

Harrison, B. (1967). 'Drink and Sobriety in England 1815–1872. A Critical Bibliography', *International Review of Social History*, vol. XII, part 2.

Harrison, B. (1971). *Drink and the Victorians* (London).

Harte, N. B. (1977). 'Trends in Publications on the Economic and Social History of Great Britain and Ireland 1925–1974', *Economic History Review*, 2nd series, vol. XXX.

Hartridge, R. J. (1955). 'The Development of Industries in London, South of the Thames, 1750–1850' (unpublished MSc Econ. thesis, University of London).

Harwell, R. M. (1973). 'A Revolution in the Character and Destiny of British Wool', in N. B. Harte and K. G. Ponting (eds), *Textile History and Economic History Essays in Honour of Miss Julia de Lacy Mann* (Manchester).

Hawke, G. R. (1970). *Railways and Economic Growth in England and Wales, 1840–70* (Oxford).

Hawke, G. R., and Reed, M. C. (1969). 'Railway Capital in the United Kingdom in the Nineteenth Century', *Economic History Review*, 2nd series, vol. XXII.

Head, P. (1968). 'Boots and Shoes', in D. H. Aldcroft (ed.), *The Development of British Industry and Foreign Competition 1875–1914* (London).

Head, P. (1960). 'Industrial Organisation in Leiecster 1844–1914' (unpublished PhD thesis, University of Leicester).

Heaton, H. (1915). 'The Leeds White Cloth Hall', in *Publications of the Thoresby Society*, vol. XXII (Leeds).

Heaton, H. (1932). 'West Riding Trade Protection Association', *Journal of Economic and Business History*, supplement.

Higgs & Hill Ltd (1948). *Higgs and Hill Limited, 1898–1948* (London).

Hirst, G. C. (1942). *History of C. & J. Hirst and Sons Ltd.* (Huddersfield).

Henry-Russell Hitchcock (1954). *Early Victorian Architecture in Britain*, vol. I (London and New Haven).

Hobhouse, H. (1971). *Thomas Cubitt Master Builder* (London).

Hobsbawm, E. J. (1969). *Industry and Empire* (Harmondsworth).

Hoffman, W. (1955). *British Industry 1700–1950* (Oxford).

Hole, J. (1866). *The Homes of the Working Classes* (London).

Holroyd, A. (1871). *Saltaire and its Founder* (Saltaire).

Hudson, P. (1975). *The West Riding Wool Textile Industry, A Catalogue of Business Records* (Edington, Wilts).

Hudson, P. (1977). 'Some Aspects of 19th Century Accounting Development in the West Riding Textile Industry', *Accounting History*, vol. 2. no. 2.

Hughes, J. R. T. (1960). *Fluctuations in Trade, Industry and Finance: A Study of British Economic Development 1850–60* (Oxford).

Hughes, J. R. T., and Reiter, S. (1958). 'The First 1945 British Steamships', *Journal of the American Statistical Association*, vol. 53.

Hunt, R. (annually 1854–82), *Mineral Statistics* (London).

Hunt, W. (1951). *Heirs of Great Adventure. The History of Balfour, Williamson and Company* (London).

Hyde, C. K. (1971). 'Technological Change and the Development of the British Iron Industry, 1700–1870'. PhD thesis, University of Wisconsin.

Hyde, C. K. (1972–3). 'The Adoption of the Hot Blast by the British Iron Industry: A Reinterpretation', *Explorations in Economic History*, vol. X.

Hyde, C. K. (1977). *Technological Change and the British Iron Industry, 1700–1870* (N. J.).

Hyde, F. E., *et al.* (1955). 'The Cotton Broker and the Rise of the Liverpool Cotton Market', *Economic History Review*, 2nd series, vol. VIII.

Imlah, A. H. (1958). *Economic Elements in the Pax Britannica* (Cambridge).

Irving, R. J. (1976). *The North Eastern Railway Company, 1870–1914* (Leicester).

James, J. (1857). *A History of the Worsted Manufacture* (London).

Jarmain, G. (1876). *On Wool Dyeing, Six Lectures to the Society for Encouragement of Arts, Manufacture and Commerce* (London).

Jeffereys, J. B. (1938). 'Trends in Business Organization in Great Britain since 1856'. PhD thesis, University of London.

Jeffereys J. B. (1946). *The Story of the Engineers, 1800–1945* (London).

Jenkins, D. T. (1975). *The West Riding Wool Textile Industry 1770–1835. A Study in Fixed Capital Formation* (Edington, Wilts).

Jenkins, F. (1961). *Architect and Patron* (London).

Jenkins, J. G. (1969). *The Welsh Woollen Industry* (Cardiff).

Jenkins, J. G. (1971). *The Woollen Industry of South West England* (New York).

Jeula, H. (1975). 'The Mercantile Navies of the World in the Years 1870 and 1874 Compared', *Journal of the Statistical Society*, no. 38.

Jewkes, J. (1892). 'The Localisation of the Cotton Industry', *Economic Journal: Economic History Supplement*, vol. II.

Jones, M. O. (1895). *On the History and Development of the Coal Industry in the Rhondda Valley for the Last Fifty Years* (National Library of Wales MSS.).

Jubb, S. (1860). *History of the Shoddy Trade* (London).

Kanefsky, J. W. (unpublished). 'Motive Power in British Industry and the Accuracy of the 1870 Factory Return'.

Kaye, B. (1960). *The Architectural Profession in Britain* (London).

Kenwood, A. G. (1965). 'Railway Investment in Britain, 1825–75', *Economica*, new series, vol. XXXII.

Kingsford, P. W. (1951), 'Railway Labour', PhD thesis, University of London.

Knowles, J. (1890). 'On the Coal Trade', *Transactions of the Manchester Geological Society*, vol. XX.

Kuznets, S. (1966). *Modern Economic Growth: Rate, Structure and Spread* (New Haven and London).

Lambert, W. R. (1975). 'Drink and Work Discipline in Industrial South Wales', *Welsh History Review*, vol. VII.

Landes, D. S. (1969). *The Unbound Prometheus* (Cambridge).

Lee, C. H. (1972). *A Cotton Enterprise 1795–1840: A History of McConnell and Kennedy, Fine Cotton Spinners* (Manchester).

Lewis, J. P. (1965). *Building Cycles and Britain's Growth* (London).

Lindsay, W. S. (1874–6). *History of Merchant Shipping and Ancient Commerce* (London).

Lloyd-Prichard, M. F. (1950). 'The Decline of Norwich', *Economic History Review*, 2nd series, vol. III.

Lones, T. E. (1898). *History of Mining in the Black Country* (Dudley).

Lynch, P., and Vaizey, J. (1960). *Guinness's Brewery in the Irish Economy 1759–1876* (Cambridge).

Lyon, D. S. (1975). 'The Denny List.' *National Maritime Museum Publications*, vol. I.

McCloskey, D. N. (1973). *Economic Maturity and Entrepreneurial Decline: British Iron and Steel, 1870–1913* (Cambridge, Mass.).

Macgregor, D. H. (1934). *Enterprise, Purpose and Profit* (Oxford).

McCulloch, J. R. (1837) *A Statistical Account of the British Empire* (London).

McGuire, E. B. (1973). *Irish Whiskey* (Dublin).

McNeil, I. (1972). *Hydraulic Power* (London).

Macpherson, David (1805). *Annals of Commerce* (London).

Mann, J. de L. (1971). *The Cloth Industry in the West of England from 1640 to 1880* (Oxford).

Marriner, S. (1961). *Rathbones of Liverpool 1845–73* (Liverpool).

Marshall, A. (1892). *Elements of Economics of Industry* (London).

Marshall, A. (1919). *Industry and Trade* (London).

Martindale, J. G. (1972). 'The Rise and Growth of the Tweed Industry in Scotland', in J. G. Jenkins (ed.), *The Wool Textile Industry in Great Britain* (London).

Masham, Lord (1904). *Lord Masham's Inventions, Written by Himself* (Bradford).

Mathias, P. (1959). *The Brewing Industry in England 1700–1830* (Cambridge).

Matthews, R. C. O. (1954). *A Study in Trade Cycle History. Economic Fluctuations in Great Britain 1833–1842* (Cambridge).

Matthews, R. C. O. (1959). *The Trade Cycle* (Cambridge).

Maywald, K. (1954). 'An Index of Building Costs in the United Kingdom, 1845–1938', *Economic History Review*, 2nd series, vol. VII.

Meade, R. (1882). *The Coal and Iron Industries of the United Kingdom* (London).

Mechie, S. (1960). *The Church and Scottish Social Development* (London).

Miall, S. (1931). *A History of the British Chemical Industry* (London).

Middlemas, R. K. (1963). *The Master Builders* (London).

Minchinton, W. E. (November 1975). 'The British Cider Industry Since 1870', *Westminster Bank Review*.

Ministry of Works (1950). Working Party Report, *Building* (HMSO, London).

Mitchell, B. R. (1956). 'The Economic Development of the Inland Coalfields 1870–1914'. PhD thesis, University of Cambridge.

Mitchell, B. R. (1964). 'The Coming of the Railway and United Kingdom Economic Growth', *Journal of Economic History*, vol. XXIV.

Mitchell, B. R., and Deane, Phyllis (1971). *Abstract of British Historical Statistics* (Cambridge).

Morier Evans, D. (1849). *The Commercial Crisis 1847–1848*, reprinted 1969 (London).

Morris, J. H. and Williams, L. J. (1958). *The South Wales Coal Industry 1841–75* (Cardiff).

Mounfield, P. R. (1966). *The Footwear of the East Midlands* (Nottingham).

Musson, A. E. (1954). *The Typographical Association*.

Musson, A. E. (1957–8a). 'James Nasmyth and the Early Growth of Mechanical Engineering', *Economic History Review*, 2nd series, vol. X, revised and reprinted in Musson and Robinson, op. cit. below, ch. XV.

Musson, A. E. (1957–8b). 'Newspaper Printing in the Industrial Revolution', *Economic History Review*, 2nd series, vol. X.

Musson, A. E. (1960). 'An Early Engineering Firm: Peel, Williams & Co., of Manchester', *Business History*, vol. III, revised and reprinted in Musson and Robinson, op. cit. below, ch. XIV.

Musson, A. E. with E. Robinson (1969). *Science and Technology in the Industrial Revolution* (Manchester).

Musson, A. E. (1970). Introduction to W. Pole (ed.), *The Life of Sir William Fairbairn* (1871; new edn, 1970) (London).

Musson, A. E. (1972a). *British Trade Unions, 1800–1875* (London).

Musson, A. E. (1972b). 'The "Manchester School" and Exportation of Machinery', *Business History*, vol. XIV.

Musson, A. E. (1975). 'Joseph Whitworth and the Growth of Mass-Production Engineering', *Business History*, vol. XVII.

Musson, A. E. (1976). 'Industrial Motive Power in the United Kingdom, 1800–70', *Economic History Review*, 2nd series, vol. XXIX.

Mutton, N. (1976). 'The Foster Family: A Study of a Midland Industrial Dynasty 1786–1899'. PhD thesis, University of London.

Neal, F. (1969). 'Liverpool Shipping in the Early Nineteenth Century', in J. R. Harris (ed.), *Liverpool and Merseyside* (London). *Essays in the Economic and Social History of the Port and its Hinterland.*

Nettleton, J. A. (1898). *The Manufacture of Spirit as conducted at the Various Distilleries of the U.K.* (London).

Nishimura, S. (1971). *The Decline of Inland Bills of Exchange in the London Money Market, 1885–1913* (Cambridge).

Nixon, F. (1956). *Papers on the Engineering History of Derbyshire* (Newton Abbot).

Pankhurst, K. W. (1955). 'Investment in the West Riding Wool Textile Industry in the Nineteenth Century', *Yorkshire Bulletin of Economic and Social Research*, vol. VII

Parliamentary Papers (1803), 1st series, vol. XI, pp. 319–804. 'Two Reports from the Select Committee on the Distillery in Different parts of Scotland and on the Best Mode of Levying and Collecting the Duties upon the Distillation of Corn Spirits in Scotland'.

PP (1816), vol. VIII. 'Reports of Woodbine Parish, Chairman of the Scots Board of Excise on Illicit Distillation, 25 April and 24 May 1816'.

PP (1818), *Accounts and Papers.* 'Accounts relating to the Distilleries in Scotland'.

PP (1821), vol. VIII. 'Report from the Select Committee on Petitions Complaining of the Additional Duty on Malt in Scotland'.

PP (1823), vol. VII. 'The Fifth Report of the Commissioners of Excise . . . for Inquiring into the Collection and Management of the Public Revenue arising in Ireland, and into Certain Departments of the Public Revenue arising in Great Britain' (cited as the Wallace Commission).

PP (1828), vol. IV. 'Report on the Office of Public Works and Buildings'.

PP (1830), vol. VIII, 1. 'Report of the House of Commons Select Committee on the Coal Trade 1830' (663).

PP (HL) (1830), vol. VIII. 'Report of the House of Lords Select Committee on the Coal Trade 1830' (9), 405. 1830 (9) VIII, 405.

PP (1831), vol. VII. 'Report from the Select Committee on the Effect of Allowing a Malt Drawback on Spirits'.

PP (1831), vol. VII. 'Report from the Select Committee on the Expediency of Admitting the Use of Molasses in Breweries and Distilleries'.

PP (1833), vol. VI. 'Report from the Select Committee Appointed to Inquire into the Present State of Manufactures, Commerce and Shipping, in the U.K.' (690).

PP (1834), vol. XXV. 'The Seventh Report of the Commissioners of Inquiry into the Excise Establishment and into the Management and Collection of Excise Revenue throughout the United Kingdom. British Spirits Parts I and II' (cited as the Parnell Commission). Part I 1834 (7), XXV, I; Part II, 1835 (8), XXX, 33.

PP (1834), vol. VIII. 'Report from the Select Committee on Drunkenness.'

PP (1841), vol. VII, *First Report* and *Second Report*, Select Committee on Exportation of Machinery.

PP (1842), 'Children's Employment Commission', *First Report*, 1842 (380, 381, 382), XV, 1: XVII, 1; *Second Report*, 1843 (430), XIII, 307, 381, No. 1.

PP (1843), vol. XIII. 'Midland Mining Commission First Report' (508), 1.

PP (1844), vol. VII. 'Select Committee on Joint Stock Companies', (119).

PP (1846), vol. VI. 'Lords' Select Committee on Burdens Affecting Real Property' (411), Part I, 1.

PP (1847), vol. XVI. 'Reports of the Inspector of the Population in Mining Districts' (844), 401.

PP (1847–8), vol. VIII. 'First Report from the Select Committee on Commercial Distress 1847–48' (395), Part I, 1.

PP (1850), vol. XLII 'Returns of the Number of Cotton, Woollen, Worsted, Flax and Silk Factories . . .' dated 10 June 1850 (74J), 460.

PP (1851), vol. XVIII. 'Report from the Select Committee on the Law of Partnership 1851' (509), XVIII, 1.

PP (1857), vol. XI. 'Select Committee on Rating of Mines, 1857', (Sess. 2), 533, 1857, (241), XI, 533.

PP (1865), vol. XXXI. 'Report of the Board of Inland Revenue to the Treasury on the Rate of Spirit Duty, 28th February', 1865, (131), XXXI, 449.

PP (1867–8), vol. XXXIX. 'Royal Commission on Trade Unions' Sixth Report 1867–8' (no. 3980–II), (in 5th–10th report), XXXIX, 149.

PP (1870), vol. XX. 'Report of the Commissioners of Inland Revenue', 1870, c. 82, XX.

PP (1871), vol. XVIII, 'Royal Commission on Coal Supply, vol. III 1871' (C. 435–II), 815, 1871 C., 435–II, XVIII, 815.

PP (1873), vol. X. 'Select Committee on the Dearness of Coal', (313), 1, 1873 (313), X, 1.

PP (1876), vol. LXV, 'Railway Returns'.

PP (1876), vol. XVII, 'Reports on the Inspectors on Mines for 1875, 1876' (C. 1499), 1876, C. 1499, XVII, 75.

PP (1892), vol. XXXIV. 'Royal Commission on Labour. First Report 1892' (C. 6708–IV), 313, 1892, C. 6708–IV, XXXIV, 313.

PP (1893–4), vol. XLI. 'Royal Commission on Mining Royalties. Final Report 1893–4 (C. 6980), 341, 1893–4, C. 6980, XLI, 341.

Payne, P. L. (1961). *Rubber and Railways in the Nineteenth Century* (London).

Payne, P. L. (1974). *British Entrepreneurship in the Nineteenth Century* (London).

Peel, C. M. (1951). 'History of Coalmining on Cannock Chase', *Transactions of the Institute of Mining Engineers*, vol. CX.

Perkins, E. J. (1975). *Financing Anglo-American Trade. The House of Brown, 1800–1880* (Cambridge, Mass. and London).

Petree, J. F. (1949). *Henry Maudslay, 1771–1831; and Maudslay, Sons and Field Ltd.* (Maudslay Society).

Petree, J. F. (1964) 'Henry Maudslay – Pioneer of Precision', *Engineering Heritage* (Institution of Mechanical Engineers), vol. 1.

Platt, D. C. M. (1973). 'Further Objections to an "Imperialism of Free Trade" 1830–60', *Economic History Review*, 2nd series, vol. XXVI.

Plummer, A. and Early, R. E. (1969). *The Blanket Makers 1669–1969* (London).

Podmore, F. (1923 edn). *Robert Owen, A Biography* (London).

Pollard, S. (1950–1). 'The Decline of Shipbuilding on the Thames', *Economic History Review*, 2nd series, vol. III.

Pollard, S. (1951). 'The Economic History of British Shipbuilding 1870–1914.' PhD thesis, University of London.

Pollard, S. (1965). *The Genesis of Industrial Management* (London).

Pollard, S. (1968). 'The Growth and Distribution of Capital in Great Britain c. 1770–1870', *Third International Conference of Economic History*, Munich, 1965, vol. I.

Pollins, H. (1969a). 'Aspects of Railway Accounting before 1868', in M. C. Reed (ed.), *Railways in the Victorian Economy* (Newton Abbot).

Pollins, H. (1969b). 'Railway Contractors and the Finance of Railway Development in Britain', in M. C. Reed (ed.), *Railways in the Victorian Economy* (Newton Abbot).

Pollins, H. (1971). *Britain's Railways*.

Ponting, K. G. (1971). *The Woollen Industry of South West England* (Bath).

Ponting, K. G. (1972). 'The West of England Cloth Industry', In J. G. Jenkins (ed.), *The Wool Textile Industry in Great Britain* (London).

Ponting, K. G. (1973). 'The Wiltshire–Somerset Border Woollen Industry', in N. G. Harte and K. G. Ponting (eds), *Textile History and Economic*

History, Essays in Honour of Miss Julia de Lacy Mann (Manchester).

Poole, Braithwaite (1852). *Statistics of British Commerce* (London).

Port, M. H. (ed.) (1976). *The Houses of Parliament* (New Haven and London).

Postgate, R. (1923). *The Builders' History* (London).

Prest, A. R. (1954). *Consumers' Expenditure in the United Kingdom 1900–1919* (Cambridge).

Railway Returns (1847–8). Vol. LXIII; (1851) LI; (1871) LX.

Ravenhill, J. R. (1877). 'Twenty Minutes with Our Commercial Marine Steam Fleet in 1877', *Transactions of the Institute of Naval Architects*, vol. XVIII.

Reed, M. C. (ed.) (1969). *Railways in the Victorian Economy. Studies in Finance and Growth* (Newton Abbot).

Reed, M. C. (1975). *Investment in Railways in Britain 1820–1844* (Oxford).

Riden, P. (1977). 'The Output of the British Iron Industry before 1870', *Economic History Review*, 2nd series, vol. XXX.

Rideout, E. H. (1930). 'The Development of the Liverpool Warehousing System', *Transactions of the Historic Society of Lancashire and Cheshire*, vol. LXXXII.

Rimmer, W. G. (1960). 'Leeds Leather Industry in the Nineteenth Century', *Thoresby Society*, XLVI.

Roe, J. W. (1916). *English and American Tool Builders* (New Haven; Humphrey Milford; London).

Roe, J. W. (1936–7). 'Interchangeable Manufacture', *Newcomen Society Transactions*, vol. XVII.

Rolt, L. T. C. (1965). *Tools for the Job: A Short History of Machine Tools* (London).

Rorabaugh, W. J. (1973–4). 'Politics and the Architectural Competition for the Houses of Parliament, 1834–1837', *Victorian Studies*, vol. XVII.

Rosenberg, N. (1963). 'Technological Change in the Machine Tool Industry, 1840–1910', *Journal of Economic History*, vol. XXIII.

Rosenberg, N. (1969). *The American System of Manufactures* (Edinburgh).

Rosenberg, N. (1976). *Perspectives on Technology* (Cambridge).

Rostow, W. W. (1948). *British Economy of the Nineteenth Century* (Oxford).

Rostow, W. W. (1960). *The Stages of Economic Growth* (Cambridge).

Rubenstein, W. D. (1977). 'The Victorian Middle Classes: Wealth, Occupation and Geography', *Economic History Review*, 2nd series, vol. XXX.

Rules and Regulations (30 June, 1856), in Leeds Reference Library.

Salter, W. E. G. (1960). *Productivity and Technical Change* (Cambridge).

Samuel, R. (1977). 'Workshop of the World: Steam Power and Hand Technology in Mid-Victorian Britain', *History Workshop*, no. 3.

Sandberg, L. G. (1968a). 'American Rings and English Mules: The Role of Economic Rationality', *Quarterly Journal of Economics*, vol. LXXXII.

Sandberg, L. G. (1968b). 'Movements in the Quality of British Cotton Textile Exports, 1815–1913', *Journal of Economic History*, vol. XXVIII.

Saul, S. B. (1967). 'The Market and the Development of the Mechanical Engineering Industries in Britain, 1860–1914', *Economic History Review*, 2nd series, vol. XX, reprinted in S. B. Saul (ed.), *Technological Change* (1972).

Saul, S. B. (1968a). 'The Engineering Industry', in D. H. Aldcroft, (ed.),

The Development of British Industry and Foreign Competition, 1875–1914 (London).

Saul, S. B. (1968*b*). 'The Machine Tool Industry in Britain to 1914', *Business History*, vol. X.

Saul, S. B. (1970). *Technological Change: The United States and Britain in the Nineteenth Century* (London).

Scarisbrick, J. (1891). *Spirit Manual* (Burton-on-Trent).

The Scotsman (1 May 1822)

The Scotsman (20 May 1826)

Scottish Record Office, series RH 15, 207/9, Beauly Distillery Company.

Scrivenor, H. (1854). *History of the Iron Trade, from the Earliest Records to the Present Period* (London).

Shannon, H. A. (1932). 'The First Five Thousand Limited Companies and their Duration', *Economic History*, vol. II.

Shannon, H. A. (1933). 'The Limited Companies of 1866–83', *Economic History Review*, 1st series, vol. IV.

Shannon, H. A. (1934). 'Bricks – A Trade Index, 1785–1949', *Economica*, new series, vol. I.

Sharpe, D. J. (1968). *A Brief History of the Morley Textile Industry, 1750–1900* (Morley Local History Society).

Shields, J. (1947). *Clyde Built. A History of Shipbuilding on the Clyde* (Glasgow).

Sigsworth, E. M. (1949). 'The History of the Local Trade at Morley', *Journal of the Textile Institute*, vol. XI.

Sigsworth, E. M. (1951–2). 'Two Eighteenth Century Worsted Manufacturers', *Journal of the Bradford and Textile Society*.

Sigsworth, E. M. (1958). *Black Dyke Mills* (Liverpool).

Sigsworth, E. M. (1965). 'Science and the Brewing Industry, 1850–1900', *Economic History Review*, vol. XVII.

Sigsworth, E. M. (1967). 'The Brewing Trade During the Industrial Revolution. The Case of Yorkshire'. University of York, Borthwick Institute of Historical Research, *Borthwick Papers*, no. 31.

Singer, C. *et al.* (eds) (1958). *A History of Technology*, Vols IV and V (Oxford).

Slater, A. W. (1965–6). 'A London Firm of Steel Makers', *Business History*, vols VII–VIII.

Slaughter, M. (1849–75). *Railway Intelligence* (London).

Slaven, A. (1969). 'A Glasgow Firm in the Indian Market: John Lean and Sons, Muslin Weavers', *Business History Review*, vol. XLIII.

Slaven, A. (1975). *The Development of the West of Scotland: 1750–1960* (London).

Smiles, S., (1863). *Industrial Biography*.

Smiles, S. (1883). *James Nasmyth, Engineer. An Autobiography*.

Smith, A. (1976). *An Inquiry into the Nature and Causes of the Wealth of Nations*, 2 vols, edited by R. H. Campbell and A. S. Skinner (Oxford).

Smith, E. C. (1938). *A Short History of Marine Engineering* (Cambridge).

Smith, W. T., 'A Shipbuilding History of Alexander Hall and Company Ltd., 1790–1953', (unpublished manuscript).

Spring, D. (1952). 'The Earls of Durham and the Great Northern Coal

Field, 1830–80', *Canadian Historical Review*, vol. XXXIII.

Spring, D. (1971). 'English Landowners and Nineteenth Century Industrialism', in J. T. Ward and R. G. Wilson (eds), *Land and Industry* (Newton Abbot).

Stamp, J. C. (1916). *British Incomes and Property* (London).

Stamp, J. C. (1978). 'The Effect of Trade Fluctuations upon Profits', *Journal of the Royal Statistical Society*, vol. LXXXI.

Statement of the Case of the Northern Coal Owners (1824). (Newcastle).

Statistical Society, *Statistical Abstracts of the United Kingdom* (1826 onward).

Steeds, W. (1969). *A History of Machine Tools* (Oxford).

Stephen Papers (1859). UGD 4/1/1; UGD 4/18/7; UGD 4/16/1; University of Glasgow Business Collection.

Strang, J. (1853). 'Progress Extent and Value of Steamboat Building and Marine Engine Making on the Clyde', *Journal of the Statistical Society*, vol. XVI.

Summerson, J. (1973). *The London Building World of the Eighteen-Sixties* (London).

Supple, B. (1970). *The Royal Exchange Assurance. A History of British Insurance 1720–1970* (Cambridge).

Sutton, G. B. (1959). 'Shoemakers of Somerset, A History of C and J Clark 1833–1903'. PhD thesis, University of Nottingham.

Tann, J. (1967). *Gloucester Woollen Mills* (Newton Abbot).

Taylor, A. J. (1949). 'Concentration and Specialisation in the Lancashire Cotton Industry, 1825–1850', *Economic History Review*, 2nd series, vol. I.

Taylor, A. J. (1960). 'The Sub-Contract System in the British Coal Industry', in L. S. Pressnell (ed.), *Studies in the Industrial Revolution* (London).

Taylor, A. J. (1967). 'Coal', in *Victoria County History on Staffordshire*, Vol. II (London).

Taylor, R. C. (1855). *Statistics of Coal* (London).

Temin, P. (1966a). 'Labour Scarcity and the Problem of American Industrial Efficiency in the 1850's', *Journal of Economic History*, vol. XXVI.

Temin, P. (1966b). 'Steam and Waterpower in the Early Nineteenth Century', *Journal of Economic History*, vol. XXVI.

Thomas, B. (1973). *Migration and Economic Growth: A Study of Great Britain and the Atlantic Economy*, 2nd edn (Cambridge).

Thompson, E. P., and Yeo, E. (eds) (1973). *The Unknown Mayhew* (London).

Thornton, R. & Sons (Dewsbury) Ltd (1960). *A Story of Woollen Rag Sales 1860–1960* (Dewsbury).

Tooke, T. (1857). *History of Prices*, Vols I–IV (London).

Topham, A. J. (1953). 'The Credit Structure of the West Riding Wool Textile Industry in the Nineteenth Century'. MA thesis, University of Leeds.

Tovey, C. (1864). *British and Foreign Spirits* (London).

Tyson, R. E. (1962). 'The Sun Mill Company Limited – A Study in Democratic Investment 1858–1959', MA thesis, University of Manchester.

Underwood, A. J. V. (1935). 'The Historical Development of Distilling Plant', *Transactions of the Institution of Chemical Engineers*, vol. XIII.

Vaizey, J. (1960). *The Brewing Industry, 1886–1951* (Cambridge).
Vamplew, W. (1969). The Railways and the Iron Industry: a Study of their Relationship in Scotland', in M. C. Reed (ed.), *Railways in the Victorian Economy. Studies in Finance and Economic Growth* (Newton Abbot).
Varley, D. A. (1959). 'An Outline of the History of the Machine-made Lace Trade from 1768 to 1914.' Part I of *A History of the Midland Counties Lace Manufacturers' Association 1915–1958* (Long Eaton).
von Tunzelmann, G. N. (1975). 'Some Economic Aspects of the Diffusion of Steam Power in the British Isles to 1856, with special reference to Textile Industries'. DPhil thesis, University of Oxford.
von Tunzelmann, G. N. (1978). *Steam Power and British Industrialization* (Oxford).
Waddington, H. (1953). *Crown Point Dyeworks, East Street, Leeds* (Leeds).
Walters, R. H. (1976). *'The Economic and Business History of the South Wales Coal Industry 1840–1914'*. DPhil thesis, University of Oxford.
Ward, J. R. (1974). *The Finance of Canal Building in 18th Century England*.
Ward, J. T. (1971). 'Landowners and Mining', in J. T. Ward and R. G. Wilson (eds), *Land and Industry* (Newton Abbot).
Watts, John (1868). *The Facts of the Cotton Famine* (London, Manchester).
Waugh, A. (1957). *Merchants of Wine* (London).
Weir, R. B. (1974a). 'The Distilling Industry of Scotland in the Nineteenth and early Twentieth Centuries'. PhD thesis, University of Edinburgh.
Weir, R. B. (1974b). *The History of the Malt Distillers' Association of Scotland* (Elgin).
Weir, R. B. (1977). 'Patent Still Distillers and Competition', in L. Cullen and T. C. Smout (eds), *Comparative Aspects of Irish and Scottish Economic and Social Development 1600–1900* (Edinburgh).
Wells, F. A. (1972). *The British Hosiery and Knitwear Industry* (Newton Abbot).
Williams, B. (1976). *The Making of Manchester Jewry 1740–1875* (Manchester).
Williams, D. M. (1966). 'Merchanting in the First Half of the Nineteenth Century; the Liverpool Timber Trade', *Business History*, vol. VIII.
Williams, D. M. (1969). 'Liverpool Merchants and the Cotton Trade, 1820–1850', in J. R. Harris (ed.), *Liverpool and Merseyside. Essays in the Economic and Social History of the Port of Its Hinterland* (London).
Williamson, J. G. (1964). *American Growth and the Balance of Payments, 1820–1913* (Chapel Hill).
Wilson, C. (1955) 'The Entrepreneur in the Industrial Revolution in Britain', *Explorations in Entrepreneurial History*, Vol. III.
Wilson, G. B. (1940). *Alcohol and the Nation* (London)
Wilson, R. G. (1973). 'The Supremacy of the Yorkshire Cloth Industry', in N. B. Harte, and K. G. Ponting, (eds), *Textile History and Economic History, Essays in Honour of Miss Julia de Lacy Mann* (Manchester).
Woodman, H. D. (1968). *King Cotton and His Retainers. Financing and Marketing the Cotton Crop of the South, 1800–1925* (Lexington).
Woodruff, W. (1958). *The Rise of the British Rubber Industry During the Nineteenth Century* (Liverpool).
Wright, G. (1973). 'An Econometric Study of Cotton Production and Trade

1830–60', in P. Temin (ed.), *New Economic History* (Harmondsworth).

Wright, J. F. (1956). 'Index of the Output of British Industry Since 1700', *Journal of Economic History*, vol. XVI.

Wright, J. F. (1965). 'British Economic Growth 1688–1959', *Economic History Review*, 2nd series, vol. XVIII.

Zabler, J. F. (1972). 'Further Evidence on American Wage Differentials 1800–1830', *Explorations in Economic History*, vol. X, no. 1.

Index